Praise for the previous books
of William F. Roemer, Jr.

ROEMER: MAN AGAINST THE MOB
"A high-speed journey through mob-land's inner sanc-
tum, with wiretaps, payoffs, shoot-outs, double-dealing,
and instant death . . . Fascinating."
—*People*

WAR OF THE GODFATHERS
"Exciting reading . . . Roemer's experience has left him
with some fascinating tales, and this is one of them."
—*Kirkus Reviews*

THE ENFORCER
"Fascinating . . . More intrigues, scams, and killings than
in almost any other book . . . Delivered with the narrative
force of a Thompson submachine gun."
—*Real Crime Book Digest*

By William F. Roemer, Jr.
Published by Ivy Books:

ROEMER: MAN AGAINST THE MOB
WAR OF THE GODFATHERS
THE ENFORCER
ACCARDO: THE GENUINE GODFATHER

ACCARDO
The Genuine
Godfather

William F. Roemer, Jr.

BALLANTINE BOOKS • NEW YORK

An Ivy Book
Published by The Random House Publishing Group
Copyright © 1995 by William F. Roemer, Jr.

Published in the United States by Ballantine Books, an imprint of The Random House Publishing Group, a division of Random House, Inc., New York, and distributed in Canada by Random House of Canada Limited, Toronto.

www.ballantinebooks.com

ISBN 0-8041-1464-1

This edition published by arrangement with Donald I. Fine, Inc.

Manufactured in the United States of America

First Ballantine Books Edition: October 1996

OPM 19 18 17 16 15 14 13 12

*To Jeannie—the love of my life.
I couldn't do anything without you.*

Acknowledgments

I want to thank the fine people once more at Donald I. Fine, Inc., my publisher for the fourth time in six years: Don Fine himself, a legend in the publishing business with many years of outstanding success; Jason Poston, his able associate and editor; Larry Bernstein, DIF's production manager and managing editor; Bob Gales, the experienced sales director with so much success in his background; and Larry Kramer, DIF's accountant extraordinaire.

I thank my wife, Jeannie, for her continued inspiration and for giving this book its first editing.

I thank some old pals from days of yore who filled me in on the background of Tony Accardo in the years before I became involved in his investigation: Bill Duffy, former deputy superintendent of the Chicago Police Department, and Virgil Peterson, the former operating director of the Chicago Crime Commission, may they rest in peace.

I thank Bill Lambie, former FBI agent, investigator for the Illinois Attorney General's office and special investigator for the Chicago Crime Commission. Bill had considered doing his own book years ago on Tony Accardo but never got around to it. He shared his research on Accardo with me and it has been invaluable.

I thank FBI agent Pete Wacks, who was assigned for two and a half decades to the Chicago FBI office.

I thank John Roberts, who worked with me on the Organized Crime Squad of the Chicago FBI and who was the case agent on Accardo for years.

I thank Mr. and Mrs. Bill Halliday for sharing photos of Accardo's house with me.

I thank Bob Fuesel, Jeannette Callaway and Jerry Gladden of the Chicago Crime Commission for sharing their records with me.

I thank Roy Suzuki of the Chicago chapter of the Court Buffs of

America, The Court Watchers, who monitor every mob trial in Chicago, for his insights.

I thank Bill Dougherty, who worked with me on the Organized Crime Squad of the Chicago FBI and kept me in shape by partnering with me in handball.

I thank Bill's wife, Lori Dougherty, our former administrative assistant in the Chicago FBI who kept our records in such an orderly manner, she could find them for us whenever we needed them. She herself knows more than most about organized crime in Chicago. I thank her especially for the day she spent with me researching material I needed to flesh out this effort.

I thank all my good pals who have kept me pumped up: Bill Hartnett, now of Here's Chicago, who was a young recruit with me at the FBI Academy at Quantico, Virginia, in 1950; Miles Cooperman of the Cook County Sheriff's Department; Bill Fudala of the Chicago Transit Authority, my former sparring partner; Jim Agnew of *Real Crime Book Digest*, for whom I write a regular column and who has helped me with my research; John Flood and Rich Lindberg of the Combined Counties Police Association and its publication, *The Police and Sheriff's News*, for which I also write a regular column; John Binder of the Merry Gangsters Literary Society and its *Prohibition Era Times*, for which I also write a column; Pat Roemer, my nephew, and Scott Hanson of Goreville, Illinois, both of whom keep me up to date on the news in Chicago; Bill Ouseley, the case agent of the FBI's Strawman Investigation in Kansas City; Larry Bergreen, who shared with me the research he did on his book, *Capone*; Bill Brashler, who shared with me the research he did on his book, *The Don*, a biography of Sam Giancana; Matthew R. Bernard, who prepared a treatise on Accardo for his Leaders in History class at Northwestern University and who shared it with me; Nick Pileggi, who has credited me with "inspiring" him to write the book and screenplay for *Casino*; George Benigni, Bob Glendon and Bert Jensen, former FBI colleagues; Lank Smith, Jack Fallon, Jim Gillis and Joe Archibald, pals from Notre Dame; Ben Bentley, the Chicago sportscaster; and the dean of Chicago sportscasters, Jack Brickhouse.

I also thank the members of the Fourth Estate with whom I share and they share: John O'Brien of the Chicago *Tribune*; John Drummond of WBBM-TV; Kup of the *Sun Times*, Zay Smith of the *Sun Times*; Roy Leonard of WGN radio; Roe Conn of WLS radio; Tony Fitzpatrick and Wendy Snyder of WLUP radio; Mark Kiesling of the Hammond *Times*; Pat McMahon and Frank

Baronowski of KTAR radio in Phoenix; and Steve Neal of the *Sun Times*.

I also thank Bill and Lori Dougherty for the photo they took of me at the desk of Tony Accardo in the basement of his former house.

I express my gratitude to Larry Heim, editor of *The Grapevine*, the official publication of the Society of Former Special Agents of the FBI. He is always most helpful and I thank all agents of the Society, including Jim McFall, the executive director, for their support and encouragement. They are a group I have the greatest respect for.

Last, but certainly not least, I thank my family for their support through the years: Bill and Bob, my sons; Earlene and Kelly, my fine daughters-in-law; and my great grandkids Chris, Matt and Tim. Keep Punchin' and Keep the Faith!

THE CHICAGO FAMILY

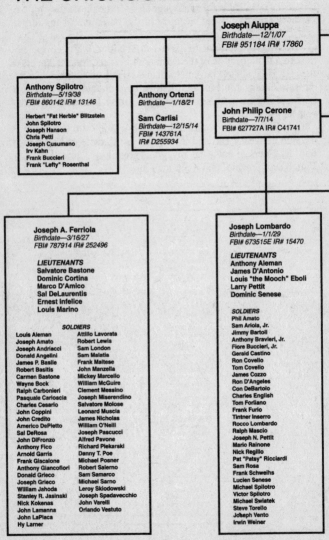

Joseph Aiuppa
Birthdate—12/1/07
FBI# 951184 IR# 17860

Anthony Spilotro
Birthdate—5/19/38
FBI# 860142 IR# 13146

Herbert "Fat Herbie" Blitzstein
John Spilotro
Joseph Hanson
Chris Petti
Joseph Cusumano
Irv Kahn
Frank Buccieri
Frank "Lefty" Rosenthal

Anthony Ortenzi
Birthdate—1/18/21

Sam Carlisi
Birthdate—12/15/14
FBI# 143761A
IR# D255934

John Philip Cerone
Birthdate—7/7/14
FBI# 627727A IR# C41741

Joseph A. Ferriola
Birthdate—3/16/27
FBI# 787914 IR# 252496

LIEUTENANTS
Salvatore Bastone
Dominic Cortina
Marco D'Amico
Sal DeLaurentis
Ernest Infelice
Louis Marino

SOLDIERS

Louis Aleman	Attilio Lavorata
Joseph Amato	Robert Lewis
Joseph Andriacci	Sam London
Donald Angelini	Sam Malatia
James P. Basile	Frank Maltese
Robert Basitis	John Manzella
Carmen Bastone	Mickey Marcello
Wayne Bock	William McGuire
Ralph Carbonieri	Clement Messino
Pasquale Carioscia	Joseph Miserendino
Charles Cesario	Salvatore Molose
John Coppini	Leonard Muscia
John Credito	James Nicholas
Americo DePletto	William O'Neill
Sal DeRosa	Joseph Pascucci
John DiFronzo	Alfred Pavone
Anthony Fico	Richard Piekarski
Arnold Garris	Danny T. Poe
Frank Giacalone	Michael Posner
Anthony Giancofiori	Robert Salerno
Donald Grieco	Sam Samarco
Joseph Grieco	Michael Sarno
William Jahoda	Leroy Skiodowski
Stanley R. Jasinski	Joseph Spadavecchio
Nick Kokenas	John Varelli
John Lamanna	Orlando Vestuto
John LaPlaca	
Hy Larner	

Joseph Lombardo
Birthdate—1/1/29
FBI# 673515E IR# 15470

LIEUTENANTS
Anthony Aleman
James D'Antonio
Louis "the Mooch" Eboli
Larry Pettit
Dominic Senese

SOLDIERS
Phil Amato
Sam Ariola, Jr.
Jimmy Bartoli
Anthony Bravieri, Jr.
Fiore Buccieri, Jr.
Gerald Castino
Ron Covello
Tom Covello
James Cozzo
Ron D'Angeles
Con DeBartolo
Charles English
Tom Forliano
Frank Furio
Tintner Inserro
Rocco Lombardo
Ralph Mascio
Joseph N. Pettit
Mario Rainone
Nick Regillo
Pat "Patsy" Ricciardi
Sam Rosa
Frank Schweihs
Lucien Senese
Michael Spilotro
Victor Spilotro
Michael Swiatek
Steve Torello
Joseph Vento
Irwin Weiner

Anthony Accardo
Birthdate—4/28/06
FBI# 1410106 IR# D83436

Gus Alex
Birthdate—4/1/16
FBI# 4244200

Dominic Blasi
Birthdate—9/9/11
FBI# 635770 IR# E8187

Willie Messino
Birthdate—1/7/17
FBI# 922367 IR#55433

Angelo LaPietra
Birthdate—10/30/20
FBI# 1777469 IR# D48410

LIEUTENANTS
Frank James Calabrese
Frank Caruso
John Fecarotta
James LaPietra
John Monteleone

SOLDIERS
Joseph Albano
Ernest Amodei
Frank Bruno Barbara
Sam Bills
Anthony Bova
Frank Butera
Frak Michael "Mike" Caruso
Rich Catezone
Charles DiCaro
James DiCaro
Paul DiCaro
Sam Gallo
Morton Geller
Jerome Gralla
Anthony Imparata
Angelo Imperato
Vincent Inserro
Joseph LaMantia
Richard LaMantia
Anthony Maenza
Nick Montos
Dominic Palermo
Flor Piccinini
Aldo J. Piscitelli
James Quarello
Carmen Russo
Terry Scalise
Tom Scalise
Nikolic Slobodan
Michael Talarico

Vincent A. Solano
Birthdate—10/12/19
FBI# 1995437 IR# D4182

LIEUTENANTS
Joseph Arnold
Joseph DiVarco
Michael Glitta

SOLDIERS
Anthony Armieri
Dan Bartoli
Ray Caccamo
Thomas Campione
Jasper Campise
Orlando Catanese
Anthony Cipriano
Anthony Cirignani
Frank DeMonte
Sal Dodero
Sid Finzelbar
Sal Gruttaduaro
Murray Jans
Walter Micus
Joseph Morici
Daniel Morsovillo
Nick Nitti
Frank Orlando
Leonard Patrick
Mike Patrick
Frank Paula
Sam Sarcinelli
Christ Seritella
Morton Shapiro
Calvin Sirkin
George Sommer
Anthony Spadafore
Ray Spencer
Arnold Taradash
Frank Tornabene
Len Yaras

Albert Caesar Tocco
Birthdate—8/9/29
FBI# 296484

LIEUTENANTS
Joseph Barrett, Jr.
Tony "Dago Tony" Berretoni
Richard Guzzino
Chris Messino

SOLDIERS
Douglas Aldridge
Harry Ansel
Daniel Bonnets
Roy Bridges
Clarence Crockett
Frank D'Andrea
Gerry Ferraro
Sheldon Fishman
Joseph Marek
Gino Martin
Seymour Miller
Tony Pelligrino
Joseph Jerome "Jerry" Scalise
Jerry Scarpelli
Eric Schmidt
Al Troiani
William Zanon
Richard Zink

Prepared by William Lambie of the office of the Attorney General, State of Illinois, with the assistance of the author, a Special Consultant on Organized Crime to the Chicago Crime Commission, then and now. Introduced by the author during his testimony on March 4, 1983, before the U.S. Senate Permanent Subcommittee on Investigations.

Introduction

Antoinette Giancana, "The Mafia Princess," gave me a call on Thanksgiving Day, 1994. Toni and I have been retained as creative consultants to the HBO movie based on my autobiography, *Roemer: Man Against the Mob*, to star John Turturro as her father, and we are friends. She had read in the Chicago newspapers that I was about to begin work on *Accardo*.

"I hear you are going to do *Saint* Accardo," she told me sarcastically.

I know it galls Toni to think that I hold the memory of Tony Accardo higher than I do the memory of her father. Toni and I have appeared on talk shows together and made presentations to audiences in Chicago and Los Angeles, among others. During those appearances my dislike of her father—and my grudging respect for Accardo—has come through, enough so that I have been asked by executives at HBO to tone down my rhetoric about Sam Giancana in the presence of Toni, in order not to alienate her and therefore hinder our working relationship. This is difficult for me.

It all goes back to the dozens of confrontations I had with Giancana and those I had with Accardo. With Giancana, they were vicious. We literally hated each other. However, those with Accardo were on a much different plane. We had a certain respect for each other. I knew that each was a torturer and a killer, each was in his own way the epitome of what a bad guy was. But it was my feeling that Accardo did his job with some class, whereas Giancana did not. When Accardo gave me his word, he kept it. I never asked Giancana to give me his word—I wouldn't have trusted it. I was also influenced by listening to the thousands of conversations we taped of the two and of their underlings talking about them and with them. Accardo was always discussed with the greatest respect by his people, much more so than Giancana.

The reason I bring this up is this: in writing this story of

Accardo, I must be objective. I cannot let my respect for the man overcome impartiality. I've tried my best to let the facts speak for themselves. When this man was guilty of the most heinous of crimes, which he was, I describe them without hesitation. But when he performed as a human being, and let his good qualities come to the fore, I write about these also.

I hope, when the reader finishes this book, he or she will agree that this biography is being presented unprejudiced and unbiased, and that he or she will fully understand exactly what made this most powerful of all mobsters—of any time in any place—tick.

This will be my fifth book to be published. In all of them Accardo has been a prime protagonist and, in fact, in *War of the Godfathers* he was one of the two main characters, Joe Bonanno being the other godfather. I should mention that in the first chapter of my autobiography, *Roemer: Man Against the Mob*, I described how I was lured to Santa Monica, California, where I was contacted by an intermediary who told me that "The Man" wanted to meet with me. At that time the only reason I went as requested was that I was told that "The Man," Accardo, felt I owed him a "marker," a debt, in view of an accommodation we had negotiated years before, as I will describe in this book. What I really thought, which I am telling now for the first time, was that the reason Accardo wanted to meet me was to tell me he was stepping down and away from the mob. He had been "The Man" in the Chicago mob for parts of five decades by that time, and he had had more contact with me than with any other law enforcement agent in his lifetime. I believed that my respect for him was mutual, and at that time, September 1987, I felt that Accardo might be choosing me to carry a message to my former colleagues. (I had recently retired after thirty years with the FBI and as the senior agent on the organized crime squads of the Chicago FBI.) It was very possible that he was asking me to meet with him to convey his message that he was giving up his role at the top of the Chicago mob because of his advanced age, eighty-one then, and his wish to be left in peace.

It didn't turn out that way. Instead, the object of the meeting was to "throw fear" at me for the expanded role I had assumed as witness for the crime commission. The mob felt that when I retired from the FBI it was "fine for Roemer to go out to Arizona and climb those mountains out there and piss down, but not on us." They felt I no longer had the "license" to testify before the U.S. Senate, write articles and give talks about the dangers presented by the mob—that when I retired, I was expected to quietly fade away. Therefore, they sent two gunsels, not Tony Accardo, to the site in Santa Monica to "kneecap" me, shoot me in the knees, cripple me. I know this for a fact.

My purpose in bringing this up here is to explain the reason I exposed myself to that potential situation. In the back of my mind I thought that Accardo was stepping down and wanted me, of all people, to be the credible one to make it known to law enforcement. Obviously, he couldn't just announce it publicly. I went because of the man's stature, because I knew I could accept his words on faith. It didn't work out as I expected, but that was my mindset. I bring it up here to give the reader my perspective of the kind of person, good and bad, that Tony Accardo was.

The encounter in Santa Monica did not deter me. Quite the opposite. I continue to adhere to my lifelong motto: "Keep Punchin' and Keep the Faith!"

1 The Man

Chicago, 1977. As usual it was a cold, blustery November. It had already snowed several times, and the snappy breeze off Lake Michigan made the pedestrians in the Loop pull up their collars as Harry Levinson made his way to his prominent jewelry store on North Clark Street.

Soon the weather didn't disturb Mr. Levinson at all. Upon entering his store, he found a lot more to be perturbed about. His store was a mess. The furnishings were thrown every which way and the counters smashed. What had been a very large inventory was gone. He had been robbed.

Levinson almost fainted. Sure, his first thought was that he was insured. But his second thought, coming immediately, was that his Christmas season would now be ruined. And in the jewelry business, as in many businesses, the Christmas season makes or breaks the year. With little or no inventory left to sell, Levinson's year would go down the drain. He would be hard pressed to stay in business.

How could this happen? Hadn't he installed the best burglar alarm system? Weren't stores in the Loop well protected by the Central District of the Chicago Police Department? Wasn't the public view from the street into his store a big deterrent to thieves?

Apparently not. Obviously, this heist had been accomplished by a professional crew of burglars. In and out without being disturbed, and with over a million dollars' worth of the best jewelry. None of the lesser jewels had been touched. These guys definitely knew what they were doing.

Levinson called 911. Within minutes police swarmed the premises. However, after a couple of hours they were scratching their heads. The robbers had left no clues. There were no leads. Sure, the burglary dicks would keep the investigation open and pursue all leads. But what leads? None of any potential. The thieves had gotten away clean. The detectives would contact their informants without, as it turned out, any success.

Levinson had an ace in the hole, however. Somebody much more powerful in Chicago than any police officer or detective. Or any official, for that matter. Levinson made the call. He was lucky. "The Man" was in town, not in California, where he spent most of the winter. Yes, he would meet with his friend.

In fact, when he arrived—at Chez Paul, a snobby French restaurant on the near north side of Chicago—The Man would be joined by two more of the most powerful people in Chicago. Number one, Jackie Cerone, had been the boss of the Chicago mob, of the Chicago family of La Cosa Nostra, the so-called Mafia, not once but on two occasions. He and Joey Aiuppa were now running the Chicago Outfit. Not many more important in Chicago than Jackie. Number two, Gus Alex, was the leader of the "connection guys," the troupe the FBI called the "corruption squad," since that more clearly defined their function, to corrupt as many public officials as needed for the Outfit to operate in Chicago. Furthermore, Gussie had been the mob's boss in the Loop for many years.

As powerful as these two were, however, there was one more powerful in the Chicago LCN. There was The Man. He commanded more respect, even from the likes of Cerone and Alex, than anyone else. He had been there since Capone, and his influence in the Chicago mob spanned parts of eight decades. He had not only seen it all but done it all. Capone had had his fifteen minutes of fame in the annals of organized crime. So had Lucky Luciano. Frank Costello. Carlos Marcello. Joe Bonanno. Meyer Lansky. Frank Nitti. Sam Giancana. John Gotti. But none was as powerful as The Man.

The Man was Tony Accardo. Not that anybody close to him ever called him that. Al Capone had nicknamed him. Once when Accardo was working for Capone, he battered two thugs, rivals of Capone's, to death with a baseball bat. Capone told his colleagues, "This guy is a real Joe Batters." The name stuck, and not just during the short lifespan in the mob of Al Capone. Accardo would outlive Capone by more than half a century, and though the newspapers would refer to him as Tony Accardo or "The Big Tuna," those close to him, even those in the FBI who got close only by physical surveillance or electronic surveillance, would call him "Joe Batters," or "J.B." or "Mr. Batters." Never Tony Accardo. Even I called him Joe on the occasions of our meetings. Even Clarice, his long-time wife, did.

Levinson was one of the privileged few. He had known The Man for years, from the time when the mob had a book joint, an "office," close by Levinson's jewelry store. When Hymie Levin was a pal of Levinson, and the biggest bookmaker in town. And Hymie was close to Batters. He introduced Levinson to Joe and the two eventually became pals—not real close, but close enough so that when Levinson put in his crisis call, Mr. B responded.

At Chez Paul, Batters and his entourage were always welcomed by the owner. He thought it was good for business with things as they were in Chicago, especially in those days. Gussie Alex, for example, probably ate there more often than anyplace else.

It wasn't long before Levinson got down to the purpose of his emergency call. When Levinson was finished telling Accardo about his misfortune, The Man reached out and patted him on the shoulder. "Not to worry," was all he said. He looked at Cerone. Then he resumed devouring his *foie gras* or whatever it is they serve at Chez Paul.

Two days later Levinson received a call. "Will you be at your store this afternoon?" Levinson recognized the voice. His heart leaped. That afternoon a million dollars' worth of the best jewelry in Chicago was returned to Levinson. Now his Christmas season would make his year. All thanks to his friend, The Man.

But that is not the end of the story.

Immediately after Accardo, Cerone and Alex left Chez Paul, a call was placed to Tony Spilotro in Las Vegas. Tony "The Ant" had been sent out there to oversee the Chicago mob's interests in the gaming capital. But he had been a Chicago burglar before he was "made," formally inducted into the LCN, and, in 1971, sent to Vegas as The Enforcer. (I've written about Tony Spilotro previously, in *The Enforcer*.) Spilotro still had his many contacts in Chicago. He suggested that John Mendell was the guy who would know most about how to circumvent or defeat burglar alarm systems. "Somebody" should talk to him.

"Somebody" did just that, and the next day the loot was retrieved from the fence who had received it for a sale when things had cooled down, when it wasn't quite so hot. It was then delivered to an excited Levinson.

Even had the Chicago PD been able to solve the case by apprehending the burglars, they probably would not have been able to recover the jewelry. And if they had, it would have been inventoried and placed in the evidence room in the Central District for months, perhaps years, to be used in the trial of the burglars.

Levinson's Christmas would still have been a disaster. Now it would save his year.

Shortly after the loot was returned to Mr. Levinson, Tony and Clarice Accardo left Chicago for their condo on Road Runner Drive, along the fairways of the Indian Wells Country Club in sunny Palm Springs, California. They left their home at 1407 North Ashland Avenue in the plush western suburb of Chicago, River Forest, under the care of their long-time houseman, a pal of Accardo's for over forty years, Michael Volpe.

On January 9, 1978, Volpe contacted Tony Accardo in Palm Springs. It must have been a difficult thing to do, because what Volpe had to tell him was unheard of. Somebody had burglarized the home of Tony Accardo! Nothing was missing but the house had been ransacked after the burglar alarm was defeated. Amazing! What demented person would dare to burglarize the home of the most important mob chieftain of his time? He would have to be crazy.

Tony Accardo gave it some thought. He called his protégé, Jackie Cerone, the guy he had elevated into the spot of mob boss. Tony Spilotro was called back to Chicago—from the warm breezes of Las Vegas to the wintry blasts of The Windy City.

The first body we found, on January 20, 1978, was that of Bernie Ryan, thirty-four, of 2727 West Eleventh Street in Chicago. He was slumped over the wheel of his 1976 Lincoln Continental, parked on a street in Stone Park, a western suburb of Chicago. His throat had been slashed from ear to ear and he had been shot four times for good measure. Ryan was holding in his hand a police scanner, a radio designed to pick up police radio calls, a device often used by burglars to monitor police activity in the vicinity of their "job."

Then it was Steven Garcia's turn. He was a known partner of Ryan. His body was found on February 2. Just like Ryan's, his throat was slit from ear to ear. But unlike Ryan, who was shot, Garcia had been stabbed many times. His body was stuffed into the trunk of a rented car in the parking area of the Sheraton O'Hare hotel on Mannheim Road.

Two days later we found Vincent Moretti and Donald Swanson, aka Donald Renno. Their bodies were in the backseat of Swanson's Cadillac in the parking lot of a restaurant, Esther's Place, at 5009 South Central Avenue in Stickney, a southwestern suburb of Chicago. Moretti was an Italian boy. He, of all the suspected Accardo residence burglars, should have known better. His face had been burned off with an acetylene torch. He had been castrated and disemboweled. And, like Swanson and his pals, his throat was slashed from ear to ear.

Then came the moment of truth for John Mendell. He had been the electronics expert who had defeated the burglar alarms at Levinson's and, still so hard to believe, at Accardo's Ashland Avenue abode. On February 20, police discovered his body in the trunk of his 1971 Olds, parked in the 6300 block of South Campbell in Chicago. Mendell had also been tortured before his throat was slashed.

It looked for a time as though the deeds had been done. Five well-known burglars had been tortured and killed. But it was only the beginning. On April 14, forty-two-year-old Johnny McDonald was found, throat slashed, shot in the head and neck, in an alley behind 442 North Racine on the west side of Chicago—not far, in fact, from the area where Tony Accardo had been born and raised. McDonald had once been tried for burglary with Bernie Ryan and had been questioned by police about Ryan's murder.

But there was one more to come before this massacre was complete. On April 26, another well-known Chicago area burglar was found as what the mob in Chicago calls "trunk music." His body, throat cut and full of bullet holes, was found in the trunk of his car in a Jewel store parking lot at 3552 Grand Avenue in Chicago. Though only twenty-two years old, Bobby Hertogs had already carved out a lucrative professional career as a member of the Ryan-Mendell-Garcia-Moretti-Swanson crew.

Although it is hard to believe all seven burglars had invaded Accardo's River Forest home, they all died for it. For decades the word has been out that if you work on "jobs" in Chicago, you stay away from River Forest. The mob bosses live there and they want no harassment from the police. For decades River Forest has been the cleanest suburb in Cook County, perhaps in the country, along with Grosse Point, Michigan, where the Detroit mob chiefs have traditionally resided. Not only had these guys invaded River Forest, they raided the home of The Man. And they paid for it. Not by being handcuffed and led to jail to receive the best that Chicago's many criminal defense attorneys could deliver (not that Chicago's justice system, where in recent years almost a hundred Cook County judges and other court personnel have been convicted of bribery to fix criminal cases, is anything to brag about), but instead to a swifter fate of death after brutal torture. What a way to go!

But the story still does not end there.

Many Chicago mob watchers could not believe this. They

couldn't believe, first of all, that Tony Accardo would be foolish enough to keep incriminating evidence in his own house. He probably didn't. But apparently these seven idiot-burglars believed he did. The mob watchers also could not believe that any Chicago-area thief would be stupid enough, or gutsy enough, to go after it in Accardo's house. But they did. Or at least they were perceived by Tony Accardo to have done so. It was one way for society to rid itself of seven of the top burglars in Chicago—something the criminal justice system hadn't done.

The mob watchers might not have believed it, but the federal government did. Our informants told us what had happened. Therefore, in September a federal grand jury in the Northern District of Illinois (Chicago) held hearings on the situation. Accardo was the first witness. He spent little time in the criminal justice system this time—like all other times. He asserted his constitutional rights against self-incrimination and took the Fifth.

Then Michael Volpe was subpoenaed. He spent a much longer time before the grand jury. Testimony before a grand jury is sacred. It cannot be revealed. Therefore, what Volpe told the grand jury cannot be revealed, not even here. Suffice it to say, it was significant. Five days after his grand jury appearance, on October 5, Volpe disappeared. He was reported officially missing by a family member. He has never been seen since, the eighth victim of this bizarre situation.

Now the FBI became involved. Ordinarily, when a victim is murdered and there is no interstate character to the crime, the federal government does not get involved. But here Volpe had been a witness before the federal grand jury. There was a strong possibility that he had been murdered because of some element in his testimony before the federal grand jury. That, then, was an official obstruction of justice.

On Friday, November 10, 1978, more than a dozen FBI agents executed a search warrant relating to the luxurious home at 1407 Ashland Avenue in River Forest, the home of Tony Accardo. Never before had the FBI been in that residence. In all the times we penetrated homes of Chicago mobsters to install hidden mikes, bugs, etc., we had never been able to get into Accardo's home. But now, just months after I had left Chicago after twenty-four years there, we would finally get inside, and this time with the paper proclaiming our right to search and seize. Oh, how I wish I had still been in Chicago! I might well have led that search party. After all, by 1978 I had been on Tony's case for twenty-one years.

But I was now assigned to our office in Tucson, Arizona, working instead on another mob legend, Joe Bonanno.

With the counsel of Douglas Roller, Chief of the Justice Department's Organized Crime Strike Force in Chicago, the agents spread throughout the house. Accardo was once more at his condo in Palm Springs. To gain entry, the agents had sought out his elder daughter, Marie, who was married to the union boss Ernie Kumerow, who lived just a few blocks away. She and Accardo family attorney Bernard Bruno admitted the agents after Bruno inspected the sufficiency of the search warrant. Soon Accardo's other daughter, Linda Lee Palermo, arrived with Accardo's criminal defense attorney, Carl Walsh. All told, the agents spent some seven hours searching every room in Tony Accardo's spacious home.

In the upstairs kitchen the agents found and seized a telephone memo pad. Interestingly enough, it contained the name and phone number of Levinson. Also seized upstairs was a police radio scanner, just like the one John Mendell had presumably used during his burglaries and which had turned up missing after his body was recovered. Also upstairs they seized a pair of gold cuff links.

Then the agents hit the basement, the location of countless mob meetings in the past. A lot of history there! Behind the basement stairs at the north end of the house, the agents found an elaborate heating and air-conditioning system as well as an incinerator. They seized the residue in the incinerator. A center hallway ran the length of that basement, and its walls were lined with pictures and cases housing what had become the famed Accardo gun collection. On one side of the hallway was a large, neat, fully equipped workshop, a utility room and a large, handsomely furnished office, of which the centerpiece was a large, beautiful wooden desk. Across the hall from the office was a very large room, also carpeted and furnished with a huge circular table surrounded by thirty chairs. How many strategies had been plotted there? How many murders sanctioned by Accardo after their reasoning had been presented to him by the likes of Giancana, Alderisio, Cerone, Aiuppa and other bosses who reported to The Man?

Adjoining this room was a large industrial-type kitchen and, back up the hallway, two pantries. In the first pantry the agents found mostly shelf items, canned goods and a lot of pasta. In the second pantry the FBI found a walk-in cellar stocked with the most expensive wines and a walk-in freezer.

It was then that the FBI agents made their most important discovery. They found a locked door which none of the keys in the household key cabinet would unlock. Marie and Linda Lee were unable to explain what was inside or how to obtain entrance. So the agents broke down the door, only to find that it guarded a vault. Rather than admit defeat, the agents called a locksmith, but before he could arrive, attorney Bernard Bruno called Palm Springs. Resignedly, Accardo gave him the combination to the lock. When the vault was opened, the agents found a ten-foot by fifteen-foot walk-in. On one shelf, in a velvet bag, the agents found and seized two .38 caliber, snub-nosed Smith and Wesson revolvers and a pile of bullets.

By now all the agents were in the vault, and it was there, in a wine box, that they found fifty-five stacks of $50 and $100 bills bound with rubber bands, each amounting, very neatly, to $5,000—a total of over a quarter of a million dollars, $275,000 in all, some still in bank wrappers from The Valley Bank in Las Vegas. Over the fierce objections of Walsh and Bruno, to say nothing of Linda Lee and Marie, and after several telephonic conferences with Roller and his associate Carl Weiner, who worked in the Strike Force offices in the Federal Building in the Loop, the agents seized the cash.

Now the attorneys of Accardo moved in court for the suppression of the seized items, the cash in particular. Even though it was highly unusual to have such a nice sum sitting idly in one's basement, this did not necessarily indicate that a crime had been committed. On the other hand, as we will see later, Accardo had been indicted for claiming that he used a red Mercedes to earn just $65,000 a year. The existence of such an amount stashed in his basement might suggest that Accardo had something to hide, for example, on his income tax return. U.S. District Court Judge George Leighton, once the attorney for Accardo's successor, Sam Giancana, thought so. He found that the government had sustained its burden of showing probable cause for the search and seizures and denied the Accardo motion to have the money returned and other items suppressed.

The government then presented its evidence to a federal grand jury. They called before it an old pal of Accardo, Linda Lee's father-in-law, Nick Palermo, a plumber by trade. They also called somebody much more important, an old foe of mine, Dominic "Butch" Blasi. Butch had started out as Accardo's driver-bodyguard-appointment secretary before becoming the close confidant of Giancana when Giancana took over the reins of the Chicago mob in 1957 at Accardo's insistence. Many people believe that Butch was also the guy who killed Giancana by gunning him down in his basement-office in Oak Park, on Accardo's orders, in 1975. Both Palermo and Blasi refused to testify. Both were granted immunity, however. If they couldn't be prosecuted due to their immunity, they couldn't incriminate themselves. Therefore, they had no recourse to the Fifth Amendment. Finally, Palermo did testify. His testimony proved worthless as far as an indictment of Accardo was concerned.

Blasi, however, was a different story. I have confronted Butch on dozens of occasions as he bodyguarded Accardo, then Giancana, then later Joe Aiuppa, when each was the mob boss. We started off as enemies, at arm's length, but we ended up not entirely so. He was one tough son of a gun. But I always respected his faithfulness to his wife, Connie. While others partied with a lady of that particular night, Butch never did. He was loyal, not only to Connie but to Accardo, and we in the force knew it. And in fact, he stood up for Accardo in the grand jury. When he refused to testify even though he had no legal right to do so, he was found in contempt of court. He would spend eighteen months in the confines of the MCC, the Metropolitan Correction Center, on the south edge of the Loop. He may or may not have had information regarding Accardo's involvement in the "trunk music," but no one will ever know—no one on this side of law enforcement, that is. Butch was what the mob calls a "stand up guy."

On May 22, 1979, the body of John Borsellino was found dead in a farmer's field near the Cook-Will county line. He had been shot several times. Then, in an apartment development in suburban Addison, Gerry Carusiello was found dead, shot seven times in the back. Carusiello had been a driver for Joey Aiuppa, in 1979 now operating under Accardo as the mob boss.

Although not connected at the time of the killings, the FBI would soon determine the reason for the gangland slayings of Borsellino and Carusiello. They had been the mob hitmen who were involved in the executions of the seven burglars, the bumblers in the Accardo house.

Aiuppa himself came before the grand jury, described by prosecutors as a "target" of the investigation. Judge James Parsons noted that he had long been under federal investigation because he "held a widely reputed position as the kingpin of organized crime operating out of Chicago." A little hyperbole to those of us who knew that Joe Batters was the true kingpin, the person who sanctioned every major move by the Outfit. But close is good enough for government work. Nothing came from Aiuppa's appearance, however. Others came before the FGJ too, even Carl Walsh, the attorney who was present during the FBI raid at 1407 North Ashland, with no results. As a matter of fact, the U.S. Court of Appeals for the Seventh Circuit (the same court which, as we shall see, overturned the conviction of Accardo years before) eventually ordered the return to Accardo of the $275,000 seized in the search of his basement.

In truth, not just ten had been executed in direct relationship to the house at 1407 North Ashland in River Forest, but eleven. The contractor in the building of this home in 1963 was a man named Sam Panveno, who used the professional name of Van Corbin. He was a trusted associate of Accardo. While he was building the home, I contacted him. Even at this point I cannot say that I got the blueprints, the architectural drawings, for the house. Let's just say they would have been invaluable if we in the FBI were interested in doing what we were doing in those days—putting hidden microphones and other listening devices into the meeting places of mob leaders such as Accardo. We had several in the homes of more than one of his closest associates in the early Sixties. Accardo learned of my contact of Van Corbin—not from us but from Van Corbin himself. It wasn't long after, on July 20, 1966, that Corbin was shot and killed by two men with silencers on their guns outside the Country Club Motel at 8303 North Avenue in Melrose Park, a western suburb of Chicago. He had been hiding out there with his wife and family. The murder has not been solved to this day and we never knew the precise motive, although it was speculated that Corbin was not convincing when he informed Accardo of my interview with him prior to his death.

This story of the burglary and its legacy is an appropriate beginning to the story of Tony Accardo, aka Joe Batters. The government took many shots at Joe. There was much excitement when we thought we had him against the ropes. A lot of flash, a lot of flurry. Years of man-hours, tons of resources, penetration of his headquarters with a hidden mike, numerous confrontations, scores of surveillances, two or three indictments, even a conviction, and yet the man often bragged, even until he passed on, that he had never spent a night in jail. What a read his story makes!

BOOK ONE

THE RISE

2 The Kid

He was a shoemaker. Francesco Accardo, Tony's father, was born in Italy on March 13, 1876. After he married Maria Tillota, they moved to Palermo, Sicily, where their first offspring, Martin Leonardo, was born on March 18 at the turn of the century.

Five years later Francesco would move again, this time all the way across the Atlantic. Soon Maria and Martin, aged twenty-one and five, respectively, would follow from Castelvetrano, where they were living. Ironically enough—their second, yet unborn, son would turn out to be the scourge of his country—they arrived at Ellis Island on the Fourth of July. They debarked from the S.S. *Gertz* and proceeded to Chicago, where they joined Francesco.

The family settled in Chicago's Little Sicily, the area around Grand Avenue and Ogden Avenue on the city's near west side. Many fellow Sicilian immigrants settled there, hence the name. At the same time most Italian immigrants were settling just a mile or so to the south, in "The Patch," around Taylor Street and Halsted Street.

Francesco continued to make his living as a shoemaker. He set up one-man shops in the different homes he maintained for his family, first at 560½ Harrison, then eight blocks west on Harrison at 1357, and then eleven blocks north at 1353 Grand Avenue.

It was there, on April 28, 1906, that the second son was born. He was baptized at the nearby Holy Name Cathedral under the name of Antonino Leonardo Accardo, the godson of Fillippo Saccomanno and Nemida Bocilla, close friends of the Accardos. During the next twelve years Francesco and Maria would have four more children—first, three daughters: Bessie, Martha and Maria; then a son, John Phillip, born in 1918.

Antonino started grade school in 1911, at the beginning of the fall term. The lucky institution was the James Otis Elementary

School, located in Little Sicily at 525 North Armour Street. By 1916 he could be found in the fourth grade of the Washington Grade School, still in Little Sicily, at 1000 Grand Avenue.

In 1920 Antonino was fourteen. Francesco and Maria were not impressed with his progress in school, and Antonino was feeling unsettled. Rather than having him continue in school where, although Antonino was at least as bright as his fellow students, he had no inclination to stick his nose into textbooks, Francesco and Maria threw up their hands and did something which was quite common at that time in the neighborhood. They filed a delayed birth record affidavit in order to beat the compulsory education law and the child labor law, laws they felt were unnecessary in their new country, laws which did not exist at the time in Sicily or Italy. Antonino's birth was listed on the affidavit as having taken place in Chicago on April 28, 1904, a full two years before his actual birth. Now he was officially sixteen, the legal age to drop out of school and obtain a job. No one bothered to check to see that Maria had not even entered the country until 1905.

Antonino's first brush with the law would hardly be a harbinger of what was to follow. On March 22, 1922, about six weeks before he legitimately turned sixteen, he was arrested for a motor vehicle violation.

In 1923 things got a little more serious. But not much. Young Tony, as he was now being called more and more by his Americanized companions, got collared for disorderly conduct. He had been found loitering in the area of a neighborhood pool hall where suspicious characters were known to frequent. He was fined $200 and costs. The record shows that he was still living at home at the age of seventeen with Francesco and Maria at 1353 Grand, and that Francesco was still at his trade as a shoemaker.

It was at this time that the teenaged Tony joined the Circus Cafe Gang, sometimes known simply as the Circus Gang. The reason for the moniker was that this gang of young toughs hung out at the Circus Cafe, at 1857 North Avenue, some eleven blocks north and three blocks west of the Accardo home. At least three of the thugs associated with the Circus Cafe Gang at that time would go on to much bigger things, and that does not count young Tony. The gang's leader was Claude Maddox, better known in his circles and later in the media as Screwy Moore. Another was Anthony Capezio, later to be known to the Chicago public as Tough Tony. Yet a third was Vincenzo De Mora. He would achieve lasting infamy as Machine Gun Jack McGurn.

Young Tony Accardo started out as just another young punk in the gang, doing his share of muggings and pickpocketing at first, usually in the Loop, located just about twenty blocks from his home. Old men and ladies, drunks were the initial prey. Then came the home invasions, usually in the more affluent neighborhoods north and west of Little Sicily, never south in The Patch or near home. Then came armed robberies, car thefts and jackrolling, where even a potentially vigorous victim could be approached from behind and smashed over the head with a brick or any other hard object. Tony Accardo was climbing his ladder of crime.

It is at this point, in the early Twenties, that the Volstead Act implemented Prohibition.

Accardo was working during the day as a delivery boy, grocery clerk and, later, as a truck driver. He did this for a brief period and only during the day as he planned his nocturnal escapades. Now, with the advent of the Eighteenth Amendment, a new cottage industry sprang up to augment the income of the residents of Little Sicily and The Patch. Almost every family, including the Accardos, cooked alcohol to be used in the manufacture of bootleg whiskey. The small quantities of alcohol produced daily in the kitchens on Grand Avenue and at Taylor and Halsted fed the speakeasies which had grown up by the hundreds in Chicago. As a truck driver, it became young Tony's duty to haul the alcohol from the neighborhood to a central distribution center, where the big boys would take it and pass it along to the thirsty populace in the Windy City.

During this period of his life, the youngster would be arrested eight times before he reached the voting age, nearly always for disorderly conduct, and never spent a night in jail for it. And it was at this time that one of the Gang made his way off the minor league team and into the big leagues. De Mora, aka Machine Gun Jack McGurn, was recruited into what had by now become the Capone Gang. The year was 1925.

McGurn would not forget his young pal, Tony Accardo.

3 The Genesis

In order to understand what was to happen to Carl Sandburg's City of the Big Shoulders in the Roaring Twenties, it is helpful to take a short sprint through Chicago's turbulent history leading up to that period.

Perhaps the best place to start in this regard would be the Great Chicago Fire. It broke out in the barn of Patrick O'Leary in the rear of 137 De Koven Street on a Sunday morning, October 8, 1871. Up until this point Chicago had been a truly great city. But since little rain had fallen during the summer of 1871, the frame buildings of the city were dry as tinder. A strong wind was blowing. Flames from O'Leary's barn whipped northward into the Loop. Soon the fire was an inferno, destroying everything in its path, including the fire engines sent to put it out. Then the city jail caught fire, freeing robbers and thieves, who spread out during the catastrophe; 2004 acres in the middle of the city were leveled by the fire, 18,000 buildings were destroyed, 3,000 people were killed. Property damage exceeded $200,000,000. And the criminals had a field day. Everything in sight was looted. Martial law under General Phil Sheridan was declared. The spirit of the citizens of Chicago appeared broken, the city prostrated. But in time, the resolute character of the people of Chicago rebounded. And the city was rebuilt better than ever, as we know.

No history of Chicago from the perspective of the mob would be complete without examination of the role of Bathhouse John Coughlin and his partner, Hinky Dink Kenna. At the turn of the century, these men were the aldermen of the First Ward (there were two aldermen, members of the city council, in each ward at that time), the most strategic ward in the city until the wards were restructured in 1992. Bathhouse John was a lowlife who operated a bathhouse at 145 West Madison Street, in the Loop, patronized by gamblers and thieves. Hinky Dink ran a saloon in the Loop.

The First Ward, until 1992, encompassed the most important area of Chicago. It contained the Loop, the Near West Side and the Near South Side. In addition to the cheap flophouses, brothels and gambling houses, the ward contained the rich downtown shopping district, fine department stores, restaurants, skyscrapers, theaters, the best hotels and the largest banks. The Loop is named for the encirclement of this area by the elevated railway tracks of the CTA, the Chicago Transit Authority. These trains brought the thousands of workers and shoppers downtown. Also incorporated inside the Loop, then and now, are scores of the largest giants of industry, commerce and finance which contribute then and now to the economic welfare of the entire nation. This, then, was the empire of Bathhouse John and Hinky Dink. Their alliance, first formed in 1893 and which continued for half a century, was a natural. As we will see, these two aldermen would be nothing but an extension of the underworld, as would their successors in the First Ward as the decades piled upon each other into the future of Chicago.

Another factor in the unrest of Chicago near the turn of the century was the Pullman Strike in 1894. Eugene V. Debs, the leader of the American Railway Union, led the strike, which resulted in violence from the strikers, who threw bricks at the locomotives of the Pullman Company. Trains were overturned, freight trains were burned. Men were shot and killed in the railroad yards. An explosion killed three more. Groups of strikers roamed the city wrecking property. Finally President Grover Cleveland ordered troops to Chicago and martial law was once again declared. At last the strike was broken, ending a startling episode of violence in Chicago's young history.

By 1907 Mont Tennes had become the czar of gambling in the city. At the time Chicago was considered the biggest handbook center in the country. Tennes ruled the roost, protected as he was by Bathhouse John and Hinky Dink, politicians who were the forerunners of many to come who were corrupted by the gangsters and who provided protection for them. Even in the early part of the twentieth century, Chicago was burdened with corrupt public officials who accepted the bribes and other considerations of the criminals in order to provide the favorable treatment needed to shield their illegal activity from the public.

It was at this time that the first battle occurred for control of the wire service, the operation which provided the handicapping odds on horse races throughout the country—the service which no bookmaker, big or small, could operate without. It was cause for war. Several homes of the people affiliated with Mont Tennes' control of the wire service were bombed in the summer of 1907, even Tennes' own home. This violence led to a grand jury investigation in September, which determined that both the mayor, Fred Busse, and the Chief of Police, George Shippy, were under the control of Tennes and his syndicate—a precursor of things to come in Chicago. The resort to violence among the rival gangs also portended future events.

Chicago's sordid history would not be complete without mention of the Everleigh Club, the notorious bawdy house. It was operated by the otherwise demure Lester Sisters at 2131–33 South Dearborn Street, south of the Loop. This area was known as The Levee and was the center, as it would be for decades thereafter, of vice, primarily prostitution. Probably at no time in our history has prostitution been as widespread, even extending at times into so-called "respectable" circles.

By August of 1911, there were fifty wide-open gambling joints operating in the Loop alone, twenty-four hours a day, seven days a week. Even the downtown hotels, the best in Chicago, operated games and employed "cappers" and "ropers" to entice patrons to their gaming tables. A gambling establishment of one kind or another could be found in almost every block of the Loop. All were provided protection from police interference by the Tennes syndicate. Horse race betting, poolroom and faro, crap games and roulette wheels were the games of choice. An investigation in 1911 by the Civil Service Commission revealed that police raids were made only on the instructions of Tennes and his key lieutenant of the day, Mike "de Pike" Heitler. Those raids were made, as the record makes clear, only on those who competed with the syndicate for gambling spots. The Commission's report included mention of the notorious First Ward Ball, which was conducted at the Chicago Coliseum and attended almost exclusively by gamblers, pickpockets, safeblowers, thugs, drug addicts and the madams, inmates and procurers attached to the bawdy houses of the district. These people contributed thousands of dollars to the treasury of the First Ward for disbursement to the police officers, judges and other public officials who turned a blind eye to their illegal activity of the day.

At this time, a soon-to-be-powerful figure in the underworld of Chicago began to make his presence felt. Big Jim Colosimo and his wife operated a prosperous restaurant in the Levee, at Twenty-first Street and Armour Avenue. Big Jim was becoming a prime figure in the First Ward, becoming closely associated with Hinky

Dink and Bathhouse John. Yet even these determined men could not save the Lester Sisters, now known more and more as the Everleigh sisters, and their brothel. They had made the mistake of circulating a brochure advertising the accommodations of the Everleigh Club and its girls to visitors to Chicago, circulating the brochure at the hotels and restaurants where guests in Chicago came to visit. It was giving the city a bad name. Then-mayor Carter Harrison ordered a crackdown in the Levee, especially at the Everleigh Club, which was raided and put out of business. This was followed by raids at other brothels in the red-light district. Violence erupted. Murders followed. On July 18, 1914, vice lords shot and killed Detective Sergeant Stanley Birns of the morals squad and wounded another officer. The Chicago *Tribune* laid the blame for the violence where it belonged, on Hinky Dink, The Bath and Police Captain Michael Ryan of the Twenty-second Street Police Station, the "Chief of Police of the First Ward." The *Tribune* charged, accurately, that Ryan had been placed there by Hinky Dink and that he was either thoroughly corrupt or incompetent. Such scandals were but shades of things to come for the next seventy years.

Harrison was a good mayor for Chicago, but his political future was tied up with The Hink and The Bath. And their power came from the Chicago underworld of the day.

It was a long way from Chicago, but events on June 18, 1914, would nonetheless open as the next chapter in Chicago's history of crime. On that day Archduke Francis Ferdinand was assassinated in Sarajevo by a Serbian member of the Black Hand terrorist organization, "Union or Death." Mayor Harrison had campaigned in a manner to cater to the huge German vote in Chicago, but with the outbreak of World War I, his reputation as pro-German backfired. His opponent, William Hale Thompson, then a relatively unknown Republican, became mayor.

Thompson would continue to hold that position, with one short interruption, for almost the next two decades, a great opportunity for the underworld of the day. Mayor Harrison, as evidenced by his raids on the Everleigh Club and the rest of the vice lords in the Levee, had been an impediment to their development. On the other hand, Big Bill, "The Cowboy," promised a wide-open city. And it was no surprise. Big Bill had been closely identified with The Sportsman's Club, the medium through which graft flowed to Chicago's politicians from the gambling industry. His name appeared on the letterhead of a letter, which shows the arrogance of the day, addressed to the gamblers and vice lords, the leaders of the underworld, soliciting membership. Also on the letterhead were the names of Mont Tennes, the gambling boss; Herbert Mills, manufacturer of the city's thousands of slot machines; Big Jim Colosimo, the boss of the Levee at the time; and two top police officials: Chief of Police Charles Healey and Captain Morgan Collins. Talk about the smoking gun! Here was a club of friendly pals, the vice lords and the top policemen whose job it was to put them away, openly consorting with each other along with the mayor of the city. If we are to understand anything about the background for corruption of public officials in Chicago, we must consider the situation at the Sportsman's Club in 1916. In the same year, the State's Attorney commenced an investigation of the situation, and indeed, on January 16, 1917, indictments charging bribery and graft were returned implicating eight men, including Chief of Police Healey; another police captain named Tom Costello; Mike "de Pike" Heitler; William Skidmore, a saloon keeper, gambler and politician of considerable notoriety at the time; and two other policemen.

Then came the race riots of 1919. When the United States entered World War I on April 6, 1917, there had been 44,000 African-Americans in Chicago. During the war there was a great shortage of workers in the stockyards, steel mills and factories. African-Americans from the South migrated to Chicago to fill those vacancies in the labor market, and by the time the Armistice was signed on November 11, 1918, the black population of Chicago had increased to over 100,000, largely concentrated on the South Side, just beyond the Levee district. These people needed places to live, and as they pushed south as far as Sixty-third Street, tensions developed with the people who had lived there in comfort for decades. During 1918 several African-American homes were bombed. It all exploded on Sunday, July 27, 1919, at the Twenty-ninth Street beach on Lake Michigan. An altercation between white and black bathers erupted, and an African-American boy was drowned. The news spread like wildfire. "The Whites have killed a Negro!" Pitched battles were fought on the south-side streets. Bands of whites roamed the black areas bombing and burning homes. There were shootings and stabbings. The riots went on for five days. The police, meanwhile, appeared to be helpless; they seemed to make no effort to protect the blacks, even those who were being physically assaulted in their very presence. Finally, on the sixth day, the militia was once again called in to protect Chicago. It was not until then that this great blemish on the history of Chicago was ended.

By 1919 Big Jim Colosimo had successfully entrenched himself as the overlord of the underworld in the city. Although there were others who operated in spheres of influence, such as the gambling boss, Mont Tennes, and Dennis Cooney, known as "The Duke," it was Big Jim, coexisting with the benevolence of Big Bill, who ruled the roost.

These were the formative years of Tony Accardo. The kid was in his developing years, as was the underworld of Chicago at the time. He was a grade school dropout, about to be inducted into the Circus Cafe Gang. This was the Chicago where he began his life of eighty-six years. In 1919 Tony Accardo was thirteen years old. It is unlikely that he knew who Big Jim Colosimo was at the time, but he would soon learn, because the elevation of Big Jim Colosimo to the top of the Chicago underworld as it existed in 1919 was the genesis of organized crime as we know it. And because young Tony Accardo would become the man to perfect it.

4 The Underboss Becomes Boss

Big Jim had immigrated from Consenza, Italy, to Chicago in 1895. He had been a street sweeper in the Department of Streets and Sanitation in Chicago, then began his climb to power by organizing his co-workers into a union, which he used as his base to attract The Hink and The Bath. He became a precinct captain under them in the First Ward. This gave him the muscle to open what would soon become one of the most famous nightspots in the history of Chicago, Colosimo's Cafe, at 2128 South Wabash in the Levee. It became the prime hangout for the racketeers of the day. The walls were covered with velvet, the chandeliers were of solid gold. The most famous singer of the day, Enrico Caruso, and the most famous attorney of the day, Clarence Darrow, were frequent patrons. They mingled elbow to elbow with the underworld and with the politicians of the day, one group indistinguishable from the other. At the same time, Big Jim built and maintained "cribs" all over town. These were mini-brothels, where the girls grinded the johns in and out. Quick, fast.

Big Jim soon became the flashiest dresser in town, with diamonds on almost every finger. He obtained the diamonds as one of the top fences for stolen jewelry and furs in Chicago. Many a cop received a weekly envelope fitted, not with cash, but diamonds. It became Big Jim's trademark. He even carried them like marbles in his pocket, and became famous for throwing a few to urchins on the streets. Big Jim became Big Flash. Nobody personified the beginning of the Roaring Twenties as he did.

His partner in crime was his wife, Victoria, née Moresco, who became the most famous madam of the day. Between the two of them, they furnished the tourist trade—and the citizens of Chicago—with what they promised was the very best sex in Chicago.

As Big Jim was reaching his zenith in his climb to the top of the Chicago underworld, he realized that he had need of a strong right hand, what in years later would be known as a *sotto capo*, or underboss. For this reason he reached out, all the way to the Big Apple, where for years Johnny Torrio had been the leader of a strong faction of the New York underworld, but not one of the top faction. They were called the James Street Gang and made the waterfront of the East River in lower Manhattan their domain. While dealing with other factions of the New York City gangs, Torrio had visited Chicago from time to time on matters of mutual interest. He had come to the attention of Big Jim when he frequented Colosimo's Cafe. Torrio, while small in stature, had brains. And Big Jim was just smart enough to recognize his abilities. Colosimo made a pitch: Johnny Torrio would be better off as the number one man to the boss in Chicago than as the leader of a small faction along the East River of New York City. Torrio agreed, and accepted Colosimo's offer.

Torrio had been in Chicago just long enough when a landmark event in the annals of organized crime occurred. On October 18, 1919, the National Prohibition Act was passed, effective January 16, 1920. At the same time, William Hale Thompson was reelected. Things were ripe for a major breakthrough. By this time, Torrio had learned the territory. He had ingratiated himself with The Hink and The Bath, with Mont Tennes and Dennis "The Duke."

Torrio had become the power behind the throne, even as Big Jim was losing his head over a singer (as would another boss of the Chicago mob some forty years later). He divorced Vickie and married the songbird, Dale Winter, on April 20, 1920. (Why, early 1920 was only one of the most important times in the history of mobdom in Chicago—or anyplace else. When Big Jim should have been thinking of the potential created by the Volstead Act, he was on his honeymoon! Truly, a case of the little head leading the big one.)

Johnny Torrio, on the other hand, had the foresight to recognize immediately what Prohibition might mean to somebody who controlled the underworld. Johnny Torrio decided that if his boss wasn't interested, if he couldn't fathom the potential, if he was more interested in his love life than in his mob life, maybe he shouldn't have a life at all.

The deed was done by an import, the consensus being that it was Frankie Yale, real name Uale. This author, who would later hear the killing discussed by top leaders of the Chicago mob on the hidden mike he had helped place in their headquarters, is not so confident it was Yale. Yale was another Johnny Torrio. He had things going well for him in New York. Very well. He did have the propensity for killing and would have been a natural for the job, but the killer may well have been another guy Torrio brought to Chicago from New York in 1919 and stashed at the Four Deuces, Torrio's headquarters at 2222 South Wabash, also in the heart of the Levee. This guy had been a member of the Five Points Gang in New York, just as tough as the James Street Gang, and he was on the lam from the police for two murders in New York. He, therefore, had the incentive and the wherewithal to do the job Torrio wanted done. And he was already in place, ready, willing and able. This guy's name was Al Capone.

In any event, the deed was done. Torrio had set it up well, arranging for Big Jim to be situated in the vestibule of his restaurant awaiting the delivery of two truckloads of whiskey by Jim O'Leary, the gambling boss of the nearby stockyards district. It would be shots of more than liquor that Colosimo received. The first of two hit him square in the head. He was dead before he hit the floor. He had had a pearl-handled revolver in his pocket but he never got the chance to use it.

When I researched this, I was most interested in attempting to learn who the pallbearers for Colosimo had been. My great interest in tracking the mob has always been their alliance with politicians. As I testified before the U.S. Senate, that alliance is the "umbrella which shields and the linchpin which holds the mob together." My research in this instance did not go unrewarded. The honorary pallbearers included three judges, an assistant state's attorney, a congressman, a state representative, numerous aldermen, including Hinky Dink but for some reason not Bathhouse John, and another who was to become a federal judge. The Bath, though not a pallbearer, was conspicuous as he knelt in prayer before the casket. Why was I not surprised? Since Big Jim was the personification of the early days of modern organized crime in Chicago, it was natural that members of the "umbrella and the linchpin" would dignify him by escorting him to his grave. After all, hadn't they held his hand all the way while he was greasing theirs? How many diamonds had Big Jim dispensed to the lot of them—and to many, many other public officials in Chicago? This official display of affection for the underworld chief clearly demonstrated that the underworld ruled the city. That is a strong statement and might be challenged by some, but I believe that after listening to the mobsters on our hidden bugs talking about those days—and many thereafter—there is foundation for that premise.

One of the other honorary pallbearers was Johnny Torrio, but Colosimo wasn't cold in his grave before Torrio began to plan his ascension to the throne. It was not, after all, as if he had been taken by surprise. And as the *sotto capo*, he had the background, experience and capability to take over the top spot, and he had a cadre of capable soldiers to leap right into whatever field he wanted to invade. What's more, he had a very capable guy he wanted to move up to be his *sotto capo*. Perhaps he should have given that further thought. After all, well he knew the story of a *sotto capo* who aspired to be the boss.

5 Another Underboss Becomes Boss

There is a popular misconception today that before Al Capone became the leader of what is commonly known as the Capone Gang what passed for organized crime was weak and ineffectual, that as the Roaring Twenties began, first under Big Jim and then under Johnny Torrio, there was no real organization at all, and that Al Capone was the guy who put it all together. That is not true.

When Tony Accardo was in his mid-teens, and an active member of the Circus Cafe Gang, the mob, although still unnamed, was a powerful force. A hearing of the United States Senate Judiciary Committee on May 10, 1920, just after the initiation of Prohibition, made it clear that Chicago was the undisputed headquarters in the country for crime and vice. This forerunner of the Kefauver and McClellan Committees, of 1950 and 1959 respectively, disclosed evidence showing that Chicago was the center of handbook gambling in the nation. Gambling was rampant but bootlegging did not lag as a source of income to the underworld. In fact, in 1921 Mayor Thompson's new chief of police, Charles C. Fitzmorris, candidly admitted that a large percentage of his officers in the Chicago PD were actively engaged in the illicit liquor business.

Soon Warren G. Harding would be elected president, and with him, his corrupt administration, perhaps the most corrupt of all time (this eventually led to the Teapot Dome Scandal). Therefore, in the early Twenties, while Accardo was growing up out of school, there was a corrupt mayor, Big Bill Thompson; a corrupt governor, Len Small; and a corrupt federal administration.

Things could have changed in 1923 when an honest mayor, Judge William E. Dever, was elected. But by then Johnny Torrio and his boys were firmly entrenched. Judge Dever would make little difference. On the contrary, Torrio, ever astute, made a move to include the suburbs of Chicago into his fiefdom, especially Cicero, adjoining Chicago on the west-southwest. Also Burnham to the south and Stickney to the near southwest. Johnny Torrio was at the height of his power, certainly as powerful as any mobster in the country, even those in New York where he had started. His move to join Colosimo had been a very wise one. He had been so successful, he couldn't count his assets. He owned the West Hammond and the Manhattan breweries and had financial interests in others in Chicago. He bought a villa in Italy in order to return his mother to her homeland.

Then on January 24, 1925, an attempt was made on Torrio's life. Three men, probably "Bugs" Moran, Hymie Weiss and Vince Drucci, rival mobsters, were the assailants. Torrio was seriously wounded and spent several weeks in Jackson Park Hospital, on the south side. He had escaped death by the narrowest of margins. In 1925 Tony Accardo, who was nineteen, was old enough to have what happened next ingrained in his mind: Johnny Torrio, wealthy beyond imagination, sitting on top of the world, had had enough. Enough money, enough power, enough headaches. He turned over what he had to his field general, his chief of operations, his *sotta capo*, Al Capone. Not that Torrio would retire altogether; he would go back to his old stomping grounds, back to the only city where organized crime could rival that of Chicago's, joining Frank Costello, Lucky Luciano, Meyer Lansky and Bugsy Siegel. He felt that it was much safer in the Big Apple than it was in Chicago. (Not that he would be safe from prosecution, however. About ten years after he returned to his beginnings, he was convicted of income tax evasion. By that time the federal government, in the persons of Internal Revenue Service agents, was demonstrating that it could cope with organized crime. Not so the FBI, however. J. Edgar Hoover, in those days, was steadfastly claiming that his bureau had more than enough to do with the crimes it was responsible for investigating, and that organized crime was not within its investigative purview. Mr. Hoover then had no interest whatsoever in the affairs of the mob. He knew there were mobs in Chicago, New York, and in almost all the major cities. But he insisted they did not transcend state lines and, therefore, there was no interstate character to their activities, the element needed to mandate federal jurisdiction. Therefore, while the mobs had to deal with the Prohibition Agency of the U.S. Treasury Department, staffed by such as Eliot Ness and his "Untouchables," and by the IRS, they did not have to be concerned in any way about the FBI. Not for several decades.)

When Al Capone took the reins of the organization from Johnny Torrio, he had a vision somewhat like that of Torrio's, when Torrio had taken over from Jim Colosimo. What Torrio had perceived had all come true. Prohibition was a gold mine for the mobsters. Torrio had taken an organization, started by Colosimo, and enlarged it manyfold, taking advantage of the special opportunity Prohibition gave him. Now he turned it over in great shape to his protégé, Capone, who would take it to even greater heights, both in the number of its members and in the amount of its income. Even Torrio would be astounded by what was to come.

Soon, therefore, Capone was in need of new "soldiers." New recruits. He needed to build his army in much greater numbers, because not only was there opportunity, but there were rival gangs. Witness the guys who shot Torrio: Moran and Weiss. Drucci too. And the Terrible Gennas. And others.

Capone found some of his soldiers in The Patch, among the 42 Gang, a gang of young toughs from the Italian enclave around Taylor and Halsted streets on the near southwest side of the city.

But there were only so many there. He needed many more. And not just anybodies. He needed tough guys, experienced guys, guys who had demonstrated abilities in the field of crime.

Of course, another gang, just as strong as the 42ers, was in existence. These guys were from Little Sicily, just north of The Patch: the Circus Cafe Gang.

Vincenzo De Mora, now known more and more by his nickname, Machine Gun Jack McGurn, had already made his way from the Circus Cafe Gang to the Torrio Gang, now the Al Capone Mob. He was readily consulted by Capone when Capone recognized the need to expand the membership. It is not known for sure, but it is probable that the first guy McGurn recommended to Capone was his protégé, young Tony Accardo. The year was 1926, and Tony was twenty. He had done many "heavy" things in the Circus Cafe Gang. We don't know if he had murdered by then, but if not, he had certainly handled nearly everything else a career criminal could get involved in, including burglaries, hijackings, robberies, muggings, sluggings, car thefts. We do know that he had already become involved in the crux of the Capone empire, illicit alcohol. He was a natural. McGurn could not have overlooked him as a prime recruit when Capone called McGurn in for his advice.

Tony Accardo would now leave his youth. He had graduated. Some of his neighbors had graduated from high school. Tony had never even gotten there. But he was now leapfrogging over all of them, at least as far as *his* ambitions were concerned. His ambition in life was not to succeed in any business world, but to become one of the most successful gangsters of his time. He had now succeeded, at least in the sense that he was now on the bottom rung of the top organization in his field. He vowed to make it all the way to the top rung of that organization, no matter what it took. He would give it his best shot. How prophetic that would soon prove to be.

6 Accardo is "Made" and "Makes His Bones"

Tony Accardo was ushered into the presence of Al Capone early in 1926, in the suite Capone kept at the Metropole Hotel on South Michigan Avenue at Twenty-second Street, just south of the Loop.

When Machine Gun Jack McGurn ushered Tony into the suite and introduced him to Scarface, the conversation probably went something like this:

"Jack says you're a good kid, Accardo. Done some good things. Can be trusted. We're gonna take a chance on you. I need some good people around me now. You know we knocked off O'Banion a few months ago and now those guys around him, like this Hymie Weiss and Drucci, we got the dope they want to revenge O'Banion. So we're being very careful. You also know there have been a bunch of guys who have been whacked in the past couple months. Things around Chicago these days are a little dangerous and we need some more good guys we can trust who can do some heavy work. So we're gonna take a chance on you on Jack's recommendation. You fuck up and it's not only your ass, it's his. You understand what I'm sayin'?" Capone put it on the line.

"Yeah," was all Accardo could reply.

"OK. Now we got a little what they call a ritual here. We call it *omerta*. Jack is your sponsor into our thing here. Shake his hand and hold it."

Accardo did as he was instructed.

Capone intoned the oath: "Do you swear to never fink on your pals in our thing? Do you swear to do the jobs we give you? Do you swear not to go after the wife or girl of any of us? Do you realize what will happen to you if you go back on any of what you are now swearing to?" It wasn't much in Chicago, unlike in New York and the Eastern mobs, even in 1926, where the oath of

32

omerta was administered with great pomp and ceremony, including the burning of a holy card common to the Catholic religion in the hands of the recruit. But it sufficed. Tony Accardo nodded his head and said simply, "Yes." He was now "made." He had been inducted as an actual member of what was now being called the Capone mob. La Cosa Nostra was still five years in the future.

Dion O'Banion had been killed on November 20, 1924. He had been gunned down by Capone's guys in his floral shop on State Street, on the near north side, just south of Chicago Avenue and across the street from the Holy Name Cathedral. If the funeral of Big Jim Colosimo was grand, O'Banion's was even grander. It took twenty-five cars just to lug the floral arrangements to the funeral home—including one from the guy who sanctioned his killing—"From Al," the card said. Some 10,000 people walked behind the hearse, and when it reached Mount Carmel Cemetery, there were 10,000 more waiting there, including Capone and Torrio, who had not yet returned to New York.

On the afternoon of January 12, 1925, the associates of O'Banion went after their revenge. Bugs Moran, Hymie Weiss and Vincent Drucci used a brand-new weapon for this, a tommy gun, which could fire 800 rounds per minute. It had been called "a broom for sweeping trenches" when it was invented in World War I. Only 15,000 had been manufactured. The trio had located Capone's car at State and Fifty-fifth streets on the mid-south side of Chicago. Three people were in the car. When they fired into it, Capone's bodyguard-driver, Sylvester Bloom, was seriously injured, but the intended victim was not—unbeknownst to the gunman, Capone had left the car shortly before their arrival.

There were over two hundred gangland killings in Chicago from 1922 to 1926, and twenty-nine in just the first four months of 1926.

Then on April 27, 1926, just as Accardo was joining Capone, Bill McSwiggin was killed. He had been an assistant Cook County state's attorney who prosecuted some of the Chicago gangsters, but who led a somewhat dichotomous life. His killing caused a furor in Chicago. Although the deed was laid at the feet of Capone and his men, probably rightfully, there is no evidence that the new recruit, Tony Accardo, participated in this murder. He had just joined the Capone mob in April, and it is unclear whether he was ready for a job of this sort. But it is conceivable that Accardo had some peripheral part to play, most likely as a spotter, lookout or driver of the getaway car.

Tony Accardo was definitely present, however, during the next major episode in the affairs of organized crime in Chicago. At midday on September 20, 1926, eleven carloads of members of the Hymie Weiss gang burst into Cicero, which Capone was using, along with his suites at the Metropole Hotel, as his headquarters. Shoppers and workers crowded Twenty-second Street, the prime thoroughfare of Cicero, located contiguous with the western border of Chicago. Capone was having lunch at a restaurant next door to his offices, the Hawthorne Inn. Weiss knew his routine; he had placed spotters in the restaurant who had called him as soon as Capone and his entourage arrived in the restaurant. Tony Accardo, now acting in his assigned role as one of Capone's bodyguards, was with Capone. As Weiss and his pals neared the restaurant in their cars, they slowed. Suddenly, they opened up, firing thousands of rounds of shotgun slugs and machine-gun bullets into the Inn and restaurant. Years later I listened as Accardo claimed that he immediately pulled Capone down and dropped on top of him to shield him. Now, if I heard that from any one of many mobsters I came to know from personal confrontations with them and from listening for thousands of hours to their private conversations, I might feel that the tale was exaggerated—at least a bit—to make the teller look good in the eyes of his colleagues. But I don't feel that way about Accardo's claim. Having listened to him and spoken to him personally, I tend to believe that Accardo generally understated his exploits, if anything. He was not, like most of his brethren, braggadocio. Some might say there were few around at the time to refute most of his stories, but there *were* a few, like Murray "The Camel" Humphreys, Paul Ricca and Joe Fusco, enough so that even if Tony were prone to exaggerate a bit, any stretching of the truth would likely have caught up with him when his story was relayed to them, guys who might not have been at the Inn, but who were all higher in the mob at the time of the incident, in the fall of 1926. I have pledged to be impartial and objective in relaying the story of Tony Accardo, but I must admit much of my story is derived from his own recollections. Now, Tony had a vast vocabulary of obscenities and he certainly was no saint; I wouldn't ask him to be the godfather of my sons, and I'm sure he wouldn't have considered that any particular honor. But he was not a loudmouth braggart or a liar. When he talked, people listened. So it is that when Tony Accardo talks about having been in the restaurant adjacent to the Hawthorne Inn, along with Frankie Rio, a major lieutenant of Capone at the time, I believe.

From Accardo's description, although thousands of bullets

were fired, only six or seven did any damage to live people. Two bystanders were wounded, people who had come to Cicero from Louisiana to attend the races later that afternoon at the Hawthorne Race Track, and a minor gangster.

Accardo's role in guarding Capone now became a daily routine. He could sit for hours in the lobby of the Metropole Hotel with a machine gun on his lap, on a shift with other young toughs who had been inducted into the Capone mob, screening visitors who wanted to use the elevator or the stairs to go upstairs toward Capone's suite. It must have been quite a sight, something we find difficult to envision these days, but obviously not unusual in Roaring Twenties Chicago, when Scarface ruled the roost.

When Capone moved around the city during these formative years in Accardo's career, he took Accardo with him. Sometimes Tony drove Capone's car, sometimes he sat in the shotgun seat, the passenger side. His youthful experience as a truck driver stood him in good stead. (Decades later, one of Capone's cars was on display for months outside the Imperial Palace Hotel-Casino on the Las Vegas Strip, Las Vegas Boulevard South. It had bullet-proof glass, extra thick steel siding, reinforced shocks, a gun rack behind the front seat, extra duty brakes and a heavy duty radiator, fully able to withstand rifle shots.)

Accardo was also assigned, we surmise, to stand guard in the hallway outside a suite in the Morrison Hotel, which served as a meeting room for the mob. (Decades later, the old Morrison would serve not only as the hangout for the mob, but as the head-quarters for Mayor Richard J. Daley and his Cook County Regular Democratic Organization, which he chaired. In fact, as we shall see later, the barber shop of the Morrison, located at 79 West Madison in the heart of the Loop, was the prime message drop for the successors to Capone in the mid-Forties.) In 1926 it was the scene of a sit-down between the forces of Capone and Hymie Weiss. Capone was not present but was represented by his ambassador, Tony Lombardo, then boss of Chicago's chapter of the Unione Siciliano, a social and political organization of Italian-Americans that was greatly under the influence of Capone and his minions—just as the New York chapter was under the influence of the New York mobsters.

At the meeting Lombardo argued that it would be insane to continue the warfare between the Capone mob and the Weiss gang. He told Weiss and the two of Weiss' lieutenants in attendance that there was enough business in Chicago for everyone concerned, and for this reason Capone was willing to make Weiss an offer: if

Weiss agreed to lay down his arms, at least not aim them at the Capone mobsters, he could have the concession of all beer sales north of Madison Street, Madison Street in Chicago being the official dividing line between north and south.

Weiss refused the offer. He was too riled over Capone's killing of his associate O'Banion to reason with Capone or his representative. He made a counteroffer. "Give me Scalise and Anselmi and then we'll talk," he said. These were the two men Weiss believed Capone had used to kill O'Banion.

Lombardo left the meeting and was accompanied by Accardo to a phone in another suite. He called Capone, who was waiting in his suite at the Metropole Hotel for word of the results of the meeting. When Lombardo informed Capone of the terms of Weiss' counteroffer, Capone angrily shouted over the phone, "I wouldn't do that to a dirty dog!" Lombardo returned to the meeting, Accardo resuming his station in the hallway, and told Weiss of Capone's response. Weiss immediately stomped out of the room with his men in tow.

Capone did not wait one minute to make his plans to kill Weiss, since he saw no reasonable possibility that the two gangs could work in harmony in Chicago. The very next day, a man who has never since been identified rented a second-story room on State Street, across from Schofield's flower shop. This is the same store where Anselmi and Scalise, if that's who they truly were, had shot and killed Dion O'Banion when he used it as his headquarters. When Weiss succeeded O'Banion, he too used the flower shop as a headquarters for his gang, which was really a continuation of the O'Banion crew. This second-story room afforded a great view of the front of the floral shop. Although I would later hear Tony indicate that he had sat in the window on Capone's orders watching for Weiss, he never indicated that he was on duty the day, Monday, October 11, 1926, that the Capone forces got Weiss. Whoever it was, they got Weiss with machine-gun fire as he was walking from the store to cross State Street, the 700 block, just south of Chicago Avenue. Weiss was in the company of three men: his lawyer, his driver and one of his bootleggers, and he never made it to the other side. The coroner counted ten bullets in his body. He was DOA, just twenty-eight years old, a little older than Capone was at the time.

Holy Name Cathedral was not immune from damage on this one. Weiss, who was a Polish Catholic—not Jewish, as most people assume—had been an altar boy at the cathedral. How ironic it was that he would die within its shadow! The building's cornerstone had borne as an inscription a quotation from St. Paul's Epistle to the Philippians: "At The Name of Jesus Every Knee Should Bow In Heaven and On Earth." On October 11, 1926, the day after Weiss' murder, mass attendees were startled to notice that the five first words of that inscription had been obliterated, shot off by the guns of the Capone killers. Nothing, it seemed, was sacred. The Chicago *Tribune*, referring to the incident, reported: "Gangdom literally shot piety to pieces."

I was again very interested in the identities of the mourners and those who showed up to pay homage to this gangster. At the time it was just before the local elections in November, and indeed, the funeral procession, once again to Mount Carmel Cemetery, looked like a campaign rally. It seemed every politician of prominence, including those running for judgeships, those who presumably would be called upon in the future to preside over mob trials, was present, their cars emblazoned with campaign signs. "John Sbarbaro for Municipal Judge" was one such slogan.

This was Chicago during the Roaring Twenties. A top gangster is slain by his rival mobster, the bullets ricocheting off the most sacred church in the city—the home of the cardinal, in fact—and here the most prominent public officials use the funeral procession to campaign for their election, some to gain a position from which they planned to mete out justice to the followers of the mob boss in the casket. Many of these, by the way, drove bumper to bumper to the cemetery, then bowed their heads to the Catholic priest, whom the murdered Weiss had served as an altar boy, and incanted the petition to the Lord for his quick arrival in heaven.

A further twist arose the next day when Al Capone called a press conference. A press conference! He told the dozens of reporters who scurried to the ballroom of the Metropole Hotel that he was "sorry that Weiss was killed," as if anybody believed that. Then he told the assembled press: "I didn't have anything to do with it. I telephoned the detective bureau that I would come in if they wanted me to, but they told me they didn't want me."

It is hard to believe the Chicago PD would not accept Capone's offer to come to their headquarters.

As Virgil Peterson, former FBI agent and long-time executive director of the Chicago Crime Commission, who researched those days thoroughly, told me: "Most of the policemen of those days were either corrupted and in no frame of mind to do anything about Capone, or they were honest but so much under the thumb of the police officials who were beholden to Capone and his political pals that it was impossible for them to be effective against

Capone and his gang." So it was not a surprise that the cops didn't want to talk to Capone, even when it was common knowledge that he had ordered the hit. Nonetheless, Capone had been cautious enough to establish an alibi; he had been in Cicero in public view at the time of the killing of Weiss. (A hat had been found in the second-story lookout room across State Street after the killers had vacated it in an obvious hurry. The label indicated that it had been purchased from a store located not far from the Hawthorne Inn in Cicero, Capone's alternate headquarters. This may not indicate that Capone had been there, but it was a clue that somebody who frequented that area had been.)

Now Capone, with Weiss out of the way, opted once again for a peace conference. This time it was held in another of the large Loop hotels of the day, the Hotel Sherman. (Ironically, the site of that mob conference is now the location of the State of Illinois Building, the large complex which houses the state's administrative offices. Of course, in those days it was located practically in the shadow of City Hall and the Cook County Building. Mayor Dever and the aldermen were meeting in the city council, while the biggest hoodlums of the day were meeting within shouting distance. This was the ambience of Chicago in the Roaring Twenties.) Tony Accardo was there once again. Not as a participant in the meeting, but as a bodyguard of Capone, who attended this meeting himself. Alongside him were Tony Lombardo of the Unione Siciliano; Harry Guzik, Jack's brother; Maxie Eisen, an associate; and Ralph Shelton. Aligned on the other side were Bugs Moran, "Schemer" Drucci, Bill Skidmore and Jack Zuta, all rivals of Capone for territory and interests. The purpose of the meeting was to find some kind of an accord to stop the killings, and it was a success. Moran and Drucci got the North Side, Capone just about everything else—everything west into the suburbs, and south all the way to Chicago Heights, some twenty-five miles south of the Loop.

The peace held, more or less, into 1927. Then Capone got a break. A tough Chicago cop, Danny Healy, shot and killed Drucci the Schemer. Now Capone had just one foe of any magnitude left: "Bugs" Moran, the last of his most meaningful rivals. Therefore, 1927 was a relatively peaceful year. Peaceful, and profitable. The Cook County State's Attorney's Office estimated that the Capone outfit took in approximately $105 million in 1927, most of it from its bootlegging empire but also a substantial amount from gambling and vice operations.

On September 7, 1928, the peace was shattered. Tony Lombardo was killed while walking with two of his bodyguards in the heart of the Loop—at State and Madison, of all places, the busiest street corner in Chicago, the intersection where all addresses south of Madison are south and all north are north, where all streets east of State are east and all streets west are west—at the height of the noon lunch hour. The mob could hardly do more to thumb its nose at authority. Capone, for one, was outraged. He had put Lombardo in as the head of the Unione Siciliano just three years before, and now he watched as rivals showed their disregard for him by taking out Lombardo in the most public of all places at the busiest of all hours.

The impact of Lombardo's death was felt quickly. Although Capone had worked closely with Frankie Yale in New York while he was with the Five Points Gang, and later in Chicago when Capone imported liquor and beer from Yale's New York operation, they had a falling-out. Here, Tony Accardo began to get into the action. Tony was working closely with his mentor, McGurn, who was by now firmly established as the top gun, the enforcer, for Capone. Working under him were Accardo, Scalise and Anselmi. Capone dispatched this foursome, along with a guy named Fred Burke, to take out Yale, which they did on July 1, 1928, in Brooklyn. Yale was driving alone in his brown Lincoln, easy prey. The group opened up with a tommy gun, the first time that weapon was used in New York. (It was also Tony Accardo's first visit to New York. He mentioned the trip once in 1959 at his mob headquarters at 620 North Michigan. Our hidden microphone, code-named "Little Al," picked up the whole conversation.)

Frankie Yale had been to the Big Apple what Capone was to the Windy City. There were others in New York, like Maranzano and Masseria, and with the demise of Yale they would become even more important, with far-reaching consequences for Chicago. For it was at about this time that these men began a gang war in New York which would match that which had been going on in Chicago for several years. When the Castellammarese War was resolved in 1931, with Maranzano winning over the Masseria forces, Chicago would feel the change. But that was down the line.

In mid-1928 Capone moved his headquarters a couple hundred yards to the Lexington Hotel, located on the northeast corner of Twenty-second Street (not yet called Cermak Road) and Michigan Avenue, address 2135 No. Michigan. He took a corner suite of ten rooms on the fourth floor, looking out on his empire to the south and west. Naturally, young Tony Accardo, who was rapidly maturing in the ways of his pals in the Capone mob, moved with him. Now he sat in the lobby of the Lexington, not the Metropole, guarding his boss and screening his visitors. In 1928 Tony was twenty-two—a man now, old beyond his years. He had done just about everything a guy could do in the mob: kill, truck the booze, guard the boss—everything, that is, except apply the grease. At this point he had not gotten much beyond the "muscle" in the two M's, muscle and money, otherwise known as "Chicago tactics." These were what it took to be successful as a Chicago mobster. As McGurn's protégé he had not yet been asked to spread any of the green stuff. Jake "Greasy Thumb" Guzik and Murray "The Camel" Humphreys were in charge of corruption for the Capone mob, the art of developing and maintaining a full stable of public officials who would do the mob's bidding and insure their favorable treatment in the police station houses, the courtrooms, the halls of the legislature and the union halls.

It was also in 1928 that the Chicago Crime Commission began to show its muscle. The CCC was founded in 1919 and had been set up to investigate and report on the efficiency of the Chicago court system, the sufficiency of its law enforcement agencies, particularly the Chicago Police Department and the Cook County Sheriff's Office, and the crime problem in Chicago and its suburbs. (The CCC was then—and is today—supported not by the taxpayers' money but by private donations from those of us, mostly corporations, who believe it performs a vital function in Chicago. I myself am honored to have served as Special Consultant on Organized Crime for the Commission since 1983, when I testified about mob activities before the U.S. Senate Permanent Subcommittee on Investigations, shortly after I retired after thirty years with the FBI, twenty-four in Chicago.) In 1928 the CCC went into a pro-active mode. Six of its top functionaries, all wealthy businessmen who believed that the crime problem in Chicago had reached a level that could no longer be tolerated, formed the Secret Six, devising what may have been the first undercover operation, the UC function so common in today's law enforcement, especially in the FBI during its fight against organized crime in the 1990s. Unbelievably, these men actually put an undercover agent inside the Capone mob. He was even able to get past the watchful eye of Tony Accardo, McGurn and the others set up in the Lexington, and take a room from which he could penetrate Capone's lair. The information he provided eventually led to the prosecution of some sixty people around Capone—not Accardo or his top people, but a significant accomplishment nonetheless.

It is hard to believe, but as 1928 was ending, Al Capone was still in his twenties. Not yet thirty years old, but a millionaire many times over, with plenty of notches on his belt for the killings he had done by his own hand and on his orders.

In fact, though it is hard to realize, Capone's entire gang was in its youth. With hardly an exception, they were all under thirty. Therefore, Accardo, at the age of twenty-four, was not out of his age group when he hobnobbed with them. He was one of the youngest, but not by far. Therefore, it is not hard to fathom why they thought he was ready to be intimately involved in what would come to be recognized as one of the crimes of the century. As we have seen, Tony had participated in much of the "heavy work" of the Roaring Twenties, not always right in the middle of it but close enough that he had become one of the most experienced and capable gunmen in the Capone mob. He was ready now that Big Al was planning his coup de grace. Tony was well prepared for what would never be forgotten, always mentioned, as one of the hallmarks of the Capone regime. He had made his bones, as the saying goes. And he was ready when De Mora, Machine Gun Jack McGurn, brought him to Capone once again.

It was on this brutal occasion that Accardo would receive the nickname which stuck with him for the rest of his life. When De Mora returned with stories of Accardo's exploits, especially how he had battered two guys to death with a baseball bat, Capone was impressed. "Why," he said, "this guy is a real Joe Batters!" The men in the room laughed—Frank Nitti, "Little New York" Campagna, Paul Ricca, Jake Guzik, Murray Humphreys. From then on Tony Accardo was known as Joe Batters, a name that followed him to his grave.

In just three more years Tony would be listed by the Chicago Crime Commission as Number Seven on their list of twenty-eight "Public Enemies."

7 The St. Valentine's Day Massacre

The job was given to McGurn for several reasons. The first was that he had seniority. By now McGurn had risen to the top ranks of the Capone organization. Although he had never finished high school, this was not uncommon in Capone's ranks; Capone himself had never graduated. But Capone, McGurn, Humphreys, Guzik, Nitti, Campagna, Anselmi, Scalise, Capezio and the rest of the top echelon of Capone's gang were no fools. Don't ever believe these guys are not swift upstairs. They have what is called "street smarts." Accardo was a real case in point. Nobody ever accused him of being retarded! Not during his salad days in the Capone mob, and especially not in his later years.

Another reason McGurn wanted this job was that he felt great animosity for the targets.

McGurn had become a walking example of the Capone gunman. He was flashy, often seen in public, sometimes at the race tracks and the then-common six-day bicycle races. He had attracted the attention not only of the public and the police, but of Bugs Moran. Moran assigned two of his top gunmen, the Gusenberg brothers Pete and Frank, to make a splash by taking out Capone's walking advertisement. They almost succeeded. They got close to McGurn, unaccompanied on this occasion by Accardo, in a phone booth on Rush Street, near the nightclub. They felled McGurn with what was now the favorite tool for such a job, the Chicago tommy gun, and a pistol. They surprised him so completely that he was unable even to get his gun from his belt. The Gusenbergs hurried back to Moran with great glee. They had poured several bullets into McGurn and were sure he had drawn his last breath. They were wrong. McGurn was tough. He spent some time in nearby Northwestern Hospital, and in time recuperated, ready now to return to the fray. Eager for the ultimate revenge against the Gusenbergs *and* their boss Moran and his motley crew.

Given the assignment, McGurn set it up carefully. One of the problems was that Moran was not Capone. He didn't eat at the best restaurants, party at the best nightclubs, show himself all over town. He was not the de facto mayor of Chicago as Capone was. He had a style, but it was not to make himself visible to anybody who wanted to go grand gangster gazing. McGurn knew, however, that Moran headquartered—not in a grand hotel like the Metropole or the Lexington—but in a garage. A garage called the S.M.C. Cartage Company, located on the near north side of Chicago at 2122 North Clark Street.

McGurn called in three of his top shooters of the time. There is a body of experts who believe that McGurn used out-of-towners for this job, namely, the Saint Louis Egan's Rats Gang and Fred Burke from Michigan. That is not what I heard from our hidden mikes in the mob headquarters in the late Fifties and early Sixties, when Murray Humphreys and Accardo himself discussed this famous incident. They said on more than one occasion that the shooters were McGurn, John Scalise, Albert Anselmi—and Tony Accardo. It figures. These were the four top hitters in the Capone stable in 1929. I have no reason to question the testimony of Accardo and Humphreys, especially since, for six years, they had no idea we had penetrated their headquarters and were listening to their every word. ("Little Al" was the first penetration of any mob by a bug. Phones had been tapped heretofore and the mobsters were alert for taps, but not bugs.) Therefore, when I read of the fine works of true organized crime experts like my friend Larry Bergreen in his well-deserved bestseller, *Capone*, I am prone to agree with what he writes, but in this instance I find room to disagree. I know that it has become conventional wisdom to believe that it was Burke and others who did the job, but from what I learned during my decades of investigation of the Chicago mob, and Accardo in particular, I feel secure in my belief that the four shooters were the four identified above. If Accardo says he was there—and this was backed up by Humphreys—and this became his reputation, never shouted from the rooftops but quietly acknowledged inside the Outfit—then I cannot in good conscience dispute this in favor of the consensus of those whose sources were newspaper and magazine articles, movies and the gossip of people who were not there and who did not have access to those who were.

Here is another rumor some have taken for gospel. In the mid-Thirties, one Bryan Bolton was arrested for a kidnapping in St.

Paul. At that time he furnished a rambling statement to the FBI in Chicago, implicating himself as the lookout man across the street from the garage where the massacre took place. He also implicated Fred Goetz, Gus Winkler, Fred Burke, Ray Nugent and Bob Carey as the shooters. He claimed he purchased the car used in the killings from a Cadillac agency on South Michigan Avenue in Chicago, using the name James Martin, and that the plot was hatched at a resort on Cranberry Lake near Couderay, Wisconsin, and that Capone himself was involved in the conspiracy. He claimed that Murray Humphreys, Little New York Campagna and politicians William Pacelli and Dan Serritella were also involved in the planning. He claimed that Claude Maddox and Tony Capezio burned the car after the massacre. This story was widely circulated in the Chicago press at the time and was accurate inasmuch as it was based on Bolton's allegations to the FBI, although the Bureau denied it at the time. However, Bolton was subsequently discredited, and although some, such as Maddox, were arrested and questioned about his claims, nothing ever came of it. I find it hard to believe for a number of reasons. The men he implicated as the killers were all losers, with the possible exception of Burke, never associated in any meaningful way with the Capone mob, and were, at the time of Bolton's allegations, either dead or in prison. It is true that a letter addressed to Bolton was found in the room rented across the street from the S.M.C. Cartage Company, and that is the reason Bolton was interrogated about this matter. But that seems to be the only corroborating or logical reason to believe what Bolton claimed: that a bunch of no-account, piddly thugs, not seasoned Capone mobsters, did this thing; that these punks accomplished one of the most notorious killings of all time. The question remains why Capone would use amateurs when he had so many seasoned, proven, expert hitmen in his own stable, all very ready, willing and able to do such a job. Some very knowledgeable and reputable former lawmen give some credence to this story of Bolton's and so I report it here—for what it's worth.

In any event, McGurn and his crew were aware that Moran and his people took delivery of their illicit whiskey and beer at their headquarters in the S.M.C. Cartage Company. As I say, McGurn was nobody's dummy. Nor were the trio he assembled to work with him. Anselmi and Scalise, after all, had been the killers of Dion O'Banion. They had also murdered another key Capone rival, one of the Terrible Gennas, Angelo, the guy who first brought them into organized criminal activity, and they had even killed a couple of police officers, for which they had served a minimal jail sentence. They were at least as experienced in the heavy work as Accardo.

Once again the Capones rented an apartment overlooking their target, this time at 2119 North Clark. Then they stole a police squadrol, a patrol wagon, from the Chicago PD, and obtained two complete uniforms of the Chicago PD from two coppers "on the pad," on their payroll.

McGurn had Moran's liquor supplier arrange to deliver a load to the garage at 10:30 on the morning of Valentine's Day, Thursday, February 14, 1929.

When the lookouts in the apartment at 2119 North Clark observed several thugs and the truck loaded with the contraband whiskey arriving, they were all set for the big bang. They telephoned McGurn, who was waiting in a phone booth nearby, knowing that the set-up was imminent.

As part of the plan, Capone was to establish his alibi. He would be at another of his homes, not the one on Prairie Avenue on the mid–south side of Chicago, but instead at the one on Palm Island in Florida, near Miami. He made sure the public realized this.

McGurn even set up an alibi for himself. He checked into the Stevens Hotel on South Michigan across from Grant Park (later the Conrad Hilton and now the Chicago Hilton and Towers) with his girlfriend, Louise Rolfe, on the night before, under what some believe was his true name, Vincent Gebaldi, although I believed it was Vincenzo De Mora. Louise would later claim, when McGurn became a suspect, that he had been with her on the morning of Valentine's Day. McGurn was leaving nothing to chance. Or so he thought.

It was a pretty good scheme. The squadrol pulled up in front of the garage, clanging with what served as its siren in those days. Out jumped two seeming policemen. Also jumping out were two men appearing to be police detectives, in plainclothes. Into the garage they hurried, all business. Passersby watched, believing that a police raid of the garage was in progress.

When the foursome entered the garage, they found seven men, whom they knew to be members of the Bugs Moran gang. The two plainclothes men pulled tommy guns from under their overcoats (it was around eighteen degrees in Chicago that morning, just about normal for mid-February in Chicago). They shouted to the Morans, "Get your hands up! Up against the wall!" They did as they were ordered. They almost certainly believed it was what it was set up to be, a police raid. But that was no problem for them. After all, the Morans had the Hudson Avenue Police Station—and the others covering the Forty-second and Forty-third wards on the near north side of Chicago—well padded. They expected this was just one more phony police raid designed to show that the cops were doing their job when they really weren't. The cops probably had gotten a little heat from downtown. They had to make it look good. But their reasoning had little time to foment. As they docilely lined up with their faces to the wall, backs to the "cops," their lives were ended. The familiar sound of the Chicago chopper echoed throughout the building, hundreds of bullets entering the backs of the Morans. All but one was dead before he hit the floor. This one was Frank Gusenberg. Although he had twenty-two bullets from the tommy guns in his body, he lived long enough to be interrogated at Northwestern Hospital nearby. Sergeant Clarence Sweeney pressed the questions.

"Who shot you, Frank?" Sweeney asked.

"Nobody," Gusenberg replied.

Then Gusenberg uttered his last words. "I'm cold. Awfully cold. It's getting dark." He was gone.

The fearsome foursome exited the garage the way McGurn had planned it. The two plainclothes guys put their Chicago choppers back inside their overcoats and buttoned them up. Then they raised their hands in the air as if under arrest. The two uniformed "policemen" marched them out in front of them, pistols trained on them, the many passersby watching in awe. They were confused. There had been the noise of hundreds of shots fired inside, but here were the cops calmly bringing out just two prisoners and calmly driving away. They weren't even able to give good facial descriptions of the "cops" or their "prisoners." Hadn't this been just another police raid during the Roaring Twenties? By 1929 the Chicago populace had been well indoctrinated in raids on stills and breweries. This, in their estimation, had been just one more.

McGurn's raid had been quite successful. Or had it? Yes and no. Except for the German shepherd watchdog, Highball by name, all the occupants of the garage—including a dentist who just happened to be mingling, as he often did, with the gangsters he looked up to with admiration—had been wiped out. But neither Moran himself nor his two top guys, Willie Marks and Ted Newberry, had gone down. They were late to arrive. They had been walking up the street about to approach the garage when they noticed the squadrol arrive. They ducked into a doorway and were as perplexed as the rest of the neighborhood when they heard the shots, then saw the masquerade as the "cops" and their "prisoners" departed. Not perplexed enough, however, not to realize they had better get the hell away from there. So the raid had not gone exactly as planned, because they didn't get the top guy himself, Moran. On the other hand, Moran would never again be a threat to Capone. He figured that anybody who killed like that was nobody to fool with. After all, he was now alone except for Newberry and Marks. O'Banion had taken it. Weiss had taken it. The Gennas had taken it. And he, Moran, would take it too. Capone certainly wouldn't stop now that Moran's gang was just a shell. He would once again send McGurn, Anselmi, Scalise, Accardo after Bugs once more, in a repeat performance of the St. Valentine's Day massacre. And this time he would probably succeed. So Bugs Moran passed from the scene in Chicago. He left town and was not seen there again.

Capone was ecstatic when he heard the news, most pleased with his four shooters. He had great plans for them. Nonetheless, three of them would soon fade into oblivion. Only one would survive. Years later, McGurn was gunned down in a bowling alley, a valentine thrown onto his bullet-ridden body—some symbolism, it was suspected, of his involvement in the massacre. Anselmi and Scalise would suffer even stranger fates. Capone himself would do the job. He came to suspect the pair, then in their glory, of being disloyal to him, even of attempting to take over the Capone mob for themselves. They had gotten the biggest of heads. So he called a victory party at a roadhouse in northern Indiana, just over the state line from Chicago. After a rousing good time, with dinner and many drinks, Capone stood behind Anselmi and Scalise. He was handed a baseball bat and promptly bludgeoned them to death.

The other killer would prosper. Unlike his three partners, he would go on to bigger and better things.

Tony and McGurn stayed close for another year at least. They were arrested together in a cab at Harrison and Clark in February of 1930. A revolver was found in the cab by the police but both denied it belonged to them.

In fact, they were returning from completing the kind of job that would become Tony's lifelong obsession: retribution against stool pigeons. Julius Rosenheim had tipped the police off to a hangout of the boys, among other things, which enabled the cops to get a line on them. Beginning a pattern which would engulf him throughout his life, Accardo and McGurn took care of Rosenheim. Offed him. Bond was set for Accardo before he had to spend a night in jail. Tony then took off and became a fugitive until he surrendered two months later. At his trial, McGurn was convicted but it was later reversed by the Illinois Supreme court. The indictment against Accardo was nol-prossed on March 13, 1931, almost a year later.

It is interesting to note that Accardo's attorney at the time was Roland V. Libonati. Later, with the support of the mob, Libby, as he was known, became a state legislator and then an influential congressman. He served for years, doing the bidding of the Outfit, on the powerful Judiciary Committee of the House of Representatives.

Just a few weeks after the indictment against him was quashed, Tony was arrested once more. On February 17, 1931, he was arrested with another man who would make a name for himself in the annals of the Chicago mob, Charley "Cherry Nose" Gioe, this time for carrying concealed weapons. Again Tony would be released the same day on bond and never tried.

Once more in 1931 he was arrested, again with a guy who would ascend the ladder and become one of the most famous names in the Chicago mob: Dago Lawrence Mangano. Accardo, Mangano and four others were arrested as suspects in the torch slaying of Mike "de Pike" Heitler, the aging gambling boss.

It was at about this time that the Chicago Crime Commission came out with their first "Public Enemy" list. On July 31, 1931, the Crime Commission published its list of twenty-eight persons prominent in the underworld and urged official action against them. The CCC described Tony, then only twenty-five years old, as public enemy number seven, "an alcohol dealer, a member of the Circus Cafe Gang, an associate of Machine Gun Jack McGurn, and a suspect in the St. Valentine's Day Massacre."

Tony would soon leave behind his mentor McGurn, who lingered in the trenches until he was murdered in a bowling alley in 1936. Tony would far surpass what McGurn had achieved or could possibly have imagined.

8 The Fall, The End and The Rise

Al Capone was at the very height of his power as the Roaring Twenties ended and a new decade began. There probably wasn't a literate person in the United States who didn't know his name—and what he stood for.

Yet there were those who thought Capone's reputation as one of the worst mobsters in history was too harsh a judgment. These people were fond of repeating, "they only kill their own." They believed that, because almost all the killers and all the killed were gangsters, Capone and his like were somehow benign. And since he supplied only what the public wanted—beer, wine, whiskey, prostitutes, gambling, loans and the places, very luxurious places some, in which to indulge themselves—then what was so bad about that? If the public officials who took their envelopes gave them the liberty to do those things, how was that so bad? That left the cops to concentrate on burglars and thieves, didn't it? The real criminals. Those who killed people who were law-abiding public citizens, not gangsters who only killed their own. So what if Big Bill and The Hink and The Bath and scores of others in public office were on the take, did the bidding of the mob? How did that hurt the ordinary Joe? Or Jane?

As if to encourage that kind of thinking, Capone set out to portray himself as a Robin Hood when the Great Depression set in after the stock market crash of 1929. He set up soup kitchens, especially in the Levee and in the Loop, giving many people who were down and out at least one good square meal a day. Hundreds, perhaps thousands, of people, every day. As a result, there were many in the country, especially in Chicago and suburbs like Cicero, Burnham, Stickney and Chicago Heights, who believed that Al Capone was some kind of saint. No wonder a great many public officials felt there were other fish to fry! Let the Big Guy alone.

Then Jake Lingle was killed. The day was June 9, 1930. Lingle was a reporter for the Chicago *Tribune*, the biggest newspaper in Chicago, then and now. That day he was on his way to Washington Park, the racetrack located in the southern suburbs of Chicago. He had descended into the underground stairs leading to the Illinois Central Railroad, now the Metra, from Randolph Street and Michigan Avenue. I guess I've taken that route hundreds of times as I took the I.C. from the Loop to my home in South Holland, the southern suburb. A lone gunman snuck up behind Lingle and, in the midst of the crowd of commuters, shot him once in the back of the head. He was dead before he hit the ground. At first the press, especially the *Trib*, was up in arms. Outraged. However, as time went by, it became clear that Lingle had not really been the *Trib*'s man. He had achieved status as a newspaper man because Capone had fed him stories, stories which were of considerable intrigue but not damaging in any way, of course, to the gang or to Capone's reputation.

Perhaps one of the most interesting episodes in the annals of the Capone Gang, which illustrates the collusion between the mob and the police, occurred when the CPD raided a hotel in the Levee in 1930. They found a carbon copy of a confidential memo from their own department calling for the arrest of some forty-one gangsters. It had apparently been submitted for approval to Capone, who had deleted the names of eight of his top men and returned the memo to the police department.

It was about this time that Eliot Ness and his "Untouchables" appeared on the scene. They were Prohibition Agency agents of the Treasury Department, not FBI agents, as many people believe. As stated previously, the FBI under J. Edgar Hoover, in those days, did not engage Capone or his men, since Hoover felt he had more important crimes to solve. Although there is no question that Ness' accomplishments were overblown by his biographer, Oscar Fraley, and by the producers and scriptwriters of his television series and his movies, he did fine work by and large. I remember one time dining in Chicago with my partner and pal in the FBI, Johnny Bassett. We were introduced by the owner of the restaurant to Al "Wallpaper" Wolf, a former partner of Ness. I understand they called him Wallpaper because the only thing left when he got through raiding one of Capone's spots was the wallpaper on the wall. Wolf, still alive in Cincinnati as I write this, told me that neither he nor Ness ever met Capone or any of his minions, such as Nitti, Humphreys, Accardo, Guzik, et al. But he was proud, and deservedly so, when he talked about the many stills and breweries they had raided, diminishing to a large extent the income to the mob. We laughed at the movie depicting Ness running Frank Nitti off a roof to his death; in fact, Nitti, as we shall see, died in a much different way.

The real guy who got Capone was not Ness, but an Internal Revenue Service agent named Frank Wilson. He put together the tax evasion case which sent Capone away. (Wilson, who spent years of tedious, meticulous perusal of records pertaining to Capone and his income, is my idea of a real hero. I couldn't have done what he did. I was at my best penetrating the mob's head-quarters with hidden mikes and developing informants inside the mob. I never have had the willpower to sit down for hours, days, weeks and months as Wilson did, checking every little entry to at-tempt to find something which could be used to put my prey away. When I think of heroes, I think more of people like Frank Wilson than I do of Eliot Ness, but each served a purpose in the fight against Capone and his people. Wilson perhaps deserved more fame than he got and Ness a little less, but all the more power to each of them. Thank God there are people like them!)

The end of Capone's reign in Chicago and the way he died have been well chronicled by gifted authors. Suffice it to say here that the IRS got him, he went away to the federal prison in Atlanta in 1931, then to Alcatraz when that maximum-security prison was built. He was released in 1939, never to return to Chicago but sentenced in-stead to suffer the ravages of the venereal disease which caused mental illness during his last several years until he died in 1947.

It is amusing to note at this point a response J. Edgar Hoover made on September 9, 1930, to a request from the Justice Depart-ment that the FBI get involved in the investigation of Capone, who seemed to personify the apex of criminality. Hoover's response to this request from the Attorney General's office:

> *"I think it is manifestly unfair and unreasonable for this Bureau to assign Agents to matters that do not come within the Bu-reau's jurisdiction, particularly when the work of the Bureau is as congested as it is at the present time. We have primary juris-diction in Bankruptcy, National Bank cases, White Slave inves-tigations, Antitrust violations, Motor Theft violations, and innumerable other major violations of the Criminal Code."*

This would represent Mr. Hoover's thinking for the next twenty-seven years until his hand was forced. One can't help speculating how it might have been had Mr. Hoover, who built the world's heavyweight law enforcement agency, come to battle with Al Capone, the world's heavyweight law violator, while Capone was at the height of his power. I guess I should be happy that he waited until I was on the scene and available to pick up that battle—not that I was anywhere near the best agent Mr. Hoover had in his stable. However, it sure made it exciting for me when we finally did get engaged.

The FBI did, however, get involved in one aspect of the investigation of Capone and his gang. Following the discovery of the list of targets of the CPD which had been edited by Capone, the IRS began looking for the guy who presumably had that list in his possession and who had been indicted for tax evasion in March of 1930: Frank "The Enforcer" Nitti. One of Capone's upper-echelon leaders, Nitti had become a fugitive and was believed to have fled the state, thereby giving the FBI jurisdiction it otherwise felt it lacked to come to grips with the gangsters. Demonstrating the efficiency of the FBI even then, Nitti was located at a den of iniquity just outside Michigan City, Indiana, some forty miles over the Illinois-Indiana border. (This roadhouse sends shivers up my spine, packed as it was with all the evils of prohibition— prostitutes, drugs, alcohol and gambling—because it was named The Roamer Inn. A real-live Capone brothel.) Nitti was followed from Michigan City back into Illinois and eventually arrested, which was just about the extent of the FBI's involvement in the fight against Capone and his men.

The IRS got not only Capone but his brother, Ralph, and Jake Guzik, as well as Nitti—Capone and his three top guys. Although McGurn, Anselmi, Scalise and Accardo were Capone's top hitters, without whom no mob can enforce its will, Ralph, Guzik and Nitti, along with Paul DeLucia, aka Paul "The Waiter" Ricca, and Murray Humphreys were his top overall lieutenants. The IRS deserved the bulk of the credit for bringing down Capone as they did in 1931.

Things might have been different had Hoover been aware of a meeting that took place before Capone went away to prison in 1931. This was perhaps the most significant episode in the history of organized crime in this country to date. The Castellammarese War, named after the village in Sicily from which many of the participants emigrated to this country, had come to an end in New York City. Joe Masseria had been executed in a Coney Island restaurant after one of his top captains, Lucky Luciano, betrayed him. Salvatore Maranzano thereby won the war. Maranzano convened a tribunal in the Bronx and initiated what he would name La

Cosa Nostra, "this thing of ours." Maranzano designated five "families" in New York and five leaders, or "bosses," as he called them, to lead them. Then he presumed to designate other families in other cities and the leaders of those families, along with the five in New York, to belong to a ruling body of La Cosa Nostra, a grand council, as it were. He called it The Commission. Al Capone was designated as the leader of the Chicago family. He then called another meeting, this one in Chicago. Capone set it up, at the Congress Hotel on Congress Parkway, on the southern edge of the Loop, still there in the mid-Nineties. In attendance were hoodlums from all over the country, including Lucky Luciano and Meyer Lansky, top people in New York. It was there that Capone was hailed by Maranzano, and the LCN, as we in the FBI would refer to it decades later when we discovered it, became a national organization. Had Mr. Hoover learned of it then, it would have given him reason to investigate organized crime at that early time, from the inception of the LCN, not after it had been solidified years and years later.

Tony Accardo had become very important to Al Capone by 1930, just a year before Capone went away. That year the national underworld called a conference in Atlantic City, attended by most of the big mob leaders from all over the country. Capone went with one bodyguard. His Joe Batters.

Lucky Luciano and Frank Costello represented New York. Jake Guzik was also there. "Boo Boo" Hoff and "Nig" Rosen represented Philadelphia. Moe Dalitz, then still in Cleveland, came with his associate, Charley Polizzi. Longy Zwillman came from New Jersey. John Lazia was from Kansas City. Also there were Dutch Schultz, Lepke Buchalter, Meyer Lansky and Albert Anastasia from New York. And one more guy from New York: Johnny Torrio. This was not an easy time for Capone. The eastern mobsters—and they outnumbered him ten to one—still had a grudge against him for the way he had sent McGurn's men, including Accardo, into Brooklyn to kill Frankie Yale without consulting them.

When Tony became aware that his hit on Yale was the reason for the animosity toward his boss, he became a little queasy. After all, it wouldn't be the least bit unusual for the New York mobsters to request retribution in the form of the person who had done the job on Yale. Fortunately, however, none of the "wise guys" were aware that it was Joe Batters who had been involved and, therefore, no move was made on him.

The conference setting, a tattoo parlor in Atlantic City, was one that would provide the occasion for something that would remain with Tony for the rest of his life. Tony, believe it or not, had the imprint of a bird tattooed between the thumb and trigger finger of his right hand. This would remain a method of identification of Tony Accardo for the rest of his life, from the ages of twenty-four to eighty-six. Knowing Tony as I did in later years, it seems incongruous that he would do such a thing. McGurn maybe, but not the levelheaded, serious-minded Tony Accardo we would get to know in later years. But I guess the Joe Batters of that age was not the same guy we came to know.

After Capone went away in 1931 and Frank Nitti took over as mob boss, Tony went to work for Nitti. Accardo was arrested in 1932 for "vagrancy," but was never convicted. The detectives who arrested him had to admit they had never seen him gambling or in a saloon. They said Accardo told them that he earned his living as a gambler, but their knowledge of his means of livelihood came from hearsay and from their suspicion of his general reputation. He was acquitted.

In May of 1933, Tony was arrested once again, this time on "suspicion." The arrest came at Canal St. and Jackson Boulevard, just west of the Loop. He was fined $25 and costs after he admitted he had not worked during the previous six months and that, when arrested, he had given the address of a vacant lot as his home.

Accardo's closest pals during these early Thirties were Charley "Cherry Nose" Gioe, Mangano, "Tough Tony" Capezio and Louis "Little New York" Campagna. He also spent time with a Cicero gambling boss, Joey Aiuppa, an ex-boxer who fought under the name of "Joey O'Brien," and some younger up-and-coming hoodlums, Gus Alex, Frank Ferraro, Sam Giancana and Sam "Teets" Battaglia.

One of Accardo's assignments in those days was to "run off" a major independent bookmaking operation which had held sway in the Loop for years. It was run by Harry Russell and his brother David. Accardo was assigned to take over their territory. Instead, he used diplomacy to absorb them, bringing them into the mob, rather than running them off, and becoming their partner in the bargain. He used no particular threats of violence to accomplish this, not being a believer in unnecessary violence. He simply convinced the Russell brothers that the time had come where it would be wise for them to yield to mob interests. He became a full partner in the entire gambling empire of the Russell brothers, a very major one, with many bookmakers. Soon the Accardo-Russell operation was making much more money than it had before and everybody was happy. Their headquarters were at 186 North Clark, in the middle of the Loop, and they flourished for the next ten years.

It was broken up in 1943 when Accardo was arrested once more, this time with David Russell and others for his part in the gambling operation. The charges against Accardo would be nolle'd, dropped, upon the promise of Accardo's attorney at the time, George Bieber, of the notorious Bieber and Brookin law firm at 188 West Randolph, that Accardo would report to his draft board for induction into the Army; most men of Accardo's age were serving their country in Europe or the Pacific in World War II. Accardo, who was living at 1431 North Ashland in the plush west suburban town of River Forest, a sign of his accumulating wealth, did report to his draft board as promised, but was soon declared "morally unfit" for Army service. The gambling charge was never reinstated and Accardo "skated" once more.

Shortly after Capone went away, so did Prohibition. The 18th Amendment, which authorized Prohibition, was repealed, and the prime source of income to the mob was lost. It was a troubled time for the Chicago mob, which was no longer called the Capone mob, but the Chicago family of La Cosa Nostra. (To be candid, however, I almost never heard the Chicago mobsters refer to their organization as La Cosa Nostra. Mainly they referred to it as the Outfit. Sometimes the press referred to it as the Mafia or "the crime syndicate," but it wouldn't be until Joe Valachi surfaced before the McClellan Committee in 1963—after FBI agent Jimmy Flynn developed him as our first real informant from inside the mob, our first "flipped," "made" member—that La Cosa Nostra became the official nomenclature in our books.)

Frank Nitti, the successor to Al Capone, would serve for eleven years as the Chicago boss, until 1943. Almost as soon as he took over, he held a conference with his top people. Tony Accardo was one of them. The conference took place in the Lexington Hotel, where Nitti took over the ten-room suite used by Capone. At this meeting Tony Accardo was designated a "*capo*," a captain of a street crew or "regime" in La Cosa Nostra terminology. He would have some ten mobsters to command, running a gambling territory. (I am not clear as to exactly the location of Accardo's area at this time, since I never heard him define it. I believe it may have been a large hunk of the west side, his old stomping ground, Little Sicily included.) One thing is clear, and that is that Tony Accardo, having made his bones time after time under Capone, stepped up when Nitti did. Thereafter, as a capo, he became one of the eight or ten top leaders of Nitti's Outfit, including Murray Humphreys, whom the Chicago Crime Commission designated "Public Enemy Number One" after Capone went away.

At Nitti's conference not only was Tony given the position of capo and the territory that went with it, but Tony was also designated to watch over Jake Guzik and Hymie Levin, two guys who couldn't be made, since they were not Italian, and who were given the handbooks to the Loop to operate. It was Tony's job to bulldog them.

Other assignments were made at the conference. Charlie Fischetti was placed in charge of the nightclubs and gambling casinos. Murray Humphreys was placed in charge of all legitimate rackets, including labor unions, cleaning plants, laundries, etc. Joe Fusco was put in charge of liquor distribution, now legal. Guzik was given the additional responsibility of overseeing racehorse betting. Eddie Vogel was put in charge of coin-operated machines, such as slot machines, then prevalent in the suburbs, cigarette machines and vending machines. Hymie Levin had the race wire. Ralph "Bottles" Capone was given the responsibility for soft drinks and tavern supplies. In addition, responsibility was given to Jack McGurn, Tough Tony Capezio, Frankie Rio, Phil D'Andrea, Rocco Fischetti, Rocco DeGrazia, Harry Russell, Ralph Pierce, Charley "Cherry Nose" Gioe, Dago Lawrence Mangano, Alex Louis Greenberg and, of course, to Nitti's underboss and top aide, Paul Ricca.

I should point out here that Chicago is unique, in that several of the most important people in the Outfit through the years were neither Italian nor Sicilian. Witness Guzik and Humphreys and, later, Gus Alex. They could not be "made," formally inducted into the LCN, but they were much more important in the affairs of La Cosa Nostra than all but a handful of made guys. Now Tony Accardo was on the rise.

I am struck by a passage in the fine book *Capone* by my friend, Larry Bergreen. Talking about this time in the affairs of the mob, as Capone went to prison, he named Murray Humphreys and Tony Accardo as the two "who vied for power." I suspect that what Larry means is that the two vied for power within the organization, not for the top spot. Tony Accardo had demonstrated by then that he was a "comer" and about as good as any of his pals in the mob. He was only twenty-six, and although Capone himself had already risen to the top at that age, now there were others,

Nitti, for example, who were better groomed at this juncture. Tony Accardo would develop into the leader that Nitti would never be, but in 1932 he had not yet developed into a leader who could command the respect that Nitti could. But just give him a few years.

9 The Terrible Thirties

One of Tony Accardo's first tasks under Frank Nitti was to take out Teddy Newberry. Newberry, of course, had been with Bugs Moran when McGurn's crew had taken out the guts of Moran's gang at the S.M.C. Cartage Company. It was 1933, and though Moran had lost his nerve and was no longer a force, Newberry had picked up where his boss left off. He had become something of a force on the north side of Chicago, a thorn in the side of Nitti. Newberry had forged an alliance with the new mayor of Chicago, Anton Cermak, which had given him the power to maintain the area on the north side that Capone had ceded to Moran.

Now Newberry had crossed the line. Using his influence with Mayor Cermak, he had caused two detective sergeants on Cermak's special police detail to arrest Nitti, on December 19, 1932, at one of his hangouts, at 221 North La Salle Street, just a stone's throw from City Hall and the County Building. A fierce gunfight erupted as Nitti resisted the arrest. Nitti was severely wounded and was on the edge of death before he recovered. Sergeant Lang was also wounded, although it appears he shot himself in order to become the hero he became.

It didn't take long. As soon as Nitti came to his senses, he ordered Tony Accardo to reciprocate. About three weeks after the gunfight at Nitti's hangout, Newberry was rubbed out. Accardo, who was now the top gun in Nitti's arsenal—McGurn had been elevated to a higher position—had put together the hit team. They caught up with Newberry in one of his spots on the near north side and shotgunned him to death. They then transported him out of the city, into a spot near where another mobster, Tony "The Ant" Spilotro, would be laid out fifty-three years later (see *The Enforcer*, Donald I. Fine, Inc., 1994). This burial spot was a ditch in Porter County, near Portage, Indiana.

Nitti, meanwhile, was targeted by Mayor Cermak to go on trial for the shooting of Sergeant Lang. But before he could see to that, Mayor Cermak traveled to Miami to meet publicly with the President-elect, Franklin D. Roosevelt. Almost before he could congratulate the nominee, a fanatic leaped at Cermak and fired several shots into his body. About three weeks later, he died.

Nitti was placed on trial for the shooting of Sergeant Lang, but at the trial the tables turned. The jury came to believe that Lang had, in fact, shot himself to bring himself glory. They hung. Lang was thereafter tried and found guilty of shooting Nitti without provocation. He was granted a new trial, however, and was not convicted, but he was fired from the police department. When Cermak died, Lang found that Nitti had a lot more clout in City Hall than he did.

Actually, the method of operation during the entire Nitti regime in the Thirties and early Forties was to "keep your head down." Acting on advice from Jake Guzik and Murray Humphreys, Nitti kept his operation low-key. He had seen what happened to his predecessor Capone, who went out of his way to court publicity. In effect, Capone was thumbing his nose at authority, although that may not have been his actual intention. Every time he appeared in public, for example at the opera, which he enjoyed, he did so in grand fashion, arriving in his expensive limousine with an entourage, wearing his expensive clothes, including his trademark fedora, even throwing money to the kids on the street. Even his charitable operations, the hundreds of thousands of dollars he spent on his soup kitchens, had the effect of flaunting his wealth. Ironically, his generosity led, at least in part, to his downfall, when the public, who were aware of the criminal source of his income, came to see him as a show-off. Thus came the eventually widespread public demand for his prosecution, which the federal government wasted no time in appeasing.

Nitti was advised not to make this same mistake. He began to move his organization out of prostitution, at least to a certain extent. He kept the strip joints but ended the wide-open brothels, whorehouses, if you will. I recall one of my first sit-downs with Murray Humphreys in the late Fifties. He went out of his way to try to convince me that the Outfit was no longer involved in prostitution. He insisted that they had no whorehouses. I was not convinced, pointing out that on South State Street in the Loop and in the Rush Street area the mob had strip joints and arcades, where prostitution ran rampant. The Outfit may not have owned the girls, but they provided the locations where they could be acquired and where an act, especially oral sex, was easily transacted. Mobsters like Humphreys had become very sensitive to the charge that they were involved in prostitution and went to some lengths to divorce themselves from the public perception that they were. All in keeping with the new philosophy of the Outfit once Capone left, based mainly on the advice of Humphreys and Guzik to Nitti when he succeeded Capone.

Hump himself got into trouble at this point. He had kidnapped Robert Fitchie, secretary of the Milk Drivers Union, and had collected a $50,000 ransom, a nice sum in those days. This was in connection with Humphreys' role in the mob as their labor specialist, in charge of the mob's extensive effort to take over as many labor unions as possible. Not only did he put his people into the Milk Drivers Union, a major union in the days when milk was delivered door to door every morning to almost all residents of Chicago and its suburbs, but he had a controlling interest, through his fronts, in one of the major dairies of the day, Meadowmoor. Hump was never convicted of this crime but he did go to prison for it. In 1943 he pleaded guilty of income tax evasion for the receipt of Fitchie's ransom. Actually, I heard Hump discuss this case several times. He was quite proud of himself because he pleaded guilty, or so he said, and I believe this, because the IRS was going after one of his fronts, Morrie Gordon. His bargain with the federal government was that if they would forget Gordon, he would plead guilty and accept his sentence. (I remember well that, years later, I too went after Hump on the theory that in another matter he had extorted money from Gordon. I interviewed Gordon about it after I saw the item on Hump's income tax. Gordon denied to me that he had given money to Hump. This is just what I wanted him to say, since it then set Hump up for false information on his income tax return. I contacted Gordon on a Friday. The next day I went to a Notre Dame football game in South Bend. The FBI office in Chicago reached out for me. I was told that Gordon had contacted the FBI Chicago office "in a frenzy." He had obviously made contact with Hump the evening of the Friday I interviewed him. Hump told Gordon, presumably in no uncertain terms, that he had undermined his claim on his return that Gordon had loaned money to him. Gordon, of course, had lied to me to protect Hump, not understanding my purpose. Apparently, when he boasted to

Hump that evening, Hump had put him straight—real straight. After that, Gordon couldn't wait for my return from Notre Dame to tell me the truth—he had indeed "loaned" money to Hump. What Hump had claimed on his tax return was factual. I was chagrined, since I lost the chance to put Hump away, but amused that Gordon was in such a frenzy.)

When Hump went away to Leavenworth in 1934, it was fortunate for him. As the Outfit's top guy in its invasion of labor unions, he would have been smack-dab in their efforts to take over IATSE, the stagehands' union, and the Motion Pictures Operators Union. These two unions controlled the motion picture industry, and organized crime, mostly the Chicago Outfit, controlled them. The New York mobsters would make their takeover, as we will see, a major design, and they were ruthless. Because Hump was in jail, he escaped possible harm.

All other activity notwithstanding in the Nitti years, gambling now was far and away their biggest revenue producer. I have been quoted several times as saying, "gambling is their lifeblood." This was never so true as it was in the Nitti era. Prohibition, the sale of illicit alcohol and beer, had been a runaway top producer through the Capone years of the Roaring Twenties. Now that was no longer available to them, when beer and alcohol became legal once again.

Tony Accardo was in the forefront of the Nitti mob's gambling operations. Now a capo, Tony was a veteran of the organization, one of its top men. There were very few mobsters more important to the mob than Tony Accardo in the mid-Thirties: Nitti, of course, Hump, Guzik, Paul Ricca. When you've listed them, you've said it all. Machine Gun Jack McGurn, Tony's original mentor, had fallen from grace with Nitti because of his drinking habits. The stress seemed to have gotten to McGurn, and he was becoming somewhat unstable, in the estimation of Nitti. Campagna, Mangano and Capezio were also top people, but they were not above Tony Accardo.

For protection of their "lifeblood," the Nitti mob needed more and more public officials on their pad. Corrupted. Big Bill was gone now, but he had been replaced by the Kelly-Nash machine.

The Hink and Bathhouse John were still the powers in the First Ward, along with Dennis Cooney, The Duke. The votes in the First Ward went overwhelmingly to the Kelly-Nash candidates. The state senator from that district was Daniel A. Serritella, also firmly on the pad.

Ed Kelly became the mayor of Chicago following the assassination of Mayor Cermak in Miami. He had been Chief Engineer of the Sanitary District since 1920, and had been indicted in 1929, 1930 and 1931 for fraud. The judge cited the testimony, which revealed "hideous corruption prevalent in the public office." Although many witnesses talked about receiving regular paychecks for one and a half years under Kelly, even though they had done no work during this time, Kelly was never convicted. When Kelly became mayor, the federal government nonetheless looked into his tax returns. It showed income amounting to more than three quarters of a million dollars in excess of his salary. Kelly settled with a payment of $105,000. Pat Nash, the other half of the Kelly-Nash machine, was the chairman of the Democratic Party of Cook County. He was required to pay the government $175,000 in back taxes after his returns were scrutinized. Virgil Peterson, the former executive director of the Chicago Crime Commission, told me that he estimated that at about this time the machine was taking in some twenty million dollars a year in graft from Nitti, Accardo, et al.

Almost never was a police captain assigned to a police district unless he had been approved by the alderman and ward committeeman in the ward to which he would be assigned, a ward controlled by somebody like Hinky Dink Kenna and Bathhouse John Coughlin of the First, all tightly aligned with the Kelly-Nash Machine. This would remain true all the way through the time I was an FBI agent in Chicago, until 1978 at least.

Gambling was rampant in Chicago in the Thirties. In the Loop, handbooks and gaming rooms were located on just about every block, fully protected by the police captain assigned to that district, the First or Central. And Duke Cooney, assigned by The Hink and The Bath to control gambling in their ward, ruled with an iron fist. Protection money from these joints rolled into the political organization of the First Ward.

When Kelly became mayor in 1933, he brought corruption with him, but this was nothing new. He also brought a certain dignity, culture and refinement into the office. He was corrupt, but he was no clown. The same, incidentally, could be said for Tony Accardo.

It was also in 1933 that Chicago celebrated its one hundredth anniversary. They did it up big by bringing A Century of Progress Exposition to Chicago. Extending from Twelfth Street south to Thirty-ninth Street on the lakefront, this world's fair was a veritable Disneyland before Disney. Sally Rand, the famous fan dancer, drew great crowds, as did the many rides and places of amusement. Tony Accardo was not shut out here. Nor was Hump or Ricca. The Outfit had a couple of the big concessions and made a mint, not only at the world's fair but from the hundreds of thousands of visitors to Chicago who stayed in the hotels around the city and who were drawn to the vice dens. Hump, in fact, owned one of the most popular rides at the fair.

In that year, which saw the celebration of "A Century of Progress," there were thirty-five gangland murders. Not just murders—gangland murders. Today a year might go by without a gangland murder. But there were thirty-five in 1933, the year when Chicago was attempting to tone it down, to cast aside its image as the home of Al Capone and his Chicago mob and attract visitors to a lovely city on which millions had been spent, in anticipation of the world's fair, for sparkling clean streets and buildings.

Perhaps the most disturbing murder that year was Gus Winkler's. He had had an interest in the Streets of Paris exhibition at the fair and was a partner of a top politician in Chicago at the time, Charley Weber, who turned out to be a close pal of Tony Accardo. Winkler operated a slot-machine manufacturing business with Weber at 1414 Roscoe Street, which is where, on October 9th, he was machine-gunned to death. In looking into the murder, the coroner's jury noted that the investigation involved citizens of Chicago, "which was honeycombed with bookmakers."

In the mid-Thirties, incidentally, Chicago also found itself "honeycombed" with gangsters not affiliated with the Outfit. Guys like John Dillinger, Homer Van Meter, Alvin Karpis, the Ma Barker gang and other notorious bank robbers and kidnappers found refuge in Chicago after committing their nefarious crimes. Dillinger, of course, was killed by FBI agents outside the Biograph Theater on the north side of Chicago after being betrayed by his girlfriend, Anna Sage, on July 22, 1934.

Virgil Peterson told me he estimated that in 1934 there were 7500 gambling establishments of one kind or another in Chicago. 7500! All operating freely under the protection of the umbrella of the Kelly-Nash Machine, which made sure no police captain was assigned to any area needing protection unless he was on the pad. In return for this protection, the politicians received a big percentage of the net, usually 50%. It was a nice arrangement for all concerned.

In 1934 one of the big events in Tony Accardo's life took place. He fell in love. She was a chorus girl who danced in some of the big shows in the nightclubs of that era, a lovely blonde named Clarice Evelyn Porter. Born Clarice Evelyn Porzadny (her parents had come to this country from Poland) on December 10, 1910, in downstate McComb, Illinois, she had come to Chicago to gain her fame. Tony's and her marriage was made in heaven. Clarice turned out to be the perfect wife for Tony. I found her to be a nice, although tough, lady and one who had a great influence over Tony. He was always faithful to her, as almost none of his pals were to their wives. They have four children, two adopted and two natural. The oldest, whom they named Anthony Ross Accardo, was born on April 25, 1936, as Baby Boy Spata. Soon came Marie Judith, born on July 3, 1939, a natural issue of Tony and Clarice. On January 14, 1941, another child, Linda Lee, was born to Tony and Clarice. In 1946, on November 30, Joseph Louis Accardo was born and subsequently adopted by the Accardos.

In 1934, meanwhile, all of the opposition to the Kelly-Nash machine was crushed in that year's election. There was now, in effect, just one party in Chicago, the Democratic Party. Even those few Republicans who held office were practical-minded enough to become Kelly-Nash people. It has been estimated that a quarter of a million votes for that year's candidates of the Kelly-Nash machine were fraudulent.

In 1935 Kelly won re-election by a plurality of four to one. Civic groups, like the Chicago Crime Commission and the Illinois League of Women Voters, were outraged at the signs, once again, of massive vote fraud. When elected, Mayor Kelly came out in favor of legalized gambling in Chicago. Nitti and Accardo supported him. Kelly had State Representative John Bolton introduce a bill to the Illinois General Assembly in Springfield, the state capital, to legalize all handbooks. Not surprisingly, it passed. But Governor Henry Horner vetoed it. Not long after, on July 9, 1936, Senator Bolton was blasted to death by a shotgun. He had attempted, with his brother "Red," to control gambling himself on the west side. Only a few months before, another state assemblyman, Al Prignano, had been slain in front of his home in what was called the Bloody Twentieth Ward, the scene of many gangland killings, and some time later to be annexed into the First Ward, giving the latter even more power.

At this time, portending things to come but unrecognized by Accardo and his pals then, the African-American population, on the south side of Chicago especially, was being exploited by a syndicate of twelve blacks and three whites who operated the policy and numbers business there. It is estimated they were reaping profits of $280,000 a week. Ed Jones was then known as the "policy king," and recipients of state aid, among others, were pouring their money into the coffers of the policy racketeers. The syndicate extended their operation to the Twenty-eighth Ward of the west side, where Big Jim Martin not only controlled the policy and numbers rackets but was the right-hand man of Pat Nash. The Nitti Outfit soon discovered the potential of policy and numbers, at Big Jim Martin's expense.

Downtown, however, was where the real action was in the Thirties. Dago Lawrence Mangano was one of the top gambling bosses there, along with Phil Katz and Hymie Levin. Jake Guzik also made the Loop his home. Gambling in the Loop in the late Thirties remained as wide open as before, with the Kelly-Nash machine providing police protection of the wirerooms and handbooks. The racketeers feared the IRS, but the boys in the dark suits, solid-patterned ties and sharp fedora hats—the FBI—were of no concern to the mob. No doubt that was a relief.

In 1939 the daily newspaper, the Chicago *News*, summed up the Thirties when it ran an editorial which read: "The average citizen of Chicago gets the privilege of being gypped in a crooked handbook joint. He gets aldermen sworn to support the law, conniving with gamblers and selling jobs on the police force. He gets a gangster in the State Senate. He gets Machine-controlled schools and courts. He gets crime and corruption."

These were good years for Tony Accardo. As racketeering flourished in Chicago during the Thirties, Tony was a big part of the operation. He gained in stature as a capo during these years, a part of everything in which the Nitti outfit was involved. Nitti was more important than he, and so was Paul Ricca, a close pal of Tony's. Hump and Guzik were also more important, but being neither Italian nor Sicilian, they could not be "made," inducted as formal members of the Chicago family of La Cosa Nostra. Nitti was on the commission, the ruling body of the national LCN, and Ricca was the underboss, the right hand of Nitti. Other than these people, however, there was nobody of any higher power than Tony Accardo.

In 1936 Tony lost his mentor and old pal, Machine Gun Jack McGurn. The former professional prizefighter, the avid golfer, the cabareter, the natty dresser, the collector of blondes, had himself a meteoric rise in Al Capone's mob. McGurn had committed at least twenty-two gangland murders for Capone, then Nitti, including his masterpiece, the St. Valentine's Day Massacre. By the mid-Thirties, however, he had fallen on tough times. Nitti was not nearly as fond of De Mora, aka McGurn, as Capone had been. He was too flashy, too mouthy, too prone to drink and dames.

On February 15, 1936, seven years and a day after his biggest exploit, McGurn was bowling in Kafora's Bowling and Billiards Parlor at 805 Milwaukee Avenue, on the northwest side of Chicago, when he was cut down by suspected members of the Moran gang, avenging the murders of their colleagues. A comic valentine was left on McGurn's body, lying flat on its back in the bowling alley. His killers were never identified.

McGurn's murder is the stuff myths are made of. And yet I doubt it was the Morans. First of all, they were nothing in 1936. The action plotted by McGurn and carried out by Accardo, et al., in 1929 effectively demolished Moran and his gang. They had no power in Chicago in 1936, were not a factor as they had been before February 14, 1929. More importantly, McGurn had turned into a bad apple in the eyes of Nitti, Guzik, Humphreys and, perhaps, even in the view of his erstwhile pal, Tony Accardo. It is likely that these men decided to chop him themselves.

In spite of the Outfit's care to maintain a low profile, there was a shadow falling over the affairs of the Chicago syndicate as the decade was closing down—one the boys in Chicago were not aware of. The shadow was falling from far off, from New York City, in fact. It was a shadow that would soon become a storm, that would sweep Tony Accardo up and up, even as his closest competition for the top spot was sent down.

10 Business

By 1940 Tony Accardo was known more and more as Joe Batters. After Al Capone had christened him, he became more and more involved in the heavy stuff. Nitti, on the other hand, had become known in the press as "The Enforcer." It was never really an appropriate name. Sure, he had done some killings, whacked some guys, but he was not one of the top men in this department. Joe Batters had *earned* his nickname the hard way, not from the press. And he had gotten his even prior to his participation in the St. Valentine's Day Massacre, his biggest claim to fame to date. Nitti had never, even on his best day, accomplished something as big as wiping out the Bugs Moran gang.

Moving up at this time in the ranks of the Chicago family of La Cosa Nostra to line up with Ricca, Humphreys, Guzik, Batters, Ralph Capone, Rio, Fusco, Campagna, McGurn, Capezio, Claude Maddox, and of course Nitti himself, were Dago Lawrence Mangano, "Cherry Nose" Gioe, Anthony "Mops" Volpe, Rocco DeGrazia, Phil D'Andrea, Ralph Pierce, Johnny Roselli, Hymie "Loud Mouth" Levin, Billy Skidmore, Big Bill Johnson, Jack Zuta, Sam "Golf Bag" Hunt, Jimmy Belcastro, the Fischetti brothers, Charley, Rocco and Joe, and Dennis "Duke" Cooney. It was an eclectic group. Not all of them, of course, could be "made."

Joe Batters handled most of the heavy stuff. Also in his street crew were Tough Tony Capezio, Screwy Moore (Claude Maddox), Sam Hunt, Jimmy "The Bomber" Belcastro and a guy named Red Forsyth, aka Jimmy Fawcett. Meanwhile, Nitti was the boss. Guzik handled the administration, such as it was, and the books. He also worked closely with Humphreys on corruption, as did Cooney.

As the decade of the Forties dawned, one of the major trials in the history of Chicago was commencing. Murray Humphreys, Frank Nitti and others had been indicted for looting the treasury of Local 278 of the Chicago Bartenders and Beverage Dispensers Union of the AFL. The president of this union was George B. McLane. (In later years I would listen on several occasions as Hump kept his colleagues in stitches as he told this story.) On October 17, 1940, McLane took the stand, testifying that in 1935 he had received a phone call from Danny Stanton, who had wanted some money to go to the Kentucky Derby. McLane said he knew Stanton to be a "labor slugger" for Humphreys. That was McLane's first contact with mobsters. He refused, he said, the request of Stanton. "Two or three days later I received an emissary from Frank Nitti," McLane continued. "He said Nitti wanted to see me at the La Salle Hotel. When I got there, I told Nitti about Stanton. Nitti told me, 'The only way to avoid incidents like this is to put one of our men in as a union officer.' I told Nitti this would be impossible. He said, 'We've taken over other unions. You'll put our man in or you will get shot in the head.' "

The hearing officer pressed forward: "Who did you see in the private dining room?"

McLane replied: "Frank Nitti, Little New York Campagna and Paul Ricca."

"And others?"

"Joe Fusco and Charlie Fischetti. Nitti continued, 'We want no more playing around. If you don't do like I say, you'll get shot in the head. How would your old lady look in black?' " McLane thought a minute, he testified, and then said, "Christine never wears black."

Then he continued. "Nitti smiled and said, 'You put my guy on the union payroll or she will be in black!' "

McLane then testified of his next meeting with Nitti, this time at the Capri Restaurant, a well-known hangout of Nitti at the time, 1935. This time he was told: "Put in our man or wind up in an alley."

McLane testified that now he was terrified. He went back to the union hall and told his people "about the threats to me—what it meant. They had no alternative. They agreed to putting a man on."

A week or so later, McLane said, he was summoned back to the Capri once more. This time Nitti brought a man over to him, Louis Romano, a man McLane had never seen before. (Romano was another of Capone's bodyguards.)

"Nitti said, 'Here's your man. His salary will be seventy-five dollars a week out of the union treasury. You'll make it raised higher later. Romano will see that all the syndicate places join the union.' "

So Louis Romano became a business agent of Bartenders Local 278. That's how it was done in Chicago in the Thirties, according to George McLane's 1940 testimony. He also described another meeting with Nitti. On this occasion he was instructed that all Chicago bartenders were to push certain brands of beer and liquor. Nitti named the brands: "Manhattan and Great Lakes draft beer, Badger and Cream Top bottled beer, all products of Gold Seal Liquors, Inc., Fort Dearborn whiskey and all the products of the Capitol Wine and Liquor Company." Manhattan Brewery was owned at that time by Alex Louis Greenberg, a front for the mob, and Joe Fusco owned Gold Seal Liquors and Capitol Liquors. (Years later I would talk to Fusco on many occasions at Gold Seal Liquors on the near southwest side of Chicago. In fact, the last time I talked to Tony Accardo may have been at the funeral home where Fusco's wife or mother was being waked. I was there just to say a prayer for her. Fusco and Accardo were standing in the mortuary with Gus Alex, another mob power later on, and I went over after" signing the register and chatted with them for five or ten minutes and then left.)

Later in the hearing McLane told of yet another meeting with Nitti, who complained that the bartenders weren't selling enough of the products they had been instructed to sell. They were selling more Bud, Miller's, Schlitz and Blatz. Nitti instructed McLane to "tell those bartenders that if they don't push our stuff, they will get their legs broken."

McLane also told that when Murray Humphreys came out of prison in 1938 he summoned McLane to a room in the Seneca Hotel on the near north side of Chicago, owned then by Greenberg. There Hump and Romano drew pistols and told McLane they wanted Romano to be installed as president of the union. McLane acceded, and Romano was shortly thereafter installed as the president of Local 278. Then, McLane testified, "I was slipped a bullet and told to get out of town." McLane testified that everybody in Chicago knew that when a mobster slipped a bullet into the pocket of somebody, that person better do as instructed or suffer the consequences. McLane said he got out of town. When he did, Romano took over the union and even established a joint council of several other affiliated unions, all of which, McLane said, were controlled by the "syndicate," his name for the Chicago family of La Cosa Nostra. McLane said that, as of 1940, Frank Nitti controlled "all bartenders, waiters, cooks and checkroom attendants" in the Chicago area through the Romano joint council.

McLane testified that he was summoned back to Chicago for a meeting with Nitti at Nitti's new headquarters in the Bismarck Hotel, on Randolph Street, just across from City Hall. Now Nitti wanted to take over the national presidency of the AFL International Bartenders, Waiters and Hotel Employees Union. At the meeting were George Browne, president of the AFL International Alliance of Stage and Theatrical Employees, and Willie Bioff, delegate for this union, who had his headquarters in Hollywood, California. Also present was Nick Circella, alias Nicky Dean, Nitti's watchdog over Browne and Bioff. These men collectively told McLane how easy it would be to put him in as international president of the Bartenders Union.

McLane continued his testimony: "I told Nitti that, as it would be known I was the syndicate yes-man, I would wind up in the penitentiary or in the alley. I told Nitti I did not favor to run."

The examiner then asked McLane: "Did Nitti make any threats?"

"Yes, he gave me to understand that I would run or I would be found dead."

McLane testified that, although he agreed to run, he secretly called his labor friends and told them that under no circumstances did he want them to vote for him. He was, therefore, defeated. This did not please Nitti, who summoned McLane once more to the Bismarck Hotel, where he told McLane he was displeased with his performance—though he did not suspect what had secretly been done. He told McLane to stop drinking and to "get on the wagon." McLane testified that he was told by Nitti "that there is an unwritten law in the Outfit which applies to everyone connected with the Outfit. They are not allowed to drink, because they might shoot their mouth off. If they shoot their mouth off, they will be found in an alley."

A few days after this latest meeting, Hump visited McLane in his office, asking him, "Why don't you have some sense? You have been in the labor game all your life. But you don't have a quarter."

"I can go to sleep at night," McLane answered. "I ain't going to push people around for you or anybody else."

"That's the trouble," Hump said. "We call it business and you call it pushing people around."

Based on this testimony, which was not at trial but at a Master of Chancery hearing, Nitti, Hump, Ricca and Campagna were indicted. They were brought to trial on November 29, 1940. (Now this is the part that amused Hump so much as I heard him repeat this story more than once on our hidden mike in the mob headquarters.) Hump had gotten to McLane after his testimony, and made McLane understand the serious business he was in if he repeated his testimony before the grand jury and/or the trial court. They made a deal. McLane would repeat his testimony before the grand jury. Then the foursome of mobsters would perhaps be indicted. But if McLane were to testify at trial, Hump told him, his wife Christine would be abducted and kept alive as her husband was daily sent one of her hands, then her feet, then her arms.

Therefore, when McLane was put on the stand at the trial, this is what took place:

QUESTION: Do you know Murray Humphreys?
ANSWER: I must refuse to answer on the grounds that to do so might tend to incriminate me.
QUESTION: Do you know the defendant Frank Nitti?
ANSWER: I must refuse . . .

This is what made Hump feel he was so clever, according to his talk years later in front of Little Al. With McLane unwilling to testify in open court after the trial had commenced, all charges against the four defendants had to be dropped. Not only that, and this is what Hump bragged about, once the trial had started and then been dropped, double jeopardy took effect. The defendants could not be charged again. They were free as the breeze. Hump laughed, "I not only had McLane, I had the prosecutor and I even had a juror for good measure. I was taking no chances."

That was Joe Batters' pal, Hump, a guy I got to know well as the years went by. He was one of my initial assignments when J. Edgar Hoover finally brought me and his FBI into the fight against organized crime in 1957, seventeen years after this situation. We had many personal contacts. Hump was quite a guy, and I did give Hump grudging respect. But when I realize the kind of threats he was in the habit of making and the nature of the "business" he was in, just like Joe Batters, I understand that the bad qualities of guys like him more than outweigh whatever good qualities they might possess.

11 More Business

Tony Accardo, known now much more inside the Outfit as Joe Batters, actually played a big part in what would become one of the most important investigations of the Chicago family of La Cosa Nostra. Even so, he would skate when push came to shove. He was phenomenal in that respect. Very quietly he was doing much of the heavy work for the Outfit, the work sometimes referred to as the ultimate discipline, and yet he was walking away without being caught. Not only without being caught—without even being implicated. Hardly ever in these days did the press write about Tony Accardo. And no reporter in those days would have known who "Joe Batters" was. The guy who was doing so much of the hitting had never, to this point, spent a night in jail. How long could his luck hold?

For at least the time being, it would hold up once again. This time the victim was Tommy Maloy. Tommy was the president of Local 110 of the Motion Picture Operators Union, sometimes called the Projectionists Union. He had not seen the light, as did George McLane of the Bartenders Union. Threats, such as those that were made to McLane, did not scare him off. He resisted the attempts of the Outfit guys to run him off and give them his union. His sudden, unnatural death was one of the reasons George McLane knew that Nitti and Humphreys were not bluffing. Any time a guy is hit, it sets a precedent. The mob will give you an example that has the effect of grabbing the mind and making you think twice.

Tony Accardo set up and carried out the hit on Maloy. He used two new guys with him on this one, Gussie Alex and Frank "Strongy" Ferraro. Hump would have been in on it too, since labor was his field, but in 1935 he was in Leavenworth for protecting his pal, Morrie Gordon, on the income tax rap.

Tommy Maloy was one feisty Irishman. He told his people he "wasn't gonna give in to those Dagos!" He had been keeping a lovely nightclub entertainer at the Windermere Hotel on the mid-south side of Chicago. Accardo learned of this, and on February 4, 1935, he, Alex, Ferraro and a couple of "spotters" followed Maloy as he left the Windermere. They drove north on Lake Shore Drive, the "Outer Drive," as it was called more in those days than now. Joe Batters and his crew caught up with Maloy, who rode in a car driven by his pal Doc Quinn, as they passed the now deserted buildings of A Century of Progress on the lakefront. Accardo's tail car pulled up alongside Maloy's and Tony leveled his shotgun. His second shot got Maloy in the head. Then Alex hit Maloy three times with a .45 caliber automatic pistol. Tommy Maloy was no more.

Of course Nitti, Ricca, Campagna and Guzik did not want Tommy Maloy killed just to take over his union; they had a higher design than that. They wanted Local 110 for more than just its treasury or for its ability to place friends and relatives as projectionists in theaters all over Chicago. (In fact, John Accardo, Tony's kid brother, would be a member of Local 110 and a movie picture projectionist almost his whole life. And Tony's son, Anthony Ross Accardo, in the middle stages of his life, before he won millions in the Illinois State lottery a few years ago, would also be a movie operator and a member of 110.) And while Tony may have played a leading role in Act I of this plan, which would forever be known as the Hollywood Extortion Case, he would play little or no role in future events associated with it.

Tommy Maloy had used his position in Local 110 to extort the Balaban and Katz movie theater chain, which owned and operated dozens of movie theaters, for $150 a week. That gave Frank Nitti and Jake Guzik, in the absence of Hump in prison, an idea: If Maloy could use this Chicago local to extort, what could *they* do if they controlled a major national movie union—a union of the American Federation of Labor, yet?

George E. Browne was the business manager and boss, at least de facto, of Chicago's 450-member Local 2 of IATSE, the International Alliance of Theatrical Stage Employees. He had become the de facto boss by slugging his predecessor over the head with a lead pipe rolled in a newspaper until the guy decided he wanted no more. The movie business was good during the Depression. For twenty-five cents an unemployed man could sit in a movie theater, out of the heat or the cold as the case may be, all day and all night. Browne had made it plain to Barney Balaban of the movie theater chain: "$20,000 a year plus $150 a week, or stink bombs in every one of your joints."

Balaban thought it over. He proposed to meet with Browne at Gibby's, a well-known restaurant in those days, operated by Gibby Kaplan on North Clark Street in the Loop. Balaban agreed to Browne's extortion on one condition: Browne had to figure out a way to put it on the books of the company without its coming to the notice of the stockholders, Balaban and Katz being a public corporation. Browne proposed putting it down as a charitable contribution. "What charity?" Balaban wanted to know. "Why, we could open a soup kitchen for our guys out of work during this Depression," Browne suggested.

They did—and served as many as 3,700 meals a week next to the Bismarck Hotel, across the street from City Hall. All unemployed stagehands could stop by every lunch hour and eat, on the ordinary menu, green pea soup, beef stew, rye bread and coffee. They could sit in comfort all day long.

Then there was the "deluxe" menu, for the politicians and coppers, which consisted of roast chicken with chestnut dressing, roast duck glazed with orange juice basting, roast prime rib of beef, broiled double lamb chops or pork chops or tender porterhouse steaks.

Browne thought it humorous. He was quoted as saying, "I never saw a whore who wasn't hungry and I never saw a politician who wasn't a whore. Let the pols eat for nix." Soon just about every politician in Chicago was eating off the deluxe menu at Browne's soup kitchen.

But did the $20,000 go for the soup kitchen? Not really. That money went into Browne's pocket. He got the money to stock his kitchen by putting the arm on the merchants in the Loop. Browne had learned the hard way, and it had paid off. He spent $100,000 to win a $25,000 job so that he could collect graft of $500,000 a year. He was no dummy—and he was also no sucker. In 1925 he had been shot in the seat of the pants in a restaurant in Melrose Park, a western suburb of Chicago. He knew who had done it but would not cop out to the police. He was in the hospital for four weeks, and when he got out, the guy who shot him was found dead of bullet wounds.

George Browne found a friend in those days, when Browne ran for office against his brother-in-law, Herbert C. Green. He tried to persuade Green to withdraw, but when he refused, this friend came to Browne's aid, smashing Green's skull with a blackjack. This caused him to withdraw. The friend's name was Willie Bioff. Willie had been a "steerer" for one of Jack Zuta's brothels. His offer was always his "fourteen-year-old sister who's only had two boys in her class at school before, never a real man." It was a good ploy, even though the girl always turned out to be someone hardly his sister, a lot older than fourteen and a lot more experienced than from "two boys in her class."

Bioff had gotten into the labor movement in Chicago after having been sentenced to the House of Correction, the Bridewell, as it was called in those days, for six months. Under the protection of a local politician, Jerry Lahey, he never had to serve his time. He was also married to a woman named Laurie Nelson, who was instrumental in his career.

Now that Browne had established the soup kitchen with its deluxe and ordinary menus, he added something else. The best entertainers in the land, when they came to Chicago to perform, were told that the curtain would not go up until they had performed earlier that day at Browne's soup kitchen. The stars of the day, people like Harry Richman, Helen Morgan, Texas Guinan, Al Jolson, Eddie Cantor, Ed Wynn, Ole Olson, Chic Johnson and many others, came by at lunchtime and entertained the pols and the unemployed stagehands. Soon the press were invited, and Browne and Bioff began to feel justifiably immune from the law and the press. Who would go out of their way to prosecute such nice guys as these? None in Chicago, it would turn out.

Browne and Bioff then began to frequent a nightclub owned by Nick Circella, aka Nicky Dean, one of Nitti's guys and a cousin of Frankie Rio, called the 100 Club, at 100 East Superior on the near north side. They knew Nick because his brother, Augie, ran some burlesque joints on South State Street in the Loop. (I later came to know Augie well, visited him there often.)

Nick told Nitti and Ricca about these labor leaders, who were flattered some time later by a special invitation to a party of Harry Hockstein, a politician close to Frankie Rio, in Riverside. When the duo arrived, they found themselves in fast company. There was Nitti, Ricca and Rio. Also another guy—Louis "Lepke" Buchwalter, the big mobster from New York, Lucky Luciano's guy in labor. He was to Luciano what Hump was to Capone or Nitti.

After a few drinks Nitti rapped on a glass for silence. He said he understood that Browne might want to run for the presidency of the international union. "Suppose we saw to it that you would have enough votes to win?"

"I'd love it," was Browne's response.

"If we help you, if we scratch your back, we expect you to scratch ours. Is that fair enough?"

"That's fair enough."

And so their alliance, not exactly made in heaven, was forged. Nitti then turned to Lepke. "Would you talk to Lucky and get Local 306 (the New York local) behind him?"

Buchwalter replied, "When you're talking to me, it's like you're talking to Lucky. The election is in the bag."

Sure enough, with Lepke Buchwalter a big presence at the convention in Columbus, Ohio, in 1934—before he was executed for the murder of a Brooklyn grocer—the election *was* in the bag. Browne was elected president of IATSE.

When Browne and Bioff returned to Chicago, they were summoned to the Riverside home of Nitti. They agreed that the Syndicate had elected Browne president and was to be Nitti's partner from then on. One of Browne's first acts was to put Bioff on the payroll as his "personal representative."

Then they got an invitation from another high position, greater, perhaps, in the mind of Browne, to that of Nitti. Franklin Delano Roosevelt, president of the United States, had invited them to move the headquarters of the union to Washington and to serve as an unofficial Cabinet to the president. They would "counsel him on domestic affairs," according to the invitation. Browne readily accepted the invitation—until Frank Nitti was informed. "What's the matter," Browne asked Nitti, "are you afraid I'd run out?" "You're goddamn right, you'd run out," Nitti replied.

The union headquarters stayed put. Browne recognized the higher power. At that point Nitti decided Browne and Bioff needed a shadow. He sent Nick Circella to New York, to their headquarters, to be his watchdog over them.

Three weeks later Frankie Rio died of a heart attack.

Nitti then started the shakedown of the Hollywood studios. Warner Brothers was first. They told James E. Coston, zone manager for Warner Brothers in Chicago, that they needed $100,000 because some "bolsheviks" in the union were pressing for a rule that each theater in Chicago had to have two operators in every projection booth on every shift rather than just one, as was required then. Coston, after flying to New York with Bioff, Browne and Circella, got the approval. The money was paid without a fight.

It seemed that Tommy Maloy's murder had not been in vain. The "greater plan" was becoming a reality.

Nitti then went to Balaban and Katz with the same scam. Balaban and Katz paid $60,000. Of these two payments, Circella used his cut to build The Colony Club on Rush Street, a popular joint for years to come.

Nitti rejoiced over all this. It set the stage for a much bigger payoff in the long run. "I think we can expect a permanent yield of a million dollars a year," he told Browne and Bioff.

Shortly thereafter, Nitti was shown something from a Chicago newspaper. It seemed that Barney Balaban was just one of seven brothers. One brother headed Paramount Pictures in Hollywood; another headed Radio-Keith-Orpheum pictures, RKO, a major studio in Hollywood at the time; another headed Publix Theaters, a major chain of New York theaters.

Bioff immediately took off to put the deal to RKO. In no time he had $87,000 to control those "bolsheviks." This was a soft touch.

In March half the Chicago Outfit was in Palm Island at the estate of Al Capone. Nitti decided to bring in Johnny Roselli, the man Capone had sent to Hollywood a few years before to handle the Outfit's interests out there. Also invited to attend this sit-down were Ralph Capone, Circella, Charley "Cherry Nose" Gioe, Little New York Campagna, Ralph Pierce, Frank Maritote, Charley Fischetti, Phil D'Andrea and, of course, Paul Ricca.

At this meeting Roselli told the Outfit leaders about Nick Schenck, the president of MGM. Roselli considered him to be the most important figure in Hollywood. As a matter of fact, he, too, had a brother—Joe Schenck, chairman of Twentieth Century-Fox.

It wasn't hard to influence them. After Browne threatened an industry-wide strike, the Schenck brothers parted with $100,000.

These sums might seem today like loose change, but when it was all counted, it would total almost $2,000,000, a very nice sum in the Depression era.

Soon the 50-50 split between Browne and Bioff and the Outfit was changed. Nitti, claiming that there were "a lot of guys in the Outfit that need taking care of," decreed that it would now be two-thirds for the Outfit. The near $2,000,000 was not reached, however, until Local 110, the projectionists' union, held a strike throughout the entire Chicago area, including Elgin, Aurora, Waukegan and Joliet, even as far downstate as Springfield, the state capital, and Peoria. This caused every movie studio in Hollywood at the time—MGM, Warners, Paramount, 20th Century-Fox, Columbia, RKO—to pay tribute.

The final phase of the "greater plan" began to take shape when Westbrook Pegler, the nationally syndicated columnist of the day, a former Chicago newspaper reporter, ran into Bioff at a party in Hollywood. He recognized him as a former Chicago pimp, and asked around. What was Bioff doing in this upscale company among the celebrities in filmdom? He was told just what a big man Willie had become. Pegler began to look into it, and discovered that Bioff still owed the state for his conviction for pandering—the time he had never spent in the House of Corrections, due to his increasing political clout at the time. Bioff was collared and brought back to put in his time at the Bridewell. Surely he wished he had served it before, when he would have been much more inclined to bear the burdens of incarceration, not now that he was living in luxury.

Six months after Bioff was released from the Bridewell, he was indicted again, charged, along with George Browne, with the movie extortion by a New York federal grand jury. Boris Kostelanetz, the assistant U.S. Attorney who questioned Browne at the trial on October 28, 1943, asked him about a conversation he had had with Little New York Campagna.

QUESTION: What did he tell you?
ANSWER: Whoever quits us, quits feet first.

He also testified that Frank Nitti had once told him he was "headed for a hearse."

Bioff, who was later backed up by Browne, testified to something else that became very significant. Each said separately that by 1939 it seemed to them that Paul Ricca was exerting more influence over the affairs of organized crime in Chicago than Frank Nitti. At meetings with them that were attended by Ricca and Nitti, it seemed that Ricca treated Nitti in such a manner that it appeared Ricca had assumed control.

Both Bioff and Browne were found guilty and sentenced. Yet they were hardly the types who could do hard time. In fact, they had started talking just after their indictment, even before the trial. As a result, on March 18, 1943, the same grand jury in New York City returned indictments against Frank Nitti, Paul Ricca, Little New York Campagna, Ralph Pierce, Johnny Roselli, Nick Circella, D'Andrea, Gioe and Maritote. They would stand trial in New York later that year, with the exception of Circella, who would plead guilty before the trial.

Two of the top people who may have been involved in the conspiracy skated. Bioff and Browne did not implicate Tony Accardo, for two possible reasons. Accardo never met with them, so far as we know. He started it all with the killing of Tommy Maloy, but Bioff and Browne could not testify to this from their own knowledge. Any information they had in that regard was hearsay. The other reason is one which became quite common as years went by. People had a certain respect for Joe Batters. They did not go out of their way to implicate him if they could avoid it. J.B. always conducted himself in an honorable fashion, fair to all he dealt with. If you were to be killed, if that was his job, sure, he killed you. But if he could handle a situation with honor—and without killing—that was his preference. Therefore, he did not alienate people. People who dealt with Joe Batters almost always came away with some respect for the man. Not that he wasn't one tough son of a bitch. He certainly was. But he had a style, a manner which left one with the impression that he played fair.

The other guy who skated on this occasion was Murray Humphreys. As Hump would often say, and which was overheard on Little Al, he was in Leavenworth doing his time on the income tax rap during almost all of the years the Hollywood Extortion Case went down. As the mob's prime labor racketeer, Hump would have been feet first in this deal. He probably was consulted by messenger at Leavenworth, but he never sat down with either of the witnesses, Bioff or Browne. Anything they might have learned about any participation on Hump's part would again be hearsay—inadmissible evidence. For this reason, no indictment of

Hump could be obtained. I believe that his messenger in these matters was Ralph Pierce, who was among those indicted. I had several sitdowns with Pierce years later and always knew him to be Hump's guy. He beat this charge, was severed from the case by the judge, and later went on to become the powerful boss of the south side of Chicago.

The Hollywood Extortion Case opened the door for Tony Accardo. In effect, it caused him to leapfrog over each of the only two people in line above him, Ricca and Nitti. Tony had done it all, but those two, had they stayed available, would have kept him in third place for years, maybe decades, maybe forever. I'm sure Joe Batters, who had time and again proven his loyalty, would not subscribe to the thinking that the Hollywood Extortion Case was the Outfit's bad luck, but it sure was *his* good luck. No matter whether he wanted it or not, he was now on his way. All the way to the top.

As a result, Tony would have only a little involvement in the trial. On September 27, 1943, during the trial, Accardo was seized by the FBI, one of their few involvements at that time in any mob-related investigations, as a material witness and placed under a bond of $25,000. It was at this time that he may or may not have broken his record of never having spent a night in jail. I can't verify it from available records, but on this occasion Tony may indeed have been housed in the clinker overnight.

At the time of his arrest, the Chicago newspapers described Tony as an "old time Capone hoodlum, reportedly being groomed as Al Capone's successor."

How prophetic that proved to be!

BOOK TWO

THE TOP

12 At the Top

Tony Accardo got a big break on his upward path almost immediately after the Hollywood Extortion Case indictments came down. Most of those indicted, especially Ricca and Campagna, were unhappy about the way Frank Nitti had handled the entire affair. After being arraigned in New York, they returned to Chicago and met with Nitti at his home in Riverside, the western Chicago suburb. Ricca, in his expanded role in the Outfit, took control of the meeting, accusing Nitti of bungling the whole affair, of being responsible for Browne and Bioff, who had proven to be so weak in the long run, of being responsible for the indictment of the top tier of the old Capone ensemble. Nitti struck back at Ricca by telling him he was just as responsible for the whole mess as anyone was, and broke the Sicilian code of honor by ushering Ricca, Campagna and the others out the door.

At two o'clock in the afternoon of the next day, March 19, 1943, Frank Nitti left his house in Riverside and walked to the tracks of the Illinois Central Railroad across the prairie, near the Municipal Tuberculosis Sanitarium. If there hadn't been two reputable witnesses who saw it, what happened next would be hard to believe. Both were stable and both saw the deed in full sight. One was a matron at the sanitarium, the other an engineer of a freight train which had come to a stop while switching cars.

Frank Nitti, the proud successor to Al Capone, drew a pistol from his pocket, put the pistol to his head and shot himself. He was dead when the police arrived.

Nitti was the only major mob boss, to my knowledge, to commit suicide. No wonder Paul Ricca had slowly, but apparently surely, assumed the top job, probably as early as four years before, although there seemed to be no ceremony or other "official" act that made it apparent. In any event, Frank "The Enforcer" Nitti had passed on, and was no longer any roadblock to the upward aspirations of Tony Accardo. Now only one man stood in his way: Paul "The Waiter" Ricca, true name De Lucia.

Ricca had first come to the United States after he murdered a man by the name of Ricca in Italy. He assumed the man's identity and immigrated to this country. In the Seventies he repeatedly faced deportation because of it, but he was never ousted; he used the strategy of sending press clippings of all his nefarious activities to all the countries that might have received him. Who would want a guy like that? They didn't.

Ricca would always remain Tony Accardo's closest friend until his death. But Tony's destiny was tied up with Ricca's, at least at this juncture.

Later in 1943, in a trial lasting seventy-three days in the U.S. District Court in New York City, Ricca and all his co-defendants (save Ralph Pierce, who had been dismissed by the judge for lack of evidence) were convicted of the charges brought as a result of their involvement in the Hollywood Extortion Case. All received the same sentence: Ten years. Ricca was also assessed a $10,000 fine. All appealed, but their sentences were affirmed by the Court of Appeals in the district covering New York, after which they all went to prison. They were eligible for parole after serving three years, but that seemed unlikely, since it was contingent on good behavior, payment of all their fines and, most importantly, the settlement of huge sums of prior tax obligations. It seemed quite certain in 1945 that Paul Ricca would remain in federal prison for the length of his ten-year sentence. Who would grant him any early parole in view of his reputation as the leader of the crime syndicate, the old Capone mob, in Chicago? Especially when other charges were pending against him. His career as the boss of the Outfit seemed over forever. It did seem so.

It was Paul's recommendation. Who else was more important in the affairs of the Chicago family of La Cosa Nostra than Tony Accardo, aka Joe Batters? Maybe Campagna, but he was in prison with Ricca. Maybe Phil D'Andrea, but he was there too. Maybe Dago Lawrence Mangano, who was not, or maybe Hump and Guzik, who were not Italian.

That left, perhaps, only Mangano as a rival to Tony. But not for long. The Chicago *Herald American* of Thursday, August 3, 1944, probably put it best. Their front page headline for that date read: *"Mangano, Pal Slain by Gang."* The lead story that day—deemed even more important than the capture of Rennes, ancient capital of Brittany and an important rail and highway center, by forces of General Omar Bradley—was that Dago Lawrence Mangano, *"chief of the Capone gang, was shot and fatally wounded at Blue Island Avenue and Taylor Street early today by rival mobsters who trailed him from Cicero. Riddled from shoulder to ankles with at least 200 shotgun pellets and five .45-caliber bullets, Mangano died in the Bridewell Hospital at 5:48 AM. For two hours and 12 minutes he begged the doctors: 'Put me to sleep!' . . . After first felling him, three gunmen in an automobile circled the block bounded by Blue Island Ave., Armington Street, Sangamon Street and Taylor Street and came back to make sure they had finished the job. In firing the final shots the gunmen also wounded Mangano's companion, 'Big Mike' Pantillo."* Pantillo, a longtime bodyguard of Mangano, also died of his wounds.

This front page of the *Herald American* contained several other stories which punctuated the times: One quarter of the page was filled with a lurid photo of Mangano, taken just before he died, if you can believe this, lying on a bed at the Bridewell (House of Corrections) Hospital, his fat stomach protruding and naked, being attended by two doctors; also on the front page was a story saying that 122,545 civilians were killed or wounded in England as a result of enemy action from the outbreak of World War II until the previous June 30; another story reported the Allied capture of six more towns in France, that the Russians were three miles from the East Prussia border, that U.S. troops in the Pacific had gained a mile against growing Jap resistance, and that Hitler was now using flying robot bombs on London, bombs which had killed another 4,753 civilians in the past seven weeks; another story told of the leading Yank air ace, Major Thomas McGuire, who had just bagged his twenty-first Jap airplane; Thomas E. Dewey, the hero of the fight against the New York mobs, Lucky Luciano in particular, was whipping into final shape his campaign plans for the November elections and was coming into Chicago to map plans for his 1944 campaign against Franklin D. Roosevelt— he would stay at the Stevens Hotel; the army announced plans to erect five discharge centers, *"a necessary prelude to wholesale releases near the end of the war"* (one of them would be the Great Lakes Naval Station, where I was discharged from the Marine Corps a couple years later); then there was the inevitable Chicago story, right under the photo of Dago Lawrence Mangano gasping his last breaths, about seven Chicago police officials, *"disgraced in public and removed because handbooks were said to be operating in their districts."* Six were captains and the other

was Lieutenant William Drury, who would later be murdered in
his garage. Chicago! Nothing seems to change. Even at a time
when our nation was involved in wars on two fronts, the two
biggest stories on the front page were of a gangland slaying and
police corruption by the mob.

I do not know whether Tony Accardo was one of the three gunmen who killed Mangano. I doubt that he was. For one reason, I
never heard him or anybody else in the mob discuss Mangano's
murder. And two, I doubt that Tony would have been involved
himself in the heavy work at this stage of his career in the mob. He
was too big for that now. On the other hand, he may well have
been involved from the standpoint that he sanctioned it. I also
doubt that Mangano was, as the *Herald American* put it, the *"chief
of the Capone gang,"* although he certainly was one of its leaders.
One thing is certain: somebody high up had to sanction the killing
of a top man like Mangano. I suspect that Accardo consulted with
Ricca and got the OK to hit Mangano. His killers were never identified, certainly not prosecuted, typical of the thousand gangland
killings the Chicago Crime Commission has charted since it was
established in 1919. But in view of Accardo's vastly increased
stature in the mob, he had to have had a role of some kind.

   With Mangano out of the way, there was nobody who could
challenge Accardo for the top spot in the mob. After Capone had
been Nitti. Then probably Ricca. Then maybe Mangano, although
it is doubtful he was ever recognized as the boss. Now came the
guy Capone himself had dubbed "a real Joe Batters," the guy
about whom Paul Ricca, who had known both so well, would say:
"This guy has more brains at breakfast than Al Capone had all day
long."

   Tony Accardo had reached the top.

13 Beyond Belief

The first thing Paul Ricca wanted to do was to have Tony Accardo arrange for the murder of Westbrook Pegler. Just as, years later, the New York mob would throw acid in the face of another nationally syndicated columnist, Victor Riesel, Ricca wanted Pegler disciplined for his role. After all, if Pegler had not devoted many columns to Bioff and the Chicago mob's takeover of IATSE and Local 110 of the Motion Picture Operators Union, there would have been no exposé of the Hollywood Extortion Case leading to the conviction of Ricca, the demise of Nitti, and the conviction of several other top leaders of the Chicago syndicate.

However, it was soon realized that hitting Pegler would be counterproductive. This was in keeping with the general philosophy of the Commission, the ruling body of La Cosa Nostra, which would have to be consulted and which maintained that only under the most extraordinary circumstances was such action allowed against law enforcement agents, prosecutors or members of the media. Accardo himself, years later, would call off the $100,000 contract Sam Giancana had put on my life.

Ricca, however, did have a sensible demand of Accardo: all efforts had to be made to get him and his people out of jail as soon as they became eligible for parole in three years. Ricca, for one, had no desire to serve all ten years of his sentence. He was told that this was utterly impossible, that no one in history had ever been granted parole immediately upon becoming eligible. Ricca was also told by his lawyers that there was no way he, of all people, the boss of the Chicago Outfit, would be granted an early parole. That, they explained, would cause a "terrible stink." But Ricca demanded it. It became the number one item on Tony Accardo's new agenda. He would oversee the plan to spring Ricca and company, but he would assign it to the master political corruptor, Murray "The Camel" Humphreys. Hump and Jake "Greasy Thumb" Guzik were still available from their days with Capone for just such matters as this.

Together Tony and Ricca devised a plan for Tony to have frequent access to Ricca at Leavenworth, arguably the most secure federal prison in the country. Eugene Bernstein, the mob's tax attorney with offices in the Chicago Temple building, across the Civic Plaza from City Hall, went to another mob attorney, Joseph J. Bulger, real name Giuseppe Imburgio. Bernstein and Bulger falsified a set of credentials identifying Accardo as Bulger. With these credentials, Accardo accompanied Bernstein to the penitentiary. In this way Tony got his instructions right from the horse's mouth, in the broken-English words of Paul Ricca, just as John Gotti is today suspected of giving instructions to his son John, Jr., from his prison cell at Marion.

Although it is a deviation from the chronological aspect of our story, there is an amusing aspect to Tony's history of, to our knowledge, never having spent a night in jail. On one occasion in particular he barely escaped breaking his record. The arrest came on a Saturday night, and Tony was taken to a police station to be housed overnight until a bond hearing could be held, probably on Monday. Proud Tony did not like that idea. Tony was allowed his one call, but he didn't call his attorney. Instead, he called the home of a judge, whose number he apparently knew from memory. (I'll not name the judge because I found him otherwise to be honorable—he later authorized the Chicago Police Department to give me two guns which had been confiscated from criminals and which were to be tossed into Lake Michigan with the hundreds of other guns so acquired by the CPD. I still have them, snub-noses, much easier to carry than my old .38 police special.) The judge was hosting a poker party that Saturday night in his home. What follows is the story as overheard by the officers on Tony's end of the conversation and one of the poker players in the judge's home.

"They are going to hold me in jail here until a judge sets bail," Tony said. "Get here as soon as you can. Set the bail so I can go home."

The judge replied, according to the listener on his end, "Yes, I understand. But it would be inconvenient for me right at the moment. I'll be there as soon as I can."

"Now listen to me, you (a word in Italian, a nationality the judge shared with Tony). You get your ass down here right now. And I don't mean in ten minutes. I mean right now."

The man listening watched the judge hang up the phone, walk out of the room and out the door. He said nothing to his guests, did not even excuse himself or get his hat.

When the judge reached the police station, he instructed that Tony be brought to him. "Set the bail," Tony said.

The judge indicated to the police they should take Tony to night court where the bail would be set. This was not soon enough for Accardo. "We don't need no courtroom. Set the bail right fucking here and let me go home."

The judge thought a minute and then told the policemen, "I order the prisoner released on one hundred dollars' bond."

Tony could pay, and he marched out of the station house and went home. The judge did his paperwork, then exited with as much grace as he could under the circumstances.

"Mad" Sam DeStefano was a "juice man." In the parlance of the Chicago underworld, that meant he was a loan shark. He loaned money at usurious rates of interest to high risk borrowers, usually small-time criminals, such as burglars and thieves. I had many confrontations with him, including the several times I went to his house in an attempt to develop him as an informant, my specialty. On those occasions his gracious wife, Anita, served me coffee and breakfast. The coffee tasted awful. Anita told me she made it with "Italian coffee beans." OK, I said. Until one day I got a call from my close pal, Bill Duffy, the deputy superintendent of the Chicago Police Department in charge of the Bureau of Inspectional Services, including their organized crime unit. He asked me, "Roemer, have you been going out to Mad Sam's house?"

"Yes, I have. Why?"

"Because, you dumb ass, he's been pissing in your coffee."

Italian coffee beans, my foot. I still can't drink coffee, even today.

In 1963 Mike Spranze died. He had been a mobster with Capone and his wake was attended by all who had known him then, including Tony Accardo and others, such as Joe "Gags" Gagaliano, Jimmy "Monk" Allegretti, Felix "Milwaukee Phil" Alderisio, Lenny "Needles" Gianola, Willie "Potatoes" Daddano, Chuckie Nicoletti and Mad Sam.

When Mad Sam left with Potatoes, he jumped into his 1962 Caddy and sped away. Chicago PD detectives Lee Gehrke and John Zitek, both friends of mine, were assigned to follow them.

DeStefano and Daddano made them almost immediately. This was right up Mad Sam's alley. He went the wrong way on Newland Avenue, a one-way street, and took off like crazy, way over

the speed limit, typical Mad Sam. Gehrke and Zitek, who knew
they had been discovered, had to make a decision—let him go or
go get him and ticket him for speeding before he killed somebody.
They turned on their flashing lights and their siren as DeStefano
turned onto Sayre, the street on which he lived, also a one-way
street at that point. He entered going the wrong way, laughing, and
screeched to a halt in the parking lot of the undertaking parlor.

While Sam laughed at him, Gehrke wrote out a speeding ticket
and stuck it under the windshield wiper of Sam's car.

Two weeks later, on May 16, 1963, the case came before Judge
Cecil Corbett Smith. The usual fine in those days was $10, and
such cases are ordinarily disposed of in two minutes.

Instead, this case went on all day long—for two weeks, in fact.
Sam, who defended himself, made a circus out of it. He was
accompanied by Bob McDonald, later married to the Mafia
Princess, Antoinette "Toni" Giancana.

Gehrke was the first witness for the prosecution. When Gehrke
identified the man with DeStefano on the night in question as
Willie Daddano, DeStefano jumped up and shouted, "I'll not have
the names of gangsters mentioned in my trial!"

When DeStefano cross-examined Gehrke, he went on and on,
inquiring into Gehrke's past history, from the day he was born, to
his grade school, to his high school, to his parentage and to all
other matters, none of which had any relevancy to the matter in
court. When the prosecution, handled by Erwin Cohen and Frank
Wilson of the City Corporation Counsel, objected, DeStefano responded: "I want to know his background. Joe Stalin may have
sent him!"

DeStefano asked for a mistrial, which was denied. At the time
he said, "Please don't handcuff me, your honor. Are you trying to
prosecute me or persecute me?"

Soon, admittance to the courtroom was barred, since it was
overflowing. The Chicago newspapers played the case up big.
Everybody wanted to attend to see the "crazy Chicago hoodlum"
make a fool out of himself. DeStefano did nothing to disappoint
them. Judge Smith allowed him every latitude. Soon DeStefano
made even Judge Smith the butt of his humor. When the judge
accidentally knocked over a glass of water, Sam made a big
point of mopping it up, saying, "I've got a million dollars and
here I am scrubbing up your stinking courtroom." When the
prosecution objected to his antics, Mad Sam informed the court
that he was "the eminent attorney who received his extensive
knowledge of law at that great institution in Waupun, Wiscon-

sin." (In 1933 DeStefano had been convicted of a bank robbery and sentenced to eleven years in the Wisconsin state penitentiary at Waupun.)

Judge Smith found DeStefano not guilty. There was some indication that all the time he had been on juice to Mad Sam. In fact, Leo Foreman, whom DeStefano would later kill after cutting pieces of flesh from his body and stabbing him with his infamous ice pick, was in daily attendance at the trial, openly identified by DeStefano as a "longtime associate of our honored presiding judge." In fact, DeStefano also announced during the trial that he too was a "longtime associate of Judge Smith." Judge Smith seemed to be in the long-standing tradition of wonderful Chicago judges.

Tony Accardo delegated the task of getting Paul Ricca and his codefendants out of prison to Murray "The Camel" Humphreys. Hump soon found that the job was twofold. One, to pay off the tax obligations of the Outfit. Two, to get dismissed a charge of mail fraud for a separate indictment. It is a federal law that no one can be paroled when there is another case pending against them.

Humphreys first set out to find some way to discharge the back taxes assessment against the mobsters. They owed a total of $600,000. The question was, how to do it without opening themselves up to a case of income tax evasion? How could they show sufficient past income to justify coughing up this huge amount of money? After all, their income tax returns, which had all been prepared by Bernstein, showed a bare amount of money. In those days it was customary for mobsters to claim around $25,000 a year from "miscellaneous" income. How could Ricca, for instance, pay the $180,000 he owed, based on previous income as small as that?

Bernstein, a former IRS official, was the key to their solution. He made the payment on behalf of the defendants. How did he get the money? "Men came into my office, strangers to me," he testified, "bringing sheafs of banknotes. They would throw a roll of bills on my desk and say, 'This is for Paul,' or 'This is for Louie.' Pretty soon I had enough money." When asked just who these kind benefactors were, Bernstein replied, "I have no idea. You don't ask such men their business."

One obstacle was out of the way. Now the mail fraud indictments had to be addressed. This would seem to present one hell of a problem. Hump attacked it. First he went to Dallas and contacted Maury Hughes, an attorney who was close to Tom Clark, the attorney general of the United States. He paid Hughes $15,000, as Hughes would later admit, for "legal fees." Hughes advised Hump to go to St. Louis, to retain another lawyer with even more clout. This was Paul Dillon, who had been the financial manager for the presidential campaign of Harry Truman. Dillon, too, got a nice fee, and he spoke to Tom Clark.

This was one of the biggest coups of Hump's career. He often bragged about it, which we overheard on Little Al, our bug in mob headquarters. "The trick," he said, "was to get to Tom Clark. He had the power to see that that indictment in New York could be vacated. But he had a lot of problems with that. What a cry would go up if the 'Capone guys' were dismissed. Finally a deal was made: if he had the thick skin to do it, he'd get the next appointment to the Supreme Court."

Well, Tom Clark (whose son, Ramsey Clark, would also become the attorney general of the United States, possibly the worst one we ever had) had the thick skin, and the indictment for mail fraud in New York was vacated.

Now there was just one more problem. The bars to the parole had been removed. Hump had done a marvelous job, just the kind of work he was known for. But now the parole board itself had to act.

It was unprecedented that the minutes of the parole hearing, held on January 16, 1945, were not open. They were not a matter of public record. Even the Congress of the United States could not get them. Neither could the press under proper subpoena. Nobody has ever seen these records to this day—nobody with the authority to do anything about it, that is. On August 13, 1947, three years and four months after Ricca and his pals had entered prison, they were released. Precisely the day they first became eligible for parole.

Two years later, for the first time since the parole, a seat on the Supreme Court opened up. Who do you think Harry Truman nominated for the vacancy? Who do you think donned the black robes of a Supreme Court Justice on October 3, 1949? None other than Tom Clark.

His appointment became perhaps the major scandal of the Truman administration. Congress held hearings and investigated the hell out of it. But, as we indicated previously, even they could not get the minutes of the Parole Board hearing. Two of the congressmen, Clare Hoffman of Michigan and Fred Busbey of Illinois, said publicly that Tom Clark "did not tell all he knew." On January 30, 1952, some five years after the parole, the Chicago

Tribune ran an editorial referring to "Clark's utter unfitness for any position of public responsibility and especially for a position on the bench of the Supreme Court." The *Trib* called for Clark's impeachment for his part in the early paroles granted Ricca and the others. It went on: "We have been sure of Clark's unfitness ever since he played his considerable role in releasing the Capone gangsters after they served only the bare minimum of their terms."

Willie Bioff and George Browne were freed from prison after a short sentence in return for their testimony against the Chicago gangsters. Bioff immediately went into hiding. He had amassed some $6,500,000 in the six years he had been in position in the union from an assessment of 2% on the earnings of the union members, most of which he had stashed in safe deposit boxes in the vault of the Harris Trust Company in Chicago.

He retrieved it, and took the last name of his wife, Nelson, calling himself "Al Nelson." He settled in the Phoenix area on a nice little farm. One of his pals in Phoenix, to whom he would someday make a contribution of $5,000 when this politician first ran for office, was a guy named Barry Goldwater. Goldwater, a pilot, loved to fly. He was a brigadier general in the Air Force Reserve. He frequently flew Nelson and his wife all over the Southwest. In October 1955, Goldwater, then a U.S. Senator preparing to run as the Republican nominee for President, flew Al and Laurie Nelson to Las Vegas for a good time and then back to Phoenix. It was their last trip together. Two weeks later, on November 4, 1955, "Al Nelson" came out of his house and turned on the ignition of his pickup truck in his garage. The explosion rocked the area. His body was found several yards from his truck. He was dead before he hit the ground.

It had taken several years to find Willie, but Tony Accardo and his guys finally did. When they did, in effect, they taught all stool pigeons a lesson. Guys like Bioff should think twice before they snitched on Chicago mobsters.

For one of the few times in its history, the FBI became involved in an investigation. This was not of the mob, per se, but if successful, it would have an impact, because one of the defendants was the then-boss of the Chicago Outfit, Tony Accardo.

In January 1948, Accardo and Gene Bernstein were indicted, as a result of the FBI investigation, for "conspiring to defraud the United States government of its privilege of selecting and designating visitors to inmates of a federal penal institution." This referred to Accardo's visits to Ricca at Leavenworth. To give Accardo credit, it was not entirely unexpected. The trial took place in November 1948. From the testimony it became clear that Accardo, using the name of Joe Bulger, had made many visits to Ricca at Leavenworth and had signed the visitors' register as Joe Bulger. In his defense, Bernstein admitted that "Bulger" had been Accardo. But he claimed that Accardo had gone with him at the insistence of Ricca, because Ricca did not trust Bernstein and he did trust Accardo. Ricca, on subpoena, had told the same story to the congressional committee which had looked into this scandal. What kind of a defense, you might ask, is that? "I did it, I falsified the record, but I did so because Ricca wanted me to"? Yet Accardo and Bernstein were both acquitted by the jury. (We never heard Accardo or Hump discuss the case, but we can assume that they got to the jury, Hump's specialty. Such was certainly the case eleven years later, as we will see.)

The Hollywood Extortion Case, with all of its amazing twists and turns, from Act I when Accardo chopped Tommy Maloy, to Act II, the extortion of the movie studios—all of them, including Louis B. Mayer, who admitted he gave in to the Chicago mob only after they convinced him he would be killed before dawn unless he did—to the "flipping" of Bioff and Browne, to Act III, the successful trial of the top "Capone gangsters," to the visits of Accardo to Ricca in Leavenworth, to the bomb blast which killed Bioff, to the acquittal of Accardo on a slam-dunk case, is perhaps the most amazing, improbable story Hollywood could imagine. Yet it is all true, told here, perhaps for the first time, in its entirety.

14 The Sub-Plot

Actually, there had been a little sub-plot stitched into the acts of the Hollywood Extortion Case. The reader will recall that one of the defendants in the case was Nick Circella, alias Nicky Dean, the brother of my friend Augie Circella. Nicky was the watchdog Nitti and Ricca assigned to guard over Willie Bioff and George Browne. He was assigned to stick to them like flies and make sure they did the bidding of the mob in the extortion of the millions from all the Hollywood movie studios. And he got a big chunk of the proceeds.

Circella, though he was indicted with the rest on September 29, 1941, did not stand trial with Ricca. Like Nitti, he escaped that—not the hard way, like Nitti, but not an easy way either. He pleaded guilty.

Nick was sentenced to eight years, not ten like the rest. Two years less for making it easy on the government, not wasting its time and causing the expense concomitant with a jury trial of several weeks. He wouldn't get off as easy as the others did in the end, however. He did six years of his eight-year sentence. And when Nick came out, the government was not finished with him. He had been in the U.S. since 1902, when he was four years old, but Nick had failed to do an easy thing, what most immigrants do when they come over from Italy as he did. He failed to take out naturalization papers. Rather than go back to Italy, Nick was able to persuade the government to let him pay his own way and go to Buenos Aires. And so, on April 21, 1955, Nick and his wife sailed off on the *SS Del Norte*, never, as far as we know, to return to Chicago. Years later his brother Augie told me that Nick was doing very well for himself. He had purchased several shrimp boats and was living in Mexico City.

Before the trial, Nick and Augie had always been attracted to the entertainment business, and Nicky had once owned a couple of very nice nightspots, described earlier, The Yacht Club, the 100 Club and the Colony Club. Augie came to own the two best burlesque houses in Chicago, both on South State Street in the Loop. Some of the top strippers in the country entertained at Augie's places, including Tura Satana, a close friend of mob guys like Gus Alex and Eddy Vogel, and Gypsy Rose Lee, probably the biggest name—and biggest something else—of all the burlesque queens of the day, or any day.

The Colony Club, located in the block north of Quigley Preparatory Seminary, where young boys studied to be priests—making it a pretty savory neighborhood—was Nick's finest and catered to a strictly upscale clientele.

Nick had fallen in love with a girl whose real name was Smith. That wasn't glamorous enough for either of them. Young Miss Smith had been a waitress at the fancy Rickett's restaurant at 2727 North Clark, further up the street, when she came to Nick's attention. Nick was one of the real cocksmiths of the mob. He had a nice wife—he would spend all of his last thirty years with her in Mexico—but at the time it seemed he needed something a little more. *Somethings*, and a lot more, that is. Soon Nick put Miss Smith, now called Estelle Carey, in an even better joint than Rickett's: The White Horse Inn, a very nice nightspot of the time.

Nick was now thirty-two, and Estelle was twenty-one. She was a very pretty, well-figured young lady, very attractive to Nick and his pals. If Nick wanted something from someone, he found he could often loosen them up after they spent a night, at his expense, with Estelle.

Now Nick felt Estelle was ready, not only to be his prime lover but his hostess at the Colony Club. Estelle at first was put in charge of the "26" game. This game, still very popular at many restaurants and bars when I first came to Chicago as a young FBI agent in 1954, was a dice board about three feet square, where customers could "throw for drinks." That was legal. But at the Colony Club and many other such places, "drinks" was a subterfuge. You threw for money, just like in a crap game. That was and is illegal in Chicago, but it was very prevalent, even in honest, well-run restaurants, into the late Fifties or so.

Every "26 game" had a "26 girl." Almost always, depending on the quality of the place, she was a pretty, well built, alluringly clad woman with a seductive wiggle in her walk. After a drink or two, a customer was inclined to have another two or three while making his pass at the board or at the girl or both.

For a quarter the customer shook the dice in a leather cup, then rolled them out on the board, hoping that they would add up to the magic number of 26. If it did, then the player won a brass check, supposedly calling for a dollar's worth of drinks at the bar. The Colony Club had a second-floor casino and dance floor. It was one of the nicest places around in those days, the early Thirties, and Nick ran the casino. It was against the law, of course, but protection from the police, as we have seen, was no problem. The captain's bagman from the Chicago Avenue Police Station, the 35th District then, now the 18th, came around the first of every month and filled up his satchel. That kept everything "honest," even if the law technically read otherwise.

Of course, even though Estelle Carey was Nick Circella's girl, she was available for the right deal to a good patron or gambler at the Colony Club, particularly to those who frequented the second floor. It would not have been good business otherwise. So were the women Estelle supervised, the other "26 girls." There was also a third floor of the Colony Club, a nice layout of suites. If it was a slow night, Estelle and her ladies of the night could be had for just $50. On a busy night, however, it might take $500. One big Tulsa oil man came in one night and fell in love with Estelle. He dropped ten grand on the second floor that night, but he claimed what he had on the third floor with Estelle easily made up for what he lost downstairs.

On September 29, 1941, Estelle was in her apartment at 40 East Oak, near what is now the Esquire Theatre. She got a call from Nick. He had just learned by phone of his indictment in the Hollywood Extortion Case. "Pack a bag, I'm on the way, I'll pick you up in half an hour," he told her. For the next several weeks they holed up in Midlothian, a south Chicago suburban village, in a roadhouse called Shorty's Place, at 147th Street and Cicero Avenue.

On December 1, 1941, the FBI found Nick at Shorty's. Not because the FBI had any particular interest in Nick's position in the Outfit, but because he was a fugitive from a federal warrant in New York and had fled interstate to avoid prosecution. Interstate flight is a federal crime assigned for investigation to the FBI. UFAP: Unlawful Flight to Avoid Prosecution.

It was obvious to all concerned that somebody had tipped off the FBI to the whereabouts of Nicky Circella. Estelle, who had harbored him, was not arrested. Tony Accardo could figure that out. That nice little bird *must* be the singer. Besides, where was Nick's money from the Hollywood Extortion Case? The mob would like to have it. Nick hadn't exactly been a stand-up guy, according to Tony Accardo's understanding of the phrase. No doubt they had high standards in this regard. Nicky had pled out, for one thing. Not like the rest of the defendants in this case. Wouldn't it be nice to kill two birds with one stone—get the snitch and find Nick's stash at the same time?

Estelle, by this time, had returned to the north side of Chicago, living now in Wrigleyville, near the Cubs' ball yard, at 512 West Addison Street. That's where Tony Accardo sent his hit squad. We may never know who Accardo sent, but those guys were tough. Not very good, but very rough. First they used an ice pick on Estelle, putting it in some parts she had used frequently for Nick and with Nick. Then they used a knife. Then the item of choice was a set of brass knuckles. There were three men: one to hold her down, one to keep her mouth gagged and one to apply the torture. She died as a result of it.

When the coroner looked her over, he was unable to tell in which order the executioners operated. She had a broken nose, several of her teeth had been knocked out, her head and face were a mass of welts and bruises, and her throat was cut with either the knife or a razor.

The killers had soaked her body, clad in pajamas and a housecoat, with lighter fluid. It's hard to know whether they doused her to scare her some more, or whether they actually intended to burn her to death. Her hands and arms were badly burned, apparently in an attempt to put out the flames which engulfed her clothing. The coroner would later rule that her heart had stopped as a result of extreme shock and from suffocation.

It is not known whether Estelle Carey stood up to the end or whether she gave up Nick's stash. (I can't recall Hump or Joe Batters talking about Estelle Carey or this incident.) Maybe Estelle protected the stash for Nick or for herself. Maybe she didn't. Maybe Tony Accardo's guys got what they wanted from her. (I doubt it though, because of what Augie told me about Nick's shrimp boats in Mexico.) But if they did, who could blame her? Three big tough guys against a little, young woman. Nobody ever accused the mob of fighting fair. Not then, not now.

On November 19, 1943, Accardo was picked up by Acting Captain William Drury for questioning about the murder of Estelle, in company with Ralph Pierce and Les Kruse, two very young, up-and-coming mobsters. As always, Tony walked away without spending the night. Although I doubt very much that Tony handled this incident himself—by this time he was too high in the

Outfit for an assignment like beating and killing Estelle Carey—in late 1943 he was in a position where he had to have sanctioned it. What a nice guy!

15 More Racketeering

Another chapter in the field of labor racketeering took place in the early Forties.

Abe Teitelbaum had been an attorney for Al Capone. Now he was retained as "labor relations counsel" for the Chicago Restaurant Association. There had been an outbreak of violence when goons were smashing windows and furnishings of restaurants in Chicagoland, and had even slugged one restaurant owner with a baseball bat. Teitelbaum's mob connections were deemed by the CRA as just what was needed to quell the violence. This was quite a ploy for the mob—create the violence, then offer to end it with their own man. But it worked and the CRA was happy. Sweetheart contracts were negotiated, and restaurant owners were required to pay dues for only a portion of their employees to the mob-dominated Local 593, the Hotel and Apartment Employees and Miscellaneous Restaurant Workers Union. The workers received no benefits like health and pension. One of the influential union leaders was a close pal of Tony Accardo, Johnny Lardino.

But by 1953 Teitelbaum had fallen into some disfavor with officials of Local 593; Carl Hildebrand, for example, who was one of the people placed in the union by Hump. Hildebrand would remain a lifetime friend and cohort of Humphreys through the years. Teitelbaum left the scene after two thugs, "Needle Nose" Labriola and Jimmy Weinberg, threatened to throw him out his office window. Teitelbaum was replaced as the labor relations counsel by Anthony V. "Tony" Champagne. Champagne, a poor attorney at the time, was a close friend of Accardo and others in the mob. His reported annual income was then $9,000 a year, but his salary at the CRA ratcheted up to $125,000. Nice boost, if you can get it. And Tony Champagne could, because he was Accardo's guy. Champagne immediately retained Sam "Butch" English as his "assistant labor agent." English was nothing but an out-and-out hood, the operator of a mob gambling joint in Cicero at the time and the older brother of Chuckie English, a major mob player. Obviously, English's background made him eminently suitable for the position of labor negotiator.

However, like Teitelbaum, Champagne, too, would fall from grace with Accardo. In 1954 he was ousted.

For the sake of demonstrating the repercussions of mob appointments, in 1959 a staff member of the McClellan Rackets Committee would testify as follows in a public hearing of the committee:

> *"During the investigation of this Chicago Restaurant Association, I had the opportunity to review some files in the Internal Revenue Service: one of the memos . . . dated March 7, 1956 . . . stated . . . there was a discussion between Anthony V. Champagne, who was the labor counsel for the Chicago Restaurant Association in 1954, and Tony Accardo. An argument ensued between these two individuals, and the arguments were over payments that Mr. Champagne was to make to the Internal Revenue Service for his retainer from the Chicago Restaurant Association, which was $125,000. Apparently Mr. Accardo became very disturbed at this and ordered Mr. Champagne murdered forthwith. Through the intervention of Mr. Champagne's friends, his life was saved, and, immediately thereafter, he resigned from the Chicago Restaurant Association . . . as counsel."*

It is most interesting to read Champagne's formal letter of resignation, knowing that Accardo had ordered his murder. It is dated June 14, 1953. In it Champagne tries to explain why he is voluntarily resigning from a $125,000 a year position to return to his law practice which had earned him $9,000 a year: "I hereby submit my resignation as attorney for your association and its members, effective July 1, 1954. . . . I have been practicing law for the past 25 years and am confronted with many legal problems and decisions to be made in behalf of my clientele. . . . In view of the established practice which I have enjoyed for many years, I feel it is my duty to continue serving these clients without interruption."

Decades later this situation would come to my attention after I had retired from the FBI. One morning in 1983 I was at home reading the *Wall Street Journal* when I noticed a small item mentioning that the New Jersey Casino Control Commission was holding up the license of Ramada to own and operate an Atlantic City hotel-casino. The reason was that Marion Isbell, the founder of Ramada, had been the president of the "mob-dominated Chicago Restaurant Association."

I did not know Marion Isbell, but one of his partners in his Isbell's restaurant on Rush Street (where Gibson's is now) had become a close friend of mine and other FBI agents, especially of Ralph Hill and Marshall Rutland. This man, Jim Saine, had opened a restaurant next to the Tradewinds, the mob-owned Rush Street restaurant, and we used Jim's restaurant, Jim Saine's (now Luciano's), as a jumping-off spot during our surveillances of guys like Milwaukee Phil Alderisio and Marshall Caifano, who ate at the Tradewinds.

I remembered Jim telling us on several occasions what a "breath of fresh air" Isbell was in the Chicago Restaurant Association when he served his term as president there. Jim, whom we learned we could trust implicitly, told us about the things Isbell had done to try to fight the mob influence in the CRA.

So I located Marion Isbell in Paradise Valley, Arizona, and eventually wrote a letter to the Casino Control Commission on his behalf. Thereafter, Ramada obtained its license in Atlantic City. (Ironically, I was later retained by the *Wall Street Journal* as a member of the defense team of attorneys who defended the libel suit Ramada brought against the *Wall Street Journal* for an article it published after Ramada bought the Tropicana in Las Vegas. The attorneys for Ramada attempted to prevent me from representing the *Journal* due to a "conflict of interest" on my part, since I had gone to bat for Isbell.)

About this time Tony was having his own problems with the dreaded IRS.

His reported income, for tax purposes, from 1940 to 1955 totalled $1,155,524.17, of which almost $300,000 was received from the Owl Club gambling casino in Calumet City and $203,000 from "miscellaneous sources"—an average reported annual income in this sixteen-year-period of $72,220. Over 43% of this was listed as coming in from the Owl Club and from sources identified as "miscellaneous." In those days, on the advice of Gene Bernstein, the mob's tax attorney, this "miscellaneous" maneuver was common. The IRS, I was to find later in my investigation of Hump, would then call the mob taxpayer in, and request him to identify just what "miscellaneous" meant. Then the mobster would resort to the Fifth Amendment. And walk. Nice deal.

When Senator Alexander Wiley, a member of the Kefauver Committee, heard about this arrangement and its success in dodging further IRS investigation, he remarked in obvious disgust: "I've got to show every calf born on my farm!" Obviously, however, Accardo had a status not subject to the same strict enforcement as an ordinary U.S. senator!

16 Capga

In 1946, while Ricca and his pals were still in prison, Tony Accardo made a major move.

Every bookmaker in the country, and there were hundreds of thousands of them now, needed the advantage of the legal wire service which supplied, via telephone and telegraph, racetrack odds, results and payoffs to the media and others. A bookmaker could not operate without them. If a bettor couldn't be advised of the results and payoff on the first race at Bowie, for instance, he was in poor shape to bet on subsequent races that day. And if the handbook, the wireroom as they are called, or the "office," as the mob called them, did not have the results, they would be unable to collect or pay off, as the case may be. The wire service, therefore, was about as much a necessity to the bookmaking business as the race itself. In those days there was very little gambling on sporting events other than boxing. It was unusual for a wireroom to take action on football, basketball or baseball. Horse racing was far and away the major action in the Forties, when Tony Accardo first stepped in as mob boss.

In that year Continental Press, owned by James M. Ragan, was the chief supplier of the racing odds. Art McBride, the Cleveland multimillionaire and holder of a pro football franchise in Cleveland, was his silent partner, but Ragan operated the service. Tony Accardo went to Ragan and made him an offer he could not refuse—but he did. Ragan told Tony just exactly where he could go. Ragan was one tough cookie. He had the monopoly in the wire service business. All bookmakers needed his services, there was no competition for it and Ragan wanted to keep it that way. He was not about to let Tony and the Chicago mob cut in on him.

What Tony did then, however, dismayed Ragan. Continental Press was headquartered in Cleveland, with distributors all over the country. In Chicago the distributor was Mid-West News Service. Since Ragan appeared to be "unreasonable" and would not let the mob in on his operation, Tony Accardo ordered that his people begin "pirating" the racing information from Mid-West News Service, then offer it, in competition with Mid-West, to the handbooks controlled by the mob in Chicago and suburbs. Ragan was furious. He went to Murray Humphreys, whom he felt might be more amenable to leaving Ragan alone. Hump suggested that the solution might be for Ragan to keep Continental Press Service, but to sell its Chicago distributor, Mid-West News Service, to the Outfit. When Ragan steadfastly refused, Hump had another suggestion. He told Ragan to keep Mid-West but to give the mob forty percent of its total profits. Ragan again refused. He had built up his business with years of hard work. Why should he give up any part of it to a bunch of thugs? He stormed out of the meeting.

Indeed, Ragan had an ace in the hole. He had contributed heavily to the Kelly-Nash machine. Nash was dead now, but Kelly was still mayor of Chicago. Ragan now sat down with two of the stalwarts of the machine—Jacob M. Arvey, Chairman of the Cook County Democratic Party, and Barnet Hodes, Corporation Counsel of the City of Chicago. Even with all their power, however, Ragan was unable to get any real help. Arvey and Hodes had no leverage over the Outfit. "The Capone gang," Ragan observed at the time, "is as strong as the United States Army."

Tony Accardo now went a step further. Not only did he continue to pirate Ragan's service, but he established a competitor, Trans-American Publishing and News Service, Inc. In order to staff Trans-American, Accardo stole many of the staff of Mid-West. At the same time he ordered all bookmakers in Chicago to cease doing business with Mid-West. Almost all of them did. They were not crazy. One who did not was Frank Covelli. On January 21, 1946, he was shot to death. Another guy, Harry "Red" Richmond, operated a handbook on the near west side, near

Ashland, at 1638 West Madison, in what was then the skid row section of Chicago. Richmond knew enough to go along with the hoodlums who told him to switch, but when Richmond found that Trans-American was inferior to the service he had been getting from Mid-West, he was crazy enough, on April 13, 1945, to switch back to Mid-West. This infuriated Accardo, who realized that if this example was not reversed, other bookmakers might see fit to follow suit. In fact, if left alone, the Chicago bookmakers would prefer to do business with Mid-West. Therefore, Red Richmond received the "ultimate discipline." Three days after he switched, Red was murdered. There was little doubt why.

Now Ragan was really in a bind. When Covelli and Richmond were slain, the die was cast. What Chicago area bookmaker in his right mind would do business with Mid-West? Ragan had two choices. He could capitulate to the Outfit and accept Hump's offer—give the mob a large chunk of Mid-West but keep Continental Press Service and the distributors in other parts of the country. Most people in such a position—then and now, to be sure—would have taken the offer they couldn't refuse. But not Jim Ragan.

Ragan took another course. First he went to the Cook County State's Attorney William J. Tuohy. He gave them a 10,000-word statement detailing his talks with Accardo and Humphreys. He identified Hump, Jake Guzik, Rocco Fischetti and Hymie Levin as the people who were attempting to muscle him. He did not, however, mention Tony Accardo, not to the State's Attorney. Accardo had come to him in a gentlemanly fashion. Tony had been smart enough not to threaten Ragan himself; he had left that to his underlings. Therefore, Ragan could not truthfully say that Tony Accardo had himself done anything illegal.

Ragan did something else. Provided with two police bodyguards at all times by the Chicago PD, Ragan went to the FBI.

As previously stated, J. Edgar Hoover had steadfastly refused to take any jurisdiction over the activity of organized crime. In keeping with his philosophy outlined in his memo to the Justice Department, when the Herbert Hoover administration had wanted the FBI to become involved in the investigation of Al Capone, Mr. Hoover continued to want no part of such investigations. In 1945 he still felt that, although there may have been mobs in all parts of the country, they did not transcend state lines, thereby giving their activities an interstate character. Mr. Hoover, of course, had the facts on his side at the time; there was no concrete evidence that the mobs had any interstate connection. On the other hand, when

Mr. Hoover wanted to do something, he generally found a way to do it.

Jim Ragan now dropped a bombshell, hand delivered, a sure-fire, slam-dunk way to justify going after the Chicago mob. Because what Ragan was telling the Chicago Office of the FBI was of direct interstate character. His company was headquartered in Cleveland. Even more than that, he was using telephone lines and telegraph lines from all over the country to bring the results into Chicago, from racetracks such as Santa Anita in California, Bowie and Pimlico in Maryland, Churchill Downs in Kentucky, and Finger Lakes and Saratoga in New York.

When the agents to whom Ragan talked in Chicago called Washington with what they had, Mr. Hoover was, by all accounts, jubilant. Here somebody was actually alleging, with direct evidence, that the Chicago mob was involved in interference with interstate commerce, and the people involved as suspects were top members of the Chicago mob, the old Al Capone mob. Now people could not accuse Mr. Hoover of being "scared" to bring his FBI into the fight against organized crime.

Mr. Hoover directed the Chicago office to open a case immediately, based on Ragan's information, and to sit down with him at great length to debrief him of his knowledge.

The case was opened as a "special." Agents from every squad in the Chicago office of the FBI, then headquartered in the Bankers Building at Clark and Adams in the Loop, were assigned to it. The case was given a code name, thereby marking the importance of the investigation: CAPGA.

This code name is indicative of the mind-set of the FBI at this time, in 1946. Such was the paucity of their knowledge of organized crime, of the mob, of the Outfit, of the Syndicate and of the "gangsters" who were its members. Because "CAPGA" stood for "Reactivation of the Capone Gang," or "Capone Gang" for short. *Reactivation* of the Capone Gang? As if the Capone Gang had dried up and blown away, and now attempts were being made to "reactivate" it. As if Frank Nitti, Paul Ricca and Tony Accardo had never been. Capone had gone away in 1931, fifteen years ago. Prohibition had ended at about the same time. The FBI seemed to be of the opinion that the mob, therefore, had ceased and desisted.

Whatever the case, now that the "special" was initiated under the orders of Mr. Hoover and CAPGA was fully staffed and given the authority to go to work on the Chicago Outfit, the agents assigned to it went full out. One of the first things they did was to institute a surveillance of Tony Accardo. Ragan was a wonderful source about the personalities and the activities of the mob. He knew from personal contact with Accardo that Tony was the boss.

Tony was living at the time in a palatial mansion at 915 Franklin in River Forest, the wealthiest western suburb of Chicago. Tony's house had twenty-two rooms and was set on one quarter of a block in the most prestigious section. The house was surrounded by a seven-foot wrought iron fence with two large electronically operated gates which controlled the entrance and exit. The interior of the house, as the agents would come to know, was a thing of beauty in its design. In addition to its conventional complement of rooms, its basement had a swimming pool and a two-lane bowling alley. One room was utilized as a gun and trophy room. Tony was an avid fisherman and hunter. Also in the home was a walk-in safe. Out back were a greenhouse and a guesthouse.

The FBI set up their surveillance. They began to track Tony to meetings with his subordinates in the mob. They found that the mob was headquartering at that time in the Morrison Hotel. The Morrison, torn down now, was located in the heart of the Loop on Madison Street. Although the agents were not successful in penetrating the headquarters with a hidden mike, a bug, they were able to put a tap on the phone of the barbershop in the Morrison Hotel. This, they found, was the "message drop" for the mobsters. The top leaders got their messages at the barbershop.

Everything was going along very well with the FBI investigation. A great volume of intelligence information was being developed, and it looked as though CAPGA would lead to a prosecution of the top leadership of the Chicago Outfit: Accardo, Hump, Guzik, even a powerful Chicago politician, Dan Serritella, a former state senator and one of the leading lights of the Kelly-Nash Machine, who was "in the pocket" of the mob. Serritella had been with Hump when Hump suggested that Ragan sell Mid-West to the mob.

Just when it was starting to look good for the government, things fell apart. On June 24, 1946, Jim Ragan was driving on State Street near Pershing Road on the south side of Chicago, Pershing being 3900 south. His CPD bodyguards were in a tail car. It was during the rush hour and that location was filled with cars and pedestrians when a tarpaulin-covered truck pulled up alongside Ragan's car, shotgun slugs pouring out of it. It may have been Hump himself in the truck. "Golf Bag" Hunt was also implicated. So were Gus Alex and Frank "Strongy" Ferraro. But the suspects most often suspected were three other mob sluggers, Davey

Yaras, Lenny Patrick and Willie Block, three mob killers from the Lawndale area on the near southwest side. Whoever it was, they were never identified and certainly never arrested or prosecuted. Ragan was seriously wounded. He was rushed to nearby Michael Reese Hospital. But he didn't die. Not then. In fact, he seemed to be recovering after six weeks in intensive care.

The shooting was the big story in the Chicago newspapers and on the radio, and the public was outraged. (Television was almost just a dream in those days, just getting started. Almost no one had a TV set. But the other media made it the big story in 1946.) It became public knowledge that Ragan had gone to the police and the FBI. His daily progress in Michael Reese was monitored for all to know.

The shooters had bungled. They had not completed their job. Unlike the hitters in the Dago Lawrence Mangano case, for instance, they had not made sure the victim was dead, had not even circled the block and come back for the coup de grace.

Accardo was furious. This was worse than ever. Ragan was still talking. The FBI was seen coming into his room daily. Accardo suspected that Ragan was now telling the FBI what he hadn't fully explained to the State's Attorney's Office—that Tony Accardo had initiated the attempted extortion of him and that Tony was fully involved in the case. Ragan was doing just that.

Accardo knew that he had to silence Ragan. By mid-August it looked like Ragan would not only survive but would be in an even more strategic position to make himself believable when he took the stand at the expected trial, which would now almost certainly follow, a trial of Accardo himself and his top people. If Accardo, Hump and Guzik—along with who knows how many more of the top people—went away, who would be left to lead the Outfit? There would be, in fact, a pause in the operation of the "Capone Gang," calling for a "reactivation" later. The difficulty was that Ragan was under twenty-four-hour CPD guard at Michael Reese.

On August 14, six weeks after Ragan's shooting, the mob got him. Probably, though it is not known for sure, they got to somebody on the staff of the hospital. Ragan didn't die of his wounds, he died of poisoning. He would no longer be available to testify against Accardo and the Outfit. Although the feds and the locals had a basic road map as to who the mobsters were and what they were doing, without Ragan's live testimony in court, they did not have enough from the standpoint of a prosecution. Accardo skated one more time. In this case he was not even arrested.

When Ragan went, so did CAPGA. Without the source, the FBI had little in the way of evidence. The phone taps, like the one at the Morrison barbershop, and the sightings of Tony Accardo meeting with Hump, Guzik and the other top people of the Outfit were nice for intelligence purposes. But they could not lead to a prosecution; the taps were inadmissible, and the fact that Accardo had lunch with Hump wasn't vastly compelling evidence of a crime.

J. Edgar Hoover gave it some thought. All evidence of an interference with interstate commerce went down the drain when Ragan gasped his last breath. There was no case there anymore. Nothing would be easy without Ragan. Therefore, Mr. Hoover ordered CAPGA closed. He terminated the "special," and all the agents assigned to it were ordered back to their old squads. The FBI's interest in "the Capone Gang" ended. It would not be regenerated for another eleven years, until 1957. That was when I came on the scene, and the first thing I did was to dig out the old files of the CAPGA investigation. I spent the first three weeks of my new assignment poring over the information from Ragan, from the tap at the barbershop of the Morrison and from the surveillance of Tony Accardo, from his home in River Forest to the Loop. In fact, while my nine partners in 1957 hit the streets I was criticized by my supervisor because I seemed to spend all my time in the office. I did, because I was most interested in what my predecessors had learned from CAPGA. It was a good foundation, a kindergarten preparing me for what would come for the next twenty years.

Tony Accardo had scored another victory. His reputation as a guy "who had more brains at breakfast than Al Capone would have all day" was reinforced. He was at the top of his game. And there were a lot more innings to play.

17 The Outfit Copes With the Pols

Two of Chicago's most infamous leaders would die within several months of each other. First it was Michael "Hinky Dink" Kenna, the alderman of the First Ward for what seemed to be forever and the single politician who did about as much as any to insure that the mob flourished. He died peacefully on October 9, 1946, in his Blackstone Hotel room suite on Michigan Avenue, Chicago's grandest roadway. The Hink was responsible for the appointment and election of literally hundreds of Chicago public officials, judges, police captains, legislators and even mayors. Unfortunately for Chicago, a great many of them had as much or more allegiance to the mob than to Chicago's citizens. Of course they did; otherwise, they wouldn't have been put in place by Hinky Dink.

The other infamous Chicago figure had not been in Chicago for almost fifteen years. In fact, he was not even able to attend the wake or funeral of his longtime pal, The Hink, confined as he was to his luxurious estate on Palm Island. Probably, he would not have even recognized The Hink, because he was suffering from the ravages of the many nights he had spent—and a lot of days, too—with ladies who weren't all that careful with their personal hygiene. For most of the latter part of his life, this guy had suffered from the effects of syphilis, and in the last years it had become not just physical but mental. Much of the time Al Capone didn't know where he was, what he was doing or whom he was with. In many ways, although it is not generous to say this, it could be said that he got what he deserved. He had never been imprisoned for any of his most serious crimes. Imprisoned for only seven years, many felt that he had come out way ahead in that regard. But few would have traded places with Big Al from 1931, when he went away, until February 4, 1947, when they lowered him into his grave at Mount Olivet Cemetery.

Capone's loyal soldier Tony Accardo did not want to make the funeral a circus. He directed that only those who had known Al well and worked with him personally should attend the funeral. This left many up-and-comers, like Gus Alex, for instance, who had accompanied Jake Guzik on a visit to Palm Island as the body-guard of Greasy Thumb, out of luck. He was instructed to refrain from attending the funeral. Guzik did, of course, as did Hump. Even Joe Batters made himself scarce. Golf Bag Hunt was seen there and, of course, Al's cousins, the Fischetti brothers, Rocco, Charley and Joe. Tough Tony Capezio was there in his derby hat. So was Claude Maddox, aka Screwy Moore, the old Circus Cafe gangbanger.

With the end of World War II, a big change had come to Chicago. Ed Kelly, after fourteen years as mayor of Chicago, was replaced. The guy who succeeded him was no Ed Kelly—or Big Bill Thompson, for that matter. Martin Kennelly was a very suc-cessful businessman and civic leader who had the backing of the influential Chicago Crime Commission as a man of integrity. He had headed the Red Cross in Chicago during World War II and was respected by all who knew him—even by those who didn't, who only knew him by reputation. More than that, he was an avowed foe of the Kelly-Nash machine.

Obviously, therefore, he was opposed by Tony Accardo and those politicians who were on the pad of the Chicago Outfit. There wasn't much Accardo could do, however. The public was by now ready to let some fresh air into Chicago after the long tenure of the political hacks beholden to the Outfit. Kennelly won the April 1947 mayoral election by a huge majority.

One of the new mayor's first steps was to bring a new procedure to the Chicago Police Department. With the help of the North-western University Traffic Institute, he shifted many of the police officers working on crime to the traffic division of the CPD. He also made it clear to his police commissioner, as that position was then known before it was changed to the current title of Superin-tendent of Police, that he had a much freer hand to function with-out political considerations. The police began to crack down on Accardo's wirerooms. The wide-open handbook, characterized by loudspeakers and wall sheets, and patronized by hundreds of play-ers, all obviously flouting the law, became a thing of the past. This is not to say gambling was obliterated. It certainly was not. It just shifted to a "sneak" basis. Anyone who wanted to could still place a bet with his favorite corner newsstand, for instance, and the Outfit's lucrative gambling business was far from dried up. There was always a way to get some action on the ponies.

I'm not about to say that Mayor Kennelly cleaned up the mob. He was a breath of fresh air but he was no panacea. In fact, he made it clear that he thought "the Capone gang is a myth." He actually said that! Here was an honest guy, sharp, straightlaced. And yet he did not believe that there was such a thing as organized crime in Chicago during his tenure as mayor. And that was just fine with Tony Accardo. If the official word was that he didn't exist, then nobody would come looking for him. They would leave him alone. And, by and large, that is what they did. As a matter of fact, Mayor Kennelly became famous when he replied to a question from an author about the continued existence of the "Capone syndicate," and what steps he was taking to combat it. The mayor's reply was this: "I don't know about any syndicate. Isn't that man Capone supposed to be dead?"

Wow! That was the honest mayor of Chicago talking, apparently in all sincerity. How Tony Accardo must have smiled when he read about that! Shades of J. Edgar Hoover, another honest, sharp man of integrity.

One of the things Tony Accardo did at this time was to put a lot more emphasis on the county, the suburbs. Because, although Mayor Kennelly was no hard-hitting knight on a white charger when it came to opposition to Tony's people, he had given the police a free rein—and there were honest policemen in Chicago; not just a few either. They went about their job of enforcing the laws, especially the gambling laws, knowing that they wouldn't be "chased" to a remote district far from their homes if they did their jobs forthrightly. As a matter of fact, it wouldn't be long—during the Kennelly administration—that the Scotland Yard Detail, the unit of the Chicago Police Department designated to investigate organized crime, would be formed. It wouldn't be around long, but while it was in existence, it did a fine job. Headed by Lieutenant Joe Morris, and staffed by such honest, capable officers as Bill Duffy, the unit banged heads, literally and figuratively, with the likes of Hump and Guzik, and many others. Morris and Duffy would each become deputy superintendents under honest police superintendents in later years, and are now recognized as among the best organized-crime experts in the history of the CPD. (The disbanding of the Scotland Yard Detail came when Mayor Richard J. Daley headed the Cook County Democratic Party, whose headquarters were in the Morrison Hotel. When the

Scotland Yard Detail put a tap on the phone of Soldier Farr, a prominent bookmaker whose headquarters were also at the hotel, Mayor Daley became incensed, fearful that Scotland Yard might learn something "too close to the flame." He ordered the unit disbanded, leaving the CPD with no viable means to investigate the Outfit.)

Tony Accardo focused on organized gambling in the county, where the sheriff was the prime law enforcement officer. Anthony Joseph Accardo had not been assigned FBI Number 1 410 106 and Chicago Police Department Number D-83436 for nothing. At first he gave much of the authority over this function to his old pal from Circus Cafe Gang days, the guy who had been with him all the way, Tough Tony Capezio. I'm sure Tony Cap would have continued to prosper in the Outfit for years, since he was close to Joe Batters, was capable and, not without significance, his wife Marie was, perhaps, Clarice Accardo's closest friend at the time. But one day while Tough Tony was playing golf, he was struck and killed by a bolt of lightning. His rivals in the mob hadn't been able to get him and neither had law enforcement. But, strange as it may seem, mobsters have the same problems with the hazards and accidents of ordinary life as do the rest of us.

The death of Tony Cap deeply saddened the "Vodka Club," the club which had been initiated many years before by Clarice Accardo. The members got together once a month to play cards, alternating at the homes of the members. They paid dues and, whenever they had collected enough, took off with each other for vacations in New Orleans, New York and other cities to see plays and enjoy the sights. The regular members were: Clarice; Marie Capezio; Clara, the wife of Jackie Cerone; Mary, the wife of Skippy Cerone, a cousin of Jackie; Gracie Aloisio, the wife of Smokes Aloisio, a mid-level hoodlum; Joanna Lardino, the wife of Johnny Lardino, a labor racketeer; and Angie Battaglia, the wife of Sam Battaglia, who, like Jackie Cerone, was one of Tony Accardo's closest pals and who would become much more important in Outfit affairs as the years passed. The Vodka Club members were Clarice's closest friends and it was, therefore, a select group. The death of Tony Capezio was a sharp blow to the club, marking the first death of one of their husbands, and they all cuddled around Marie in an attempt to soften the blow. Tony Cap's death was, therefore, not only a blow to Tony, because Cap was a good pal, but also because it affected Clarice. And anything that affected Clarice affected Tony, the good and loving husband that he truly was.

Perhaps the best example of Tony Accardo's attempts to increase his income from gambling in areas outside Cook County was in Cicero. For decades Cicero, which is contiguous to the western borders of Chicago, just a trifle south of mid-Chicago, had been a Capone stronghold, the site of one of his two prime headquarters. On April 19, 1948, another man of principle in the Chicago area, John C. Stoffel, was elected mayor of Cicero. He appointed a man in his own image, Joe Horejs, to be superintendent of police. Joe had been one of the honest, capable policemen on the Cicero force for years, and Mayor Stoffel knew he was the man for the job he wanted done—that was to clean up Cicero. Tony Accardo promptly had an associate of Horejs approach him with an offer of $100,000 if he could "see the light." Horejs declined the honor. Accardo then attempted other methods. First, under "Chicago methods," you try the offer of money. If that is rejected, then comes the other "M." Muscle. It was tried on Stoffel and Horejs on several occasions, to no avail. They were tigers. It was unusual for Accardo to come up against such people, least of all people in public office.

As a result, many of the old Capone syndicate operations in Cicero were closed down, their operators arrested. They had to move out of Cicero to the unincorporated areas where only the sheriff had jurisdiction. Tony knew something had to be done.

He resorted to another method. Other than Stoffel and Horejs, there weren't many men of principle in office in Cicero. After all, this had been a stronghold of the mob even after Capone. Hump had the idea. Change the city ordinance which gave the mayor control over the police department in Cicero. Take the police function away from the mayor's office. Sure enough, that was the answer. The ordinance was changed by vote of the village board. Then, when Mayor Stoffel no longer had control of the police department, Horejs was ousted as police superintendent. The former superintendent, who had been noted for tolerance of widespread, wide-open gambling in Cicero, was put back in place, and gambling began to flourish once again. Accardo's gang had prevailed again.

Things didn't quiet down in Cicero, however. Not right away. Stoffel resigned as mayor in protest of his village board's obvious misfeasance in office, but he didn't give up. He and a close friend and associate, Frank Christenson, a former Assistant Cook County State's Attorney, waged a vigorous campaign to rid Cicero of the corrupt influence there. Christenson got out in front on this issue, and he paid for it. On December 9, 1949, he was murdered. Soon thereafter, gunmen cornered Stoffel, blocking his car in his drive-way. He was able to escape, but the lesson was not lost on him.

Another voice that was unheeded in those times was that of Nona Ackley. It seems that a busy handbook operated at 3025–29 North Greenview in Chicago. Operate it did, but it did not have any sani-tary facilities. Every day the dozens of patrons in the handbook would go out in broad daylight and do their business in the alley out back. There was a constant stream of men and urine. Now it just so happened that Ms. Ackley happened to own and operate a very nice, clean restaurant on the other side of that alley. Every day, all day long, she and her diners were subjected to the sight of the gamblers letting loose just a few yards from the area where they were attempting to enjoy their meal. Ms. Ackley didn't like that at all; it was not real good for business. So, being of some courage, she went over to the wireroom one day and asked two of the employees if they couldn't handle their problem in some other way. She thought she did it in a reasonable, courteous manner.

Almost immediately she realized she was out of her league. A convoy of city inspectors immediately descended on the estab-lishment—not on the wireroom but on Ms. Ackley's restaurant. The city license department investigated her right to a license. The health department inspected every nook and cranny of her facili-ties. The building inspector looked for any possible violation of the building code. Then the police arrived. They stationed a twenty-four-hour watch on her restaurant outside the front street, which had the result of scaring away even more of her patrons. Then the precinct captain of her ward called her and told her to get out of town. She began to receive a bevy of anonymous, threaten-ing calls. Reservations were made for dozens of people who never showed up. It didn't take long before Ms. Ackley was out of busi-ness. Who was she to complain, they seemed to be saying, about who frequented Tony Accardo's gambling joint just because they might create a nuisance in view of her dining room? Who was a private citizen, even an employer of several people, an honest businessperson, to complain, period? What was more important to the public officials of that ward? Some unconnected legitimate businessperson or the operator of an illegal mob handbook? The answer was clear.

During two successive sessions of the Illinois General Assembly, in 1947 and 1949, the Chicago Crime Commission submitted five bills designed to improve the administration of criminal justice.

They could hardly be considered controversial. (Virgil Peterson, then the Operating Director of the CCC, told me this story years later.) The main bill, for instance, merely proposed that the term of the grand juries in Cook County be extended, like all other grand juries in Illinois, from just thirty days. There were 101 counties in Illinois, and all but one had extended the term of their grand juries, many to as long as six months. But in Cook County the life of the grand jury was just thirty days, hardly time for the prosecutor to fully explain and have witnesses elucidate the nature of the most important cases, such as organized crime cases. The CCC proposed merely to put Cook County, Illinois' biggest county, on an equal footing with the other hundred counties in Illinois. Did Tony Accardo want that? No way.

At this time and for decades thereafter, the West Side Bloc was in existence in Chicago. This was a large group of politicians, generally from the West Side of Chicago, but certainly including the First Ward, the centerpiece of political corruption in Chicago, all of whom were either under the considerable influence or the absolute control of Tony Accardo and his two top lieutenants at that time, Murray Humphreys and Jake Guzik.

The West Side Bloc, under the orders of Accardo, as passed on by Hump and The Thumb, vigorously opposed the five CCC bills. The Bloc was then led by Roland V. Libonati, a state senator of some stature. Libby, as he was known, was from the Bloody Twentieth Ward, later to be annexed to the First Ward. He had once been photographed attending a Cubs baseball game with none other than Al Capone, his pal. Later he had been arrested in the company of such luminaries as Hump, Paul Ricca, Frankie Rio and Ralph Pierce. (I would later initiate a tail of Hump from Midway Airport in Chicago, before O'Hare was constructed, to Washington, D.C., where Hump often visited Libby, bringing a package we suspected was filled with one hundred hundred-dollar bills. Hump never went home with a package.) You would think that Libby's well-known background as a mob associate would count against him when he ran for Congress—or for any other office—but not so in Chicago. In fact, Libby became a most influential congressman, serving on the Judiciary Committee, a committee that is vital in so many areas, as important as any other in Congress. Witness, for example, the Anita Hill/Clarence Thomas hearings. As a member of that committee, Libby visited the federal penitentiary at Terry Haute, Indiana. According to the warden, he extended congressional courtesy a little far, hugging and kissing the prisoner he had come to visit—Paul Ricca. In fact, he even went so far as to move for the transfer of Ricca from Terre Haute to Leavenworth, where he would be more comfortable—and in a position to receive the frequent visits of Tony Accardo, that master of disguise. That was Roland Libonati.

Libby, ably assisted by another of his ilk, Pete Granata, from the district covered by the First Ward, and aided by the counsel of the law firm of Bieber and Brodkin, was able to prevent a vote on the Grand Jury Bill. It never came to the point where it could be passed. The law firm of B and B, as it was known, represented many of the big guys in the Outfit, like Paul Ricca and "Milwaukee Phil" Alderisio, a terrible man, a real killer. In 1947 alone, the firm represented over 1,000 defendants charged with gambling violations. Over one thousand in one year!

Also a key member of the West Side Bloc in the 1949 Illinois General Assembly was John D'Arco. D'Arco later would become the alderman and ward committeeman of the First Ward, and, as alderman, he sat in the Chicago city council. The ward committeeman was even more important. He dispensed the patronage—gave out the city jobs where a "ghost payroller" could come to work only to pick up his paycheck every week. Even Mad Sam DeStefano had a job on "Streets and San," the Streets and Sanitation Department. No one who knew him could ever imagine Sam sweeping the sidewalks or shoveling snow, but they paid him handsomely for it.

I would get to know John D'Arco well when he was the figurehead of the mob in the First Ward. In 1983 I testified before the U.S. Senate that the First Ward was "the conduit through which the orders of the mob were passed to the politicians and public officials under their control." D'Arco once bragged to my face, before he walked out of his office where my interview of him was conducted, that he was "too big a man in this town to be embarrassed by the FBI." Afterward, I walked into a private dining room, where he and the successor to Tony Accardo, Sam Giancana, were having a private meeting. D'Arco was pleading to be retained as the First Ward alderman when I hollered "Ho, Ho, Ho, it's Mo," using Giancana's mob code name. D'Arco, not quite grasping the situation, jumped up and, with the reflex of a politician, which he was, shook my hand. Giancana, who recognized me from our many confrontations, kicked him in the shins and growled, "This is Roemer, you fool!" The next day it was announced that D'Arco was resigning his position as alderman. I had to wonder if he still felt he could not be "embarrassed by the FBI in this town."

In 1949 the Chicago Crime Commission issued a report on the conditions existing in the Chicago Avenue Police District, then the Thirty-fifth District on the near north side, the nightclub area, including Rush Street. The report reflected that protected vice, gambling and flagrant liquor law violations and a number of "perversion dens" were flourishing in this district. There were charges of widespread graft. The commissioner of police denied the CCC charges, but almost before his denial hit the newspapers, two out-of-town businessmen, who had wandered into one of the nightclubs mentioned in the report, complained that their bill had been padded, not an unusual occurrence, and they had been assaulted by thugs. One of the businessmen got a cut on the head that needed stitches, and the other out-of-towner had his ankle broken with an iron bar.

By 1950 the population of Chicago had increased by more than six percent, to 3,606,436 people, over the previous ten years. Even with the election of a mayor of integrity, the virility of the mob under Tony Accardo was increasing. This was the year that all would be laid out for the whole country to see.

18 The Kefauver Committee Leaves Its Mark on Chicago

1950 was the year Estes Kefauver came to Chicago. Senator Kefauver was the chairman of a Special Committee of the United States Senate that had been appointed to investigate organized crime in the United States. All roads would necessarily lead to Chicago when such an objective was mandated.

The Kefauver Committee started its investigation in Florida in order to get its feet wet in preparation for the major event. In the meantime they sent an associate counsel of the committee, George Robinson, to Chicago to work with the Chicago Crime Commission and its Operating Director, Virgil Peterson, who at the time was undoubtedly the most knowledgeable expert on organized crime in Chicago. Pete immediately suggested to Robinson, as we later discovered, that he should serve a subpoena on Tony Accardo, for him to appear before the committee at a later date. Joe Batters was without question the most important active mob figure in Chicago, and the idea was to serve him before it was made public that Robinson and the Kefauver Committee were in town. It was too late. Tony had gotten the word and skipped. Some politicians had gotten wind of Robinson's arrival and the interest of the Kefauver Committee in the situation in Chicago. It was September, and with the national elections coming up in November, the pols wanted Chicago to be very quiet at least until after that.

It was not to be. At seven o'clock on the night of September 25, 1950—the same day I took my oath in Washington as a new FBI agent—Chicago Police Lieutenant William Drury, one of the seven top police officials who had been fired the day after Dago Lawrence Mangano was whacked, was backing his Cadillac into the garage in the rear of his home on the northwest side. He had been reinstated and was acting captain. He took four blasts from a shotgun and was DOA before he could reach for his revolver in the glove compartment of his car.

Drury had had a checkered career in the CPD. He had once been known as the "Watchdog of the Loop," when he rousted any mobster who ventured there. He had made a personal vendetta of Charley Fischetti, the top mobster and cousin of Al Capone. But he had his secrets too. For instance, he had been discharged from the force and had refused, for some unknown reason, to honor a subpoena to testify before the grand jury which investigated the murder of Jim Ragan in 1946. Most interesting of all, he had been scheduled to furnish information to the Kefauver Committee on September 26, the day after his killing. Obviously, Tony Accardo did not want him to talk.

There was one cop who did talk, but not about the mob. This was Dan "Tubbo" Gilbert, a longtime captain who was at that time the Democratic candidate for Sheriff of Cook County. Gilbert appeared before the Kefauver Committee on October 17, in executive session so as not to embarrass the Democratic Party just before the election. But on November 2, just a few days before the election, the Chicago *Sun Times* published several pages of his testimony, in which he freely admitted that he had amassed the huge sum of a third of a million dollars during his tenure as a Chicago cop. He was promptly dubbed "The World's Richest Cop," a moniker which lasted him the rest of his life.

One of Captain Gilbert's admissions, that he was a gambler, is of particular interest:

QUESTION: Where did you place your bets?
GILBERT: With a handbook of John McDonald at 215 North
           LaSalle.
QUESTION: That is not legal betting, is it?
GILBERT: No, sir, it is not. Well, no, it is not legal, no.

Gilbert sounded as if he had never considered, one way or another, whether he was violating the law. It is interesting that a captain in the Chicago Police Department, then the Chief Investigator for the Cook County State's Attorney, the top prosecutor's office, and the then-current candidate for Sheriff of Cook County, could admit under oath that he gambled at a well-known Chicago handbook, right in the financial district of the Loop, and then act surprised that anybody would wonder if that was illegal.

It is a tribute to the voters of Chicago that five days later Gilbert was soundly defeated in his bid to be sheriff. In fact, the voters were so aroused that many of them in Cook County voted the straight Republican ticket and sent the longtime senator, Scott Lucas, down to defeat, thereby electing a man who would make a huge contribution to Chicago, Everett M. Dirksen, for whom the Federal Building in Chicago was later named. (The only blot I would find on Senator Dirksen's career came years later, when his office petitioned for the reinstatement of a visa for Gus Alex after the Swiss government had revoked it. Alex, at the time, had risen to become one of the upper echelon leaders of the Outfit.)

Lucas, of course, blamed his defeat on the Kefauver Committee for having smeared Captain Gilbert. But Captain Gilbert was not the only Chicago police captain who had been flushed out by the Kefauver Committee. Captain Tommy Harrison, who commanded the notorious Chicago Avenue Police District on the near north side, had also become very rich. He admitted that he himself had gotten started on his way to wealth by moonlighting. That was fine and allowable by any police department standards. But Captain Harrison testified that his moonlighting job was as a bodyguard. Bodyguard? Explain. To Whom? To John J. Lynch. Well, that would have been all right, except that John Lynch was one of Chicago's best known bookmakers. It seems unbelievable that Captain Harrison even testified that on one occasion, while dining with the notorious Accardo bookmaker, he had been handed an envelope by Lynch. He said, under oath, that when he opened it, he found it to contain $30,000. A very nice sum in the Forties.

Speaking of seemingly unlikely windfalls for public officials in

Chicago, former mayor Ed Kelly died on October 20, 1950, just as these revelations were being elicited by the Kefauver Commission. His estate listed homes in Chicago, Wisconsin and Palm Springs, in addition to "only" some $600,000, which his widow soon claimed should have listed another million; she was being cheated. This, from the estate of a man who probably never earned more than $20,000 a year in his life. It was quite evident that Kelly had breached his mother's advice to him when he was a boy: "Always keep neat and never drink out of another man's beer can." It would seem that was the least of his transgressions.

When the Kefauver Committee released its report on its investigation of the mob in Chicago, they summed it up: "The Accardo-Fischetti crime syndicate in Chicago is now one of the two major underworld organizations in the nation." The other, of course, was one of the five families in New York. I am at a loss to explain why it was called the Accardo-*Fischetti* crime syndicate. This was apparently a reference to Charley Fischetti, one of the three Fischetti brothers who were top Chicago mobsters. But neither Charley nor any of his brothers reached the stature of Tony Accardo, then or ever.

Tony Accardo had disappeared from Chicago when he learned that he was to be subpoenaed for an appearance. He took off for Mexico in July when the hearing commenced and was not seen in Chicago until he and Charley Fischetti returned through Brownsville on October 10, 1950. Finally he and his attorney, George Callaghan, appeared in the Chicago office of the Kefauver Committee and accepted service of the subpoena calling for Tony's appearance on January 5, 1951.

In the meantime, Virgil Peterson testified, identifying Tony as the top man in Chicago, a successor to Al Capone, and telling some of the intricate workings of the Chicago crime syndicate, as it was known in those days. He testified that gambling and vice were its prime income producers; that it had political influence and penetrated into broad areas of legitimate business. Pete made a huge impression, not only on the members of the committee, but on the large audience the hearings attracted from the television-viewing public. Television was a new medium at the time; many families were just now buying their first TV sets and the Kefauver hearings were a big attraction.

Before Accardo testified in early 1951, Eugene Bernstein, the tax attorney who represented Tony and most of the other Chicago mobsters, appeared. Among other things, he testified about Tony's tax returns. President Truman had issued an Executive Order making copies of tax returns of the mobsters available to the Kefauver Committee. Tony's returns showed that he and "Greasy Thumb" Guzik had formed a partnership to run the Erie and Buffalo policy wheel and that during 1949 they reported $278,667 from this source. Bernstein also confirmed that Accardo had reported income of $33,000 from the Owl Club. The Owl Club was the largest casino-type gambling operation in the Chicago area, featuring organized games ordinarily available only in Las Vegas, such as craps, blackjack, roulette and poker, as well as slot machines. It had originally been set up in Calumet City, Illinois, a southern suburb of Chicago which was wide open to vice at the time. (I'm not pleased to say that while I was a student at Notre Dame, we would occasionally travel the seventy miles or so to watch the strippers in the clubs on State Line Avenue in Cal City. This was in the late Forties, before I got married.) Tony's return also showed that in 1948 Accardo reported $60,000 from "various sources." The returns also showed that Accardo and Guzik were partners in the R & H News Service, a Chicago wire service for bookmakers.

In response to the subpoena, Tony dutifully appeared before the Kefauver Committee on January 5, accompanied by his attorney, Callaghan. As was typical of most of the "unfriendly" witnesses who appeared before the committee, the questions put to Tony shed more light on the Outfit and his role in it than did his answers. Indeed, about a full one hundred of his answers consisted of a terse repetition of his refusal to answer on the grounds that such answers would violate his rights under the Fifth Amendment to the U.S. Constitution, the right against self-incrimination. Much of Committee Counsel Rudolph Halley's interrogation, if it can be called that, concerned the fact that, as fully reported elsewhere herein, the Chicago mob had muscled in on the twenty-six-million-dollar-a-year S & G gambling syndicate in Miami Beach, with Harry Russell in charge. "The Russell Muscle."

Accardo took the Fifth with regard to his efforts to obtain the parole for his pal, Paul Ricca, and his codefendants in the Hollywood Extortion Case. After giving his name, he refused to answer whether he was known as "Joe Batters." He declined to acknowledge that he had known Al Capone. Or Ricca. Or Hymie Levin, the major Chicago bookmaker. He did admit knowing Bernstein and that Bernstein represented him, but Tony declined, once again, to admit to any knowledge of the Ricca tax matter.

The questions continued:

Q: Do you have any connection with gambling?
A: I refuse to answer.
Q: Narcotics?
A: I have nothing to do with that.
Q: Vice?
A: No.
Q: Do you belong to the Mafia?
A: I don't know what the Mafia is all about.
Q: Where have you been the last few months?
A: I refuse to answer.
Q: Were you in Mexico? Was it hot down there?
A: (Callaghan) Not as hot as it is here!

Halley produced Accardo's arrest record, which reflected 23 arrests through 1945 but no conviction later than 1924. He asked: "How have you been able on so many occasions to beat the rap?"

A: I don't know what you mean, 'beat the rap.'
Q: Did you use political influence?
A: I refuse to answer.
Q: Do you have friends in Chicago?
A: I refuse to answer.
Q: Do you have any friends?
A: I refuse to answer.
Q: Do you keep the books?
A: No.
Q: You had a quarter of a million dollar profit from one partnership in 1949. How can you indicate the correct amount to the person who prepares your income tax return if you don't keep books?
A: I refuse to answer.
Q: You are perfectly willing in these trying times to pay whatever is just and equitable in taxes?
A: (a shout) YES, SIR!

Following Accardo's appearance, the Committee voted unanimously to cite him for contempt of Congress based on his refusal to answer some one hundred questions. It should be noted here that, following the hearings of the Kefauver Committee, it generally became the rule that, once a witness "opened the door" by answering any question other than his name and address, he thereafter had no recourse to the Fifth Amendment. However, at this time, the witness was able to "pick and choose," as Tony did, when he wanted to answer questions and when he wanted to resort to the Fifth. It should be noted that Tony apparently did not think it could be proven that he was engaged in vice (prostitution) and narcotics. As has been indicated elsewhere in this book, mob figures, such as Murray Humphreys, were quick to deny participation in prostitution, and all throughout Tony Accardo's reign in Chicago, the Outfit prohibited its members from having any involvement whatsoever in the drug business. In fact, when one, Chris Cardi, violated that prohibition, the mob allowed him to serve his sentence in prison and then, almost immediately after he was released, killed him as an example to any others who might become interested in the great money that narcotics could offer.

No sooner did Tony return to Chicago than he was served with another subpoena. This one called for his appearance before a Cook County Grand Jury. Within a week he was on the stand again. Grand jury testimony is sealed and sacred, but it was leaked that he was mainly asked the same questions put to him by the Kefauver Committee. After all, these seemed to be the logical questions. According to the leak, however, Tony did answer some questions, just as he did before the Kefauver Committee, the "open the door" policy still not having come into effect. When asked about whether he owned any stocks or bonds, Tony reportedly answered, "Only government bonds."

At the close of his testimony before the local grand jury, Tony was handed one more subpoena calling for another appearance before the grand jury, on January 18, 1951. State's Attorney John Boyle announced that if Tony continued to refuse to answer questions at that time, he would seek a contempt of the grand jury citation.

So it was that Tony, getting used to this now, appeared once again, for the third time in six weeks, before a proceeding. He continued his stance of hiding behind the Fifth.

As promised, Boyle petitioned for a contempt citation. It was denied by the Chief Judge of the Cook County court system on constitutional grounds.

Tony wasn't finished yet, however. On January 23, 1951, the full U.S. Senate voted to cite Tony and seven other reluctant and unresponsive witnesses for contempt of Congress. This proved to be fruitless, and Tony was never arrested or convicted of this charge. It was ruled that he had properly asserted his rights under the conditions of the Fifth Amendment. This was decided by the U.S. Supreme Court in November of 1952, and although Tony might have had some concern about whether his string of consecutive days (and years) of never having spent a night in jail might be at last broken, he need not have been.

The hearings of the Kefauver Committee had an immediate effect. Mayor Kennelly announced on November 14 that he was selecting a new police commissioner, naming Timothy O'Connor. O'Conner would remain throughout the decade of the Fifties. I would get to know him and to respect him. He was a good and honest man. Not that he wouldn't have his problems, and not that Tony Accardo and his minions wouldn't flourish while he was at the top. He started the Scotland Yard Unit, which brought in Joe Morris and Bill Duffy into a position where they could bring their extraordinary talents into the fight against the mob, and he tried his best. Unfortunately, as we shall see, it wasn't good enough and he would leave his office, not disgraced, as they say, for he did a good job, but under some fire. Things in Chicago would not change.

19 Accardo Moves

At the same time that Tony Accardo was consolidating things in Chicago, the New York mob, under the aegis of Frank Costello and Meyer Lansky, had opened up a new venture which would be a godsend, not only to the New York families of La Cosa Nostra, but to the Chicago family under Accardo.

In 1946, after Costello and Lansky had sent Ben "Bugsy" Siegel out to Los Angeles, Siegel got a bright idea. He saw the vision of gaming in Las Vegas. At the time Highway 91, called the Gay White Way then, had almost nothing in the way of casinos. Today it is Las Vegas Boulevard South, better known around the world as The Strip. But then there were no neon lights on Highway 91. There was almost nothing there. Nevada had legalized gambling in 1931, but until 1946 most of the gaming which attracted the visitor was in Reno. In 1946, however, at Christmas time, Bugsy opened the Flamingo. It was not an immediate success. It closed for a while and then reopened again. Then it boomed.

When Tony Accardo attended his next meeting of the "Commission," the ruling body of the mob nationwide, he learned of the promise of gaming in Las Vegas. He immediately dispatched Murray Humphreys out there to take a look, and Hump concurred that the potential was outstanding. Tony, always disposed to listen to the wise Humphreys, became alert for an opening.

But it would be some time before Accardo found the right opportunity to move into Las Vegas, 1955 to be exact.

In the meantime things almost slipped away from him. In 1949 Morris Barney Dalitz, soon to be known as Moe Dalitz, "The Godfather of Las Vegas," arrived. He built the Desert Inn. By the time Accardo would get to Vegas, the D.I., the Riviera, The Royal Nevada and the Dunes were all in operation on The Strip.

Moe Dalitz was some piece of work. He had started off as a leader of "The Little Jewish Navy" in Detroit during Prohibition. His boats brought illicit whiskey over the Detroit River from Canada, but the Purple Gang in Detroit had proven too much for Dalitz. He moved across Lake Erie to Cleveland, where he became the leader of what was then known as the Mayfield Road Gang. With Charley Polizzi, Morris Kleinman, Sam Tucker and Lou Rothkopf, aka Lou Rody, he took over the rackets in Cleveland, and as a result, he became very close with mobsters all over the country, especially Frank Costello and Meyer Lansky in New York, but also Accardo, Guzik and Humphreys in Chicago. Soon Dalitz had outposts in northern Kentucky, where he had the Lookout House and the Beverly Hills Club, two gigantic gambling casinos in Newport and Covington, across the Ohio River from Cincinnati. He had established himself as a major player in the gaming industry.

Costello and Lansky needed an expert like Dalitz to run their operations in Vegas. They approached Dalitz and persuaded him to take over the operation of their Riviera and their Desert Inn, two magnificent hotel-casinos up on the north end of The Strip. In 1949 Dalitz made his move. He completed the construction of the D.I. and opened it in 1950. From that time on, Las Vegas has been the focal point of legal gambling in this country.

In 1950 Tony Accardo had not been sufficiently convinced that Vegas was an opportunity he needed to pursue. At least, he hadn't yet found the right spot to move in.

As a matter of fact, the move Accardo made in 1950 was in just the opposite direction, to Miami Beach. With Jake Guzik and Harry Russell, he moved on what was called the S & G Gambling Syndicate, which furnished wire service to practically all bookmakers in southern Florida. S & G was owned and operated by five local residents of Miami. The books of the S & G Syndicate showed that they had a gross income in 1948 of twenty-six million dollars! It was quite a nice operation. In payment, the bookmakers were required to turn over half their net to S & G. Some cheated on the owners of S & G, but most reported their income as contracted, making S & G a very going concern. In fact, since just twenty-six mil was *reported*, Tony Accardo thought that the real income to S & G must be close to twice that. Tony felt it was ripe for the taking. After all, what muscle did these five Floridians have to keep Tony Accardo out?

Russell already had an inroad in Florida. He was involved in a dog track there and had become close to a man named Fuller Warren, backing Warren financially. Warren became the governor of Florida in 1949, after he was already in Russell's pocket.

At Russell's behest Governor Warren gave him a prize for his backing. The governor thought it a small prize. He appointed William "Bing" Crosby (not the entertainer), a pal of Russell, as his special investigator.

Ten days after Crosby became the governor's "special investigator," he went to Miami, where he told Sheriff James A. Sullivan that he had been sent by Governor Warren especially to investigate gambling. He requested that the sheriff assist him in making raids on gambling places in Miami's Dade County. The sheriff was amazed at Crosby's knowledge as to the location of so many handbooks in Dade County, something he himself knew little of. Crosby had an ace in the hole, of course. He had gotten the list from none other than Harry Russell.

Of course, there was a big reason for Russell to become a snitch for the state investigator. Only those bookmaking establishments doing business with S & G were on Crosby's list.

Crosby and the assisting sheriff's deputies had a ball. They conducted dozens of raids on the S & G establishments, causing a great rip in the fabric of S & G's income sources. They reported less than $26 million in 1950.

Accardo made another play at this time. He had already done away with Jim Ragan, the operator of Continental Press in Cleveland, and established Ragan's successors. Now he encouraged Continental Press to cut off service to all bookmakers in Florida, which had the immediate effect of practically putting them out of business, S & G in particular.

S & G remained "down" for two weeks. When it reopened, Harry Russell was a partner; the books showed that he had paid $20,000 for a full partnership, a pretty nice deal for a concern that grossed about $50 million a year. Accardo himself began to show income from S & G on his tax returns, and the books showed that S & G paid Tony $20,000 for his yacht, the *Clari Jo*, that he kept anchored in Biscayne Bay.

There was one other development when Harry Russell became a partner in S & G. Mr. Crosby never again made a raid on an S & G bookmaker.

Sam Giancana had been a member of the 42 Gang, the rival gang of the Circus Cafe Gang of young toughs. The 42 Gang was head-quartered in The Patch, around Taylor and Halsted streets, a mile or so south of the Circus Cafe Gang turf in Little Sicily. When Tony Accardo joined Al Capone in 1926, Giancana was still young enough to still be a "42er." He went away for a stretch in prison for bootlegging. While in prison, in Terre Haute, he be-came acquainted with some of the African-Americans who were there for their participation in policy and numbers games on the south and west sides of Chicago, in the "black belts," as they were referred to at the time.

Policy, at the time, was an offshoot of the lottery. It preyed on poor folks who saw it as their one chance of a big payoff. Policy players purchased numbers from runners or in policy stations. The operators of the game placed seventy-eight pellets in a cylinder, usually called a wheel, and the winning numbers were drawn from this cylinder. At least, that was the way it was supposed to work. For the most part, the operators simply looked for a number which had not been played, or hardly played, and announced that number as the winner. Of course, even when the game was honest, the odds against winning were astronomical.

When Giancana was released, one of the first things he did was to look up Tony Accardo. This took some doing because Sam had not yet been "made," and to have an audience with the boss of Chicago was not usual. But he managed it. Giancana had devised a scheme which he hoped would attract Accardo's interest and become the vehicle which would "make" him. His presentation to Tony, which he had developed through lifelong contacts with people who knew policy and numbers, was persuasive. Tony thought that there might be something to Giancana's plan to move into the black belts. When piled up, those nickels and dimes added up to many dollars—millions of them—a year.

Accardo recognized the potential in Giancana. This kid seemed to have what it took. He wasn't much younger than Tony but had gotten off to a much slower start. He hadn't had a Machine Gun Jack McGurn to recognize his potential. Besides, Giancana had spent a good portion of his early days in the can, whereas Accardo had skated time and time again. He was much further advanced in the Outfit than Giancana—and always would be.

Accardo took the position that there wasn't much to lose in giving Giancana his head and lending him several "soldiers," the lowest rung of membership in the Outfit, to assist him. After all, after Prohibition had ended, there were many soldiers with wrinkles in their bellies, unable to lead a life of luxury on their income from gambling and the other income-producers now available to the Outfit. None of them were living in twenty-two-room mansions in River Forest like Tony Accardo.

Actually, the initial move on policy and numbers had commenced in 1946 and was only now, in 1950, coming to fruition. It had commenced when Giancana, with Accardo's sanction and with the assistance of Accardo's soldiers, went after one of the biggest policy racketeers on the south side, Eddie Jones. In May of 1946, Giancana and his helpers ambushed Jones as he left his headquarters, the Ben Franklin Store at 47th and South Parkway, in the heart of the "black belt." They yanked him out of his car (he was riding with his wife and secretary), hit him over the head and threw him into their car. With a second car as a backup, they sped away. However, they had the bad luck to run into a patrol car that had been cruising the neighborhood. Giancana fired shots at the two policemen inside, and Officer Michael Derrane was hit in the shoulder. Giancana and the rest of the kidnappers got away clean.

Jones' abduction was one of the biggest in Chicago's recent history. It became a major item in the press of the day, especially the community newspapers on the south side, but also in the Chicago dailies like the *Trib*, *Sun Times* and *Herald American*.

Jones was held captive for almost a week. It was not ransom the kidnappers wanted; they wanted to scare the hell out of Jones, to impress upon him that what they wanted was his policy wheels, the Maine-Idaho-Ohio wheel, for example, Chicago's biggest at the time.

The Outfit, thanks to Giancana, got what it wanted. Soon after Jones was released, as he had promised, Jones left for Mexico. He had enough to live comfortably there and had apparently had enough of dealing with the Outfit. Immediately thereafter, the Maine-Idaho-Ohio wheel was in Accardo's hands. A very nice coup.

Now some more muscle was needed. It was nice to have the Maine-Idaho-Ohio wheel, but wouldn't it be nice to have a couple more? Another big policy officer in Chicago at the time was Ted Roe. Roe was nobody's fool. He had seen what happened to Eddie Jones. He hired two Chicago police detectives to guard him at all times, carried a gun himself and was prone to use it. So Accardo sent Gus Alex, a tough young mobster, with Giancana to "reason" with Roe and make sure he knew the facts. "Go fuck yourself," Roe told Alex and Giancana. He knocked Giancana to the floor.

Giancana and Alex quickly left, but they would be back.

The next time there were four of them: Giancana, "Fat Lenny" Caifano, Fifi Buccieri and Vince Ioli. But the results were no better; Roe and his two police-officer bodyguards were a good match for the mobsters. Fat Lenny was killed, Ioli badly wounded. It was the first known "heavy work" that Buccieri participated in, but it certainly would not be his last.

Now Teddy Roe was lionized. He had once again beaten the Chicago mob. He was arrested for the killing of Fat Lenny, but he was never brought to trial. After all, he had a good defense. He had only been protecting himself.

For the next several years, Teddy Roe held out. He became a hero on the south side, known as a man who had beaten the mob. A black who was more than a match for the white guys. He became known as "The Robin Hood of Policy," a major benefactor to so many down-and-out blacks in his part of town. Not only did he hold on to his policy wheels and his numbers racket, he expanded them; it had become a matter of pride for the locals to patronize his wheel over the Outfit's.

It therefore became more and more necessary to take out Roe. On August 4, 1952, two men parked behind a billboard across the street from Roe's residence at 5239 South Michigan. They were white men and they stuck out, but most who observed them took them to be cops. Unfortunately for Roe, by this time he had gotten careless. It had been years since the Outfit had come after him.

It was after ten at night; usually Roe would have been accompanied by his bodyguards, but on this night he was not. As he left his front door to walk to his Buick, which was parked on the street, the two men leaped out of their car and headed for him. They fired five shots from their shotguns point-blank at him. Roe was dead at last, just like Fat Lenny.

The Roe murder caused outrage on the south side. The alderman of the Third Ward, in the heart of the south side, Archibald Carey, was a big voice in African-American affairs at the time. He attacked Mayor Kennelly in the press, saying: "The responsibility is on you, Mr. Mayor. We appear before the world as the most godless and callous group of public officials anywhere."

This got Mayor Kennelly's immediate attention, since he considered he had the black vote to thank for his election. Carey was not to be trifled with; Theodore Roe had been a policy operator, for sure, but he had become an icon in the eyes of his fellow citizens on the south side. In their eyes, to do nothing to solve this heinous crime would be outrageous.

The police, much to Kennelly's horror, interrupted Roe's funeral, at which several thousand people were present, and arrested Roe's five pallbearers. Roe's supporters were stunned and outraged. Everybody knew the killers had been white, had been members of the white Chicago crime syndicate. Roe had not been killed by his black pallbearers.

Homicide detectives contacted Scotland Yard in an effort to elucidate the situation. Who could have done this? Lt. Joe Morris and Sergeant Bill Duffy smiled. "Go look for Sam Giancana," they advised, wisely. "Then go pick up Fat Lenny's brother, Marshall. Then go look up Tony Accardo." They gave the homicide boys a list of the top dozen people in the Outfit then. It should not come as a surprise that none were arrested.

Now that Tony Accardo had gotten what he wanted on the south side, taking over Roe's Delta, Indio and Alcoa wheels, he needed to do the same in the other predominantly black area in Chicago, the west side. This job he assigned to another up-and-coming Chicago soldier. Another guy who, like Giancana, would use the job as his springboard to much bigger things. His name was John Philip Cerone, better known as Jackie.

Cerone, about eight years younger than Giancana, had come to Accardo's attention as he searched for rising stars in the Outfit. Jackie's job was to hit the big policy operator on the west side, "Big Jim" Martin. Martin not only ran policy and numbers, but was a key political figure on the west side, especially in his area of the 28th Ward, even though that ward was mostly white in the early and mid-Fifties.

A bug we placed in the early Sixties picked up a conversation of Jackie Cerone, who was then working under Giancana as a capo. The following conversation is quoted verbatim from official FBI tape.

CERONE: So when I banged the guy, I caught him with a full load . . . but it had to go through a Cadillac. I blasted him twice. Joe says, Is the guy dead? And I said, Sure. Because when I nailed him, his head went like that, you know? The next morning the headlines are in the paper. The guy is still living—this double-ought buck was ten years old. It wasn't fresh, so the guy lived. . . . That guy was a big nigger. He left the country and went to Mexico. That's what we wanted anyway. We grabbed up all his policy games. The next day I'm on the corner where he was shot. I went to the place all dressed up. The police squads are all around. I'm right there. And everybody is talking and I say, "Oh, isn't that terrible! But them fucking niggers are always fighting each other, you know."

The man Cerone referred to was, we firmly believe, Big Jim Martin. When Martin abandoned his west side policy and numbers operations, Tony Accardo had just what he wanted. The policy and numbers racket in the black belt proved to be well worth the effort. Sam Giancana had been well informed when he came to Tony with the idea. The income from these operations came to be a big hunk of the new annual income of the Outfit.

Not only that, the invasion of the black belt had been a proving ground for four guys who would prove to be just what Tony Accardo was looking for. They had made their bones in this effort. Marshall Caifano soon became the Chicago mob's man over Las Vegas until 1971, when Tony "The Ant" Spilotro replaced him. Fifi Buccieri became the capo in charge of the entire west side, a most lucrative area for Accardo. Sam Giancana would one day be named by Tony as the "caretaker" of the Outfit. And Jackie Cerone would himself become a successor to Giancana.

Tony Accardo was a most happy warrior in those days. He was proving that what Paul Ricca had said about him was true: he did have more brains at breakfast than Al Capone had all day. The invasion of the black belts of Chicago reinforced his reputation. Tony Accardo was on his way to becoming the most capable of leaders of the Chicago family of La Cosa Nostra. He was doing it all. And there was more to come.

20 Dallas Debacle

Joe Batters, as Tony's friends were now calling him, came to find that, as well as he managed the Chicago Outfit, there would always be a bump in the road, even in the years when there was no interference from the federal government, little from the cops and little from public officials.

Joe was approached with a second scheme, in 1946, this time from a guy named Paul Jones. Jones had a tenuous affiliation with Murray Humphreys and Jake Guzik, but was not really all that close to them or to anybody else in the Outfit. However, recalling his initial doubts when Giancana had approached him about invading the south and west sides of Chicago, Accardo decided to give Jones the go-ahead on his plan.

Jones had been in Dallas, Texas, dealing in drugs. He felt that he knew the town and its players. So, with little or no help from Joe Batters, but with his sanction, Jones flew from Chicago to Dallas to set his idea in motion.

No sooner had he arrived, however, than the local gamblers got a sniff of what he was up to. Obviously, they had things going for them in Dallas and did not want to share it with any Chicago people. Therefore, they reached out to one of their contacts in the Dallas Police Department, who passed on the information as if it were from an informant, indicating that Paul Jones, a representative of the Chicago mob, was in town in an attempt to start proceedings to invade Dallas.

This information, in the form of an official memo, got the immediate attention of the top powers of the Dallas PD. They immediately assigned one of their top officers, Lieutenant George Butler, to locate and interview Mr. Jones. When he did, Jones made a huge mistake. He assumed that he was dealing with the likes of a Chicago cop and admitted what he was up to. He began to give Lt. Butler a rundown of how organized crime worked in Chicago, explaining that they had many Chicago-area law enforcement officers "on the pad." Jones then made another bad mistake. He offered Lt. Butler $150,000 a year if he would emulate his Chicago brother cops. He then asked Lt. Butler to approach the newly elected sheriff, Steve Guthrie, and determine if Guthrie might be willing to sit down with Jones and "talk business." Jones then went further, referring to Murray Humphreys and Jake Guzik and identifying them as people he was representing. He told Lt. Butler that Paul "Needles" Labriola, the Chicago gunman who was the stepson of Dago Lawrence Mangano, would probably be one of those who would come to Dallas to be involved in the takeover. Jones also told Lt. Butler how the Chicago Outfit had taken over the policy and numbers rackets from the blacks in Chicago. He indicated that the same Chicago methods might be useful in Dallas.

Armed with all this, Lt. Butler returned to police headquarters in downtown Dallas—the same headquarters where, years later, Jack Ruby shot and killed Lee Harvey Oswald. Butler faithfully reported to his superiors every bit of his conversation with Jones.

Lt. Butler was instructed to go ahead and contact Sheriff Guthrie, which he did. Together, the police made an elaborate plan to set up Jones. They contacted the Texas Department of Public Safety, who sent a ranger to Sheriff Guthrie's residence, where, in a separate room off the living room, a recording device and a camera were installed. Sheriff Guthrie invited Jones to his house to confer over the plan to bring the Chicago mob to Dallas.

The first meeting between Jones and Sheriff Guthrie took place on November 1, 1946. They were introduced by Lt. Butler. The meeting lasted from eight at night until early the next morning, all under the watchful eye of the camera and the attuned ear of the bug. Lt. Butler and Sheriff Guthrie led Jones right down the primrose path. When Jones left, he was elated. He hurried back to Chicago, where Joe Batters had put Pat Manno in charge of the operation. This was Accardo's standard operating method, his modus operandi, and the reason he could brag that he never spent a night in jail. Paul Jones might identify Manno in this conspiracy, but he would not be able to implicate Joe Batters in its details because J.B. had not participated in them.

On November 6, 1946, Pat Manno flew to Dallas and checked in downtown at the plush Adolphus Hotel, one of Dallas' finest. Early the next morning Jones took Manno to the residence of

Sheriff Guthrie, where DPS had once again set up their elaborate film studio.

Manno spoke to the assembled group: "Once we get organized, the money will flow in. You don't fucking have to worry about it personally. Everybody will be happy. I don't like fucking five or six joints in the radius of six blocks. Every block. That's one thing I've always talked against. I like one big spot and that's all. Out in the county. Out of the city entirely. Policy is my business. That I can run." Manno told the sheriff and his men that he was the advance man for the Chicago people. "I am here to look things over and report back to my people."

After the meeting Manno returned to Chicago. Hardly had he landed in Chicago, when the Dallas police exposed him, Jones and the plot. They were not able to extradite Manno, but they had latched onto Jones before he could leave Dallas. He was subsequently tried for bribery, found guilty, and sentenced to three years in the state penitentiary.

For himself, Pat Manno was happy to be back in Chicago. He had never expected, after years of dealing with Chicago cops, that there were cops who could pull such a "dirty" trick as this. Never had such confidences been betrayed in Chicago, never had there been arrests for such things as "bribery." What was that?

J.B. could only shake his head. He had lost a little face in letting Jones try his luck in Dallas, but not much. You can't win them all.

21 Accardo's Rap Sheet

The Internal Revenue Service proceeded to review the income of Tony Accardo, or at least that which he had reported, during the Forties. Obviously, this was but a small percentage of what Tony actually received from his mob activity. However, all mobsters learn at an early age that they have to report enough of their actual income in order to support their lifestyle. In other words, if Tony was now living, as he was, at 915 Franklin in River Forest in a twenty-two-room mansion worth half a million, and sojourning in Bimini, Puerto Rico, Europe and South America (where Clarice journeyed occasionally), he had to show sufficient income on his tax returns each year to justify his expenses. The IRS prioritized "net worth and expenditure" cases on people like Accardo. Obviously, Tony was reaping millions a year. He didn't have to report anywhere near that amount to keep the IRS off his back, but he couldn't report just a pittance either.

Following is what he reported to the IRS on his annual income tax returns during the decade of the Forties, as recorded by the IRS!

From the partnership of DAVE RUSSELL, HARRY RUSSELL, TONY ACCARDO and LAWRENCE IMBURGIO, also known as "HINDU" IMBURGIO, ACCARDO received from 1940 to 1942 inclusive, $11,300, for an average of $3,767 per year per partner.

From the partnership of JOE BATTERS, "HINDU" IMBURGIO, FRANKIE LA PORTE and PERRY, ACCARDO received an income from the Owl Club in Calumet City during the years 1940 to 1949 inclusive of $179,000, for an average of $19,889 per year per partner.

ACCARDO also received a total of $170,000 during the years 1940 to 1949 from what he identifies as miscellaneous income, for an average of $18,888 per year.

ACCARDO received an income of $26,200 from the OK Motors during the years 1943 and 1944 inclusive, for an average of $13,100 per year.

From the partnership of GUZIK and ACCARDO, Tony's income in 1946 was $65,000.

During 1947 and 1948 inclusive ACCARDO received $6,900 from the Illinois Simplex Distributing Company for an average of $3,450 per year.

In 1949 ACCARDO received $134,207 which is identified as one-half of sale price of the Erie Buffalo Wheel to SAM PURDY and PAT MANNO.

This gives a total known income for the years 1940 to 1949 inclusive of $592,600, for an average of $65,845 per year.

At the same time, in 1949, Tony had amassed the following criminal record under Chicago Police Department Identification Number C-25251:

IV—CRIMINAL RECORD

ACCARDO, Bureau of Identification No. C-25251, has the following record:

Date:	Charge	Disposition
3-22-22	Sec. 7 CC, Sec. 27 MVL	Fined $2. Dismissed 3-24-22
5-26-23	2655 (D. C.)	Fined $200 and costs 5-31-23
12-10-23	2655 (D. C.)	D.WP 1-3-24
1-18-24	2655 (D. C.)	Fined $10 and costs 1-19-24
4-5-24	2655 (D. C.)	Fined $25 and costs 4-7-24
10-12-24	2655 (D. C.)	Dismissed 10-13-24
11-16-25	Sec. 22 MVL	Dismissed 11-17-25
1-5-26	2655 (D. C.)	Dismissed 1-6-26
3-3-27	2655 (D. C.)	Dismissed 3-3-27
5-30-27	2655 (D. C.)	Dismissed 6-6-27
10-13-27	2655 (D. C.)	Dismissed 10-14-27
1-28-28	2655 (D. C.) Par. 155 Sec. 4 Ch. 38 (CCW)	Dismissed 1-30-28
1-1-30	CCW	S.O.L. 1-30-28
7-29-30	CCW (reinstated)	NP 3-13-31
9-30-30	2655 (D. C.)	Dismissed 10-2-30
10-4-30	Investigation (murder)	
11-12-30	2655 (D. C.)	Dismissed 11-13-30

2-17-31	CCW	
5-9-31	DC	Dismissed
3-3-32	Vagrancy	Not Guilty 5-24-32
5-16-33	DC	Fined $25 and costs
5-5-33	Investigation	
3-4-43	Investigation (murder)	
9-27-43	Material witness (extortion)	Held under $25,000 bond
12-4-43	Conspiracy (operation handbook)	Agreed to accept subpoena and appear in New York
12-17-43	Gambling	
2-13-45	DC	Released on habeas corpus
January 1948	Conspiracy to defraud US Govt	Not Guilty

One particularly amusing note is his arrest on May 16, 1933, for "DC," disorderly conduct. On that occasion he was arrested "on suspicion" at Canal and Jackson streets, on the near west side of Chicago. At his hearing, which took place the next day, he was fined $25 after he was found with $500 in his pockets and after admitting that he had not worked "for six months" and that he had given the cops a vacant lot as the address of his residence. When the judge threw that at him, Tony explained: "If I gave my right address to the police, they would be all over my place all the time." One has to wonder what it was he didn't want the cops to see.

Another noteworthy arrest was on February 1, 1930. It was effected by a Chicago police officer who later became quite famous and controversial. He was Officer William J. Drury, later Lieutenant Drury, then Acting Captain Drury.

He described the incident:

"On February 1, 1930, my partner and I left Chicago police headquarters on a routine tour of the Loop. We were riding south on a Dearborn streetcar when a collision between a taxicab and a light delivery truck attracted our attention. Looking from the streetcar into the cab, I observed one of the passengers in the cab as 'Machine Gun Jack' McGurn.

My partner and I jumped from the front platform of the streetcar and surrounded the cab. We pulled the two occupants out and searched them. McGurn had a .45 on him, as usual, and his companion, whom I did not know at that time, was carrying a loaded .38.

After taking their guns away from them, I said to McGurn: 'Who's this new punk, Jack?'

He said: 'Sarge, he's not a punk. He's a solid fella. This boy is going places. He's a good standup kid.'

I said: 'I know, but what's his name?'

McGurn said: 'Tony Accardo.'

How true his predictions were."

The arrest on March 4, 1943, was also made by Acting Captain Drury. Tony was arrested in the company of Ralph Pierce and Les Kruse. (Pierce would go on to be the boss of the south side of Chicago; Kruse would boss the northern suburbs of Chicago in Lake County.) They were arrested in connection with the murder of Estelle Carey, the sweetheart of Nicky Circella. Captain Drury made it public at the time that he believed the torture-murder of Estelle Carey was meant to send a message to Circella, that he should not talk after he pleaded guilty in the Hollywood Extortion Case. Captain Drury admitted that after he arrested Accardo on this occasion, he received several threatening phone calls.

At the time of the arrest shown on December 4, 1943, for Tony's conspiracy in the operation of a handbook, David Russell appeared voluntarily in the offices of the Chicago Crime Commission and advised that he, his brother Harry, Tony Accardo and Lawrence Imburgio had operated a handbook at 186 North Clark Street, but that this partnership had been dissolved at the end of 1942. That arrest was made in cooperation with the FBI, which was then seeking Tony as a material witness in the Hollywood Extortion Case in New York. Tony was released when the subpoena in this matter was served on him commanding his appearance there.

An arrest not listed above was that of Gus Alex on October 4, 1944. He was arrested for no reason other than because he had been observed talking to Accardo while Accardo was under surveillance. That was good enough reason to arrest anyone, according to Chief McGinnis, who personally snapped the cuffs on Gussie.

Accardo's arrest on February 14, 1945, occurred in the 500 block of West Worthington Street in Chicago. It was for questioning in the kidnapping of Greasy Thumb Guzik, of all people. Guzik had been missing for a few days in 1945, and when he turned up, he indicated that he had been kidnapped. Tony was also wanted for questioning in the slaying of Jens Larrison in a tavern of Matt Capone, Al's brother, at 3844 Ogden Avenue on the west side of Chicago. Giancana was with Accardo at the time of his arrest.

(It was at this time, incidentally, that a bill was introduced before the Illinois State Legislature in Springfield which would remove the personal liability of policemen for damage they might do to personal property when engaged on official business. The support of State Senator James Adduci was sought for the bill. Adduci was a member of the "west side bloc," that group of politicians "on the pad" of the mob. He advised a source that "in order to get such a bill enacted, it would be necessary first to get the approval of Tony Accardo." Apparently Tony did not give his approval; the bill was defeated in the legislature.)

The arrest in January 1948, for "conspiracy to defraud the U.S. Govt," and the decision of "not guilty," was, of course, the arrest for his visits to Paul Ricca in prison at Leavenworth, when Accardo falsified his identity as the lawyer, Joe Bulger.

At the end of the decade of the Forties, the Chicago Police Department Identification Division described Tony physically as follows:

Name:	ANTHONY JOSEPH ACCARDO alias TONY ACCARDO, JOE BATTERS
Age:	45 (born 4-28-06), Chicago, Ill.
Height:	5 ft. 9½ in.
Weight:	195 pounds
Build:	Heavy
Eyes:	Hazel
Hair:	Dark chestnut
Complexion:	Ruddy
Scars & Marks:	Flying dove on back of right hand Scars on back of left hand
Occupation:	Gunman, gambler
P.P.C.	31 W MO 4 W OI
Residence:	915 Franklin Avenue, River Forest, Illinois

Relatives: ANTHONY ACCARDO, son
                  MARIE ACCARDO, daughter
                  LINDA ACCARDO, daughter
                  CLARICE ACCARDO, wife
Marital Status: Married
Photograph: In file

The Forties had been good to Tony. He had entered the decade as a capo under Frank Nitti, then stepped up to acting boss under Paul Ricca, officially emerging as the top gun, "the boss" in the lexicon of La Cosa Nostra. It was a heady role for a guy in his mid-forties, but it was nothing Joe Batters couldn't handle, and handle just as well as any of his predecessors. Certainly as well as Capone. Better than Nitti, who had committed suicide after being disrespected by his people. As well as Ricca. And importantly, Accardo had not gotten himself imprisoned. As the Forties turned into the Fifties, Tony was riding high.

22 Bigger and Better

It was about this time that Tony began to host the parties at his River Forest mansion that were to become infamous. Each year Tony hosted anybody who meant anything to his organization on the Fourth of July. For the first several years they went virtually unnoticed, but the top investigative reporter in Chicago at the time, Sandy Smith, then of the Chicago *Tribune*, got wind of the parties and began publicizing them, somewhat at his personal risk. (Sandy became one of my best friends, and we were later able to afford him some protection, but not in the beginning. I recall, for instance, when Claude Maddox, aka Screwy Moore, died in 1959, we took Sandy with us. In those early days of the FBI involvement, when we knew so little about the mob, he could point out the several mobsters who attended the wake, so we could photograph them and use the photos for subsequent surveillances. After a little while, of course, the mobsters who attended the wake, as almost all did in those early years, got wind of our photographic surveillance. The next day, the day of the funeral itself, when Sandy brought his own *Tribune* photographer to the site of the funeral home, the photographer was attacked by mobsters. Unfortunately, I was at a firearms training session at the Great Lakes Naval Station, where we fired monthly during the warm weather months. But Frank Mellott, a fine agent, was there. He rescued Sandy's picture taker.) Sandy soon identified not only many of the mobsters who attended Tony's functions at his mansion on the Fourth of July, but some of the pols who showed up as well. To get an invitation to Tony's parties in those days was a prestigious event. If you were anybody on the shady side of the law—on the bench or before it—you were honored to be invited to 915 Franklin in River Forest. Not only to greet Tony, a successor to Al Capone, but to see his mansion and to mingle with the cream of the crop.

In the first years things were wide open. There was no stigma, no danger of being identified as a bad guy, even if you were a judge or an alderman. I don't believe corrupt cops were dumb enough to show up, but public officials certainly did. One judge, for instance, who made at least one appearance was the one who jumped from his poker party late on a Saturday night to hurry to the station house to release Tony on bail. This was when Tony was picked up for questioning on June 23, 1951, about the murder of Fat Lennie Caifano, after Caifano had been killed by Ted Roe.

In the early and mid-Fifties Tony was well on his way to becoming perhaps the top gangster in history. Al Capone had captured the public imagination with his high-flying manner. But Big Al had lasted, what, ten years? Lucky Luciano was the big mob star in New York, but how long had he lasted before he was sent to prison by Tom Dewey in 1935? He was never to be important again—either in prison or out of the country. Frank Costello might have lasted longer and been of prime importance to the New York mob, but in 1957 he was shot on Central Park West and was never again active. Joe Bonanno lasted longer than Joe Batters, but he commanded a small family, responsible for only a portion of Brooklyn—and he ran that for a long time by remote control from his comfortable home in Tucson. John Gotti rose like a shooting star in New York in the Eighties, but by the early Nineties he was in federal prison for the rest of his life.

It was at this point that Tony made a huge effort to prove that his reputation would be his legacy.

He undertook it in a time of aroused interest in the affairs of the Chicago mob, thereby making his move more difficult. The reason for the public's arousal at this time was the murder of Charles Gross, one of the very few times in Chicago's history that a public official had been slain. It was February 1952. Gross was the acting Republican ward committeeman of the 31st Ward on the north side of Chicago when he was shotgunned to death, after being warned by the mob to abandon his campaign for election. The Chicago *Tribune* put up a $10,000 reward for any information leading to the arrest of the murderers of Gross. Then the Chicago Crime Commission, always in the vanguard of efforts to arouse public outrage against the Outfit, and the Chicago Association of Commerce organized a mass meeting of some four hundred civic leaders at the La Salle Hotel. These civic leaders in Chicago together agreed to fight "Capone gangsters and their political henchmen until the threat is destroyed." The CCC and the CAC decided to follow in the footsteps of the 1912–1915 reform wave that washed away Chicago's red-light districts, the vice dens on the Levee and elsewhere. They now massed in open defiance of the Outfit's obvious intent to take political control of Chicago.

It was into this public outcry that Tony Accardo now made his move to expand his income base. It was a move that Tony felt was long in coming.

For years there had been hundreds of bookmaking establishments, wirerooms, "offices" throughout Chicago, its suburbs and the surrounding counties that were, for the most part, controlled by the Outfit. These included offices in the two Lake counties, one in Indiana and one north of Chicago, DuPage County, McHenry County, Kankakee County and Will County. Many of those offices not in the Outfit's control had been pressured to turn over a percentage of their net, their "win," to the Accardo syndicate. Even those, however, did so on the basis of what they told the mob their "win" was. There had been no real effort to determine whether these bookies were being straight with the mob. And there were many who weren't kicking in at all.

Tony set out to bring every one of the gamblers into his domain, under his sanction. Not that he wanted to take over their control, but he wanted to make sure he got a big cut—half—of their win. He held a meeting of his top guys at the time: Murray Humphreys and Fifi Buccieri, who had just taken over the west side; also Gus Alex, who had just taken over the Loop; Ralph

Pierce, the south side boss; Caesar DiVarco on the near north side; Frankie La Porte, the longtime boss of the southern suburbs; Joe Amato in DuPage and McHenry counties; Les Kruse in Lake County and the northern suburbs; Tony Pinelli in Lake County, Indiana; Lenny Patrick in Rogers Park, the Jewish section of Chicago on the far north side; Ross Prio, who had the rest of the north side other than the near north and Rogers Park; Sam Giancana, who had become Accardo's underboss; Butch Blasi, Tony's appointment secretary and driver; Felix "Milwaukee Phil" Alderisio and Chuckie Nicoletti, the mob "heavies"; Frankie "Strongy" Ferraro, the partner of Alex in the Loop; Eddy Vogel, the slot machine king since the days he worked under Capone and Nitti; Jake Guzik, the king of corruption since Capone; Turk Torello, a fast-rising young tough; Sam "Teets" Battaglia, who eventually would rise even higher; Jackie Cerone, who was now the boss of the western suburbs, with a headquarters in Elmwood Park; Donald Angelini and Dominic "Large" Cortina, two very young but rising specialists on gambling; Rocky De Grazia, a veteran specialist on casino gambling and the operator of Casa Madrid, the casino in Melrose Park; Charley "Cherry Nose" Gioe, a veteran mobster and expert on gambling; the Fischetti brothers, Charley, Rocco and Joe; Davey Yaras, one of the shooters of Ted Roe. They were all there, the most prominent guys in the Outfit of that era, almost all specialized in the "lifeblood" of the mob: gambling. Others were enforcers, guys like Alderisio, Buccieri, Cerone, Nicoletti and Alex.

The meeting was one of the landmarks in Tony's rule. If all bookmakers in the vast area of several million people where the Chicago mob held the power could be brought honestly and candidly to fork over 50% of their "win" to the Outfit, it would become the single major source of income to the mob. Many of the bookies in question had operated without the knowledge, even, of the Outfit. Many of those who were known by them operated with impunity, without cutting the mob in on their take. Many had been influenced to share with the mob, but were doing so on just a small part of their income.

It would take muscle. A lot of it. How else could a Chicago area bookmaker be influenced to hand over half of his income?

Those who participated in Tony's conference fanned out all over their assigned areas and the word was spread. Some bookmakers, knowing the reputation of the people they were dealing with, readily coughed up the full 50%. Without argument, because they knew what could happen if they did not. Others reluctantly agreed, but appeared to hold back on the true count. Not many told the mobsters who came to see them to go to hell.

Those who did lived to regret it. There were many broken heads and broken legs in Chicago in those days. And there were some who paid the ultimate price. Even one of the guys who had been at the meeting went down. On August 18, 1954, Charley "Cherry Nose" Gioe got his.

Cherry Nose had been one of the top leaders of the Outfit almost as long as Tony. In 1954 Tony was the boss and Gioe (pronounced Joy) was one of his top people, a potential rival. But he was no more after Wednesday night, August 18, 1954. His body was found on the front seat of his car. Five bullets ended his life. Fortunately for Cherry Nose, he had parked right across the street from St. Maria Addolorata Catholic Church at 1148 West Erie, on the near northwest side of Chicago. When Father Alexis Peloso saw and heard the commotion, he ran from the rectory and arrived even as the cops did. He gave the last rites of the church to the man he recognized as a parishioner.

Gioe had been ambushed before he even had a chance to turn the ignition. The car keys were dangling in his hand as he lay dead. As usual, the CPD conducted its investigation. Although the hit had taken place on a busy street close to the restaurant Gioe owned (in his wife's name), Angelo's Pizzeria, the cops could find no witnesses. No one would admit they had seen the ambush (or the killers). Such was the end of yet another participant in the Hollywood Extortion Case.

Cherry Nose was murdered with the sanction of Joe Batters. Gioe had been in charge of a chain of handbooks in the Loop, and it seemed that, although he was high up in the chain of command of the Outfit, he was a cheater. He wasn't sending enough of his win to the "west side." J.B. *was* the "west side," the boss, and this didn't sit all that well with him. Cherry Nose felt he had paid his dues in the Outfit, especially since he had gone down in the Hollywood Extortion Case and spent some time in prison. He, therefore, felt he was immune from Accardo's edict that all books were to be 50-50, with no take for the middleman.

In addition to that, it was also said that Gioe had talked a little too much to the Kefauver Committee. Unlike Accardo, Ricca, Campagna and the others from Chicago who had resorted to the Fifth Amendment, Gioe had answered questions. Evasively and without bringing anybody down, but he did not follow the example of the other top Chicago Outfit people who had appeared before the Committee. In fact, he had appeared the same day as

Ricca and "Little New York" Campagna. Ricca and Campagna had flown to Washington in answer to their subpoena. Cherry Nose traveled to Washington alone, by train. When the three had gone through the ritual, a reporter heard Senator Kefauver remark that "Gioe appeared to be the most forthright and his testimony was the most complete" of the three. He added that Gioe seemed to have told "everything he knew of value to the Committee." When the reporter conveyed this to Gioe, he saw Gioe flinch. He later remarked that he was convinced that here was a man who would rather have heard himself accused of a crime than of having told what he knew of gangster operations.

Gioe had rubbed his people the wrong way; therefore, he was rubbed out. A lot of people in his element were eliminated for far lesser infractions. Tony Accardo might have had some human qualities—more than most of his pals—but he ruled with an iron fist. It might be the velvet glove, all right, but that didn't mean you could horse around with the rules of *omerta* and expect that he would not send someone after you. He would and he did. When one considers that Charley Gioe had been arrested on one occasion with Tony as far back as 1931, and had been his partner in a concession at the Century of Progress, Chicago's World's Fair, it is clear that Joe Batters played no favorites when it came to discipline.

Eventually everybody came into line. Soon there would be hardly a bookmaker in Chicago who wasn't giving the mob its honest count and a 50% split. As a result, the coffers of the Outfit swelled. For the first time in the quarter century since Prohibition ended, the income of the mob matched that of the old days. Now the bellies of even the lowest rung of soldiers were filled. And the respect paid to Tony Accardo by his underlings was unmatched. Nobody failed to understand that Tony Accardo had brought the mob to its highest point ever.

Then Tony enforced another edict. For years, Chicago area burglars and thieves—from every small-time punk to the career jewel and fur thief who made hundreds of thousands of dollars a year—knew they had to pay the "street tax." He had to cough up a large percentage of his scores to the Outfit. If he hit a place in the Chicago area, he had to fork some of it over. Even if he moved outside Chicago, if he hit a spot in the city, he had to give up his tribute to the Outfit. If he was a fence who fenced the burglar's score, he had to pay his street tax. If he was a pornographer or an abortionist, he had to give up a fee to the mob. In fact, if anybody in the Chicago area operated professionally on the shady side of the law, he was under orders to fork over to the mob. Even some legitimate businessmen, who for one reason or another seemed to be shady, were forced to pay a street tax. The street tax, however, was not being uniformly enforced at the time. Many was the burglar who winked at this rule and went about his business without paying attention.

Under Tony Accardo in the Fifties, this became a very unwise thing to do. The hitters again went out, this time to enforce the street tax. Now even if a Chicago area burglar ventured to Beverly Hills to rob a jewelry store, he would be kneecapped and get his arms broken if he did not immediately report his success to the Outfit boss in his area and dish up some of the score, either in jewels or furs or in a big percentage of the cash he received from his fence for them.

It would take some trunk music before the burglars were convinced. After all, they were tough guys all. Joe Batters had a reputation and nobody fooled with him or his edicts, but there were some stupid burglars in Chicago. Some had a wake-up call. Their elevator button had to be punched now and then before it ran up to their top floor, if you will.

Paul "Needle Nose" Labriola and Jimmy Weinberg were two such men. (They had been involved, the reader will remember, in the move on the Chicago Restaurant Association. They were the guys who threatened to push Abe Teitelbaum out the window of his high-rise office when the old Capone lawyer didn't register the mob's "request" that he leave his plush spot in the CRA.) It was mid-March of 1954. Labriola had a connection to the mob, a relative, and he had been "made." He should have known better.

The bodies of these two punks were found at the end of the gangland trail, scrunched in the trunk of a cream-colored Pontiac sedan in a lot adjoining an alley behind 5018 Armitage, on the northwest side of Chicago. Just to demonstrate the mob's versatility, they were not shotgunned or stabbed. They were strangled.

The message was delivered loud and clear to everybody on the wrong side of the law in Chicago: "Don't fuck with Tony Accardo."

One problem Tony had in the mid-Fifties was sorrow for his older brother Martin. Martin was hit with an income tax rap, and on November 1, 1954, he went away to the federal penitentiary in Terre Haute, Indiana, to serve a three-year sentence. He had failed to report sufficient income from his operation of a tavern and handbook in Cicero which Tony had set him up with. Tony believed that if he hadn't become recognized, especially after his much-publicized appearance before the Kefauver Committee, as the Chicago mob boss, the IRS would not have honed in with all their resources on Martin. Actually, Tony had taken pretty good care of his family. Along with setting Martin up as a tavern owner and handbook operator, he had put younger brother John into a job as a movie projectionist. John was a member of the mob-dominated Local 110 of the Motion Picture Operators Union, Tommy Maloy's old union, which the mob took when they whacked Tommy in 1935 and had controlled ever since. Tony's sister married a man named Dominick Senese, whom Tony put into the presidency of a Teamsters' local in Chicago. It wasn't his fault that Dominick was shot in the face years later. Tony's sister Marie married Tarquin "Queenie" Simonelli. Tony brought Queenie into the mob. Queenie, who never really had the talent, never became a capo. The other sister was Bessie, who was on the payroll of State Auditor Orville E. Hodge, who was subsequently removed from office and sent to the penitentiary for embezzling state funds. Tony put his son, Anthony Ross, into a travel agency, Plan-It Travel Service, in Oak Park, with a relative of Frank Nitti. After it failed, he moved him into Local 110. One of his daughters is now married to Ernie Kumerow, the ex-president of a union long under the influence of Accardo, the Laborers Union. No one can say Tony Accardo was not loyal to his family.

Another move Joe Batters made in the Fifties was on the loan sharks, the juice guys. Concomitant with gambling is shylocking, called "juice" in Chicago. Many people on the dim side of the law need cash from time to time, in between scores. Even bookmakers who get hit hard on occasions. Bookmakers almost cannot lose. Not as long as they balance their books. In Chicago most people want to bet on the Cubs, White Sox, Bears, Bulls and Blackhawks. Even on Notre Dame, Loyola and DePaul, on the University of Illinois and the U. of I-Chicago. And on Northwestern. And Purdue and Michigan, even Indiana. So a bookmaker can quickly become overloaded. His books get out of balance. When the Bulls are playing the Knicks, for instance, or the Bears are up against the Bengals, a Chicago area bookie, quite naturally, will receive many more bets on the Bulls and the Bears than he will on the Knicks and the Bengals. Now, unless there is a procedure to overcome this, he will be in jeopardy if the Bulls and Bears don't beat the point spread. What he can do to prevent this is to "lay off." He balances his books by making an arrangement with other bookmakers who are overbalanced the other way, like bookies in New York or Cincinnati in the cases cited. Then he can't lose. In fact, he must win because of the "vig." If a bettor wants to bet, he must give 11 for his 10. That's the way the odds are set, in Las Vegas and Atlantic City, as well as with the illegal bookmaker. So if a bookmaker gets two $100 bets on the Bulls and none on the Knicks, he lays one off. Then he is safe, no matter who wins, because he gets the $10 vigorish. Multiply that two hundred times, not at all out of line for the action an average bookmaker will take on any major ball game, and the reader will understand why this is a nice business for making money. Multiply that on any given Saturday or Sunday, on a fall afternoon when scores of games are being played, and it can be even more profitable.

But what happens to the bettor? It is the bettor or "player," as he is called in the book, who loses. And face it, due to the vig and the always equalizing point spread, almost all players are "grinded out." They might win today and even tomorrow. But over time it just is not a safe way to enhance one's income. So what does this player do when he is down on his luck and doesn't have the money or the credit standing to go on? He usually can't go to a bank or savings and loan, so he goes to his juice guy, the loan shark, who readily loans him what he wants. Why does the juice guy give him the money when the bank won't? Because the juice guy has an edge. He will break your head or your arms and legs if you don't find some way to pay up. If you have an attractive wife, he may even suggest that she hire out as a prostitute. Anything to get you to cough up what you owe. He won't do it the easy way as a bank would, by taking you to court. His courtroom will be in any prairie when the moon is down. Or on any street, even when the sun is up.

Since juice drips off every handbook, Tony Accardo made sure that this phase of his business was well handled. He made sure every juice guy in Chicago was either a member of the mob—like, say, Willie "Potatoes" Daddano—or was a guy well connected and well enough educated to make sure he forked over the "street tax" that would become due. A good example of the latter is a guy like "Mad Sam" DeStefano, who was too demented to be "made" but who had ingratiated himself with Paul Ricca. (Ricca interceded on his behalf, asking J.B. to grant DeStefano this lucrative concession.) Everybody understood that even a retarded guy like Mad Sam had to give the street tax out west every month.

So it was that in every avenue of opportunity available, Tony Accardo was bringing the Chicago Outfit into its glory days. Things were great in the mid-Fifties. It was truly the heyday of organized crime, particularly in Chicago. Prohibition had been great, but it had been marked by all kinds of danger for its membership. Rivals of Capone had killed many of Capone's men, had even come after him. Such rivals had to be taken care of and they were. But it was an uneasy time. Those who survived prospered. Many did neither.

Once Tony Accardo took over, however, things were just great. Sure, there was some violence as he got things squared away the way he wanted, until they had achieved the pot of gold at the end of the rainbow. But the violence was all the other way. The gun was in his hand. There were no rival mobs to be taken out. Capone had taken care of that. Tony's job had been to bring the operation up to speed and he did that; he didn't have to fight for territory. That had been deeded to him. Into the mid-Fifties Tony enhanced every opportunity, including some which had not theretofore been taken. Now things were going smoothly—and richly. The Chicago Outfit was on top of the world. So was its leader, Joe Batters.

Typical of Tony Accardo, there was yet one more opportunity to be taken. And he went after it with all his might.

23 Las Vegas

Tony's next move was into Las Vegas. He had already made a tentative move there, sending out Hump to look over what Bugsy Siegel was building and to evaluate the potential. Hump, with his usual wisdom, had informed Tony that there *was* something there.

Moe Dalitz had himself been sent by New York to Vegas. He had constructed the Desert Inn and the Riviera, both on the same side of the street as the now-functioning Flamingo. Things were heating up. From what would become Sahara Road to Flamingo Road, things were filling the void which had been Highway 91 and which was now about to become the Strip, Las Vegas Boulevard South.

Tony had sent one of his top casino operators, a guy who had gotten his start at Tony's Owl Club in Calumet City, Johnny Drew, to Nevada and he had done well there. But that was in Reno, "The Biggest Little City" in the country, where Drew had gotten the Chicago Outfit's feet wet with his Bank Club, which Chicago operated with Bill Graham, a veteran Reno area gambler. But now three years had gone by and Joe Batters hadn't yet made the move to Vegas.

J.B. decided to take a look himself. The easiest way in those days was to fly to Los Angeles from Chicago and then drive a rental car to Vegas. Tony took another of his protégés with him this time, the guy who had demonstrated his capability by invading the black belts of Chicago and taking over the policy and numbers racket, Sam Giancana. Also along for the ride was Colonel Eugene Chesrow, the medical superintendent of the state-run Oak Forest Hospital, a job Tony's clout had helped Chesrow obtain.

The two mobsters and the good doctor arrived at LAX on TWA Flight 93 at 8:15 on the evening of January 15, 1953. They had intended to stay a couple days in Los Angeles conferring with their man there, Johnny Roselli, and then drive to Las Vegas to look things over. They were met at the airport by two more of Tony's people, Tony Pinelli and Frank "Strongy" Ferraro, long-standing allies.

The group did not figure on the abilities and the interests of the Los Angeles Police Department, however. At the time, the Intelligence Unit of the LAPD, under Jim Hamilton, rivaled the intelligence units of the New York PD, under Ralph Salerno, and the Chicago PD, with Lt. Joe Morris and Sgt. Bill Duffy. They put a tail on this group when they were recognized as they stepped off the plane at LAX. The LAPD tailed them to Perino's, then a fine restaurant in Beverly Hills, where they watched them dine. Then they took them into custody. Tony had flown on the plane as "S. Mann." Prophetic. "Strong Man."

It wasn't long before Tony admitted his identity and stated he had known Dr. Chesrow, his personal physician, for twenty years. He admitted that they were on their way to Las Vegas. It is interesting to note that Tony was carrying seven thousand dollars in his pocket, Giancana five thousand. Chesrow, to complete the picture, was carrying just two hundred and fifty dollars. The trio was ordered to get out of town.

Two years later, Tony made his move into Las Vegas in spite of attempts to thwart him. Tony Cornero, who owned and operated gambling boats in the Los Angeles area, whom Tony, Giancana and Dr. Chesrow were presumably in L.A. to visit before they were tossed out on their ear, had begun to build a hotel-casino in Las Vegas. It was to be called the Stardust. But before he could finish it, Cornero died. (Although it cannot be documented, I believe Tony Accardo was behind this deal from its inception.) When Cornero, Tony's front, died, Tony was in something of a pickle. However, Hump came up with the solution. He brought Jake "The Barber" Factor to Accardo's attention. Factor, the brother of Max Factor of cosmetics fame, had been associated with Hump on the q.t. since Factor had been kidnapped by Roger Tuohy, the leader of another Chicago gang in the early Thirties. Hump had been instrumental in Factor's release. (In fact, it wasn't long after Tuohy was released from the prison and killed that Hump was picked up for questioning.)

Tony installed Factor as the front for the Chicago Outfit in the Stardust and completed its construction. It would remain the flagship casino for Chicago until sold to the reputable Boyd family in the mid-Eighties. The Stardust catered to the "low rollers" who visit Vegas. It has been beautifully renovated now by the Boyds, with a big new building, but in 1955 when it was opened, it was also very nice. It sits across the Strip between the Riviera and the Desert Inn on the north and the Flamingo on the south.

Tony had a gold mine in the Stardust. In 1955 there were few hotel-casinos on the Strip, and the Stardust was unique. While the Desert Inn and the Riviera catered to high rollers, big spenders doing their business at high-minimum-bet tables, the Stardust catered to the blue-collar player. And when sports betting began to be a big thing, the Stardust had one of the best locations for betting on everything from the major sporting events, such as football, buckets, baseball and boxing, to tennis and golf, even car racing. And, of course, with the advent of the satellite dish later, all these events, plus horse racing from the big tracks around the country, could be viewed by the players as they took place. Anything to grind the bettor down, albeit with some enjoyment.

Three years after the mob built the Stardust, they leased it out to the United Hotel Corporation. That was Moe Dalitz's outfit, which also operated the Desert Inn and the Riviera. Now Dalitz would partner not only with New York, but with Chicago. "The Godfather of Las Vegas" was some kind of guy!

In 1949 the Teamsters Union had begun its Central States Pension Fund. That had meant little to Tony at the time. But when he found that he could use funding for the operation of the Stardust, he got a bright idea. Why not milk the Teamsters from their pension fund? At just about that time, the Outfit had forged a very nice relationship with just the guy who could do it for them. His name was James Riddle Hoffa. Some time before, a labor hack in Chicago with close ties to the mob had brought Jimmy Hoffa to the attention of Hump, who had been Nitti's guy in the labor racketeering field. He had spearheaded the mob's influence over some of the biggest unions, like the Teamsters, the Laborers, the Laundry Workers, the Movie Picture Operators, the Hotel and Restaurant Workers and, to some extent, the International Brotherhood of Electrical Workers. When the labor hack, Paul "Red" Dorfman, recommended Hoffa to Hump, the Chicago mob began working toward his advancement in the Teamsters, right up to its presidency. In return for this assistance, Hoffa had shown his gratitude by giving Red Dorfman's son, Allen, the spot in the Pension Fund where he was instrumental in deciding who should benefit by obtaining huge loans. Allen Dorfman decided that the Stardust was a nice investment for the fund. So Accardo, who had helped put Hoffa in place, who, in turn, had put Allen Dorfman in place, now had a nice payback, one that would be far from the last loan the mob's various properties would get from the Teamster pension fund.

In early 1961, the underpinnings Tony had initiated would bear fruit when Moe Dalitz would come into Chicago to meet with Sam Giancana, Murray Humphreys and Gus Alex, then upperechelon leaders of the Chicago Outfit, in order to put a deal in place where, through fronts, the Chicago and New York mobs would exchange "points," hidden interest, in the Desert Inn, the Riviera and the Stardust. (I recall well listening to Hump discuss the details of this deal on "Little Al," our bug at the mob headquarters. He stated then that the deal, which culminated in January of 1961, had been initiated by "Joe," referring to Joe Batters.)

Tony Accardo had gotten the Chicago mob off to a great start in Las Vegas. It would turn out to be only the beginning. But his recognition of what might be—and his implementation of that vision—once again swelled the coffers of the Chicago Outfit treasury as a result. It would also make possible the continuation of that progress; the mob could go on to even bigger and bigger rewards in the future. Las Vegas became very possibly the largest producer of income for the mob in years to come, and it was Tony Accardo who recognized that and got the Outfit into Vegas almost from its beginning.

24 A Big Decision

Under Joe Batters the Chicago Outfit had truly climbed to heights it had never reached before. He had consolidated every aspect of the operation. At this point the Chicago family of La Cosa Nostra was at its pinnacle. The Chicago Police Department had caused it some trouble when it had put its Scotland Yard operation into effect. Its duties did not require arrests or investigation for prosecution but, instead, its function was to be informed of the inner workings of the mob for intelligence purposes. It was staffed with some of the best and most honest policemen in the history of Chicago. Unfortunately, just about the time it began to perform at its best, two or three years after its creation, it was disbanded on orders of Mayor Richard J. Daley. There was now no law enforcement unit watching the mob exclusively. Harry Ainslinger, the director of the Treasury Department's Bureau of Narcotics, the forerunner of the DEA, was often quoted as saying he believed there was a Mafia, but his jurisdiction precluded any investigation outside narcotics trafficking. The Chicago mob wasn't involved in narcotics. As far as Tony Accardo was concerned, Ainslinger could trumpet all he wanted about the existence of the Mafia. It didn't impact on Tony or his crew. Sometimes there was a sheriff's deputy who got a little too big for his pants and raided a mob gambling joint, but that did not occur often and, in any case, only affected one spot. When it did happen, Tony saw that the culprit deputy was transferred to a traffic detail. Acting Captain William Drury had caused a problem, had even picked up Tony himself for questioning about the brutal killing of Estelle Carey in 1943. But that was handled, too, when Drury was murdered. The Illinois Bureau of Investigation tracked mob activities, but it was not created until Richard B. Ogilvie became governor in the late Sixties. (I was offered the directorship of the IBI by Governor Ogilvie, but declined.) Not even the world's greatest investigative body, the FBI, would have an investigative interest in the Chicago mob or any other organized crime group, at this time.

In 1957 the tightly disciplined, monolithic, strictly structured, highly prosperous Chicago family of La Cosa Nostra was flying high. There were no problems, none even on the horizon which could be discerned.

Tony Accardo had become a little bored. The great Joe Batters had accomplished just about everything a mob boss could accomplish. He had become the very best ever, at any time in any place. When he was not bored, it was because some mundane problem had come up, the likes of which he had handled a million times. The truth was, he had had enough. Enough power, enough money and enough headaches. By this time he and Clarice and the kids were spending some time at a winter residence at 9199 Collins Avenue in Surfside, Florida, enjoying the time and the lifestyle away from the dreaded Chicago winters. Life there was good.

Joe figured it was as good a time as any to retire. He was just about fifty years old. There had been some stress involved, as there is in the life of any mobster, although J.B. had handled it as well as any ever had. But why continue on? He had done it all. Besides, Clarice wanted him to get out while he was in such good shape physically, mentally, emotionally, financially. And what Clarice wanted, she usually got. She was a very determined lady, and Tony loved her deeply. Tony Accardo was a bad man, involved in the worst kind of crime—a murderer. But he had good qualities, which most of his pals did not. This may well have been the reason he had skyrocketed to the top. And it was what ultimately led him to his decision to step aside.

Joe Batters listened to Clarice and then took his own counsel. She was right. He had come this far, gotten everything a guy in his tradition had ever achieved. Why keep going? What was in it? More money? How could he ever spend what he had stashed away now? More glory? What glory? He had kept his light under a bushel; it was only due to the accumulation of his years that the press had gotten a handle on him. Witness the Kefauver Committee when they reported that the Accardo-*Fischetti* syndicate was one of the two most important in the country. Fischetti? Joe didn't even understand which of the brothers Fischetti they might have meant. Charley and Rocco weren't all that much, compared to him at least, and Joe Fischetti was little more than a pimp for guys like Frank Sinatra.

And the time might come when the law would catch up with

him. Why jeopardize all he had now? Why take a chance that he might have to spend a night in jail—or thousands of nights in jail? Look at his good pal, Paul Ricca. The Waiter had gotten out of prison, thanks in no small measure to Tony Accardo, in just three years. Soon, however, he would be going back again. About the only people bothering mobsters—and this had been true since 1930—was that IRS, but they were damned effective.

So it was that Tony once again made a decision. A big one, and just in time.

BOOK THREE

THE CHAIRMAN

25 Tony Steps Aside

After he had given it some thought, Tony Accardo decided that he *had* had enough. Enough of the daily grind, at least. It was early 1957.

First he sat down with Paul Ricca, his longtime associate. Paul would have been the Chicago boss had he not had the misfortune at the time the job became available—when Frank Nitti had gone out to the railroad tracks and shot himself in the head—to be sentenced to three years in prison. Paul was of the absolute opinion that the Chicago mob could not do without Tony.

"You can't just pack up and leave and expect to get away that easy," Ricca told Tony. "You remember the old saying, 'You can only leave feet first.' "

Ricca smiled when he said that. Tony knew he didn't expect that anybody would do away with him physically if he decided to get out. But he got the message from his trusted friend. He knew that he could not just say goodbye and walk away.

They talked it over and came up with a plan. Tony would become the *consiglieri*, the counsel to whoever it was who would succeed him as boss. The boss would handle the day-to-day machinations of the Outfit and generally act as general manager or operating director. All the little, mundane problems of organization would be his. He would be expected to be on the job almost daily and in direct contact with the capos at least, and sometimes even with the soldiers.

At the same time Tony could get away, more or less, to enjoy himself more. Tony had enjoyed deep-sea fishing in Bimini for years. This would give him a chance to get there more often and to travel to other places he had come to enjoy.

At the same time, however, when pressed by Paul Ricca, Tony agreed to be available, either in person or, minimally, by messenger, to counsel on any matter of more than routine importance. He would not be allowed to walk off into the sunset with all of his capability and experience. Or, perhaps most importantly, his contacts.

The Outfit had recently lost one of its best, experienced men just the year before and didn't want to lose another. Jake "Greasy Thumb" Guzik, the wily corruptor who had been a key figure in the mob even under Capone, had passed on. He was at his favorite hangout, St. Hubert's Olde English Grill on Federal Street, just south of Jackson in the Loop, when he collapsed with a fatal heart attack. Not wanting the body to be found in a mob hangout, Murray Humphreys, who had been with him, had his men carry Guzik's body to his home in the South Shore neighborhood of Chicago's south side, where the amazed widow was instructed to advise police he had died there. Guzik had for years been one of what the mob calls the "connection guys." It was Guzik's job to lead a group of Chicago mobsters whose prime function was to corrupt, to influence public officials such as cops, judges, politicians, labor leaders and anybody else who might be in a position to lend favorable treatment to the Outfit. The loss of Guzik would have been serious, except that there was one other guy who was available to fill his shoes. Murray Humphreys. Hump, the Camel. Code-named "Curly" in the Outfit, a play on the curly hair he had in youth. The Outfit was very fortunate indeed to have someone just as capable, just as experienced and with as many contacts in the outside world as Guzik did, many of whom were the same contacts as Guzik's.

Realizing this, Ricca did not want to create a vacuum that could not be filled if Tony was allowed to walk away and be unavailable to the people he had led for so long—through tough times into the bright world they were enjoying in 1957. And Tony realized the wisdom of Ricca's thinking. He probably had not really expected that he would be allowed to walk away. And when he thought about it, Tony knew he didn't really want to. The solution proposed by Ricca sat well with him. What he was tired of was the daily grind, the everyday problems and the dealing with a lot of guys he really didn't care for. By 1957 Joe Batters had come a long way. His close circle of friends did not include just mob guys. A lot of his friends were legitimate people, businessmen like Jeffrey Stern, a Cadillac dealer; John Marino, a Pontiac dealer; Sal Marino, who owned the reputable Farmers Market on Elston in Chicago; Isadore Goldberg, another car dealer; Tony and Ben Fillichio, the owners of the flourishing liquor stores, Austin Liquors; Ray Basara, owner of Mohawk Construction Co.; and Tony

Marino, who owned Uptown Auto Supply, and whose wife Bettie Jo was one of Clarice's best friends. Tony wanted to spend more time with these people and other legit people, and less of his time with mobsters. Let's face it, even Joe Batters liked to get a breath of fresh air once in a while. And there wasn't a whole lot of fresh air inside the mob. There were those, like Paul, Hump and Jackie Cerone, who were good to be with under any circumstances. And Tony had become close to another younger guy, Gussie Alex, whose company he enjoyed. Jackie and Gussie were eight and ten years younger than Tony, but they were sharp younger guys, maybe as sharp as J.B. He was also very friendly with Sam Battaglia, and seemed to enjoy the company of another guy, one Joey Aiuppa, although Aiuppa never seemed to be in his class as a person. For some reason Joe Batters allowed Aiuppa, called "O'Brien" after the name he had used in his youth as a boxer, to hang around. One other mob guy was also close to Accardo: Dominic "Butch" Blasi. Butch was more than just the appointment secretary and driver-bodyguard of Joe, as Joe had been for Capone. He was a true friend in whom Joe confided. Butch knew most of J.B.'s secrets and Joe was comfortable with that. Ralph Pierce was another guy Joe could tolerate, Pierce being the boss of the south side. But when you mention those guys in the Outfit, that was about it. The rest were thugs, common. A little bit of their company went a long way. It would be good to divorce himself from daily contact with them. Sam DeStefano, for instance, who had pushed himself in with Accardo a great deal. In fact, he had maneuvered his way into Tony's elite poker group through his friendship with Paul Ricca. It would be good to get away from this thug, and from guys like Philly Alderisio and Chuckie Nicoletti, the mob killers. It was necessary to keep them on an even keel by stroking them, but now he would no longer be the guy who had to do that. He could keep away from such guys as that, and there were some three hundred "made" guys of that stripe in the Outfit. Joe understood that when he started with Capone and advanced under Nitti, he himself probably was considered just a thug. But as his life and experience matured, he came to believe he was somewhat of a large cut above those kinds of guys. Nobody ever considered that the huge bulk of the membership of the Outfit were nice guys. They aren't. Joe Batters knew that better than most. A large percentage of the public go to movies like *The Godfather*, *Good Fellas* and *Casino* and come away fascinated by the mob characters portrayed by Brando, De Niro, Pesci and the like. How different those mob characters are in real life. Who would want to live with them? Not even Tony Accardo.

So the decision he had been pondering for some months had now been finalized. He would step *aside*, not *down*. Let somebody fresh handle the day-to-day, mundane, routine problems. Instead, he would be the *consiglieri*. In most families of La Cosa Nostra, the *consiglieri* is a wise, older guy who has done most of what his family does. He is available to advise. In Joe's case, it would be to advise *and consent*. He had the final word, the veto power—much more, actually, than his title would indicate. The chairman of the board would hold sway over the president of the company. Nothing important was to be conducted without his sanction. The chairman emeritus.

That part of his move was complete. Now the other part: whom to appoint as his successor. Jackie Cerone came immediately to mind, but Jack was just a little too young yet, not yet forty. He was the most intelligent, but as the leader of the Elmwood Park Street Crew, he had not yet gained the experience of the overall mob. Sam Battaglia? Joe liked "Teets" and he was older, but again, not quite ready. Alderisio? No, not the killer. Aiuppa? Maybe someday. Hump and Alex? Not Italian. That ruled them out.

That left one guy. One guy who had come to Accardo's attention when he led the Outfit into a new area of income. He had handled it almost perfectly. He had the experience and, in Tony's mind, the capability to be the new boss. And always the strong hand of Accardo would be there to advise and guide him. When he talked to Paul and to Hump about his thoughts about his successor, he found that, although they had some reservations, they were unable to recommend anybody else. They would go along. So Tony had his man. Not that he was perfect, but he was considered the best available at that time. He was tapped.

26 The New Boss

He was not going to be my favorite guy. Not at all! But looking back, I guess he was the right guy, or at least the best guy, that Tony could find to step into his shoes. After all, this guy didn't have to be Einstein or George Foreman with Tony available to backstop him.

Born in 1908, at forty-nine Sam Giancana was just two years younger than Accardo. In the last couple years, since his success with the black belts of Chicago, he had become the underboss, the *sotto capo*, under Accardo. As such, Tony had assigned certain tasks to him and Sam had performed well. He wasn't as intelligent as Accardo, not many were other than Hump and Guzik, maybe the developing Cerone and perhaps Gus Alex, but he was just as tough. He had not acquired the polish of Accardo, and I'm sure that most Outfit guys recognized that he was a step down, at *least* one step down, from Joe Batters. But with J.B. available, even if from a distance, to advise and counsel, they undoubtedly felt that they would be well cared for.

In actuality, Giancana was the iron fist in a leather glove, whereas Accardo was the iron fist in a velvet glove. I would also get to know him well, and would never equate Giancana's capability with that of J.B.

With this arrangement, the Outfit was in good hands. Things were not going to change drastically under the new president. Giancana, who had a temper and a rough way, would not be as easy to deal with, and there were matters outside his experience that were old hat to Batters. But isn't this pretty much the case in most takeovers—in U.S. presidential elections, for example? It was not much different in this sense when Bill Clinton took over from George Bush. Here is a brash new guy taking over from the more refined older man. The only difference, perhaps, is that the

voters, the "made" guys, would never have cast their ballots for
Giancana had Accardo wanted to stay on.

When Sam took over, he established his headquarters in the Armory Lounge on Roosevelt Road, just west of Harlem Avenue in
the western suburb of Forest Park. The mob retained their general
headquarters at 620 North Michigan on the Magnificent Mile,
Chicago's answer to Fifth Avenue and Rodeo Drive. Just as Accardo had established his special meeting place with his capos in
an alcove at Meo's Norwood House Restaurant in Norridge, another northwestern suburb of Chicago, where it was difficult to
observe him, Giancana now made his headquarters in a private
room in the rear of the Armory Lounge.

The Armory Lounge (now Andrea's) had been a speakeasy.
The room in the back had a peephole and was guarded, whenever
Giancana was on his throne, by Butch Blasi. Blasi had held the
same position with Accardo; now that Tony had no use for him,
at least not on a full-time basis, Butch spent his time almost
continuously with Giancana, his new boss. Whenever anybody
wanted a "sit-down" with Giancana, he contacted Butch at the Armory. Butch then arranged the meeting in the back room—unless
the meeting was with one of the public officials Giancana wanted
to get to know. Then the sit-down would be at a remote area,
sometimes at Waldheim Jewish Cemetery, on Des Plaines Avenue in North Riverside, just two or three miles away, or in Columbus Park, across from Loretto Hospital at Eisenhower and Central
Avenue on the west side of Chicago. Butch would drive Giancana
to the spot where Giancana, depending mostly on the weather,
would either talk in the car or while walking in the area.

In the meantime, Joe continued to meet with Giancana at
Meo's. Giancana came to him most of the time. As the years went
by, this changed somewhat.

It soon became Joe's practice to be picked up by Jackie Cerone,
who was now spending more time as the go-between between
Giancana and Joe. Usually they stopped by Paul Ricca's house,
where they would pick up Paul and head to the alcove at Meo's for
the Italian lunch they all enjoyed. Most of the time it was like a social visit, but occasionally Jackie himself brought word to Joe as
to what was going on inside the Outfit and what Giancana was up
to. J.B. began to spend most of his daytime hours with Ricca and
Cerone, the wise old man and the sharp younger man. The combination of the two was just what Accardo was interested in. Paul
and he shared memories of their days with Capone and Nitti and
Campagna and D'Andrea. Cerone, on the other hand, was in tune

with the modern world, not only inside the mob, but outside of it. Paul didn't speak good English, but a blend of English and Sicilian, very broken, but Cerone read bestsellers and the daily newspapers. He was a scratch golfer, won some tournaments at Riverwoods, the country club he joined after Tam O'Shanter, his longtime favorite, went down.

Following a long, leisurely lunch, Accardo usually drove home with Cerone after dropping off Ricca at his place, then took a leisurely nap. That evening he would either stay home to eat a nice dinner his houseman, Mike Volpe, had prepared, with Clarice and maybe one of his four children, now mostly grown. Sometimes he went out for dinner with Clarice and one or two of the couples with whom they were friendly. Almost never did he go out in the evening on business, nor did he go out socially without Clarice. They remained a very loving couple. Clarice was nobody's patsy. She took care of her man. Nobody ever had a more loving, dutiful wife than Tony Accardo did. He knew it and made sure he did nothing to impact on his marriage. About the only time he and Clarice did not spend their evenings together was when Tony took off with some of his pals, including Jackie Cerone and Joey Aiuppa, also Ray Basara and others of his circle, to Bimini or to Florida for the deep-sea fishing. This is how Accardo got his media nickname. On one occasion, while in the West Indies on a fishing trip, he caught a mammoth tuna. He was photographed with it, proudly displaying his trophy. The picture got publicized. Soon the press was calling Tony "The Big Tuna." It was a name which, along with Joe Batters, would stick with him forever. It somehow fit.

Giancana, in the meantime, loved his new spot. He had been accustomed to some bowing and scraping from his underlings when he was Accardo's underboss, his chief aide. But now, by God, he was *the* boss. Not only did his subordinates pay him homage, but the general public as well. As the papers and the TV publicized his new position as the successor to Capone, Nitti and Accardo, three of the most infamous names in gangland history, the fascination the public has with such people attached to him, and Giancana ate it up. Giancana was a forerunner to John Gotti, the Dapper Don, the New York boss who would be in New York what Giancana had been in Chicago, a man who loved the limelight. The brighter and more public the spotlight, the more he loved it. This was in stark contrast to Accardo, who had played down his role. And it would cost Giancana dearly.

Tony Accardo could see it coming, though it took some time to hit. He warned Giancana from the beginning, both directly and through Jackie Cerone, that he should tone it down, keep a low profile, "keep your head down," as he put it.

Giancana, for his part, was over whatever grief he had suffered after his wife Angeline died three years before, and he was out on the town. (Angeline died in 1954. She and Sam had raised three daughters, Antoinette, Bonnie and Francine, in that order. Antoinette, "Toni," would take after her father, whereas the two younger daughters would take after Angeline. Toni aspired to acting and would even, in later years, show her good figure in all its natural beauty in *Playboy* magazine. A real chip off the old block!) His girlfriends were legend, at least in their number. Two even had the same last name, Clark, although they were not related, but that is how many he squired. (I recall scaring Bridget Clark one evening in her home after she had taken a diamond ring to Peacock's for repair because a baguette had fallen out. The sharp people at Peacock's, the jewelry store located in the Palmer House Hotel in the Loop, recognized the ring as having been part of a score during a burglary in Beverly Hills. They notified the FBI, and I went out and told Bridget that unless she advised where she had gotten the ring, we would take her before the grand jury to testify under oath, and might even charge her with possession of stolen property. Even though she whispered, "You must know who I got it from," she stood fast. She would never tell me that it was Giancana who had given her the most expensive present. She was "stand up," as they say. I respected her for that, and we never charged her or brought her before the grand jury. Obviously, the ring was part of the "street tax" the Outfit had put on burglars from Chicago, even when they operated elsewhere. Sam was foolish to give it to a girlfriend, but that was him all over.) The other Clark, Patty, conned Giancana into believing she was pregnant. He bought a home for her in Florida. Vintage Giancana.

Of course there would be two other girlfriends of greater magnitude—in some ways at least. One, Judy Campbell, went to bed with Giancana, the leader of the underworld, on one day and with John Kennedy, the leader of the free world, the next. We followed her when she did. The other girl was one of the most famous and talented singers of our time, Phyllis McGuire, of the great McGuire Sisters. They had many number-one song hits like "Sugartime," "Sincerely," and "Picnic" in the Sixties, appearing regularly on the *Ed Sullivan Show* and the Arthur Godfrey program, the two top entertainment television shows of those days. Phyl was the middle sister, the one with all the talent. She was admittedly Giancana's girl for years. Beautiful and talented as she was, it was hard to believe, especially since Giancana was not handsome, refined or particularly smart. But power is, some say, an aphrodisiac. People who have the ability—the character defect, rather—to shoot people in the back seem to fascinate. This is the only reasonable explanation for Phyl's attraction to this man. Whereas his other girls may have been attracted because of his wealth and his willingness to spend it on them, Phyl did not have that excuse. She had plenty of her own. And being seen on Giancana's arm gave her no cachet, at least as far as we could see. *She* was the celebrity, not he. Or at least one would think so. Apparently she didn't.

Sam Giancana, in spite of all his flash, never really filled Accardo's shoes. But in all fairness, there was not a man in Chicago who could.

27 Apalachin and the Top Hoodlum Program

1957 would be some year! The watershed year in the affairs of the Chicago family of La Cosa Nostra. Early in the year Sam Giancana had stepped in for Tony Accardo. A major event. There was more to come.

It was all the fault of the New York mobs, the five families of La Cosa Nostra in the Big Apple who were later designated the Gambino family, the Colombo family, the Genovese family, the Bonanno family and the Luchese family, after the names of the bosses who headed them in 1963. Between them, they divided the five boroughs of New York City, though not equally, into spheres of organized crime.

Because there were five such families, populated by greedy and sinister people, they were constantly at war with each other. Each of them was represented by their boss on the Commission, the ruling body of La Cosa Nostra, but each had his own agenda and was much more interested in his own well-being rather than that of La Cosa Nostra in its entirety. It was as if the quarterback of the Notre Dame football team was more interested in his personal glory and what it could do for *him* than in the success of his team. A great temptation, of course, and one that mob leaders often succumbed to. For instance, we suspected that Joe Bonanno, whom I would get to know personally, would conspire against two of his fellow Commissioners—to murder them.

This was as true in 1957 as at any other time. First, Frank Costello, "The Prime Minister of Organized Crime," who, like Bonanno, had been a boss since La Cosa Nostra was formed in 1931, was shot in the head as he entered his apartment house at 115 Central Park West. Although he survived, it was the start. Then two brothers, both top people in another family, were shot and killed. In the fall of that year, "Double A," as he was called, Albert Anastasia, took a stroll to his barbershop for his daily shave in the Park Central Hotel on Seventh Avenue, not far from Carnegie Hall. When his favorite barber covered his face with a hot towel, two gunmen burst in. They filled the fat body of AA with lead.

The Commission decided something had to be done about this internecine war. The Commission called the most extraordinary meeting of all time in the affairs of the LCN. All twelve members of the Commission attended, with many of their top aides. Chicago was represented not only by Giancana, but by the guy he had just succeeded, Tony Accardo. Representatives from Los Angeles, Denver, Kansas City, Milwaukee, San Jose, San Francisco, San Diego, all of the subsidiary cities controlled under the Chicago Outfit umbrella, were represented at this meeting.

Some eighty invitees to this sit-down came from all over the country. From New Orleans, Tampa, Boston, New York, Buffalo, Detroit, Cleveland, Philadelphia and New Jersey, in addition to those cities west of Chicago.

The meeting took place on November 14, 1957, at an unlikely spot. Unlikely, because that seemed to be the safest spot for this meeting of the top people in every La Cosa Nostra family in the country: Apalachin. Where? Apalachin is a small village located in the western part of New York state. At the time, Joe Barbara, a businessman in nearby Buffalo, had a large estate in Apalachin. Joe, although he had been voted Man of the Year in Buffalo, had some unlikely friends who recommended his estate, when they found he was willing, to the powers that be in the Commission.

Who in that village would ever recognize the top mobsters from all over the country, any of them? It was the perfect place.

No one did recognize them, although one guy was suspicious. He wondered about just why so many visitors were converging on this small village at one time. After all, Apalachin, New York, is not Niagara Falls.

This guy made it his business to find out, and he did. He was Sgt. Edgar Croswell, with the New York State Police. He gathered together a few of his troopers and alerted the Alcohol and Tobacco Tax and Firearms Bureau of the Treasury Department. (We know why he didn't alert the FBI. What would they care on November 14, 1957?) Sgt. Croswell and his troopers and the ATF agents rousted the people at Joe Barbara's estate, stopping some in their cars as they arrived and hustling others who had already arrived. They identified some of them. Sam Giancana and Tony Accardo, they didn't; when the ruckus started, they escaped through the woods out the back door. But Sgt. Croswell had nonetheless become the number one Edgar in law enforcement in the country. He had had personal contact with real live mobsters, as the other Edgar never had. He had taken it upon himself to grab these guys and find out who they were, even if he had no evidence that they had broken any laws. Interstate character was not a concern to him. When Sgt. Croswell and his crew were finished, they had determined who many of the conferees at Apalachin really were—the top gangsters in the country! A press release was issued to this effect.

The media went into a frenzy. So many of the leaders of all mobs across the country had gathered in this remote area to hold a gang conclave? Wow! The public then became aroused. This was major news in 1957—as it would be at any other time. When the public becomes aroused, of course, so do their representatives. Congress called for hearings, as did New York state. They would have them, but before they could, somebody else was aroused.

By 1957, J. Edgar's enthusiasm for his top investigative priority, the investigation of Communism, had waned. For two decades he had pursued the real, live, actual menace presented to the national security of this country by the Communist Party, USA, people like Alger Hiss and the Rosenbergs, people who betrayed their country by disclosing our secrets to our archenemy at the time, the Soviet Union. There can be little doubt that Mr. Hoover had his priorities straight when he threw the resources of the FBI into this fight, but by this time, two things had transpired. First, the FBI had effectively exposed and prosecuted the threat. Joe McCarthy had come on the scene. The country went through the McCarthy era, when the menace had become greatly exaggerated, played up by Senator McCarthy for much more than it was. The country had sickened of the situation, realizing that McCarthy was using his Senate committee for his personal aggrandizement. As a result, the communist threat to national security was now perceived to be overblown. Mr. Hoover began to recognize this perception.

Apalachin couldn't have come at a better time for Mr. Hoover. Here he had all these FBI agents working on the CP-USA, and now it seemed they weren't needed. With the exposure of this new menace, he could choose to take the agents and throw them into a fight against organized crime. It was certainly, he recognized, a worthy cause. Not only was this dangerous group undefeated, no law enforcement agency had yet come to grips with them and taken them on. If Apalachin was what it looked like, it was now the time to shift priorities from Communism to organized crime, not with any political purpose, but for a more legitimate reason. If these people were so strong that eighty of them from all over the country could brazenly meet with each other, the scope of their operations, which were certainly illegal, must be very great indeed. And here was proof at last that there was an interstate character to the organization. Federal laws were being broken.

Mr. Hoover called his top legal people into a conference. "How can we proceed? We want to get the Bureau involved in investigation of organized crime now, but what hook do we have? What statute can we use to peg our jurisdiction?" The FBI legal team gave it some thought. They came up with the Hobbs Act. This act, sometimes called the Racketeering Act, had been passed almost twenty years before. It was little used, almost always in labor racketeering cases, never in a broad spectrum and never as an umbrella to justify what Mr. Hoover had in mind. But it was the best the FBI legal eagles could come up with. Mr. Hoover agreed that it would have to do.

On November 27, 1957, Mr. Hoover sent a directive to all field offices of the FBI. It was captioned "The Top Hoodlum Program: Anti-Racketeering," and directed all field offices of the Bureau to institute such a program, to assign agents to investigate organized crime in their field divisions. New York was instructed to assign twenty-five agents to the Top Hoodlum Program, to be known internally as the THP. Chicago was directed to assign ten. Each office was to make this its number one priority; therefore, top agents were to be assigned, experienced agents with a solid record. New York was notified to designate twenty-five "targets," twenty-five of the top hoodlums. Chicago, ten. Other cities: Philadelphia, eight; Detroit, six; Kansas City, four; Denver, two; Buffalo, one.

Mr. Hoover, via the grapevine from his supervisors in Washington at what was then called S.O.G., Seat of Government, and what is now called FBIHQ, put the word out. "This will be our top priority." The supervisors knew what that meant—get the job done, perform well, or suffer the consequences. Mr. Hoover would now be on the backs of his people at S.O.G., and they, in turn, would be on the backs of the supervisor of each Top Hood Squad in the field. And those supervisors in the field would be on the backs of the agents assigned to this new program. It would become the best way for an agent to break his pick. Be assigned to the THP and fail to perform, fail to make sense of it, fail to come up with the intelligence to determine who, what, why, where and when the Top Hoods are, then put them away, and you were off the team. Agents had to neutralize them. Prosecute them. And anybody Mr. Hoover perceived to be falling down on the job, his number one priority, was out, and that went for everybody— supervisors at S.O.G., supervisors in the field and the agents assigned to the program. Sparks were flying.

Soon after the directive arrived in the field, and even before when the grapevine had buzzed with the scuttlebutt, the "field" became aroused. Who would be assigned to this program? Who wanted to be? Many agents did not. They knew heads would roll when Mr. Hoover became impatient with results. Most agents were comfortable with their current assignments. Why get involved in the THP? That's a good way to fail to impress Mr. Hoover and, at the least, get transferred to his favorite disciplinary office, Butte, Montana. That was why some of the best agents in the Bureau were in Butte. Most of the older agents, now comfortable in their "O.P.," their office of preference, had no desire to go to Butte. They had no desire to accept assignment, if they could help it, to the THP under these conditions.

There were some eager ones, however. Some naive, younger agents who thought the THP would be a good challenge. These, you will now meet.

28 Coming to Grips With the Mob

In 1957, I had been in the FBI for seven years. I had been assigned to field offices in Baltimore, New Haven, New York City and now Chicago, where I was assigned to Security Squad Number One, the "underground squad." We were assigned to the investigation of those hard-core communists who had gone underground, had transferred from the areas where they had been active and were now undercover, working under assumed identities, mostly in strategic industries which, upon the outbreak of an emergency, such as war with the Soviet Union, we believed they would sabotage. There were a score or so of them who had gone under in the Chicago area. It was the job of the S-1 Squad to locate them and keep tabs on them so they could be rounded up in an emergency. We were penetrating the homes and offices of these people, and the members of the CP-USA who were out in the open, by placing hidden mikes in their headquarters and by "black bagging" their communications and documents, photocopying them with a Minox camera. We had some good, sharp agents on S-1 and by late 1957 we felt we had our subjects under control. As to the rest of the CP-USA in Chicago and the rest of the country, I, at least, was not all that enthusiastic about deeming their menace something that was now a matter of great concern. I felt that we had beaten the Communist Party. I did not deem my work now to be of great import. It had been, I thought, but now I, too, perceived the threat to be greatly exaggerated. As a result, I had lost some of my zest for my job.

When they realized my apathy, two of my brothers suggested that I should join them in their law practice in South Bend, Indiana, our home town. I was very interested. However, I had never taken the Indiana bar exam, making me ineligible to practice law. I began to study, trying to recapture my knowledge of contracts and torts and the other subjects which would be examined on the bar exam, four hours every night and sixteen hours on weekends. I fully intended to leave the FBI in the fall of 1958 and join my brothers in their law firm.

Something happened on the way, however. Earl Stark was my supervisor. He was not my biggest fan. He caught on that I was not enthusiastic about my duties on S-1. He could see I was not his hardest worker. To be quite honest and candid, I was extending my lunch hour, studying my law books at the Chicago Library, then at Michigan and Randolph, right at the corner where Jake Lingle had been clipped. One day Stark called me into his office. It was around Thanksgiving, 1957.

"Bill," he said to me, "I don't know if you've heard about this new Top Hoodlum Program Mr. Hoover has commenced."

"Yes, I have," I replied.

"Well, Mr. Hoover has instructed that ten agents in this office be assigned to that program."

Now I caught on.

Stark continued. "It has been decided that only those agents who want this work will be assigned to it. In other words, only volunteers will be considered."

"Yes?"

"I suggest you volunteer." Stark gave me a half-smile.

I got the idea, of course. He was designating me as the agent the front office had decided S-1 would give up. But I had to "volunteer." I had some mixed emotions. First of all, I was set in my decision to resign from the Bureau within the year. Secondly, my primary interest had become the law. Of course, I had heard the scuttlebutt in the office. This was going to be one tough job. The other side of the coin was that this was precisely the kind of work I had come into the Bureau to perform. I had grown up ninety miles from Chicago, in South Bend, listening to the radio and reading the newspapers about the Capone gang. I had heard of Tony Accardo and Greasy Thumb Guzik and Murray the Camel. I didn't know the monikers "Joe Batters" or "Hump" at that time, but I did have *some* sense of what the Capone gang was. The prospect of coming up against them excited me. It did get my heart pumping to think that I could be a part of this new Top Hoodlum Program and come to grips with the worst criminals in the world. Earl Stark might not have been such a bad guy after all.

I gave it some quick thought. "I volunteer," I grinned.

"OK, clean up your work here as soon as you can and go up and report to Ross Spencer on C-1."

I cleaned up quickly, then hurried upstairs to the floor in the FBI office where Criminal Squad Number One was located, then at 212 West Monroe, on the far west edge of the Loop.

Roswell Spencer was reputed to be the best supervisor in the FBI. I would grow to respect and admire him greatly and to enjoy his company. He was my kind of guy. He gave it to me bluntly.

"Look, kid, if you want to be here, fine. I remember you from the Greenap Special. You did a good job." (I had been "volunteered" by Stark for previous absence from his squad, mainly for the same reasons I was now being "volunteered." A young boy had been kidnapped in Missouri and the ransom money had shown up in Chicago. A "special" had been set up, meaning that agents from different squads were assigned on a temporary basis to investigate the kidnapping of this young boy. His name was Bobby Greenlease, hence the code name for the investigation, Greenap. I had worked the case for about six weeks, a year or so before my assignment to C-1. Since it had been supervised by Spencer, he remembered me. Vaguely, I guessed. I was not one of the key agents he had assigned the more important leads to.) Ross Spencer continued: "But this you've got to know. Mr. Hoover is going to put a lot of heat on this project. He'll be on my ass and I'll be on yours until we get it under control. And who knows when that will be. Maybe never. We just don't know enough about this program to know what it's going to take. But we do know one thing. If we don't do a job in Chicago, it's going to be bye-bye, baby. Mr. Hoover expects the New York office and us to carry the ball on this. This is where the heat will be. You must know what you're volunteering for. Be sure you want this, because if we don't get the job done, whatever that may entail, it's going to be my ass, and then I'll make sure it's your ass."

That was laying it on the line alright. But the more I listened to Spencer and observed him, the more I felt that I was finally going to get my teeth into what I had expected when I first joined the FBI. I made it clear that I wanted to be on C-1 to work on the THP. Very clear. Not only did I want Spencer to see that I had the zeal for the assignment, I now recognized within myself that I had it. I was, all of a sudden, enthused about my new job. "Count me in," I said.

At the time, C-1 was the "major case squad" of the Chicago office. All of the major criminal cases were handled in that squad by the most experienced agents in the Chicago division. We handled bank robberies, kidnappings, extortions and other important crimes under the jurisdiction of the FBI. No matter what we worked on, the THP or what have you, when a bank robbery went down, we all responded immediately, no matter where we were when the car radio squawked.

Ross Spencer assigned two "relief" supervisors, assistant supervisors, to handle the routine aspects of the THP, namely Ray Connelly and Harold Sell. Two top guys. They had gotten together before I hit the squad and assigned the agents to their subjects. Obviously, targeting the appropriate hoodlums was problematic. How did any FBI agent in 1957 know who the top ten leaders of the Chicago Outfit were? We didn't even know to call it the "Outfit," to say nothing about "La Cosa Nostra" or the "Commission." But Connelly and Sell had looked up the veteran officers of Scotland Yard, the ill-fated Chicago Police Department's intelligence unit. (Especially helpful at this time was Bill Duffy, the epitome of the incorruptible Chicago cop, who would become the CPD's most knowledgeable mob expert.) They gave the FBI the scant knowledge they had about who the ten major Outfit leaders were. They told us Tony Accardo was the boss. Close. They felt that Murray Humphreys had to be included. Ralph Pierce, the boss on the south side, also. Sam Giancana, Paul Ricca, Rocco Fischetti, Lenny Patrick, Eddy Vogel, and Jimmy Allegretti, the boss then of the near north side, who we believed to have the entire north side. One guy was left, as important as most of the rest, but a guy who kept his "head down," who was mysterious, who was so careful, his residence was not known.

I was the last new guy to report to C-1 and the THP. By the time I had cleaned up my work on S-1, even rushing as I did, all of the targets were selected by the agents who had beaten me to the punch. I would have liked to have been able to select Accardo. Or Giancana. Or Humphreys. They would have been my choice for November 1957. But I had no choice. The one guy who was left was the mystery guy, Gus Alex. As it turned out, Gussie was a lot more important than we realized and, unfortunately, since I never really impeded his progress, he became even more important as the years went by. Although we didn't know it in 1957, Gussie was not only the boss of the Loop, the most strategic area of Chicago, but he was a member of the "connection guys." We didn't even know what they were in 1957—or 1958, for that matter.

It wasn't long before I doubled up. Hump would also be assigned to me. He was another guy whose residence we would have trouble locating.

Fortunately, Tony Accardo and Sam Giancana were never far from my interest. Tony had been assigned to John Roberts, a sharp young guy about my age and experience in the Bureau. He and I played handball against each other three times a week and were close friends. I would work with him a great deal on Joe Batters, and he with me, on Gussie and Hump. Another guy I worked with a great deal was a guy who more or less became my partner in those early days, Ralph Hill. He was also one of the younger guys on the squad and we became good pals. He had Giancana as his target. Therefore, even though neither Joe Batters nor Giancana was my target at the time, I spent a good deal of time tracking them.

Soon, working with Roberts, who became the case agent, I would spend much of my time working on Tony Accardo.

29 Accardo's Qualities— of a Sort

One of the first things John Roberts found out as he commenced his investigations of Tony Accardo in December of 1957 was that when Frank Nitti passed the torch to Tony when he committed suicide in 1943, Tony had imposed a ban on the sale of narcotics by any "made" member of the mob. In fact, the prohibition extended to association with anybody who did deal narcotics.

John found that the reason for Tony's ban on narcotics was not altogether altruistic. On the advice of Hump and Guzik, Tony believed that many public officials, such as cops and judges, could be influenced to jump on the pad of the Outfit if they could be conditioned to believe that the mob "only killed their own," as the myth went. However, if they believed that the Outfit was involved in so-called heinous crimes like narcotics, they might be much more reluctant to accept the money or position or whatever leverage was put on them and close their eyes, in the cases of the cops, or acquit, in the cases of judges.

Whatever, those of us who were informed by John Roberts of Accardo's position gave Tony a grudging respect for it. From the outset of the THP, I shared the feeling with all my colleagues on the THP that Tony Accardo's character was a notch above that of most of his confederates. He was a bad guy, we had to start with that premise, since he could not be otherwise if he had murdered and sanctioned murders, as he had on many occasions. After all, he started with Machine Gun Jack McGurn. There have been some exceptions, "made guys" like Donald Angelini and Dominic Cortina, who might get there due to their expertise and not because of their animal qualities. But they are very, very few and far between. Very, very few. In speaking of Accardo, John Roberts later reported: "Another facet of the Accardo leadership was to low-key the image and involvement of the organized crime member. It was necessary to extort in order to gain an entry into a legitimate business and to maintain that extortion until control had been achieved, but it was Accardo's philosophy that it was not necessary to accomplish this with brutal, gaudy, dramatic manhandling. There were more subtle ways of achieving the same purpose and ways which were not as easy to uncover, thus adding a dimension which afforded difficulty in discovery and proof of a crime." In his report Roberts went on to discuss Accardo's "retirement." He reported: "Even though Accardo was in a state of retirement, he was in contact with Giancana on a regular basis. He was believed to be counseling Giancana regarding problems. It is believed, in this regard, that one of the things Accardo counseled Giancana on was 'hits' that occurred during Giancana's tenure . . . It is known that Accardo told Giancana that ten years in this job is like thirty years in any other job. He went on to counsel Giancana about the hazards, stress, diplomacy, demands and, sometimes, humiliations of the job (being the Outfit boss)."

Roberts reported that "Accardo always tries to maintain a low profile. He never loses his cool when confronted by police or other law enforcement agents, like some others, such as Giancana. He merely says nothing or responds in the briefest manner if forced to talk. He had always been considered to be fair, a person who will listen to both sides before making a decision, and will then make a just and impartial finding. He is firm, not vacillating, and once a decision is made, it is final. He is respected and loyally followed by his underlings for many years, and in times of trouble he is looked to for leadership and help."

Agent John Roberts had the best handle on Accardo during the early years when Tony became the chairman of the board of the Chicago Outfit. Later, when John left C-1, as he was promoted to be the supervisor of another squad, I would get to know Joe as

well as John did. In those early days, John Roberts obviously had
gotten inside Joe's head and under his skin and had learned his
personality, and I went to school on what John Roberts told me. I
never found him to be mistaken about anything he felt strongly
about. Obviously, he had a respect for Tony. I suppose it is, therefore, not surprising that I would come to feel the same regard, but
I always started with the knowledge that Joe Batters had gained
his moniker from Al Capone legitimately. He was a killer. Capone
hadn't fastened it on him because he was "Saint Accardo." He
gained it because he was one of the baddest of the baddest. And
J.B. carried his brutality into his later years; he didn't reform all of
a sudden. Yet when you're dealing with the worst kind of people,
some stand out above others. Some have good qualities to go with
their bad qualities. Most of the mobsters I know, almost all, are
awful creatures. In that company, Joe Batters stood a little taller
than most of his pals. That's the best that can be said about him.

30 The Accardo Trial Begins

Agent John Roberts didn't spend his time looking
for Tony Accardo's good qualities, as hard as they were to discern.
Soon after the Top Hoodlum Program was commenced by Mr.
Hoover, John started an investigation which would lead to extreme difficulty for his target, Accardo. I was assigned as the "alternate" agent, the number two man on the case.

We began in March of 1958, shortly after John had put together
a preliminary report of all the information he had uncovered in the
files of the FBI (almost all from the CAPGA investigation); from
the files of the Chicago Crime Commission that Virgil Peterson
had accumulated; and from the files of the Scotland Yard Unit.
John had gone over to the IRS to take a peek at Tony's recent income tax returns, as shown on pages 133–34.

John's pulse quickened when he spied one particular item on

the return of Accardo for 1957. He noted that Tony claimed a legitimate employment. The great Joe Batters claimed that he was a beer salesman for Premium Beer Sales, Inc., the Chicago distributor of Foxhead 400 Beer, brewed in Waukesha, Wisconsin.

On several occasions John and I went out and interviewed the owner and president of Premium Beer Sales, Inc., located at 2626 West Armitage, on the west side of Chicago. The president was named Dominic Volpe. He advised us that, yes, Tony Accardo really was his employee. He really does sell Foxhead 400 beer. To whom? Why, to many taverns, restaurants, bars and retail outlets. Even to the race tracks. All over the Chicagoland area. Really? Yes, and as a matter of fact, an associate of his does also. His name is John P. Cerone.

Armed with this information, we made contact with one of the people I respected as much as anyone I would ever know. We became very close personal friends until he died in 1988, on May 9. This man would go on to become Sheriff of Cook County, Chairman of the Cook County Board of Commissioners (called the mayor of Cook County) and governor of the state of Illinois, one of the most respected public officials I would ever be privileged to know. Richard Beale Ogilvie.

At the time Dick Ogilvie was the head of the Attorney General's Midwest Office on Organized Crime, formed after Apalachin had caused William Rogers, the U.S. Attorney General, to form a special unit to investigate organized crime. We presented the case to Dick, feeling that if Accardo and Cerone were really selling beer to outlets in Chicago and suburbs, it must be with muscle, intimidation and extortion. We asked Dick whether, if we went out and interviewed employees at these sales points and got a few to testify that they were muscled in any way to sell Foxhead 400 beer, he would then prosecute based on such evidence. He said he sure would. His mouth almost watered. If we could legitimately get Tony Accardo for extortion, our Top Hood Program would be off to a flying start. Furthermore, Mr. Hoover would get off Ross Spencer's case and he would get off ours.

Ross formed a "special." He assigned all the agents on C-1 to go out and interview every one of the people shown as customers of Accardo and Cerone on the records of Premium Beer. There were perhaps seventy or eighty listed.

Oh, how we struck out! None of them would even admit they had ever been visited by Accardo. They had never met him. The only one who admitted being visited by Accardo said that Accardo had been accompanied by Jackie Cerone and that it was

Cerone who did all the talking. Accardo never said a word, and neither man used any persuasion other than any other salesman might use. We hung our heads at this defeat.

Dick Ogilvie, however, had jumped one step ahead of us. He had had the foresight to take another look at Tony Accardo's tax return. It showed that he had taken a $3,000 deduction thereon for the use of his Mercedes. It was a business deduction, for the business of being a salesman for Premium Beer. So? If he says he uses his Mercedes to sell beer, Ogilvie told us, and you guys go out and talk to every one of his accounts, and only one admits he was ever sold any beer, even met the guy, then how can he take a business deduction for the use of his car? This is his only business, according to his return. That, my friends, is income tax fraud.

We had him and didn't know it. At least, we had him if we could prove that he never sold beer. We had already contacted every one of his accounts, and they all told us what they thought Tony wanted them to say. He had never muscled them, never even talked to them. Now that would backfire. Dick Ogilvie, it was clear to us, didn't get where he was because he was dumb.

Before the trial would commence, the indictment of Accardo for the tax fraud was obtained after the grand jury voted a true bill. The first witness before the grand jury was Dominic Volpe, the president of Premium Beer Sales. He testified that Accardo had earned his $60,000 a year salary. Ogilvie asked him whether Accardo actually made sales calls. Volpe said, according to Ogilvie, "I assume so." When Maurie Walsh, Accardo's lawyer, was subsequently questioned about whether it had been Accardo's sales technique to "buy-or-else," Walsh responded, "I don't think the grand jury will find any muscle in this. I really don't." After Volpe testified, so did Jackie Cerone. Then another appeared. This was Anthony Cosentino, the president of OK Motor Service, at 2513 West Armitage. He testified that he had borrowed $15,000 from Accardo in 1942. "That was before Accardo was a big shot; he was nothing then," Cosentino said. Not quite accurate but Ogilvie let it pass. In 1942, Accardo was just about to assume the top job in the Outfit. Cosentino continued: "I soon found out he wanted half of my company, so I borrowed from somebody else and gave him his money back. He hasn't spoken to me since." Cosentino had some guts.

Following the return of the true bill, the grand jury indicted one of the witnesses before it, on May 2, 1959. Joseph Bronge of Melrose Park, owner of West Towns Distributors, was charged with two counts of perjury. He had been forced, it was alleged, to do something similar to what Volpe had done—put a mobster on his payroll. The grand jury was interested in the methods used in that case. The alleged mobster was Joe "Gags" Gagliano, the prominent gangster who was later designated by Hump to approach a gas station owner in Wood Dale, a prospective juror in the Accardo tax fraud trial. "Gags" was on Bronge's payroll, and Bronge was charged with lying when asked if he had discussed the hiring of Gags with anyone at the Foxhead Brewing Company.

Before Bronge could be brought to trial, he was shot several times in the face and head by two gunmen who ambushed him at West Towns Distributors on July 19, 1959. He remained in a coma for days after the shooting, raising hopes that he would regain consciousness and possibly identify his shooters. He subsequently died without regaining consciousness. Because of the circumstances surrounding the shooting of Bronge, Accardo became an immediate suspect in his murder. This, although the sons of Bronge and Accardo had been college roommates and were close friends.

Nothing ever came of the Bronge shooting. Tony was never charged and it remains unsolved to this day. The trial would take place without Bronge, a key witness. The trial was scheduled to start—and did—in September of 1960, after all kinds of motions, continuances, etc. Justice moves very slowly.

By 1960 we were much more adept at our game. By the time Tony's trial was scheduled to start, originally in the summer of 1959, we had placed a bug, a hidden mike, in the mob's headquarters on the Magnificent Mile. It wasn't long after that bug was in operation, starting on July 29, 1959, that Tony was arraigned. He posted bail and immediately made his way, circuitously, to the mob headquarters, where he sat down with Murray Humphreys, Gus Alex and Jackie Cerone. They discussed the facts of their case, and decided to fix the jury.

At the time we didn't exactly have a statute authorizing us to plant bugs. The information we got off them was, therefore, inadmissible in court. But we could certainly use the information to thwart the mob's plans. This is what we set out to do.

For a couple weeks, Hump masterminded the fix at headquarters. He got hold of the jury panel, the list of a hundred or so prospective jurors from which the twelve jurors and two alternates would be selected. He parceled each one of those prospective jurors out to a mob member, for their backgrounds to be checked. For instance, one of the prospective jurors was listed as a truck driver. Hump immediately dispatched Frank "Strongy" Ferraro,

the new underboss to Sam Giancana, to go outside—fearful of a
tap, but not a bug at headquarters—and call Jimmy Hoffa on the
phone, find out whether this truck driver was a member of the
Teamsters, and if so, what local did he belong to and who could be
contacted within the Teamsters to approach this possible juror to
understand what a bummer of a case against Accardo this really
was. Another prospective juror was a gasoline station attendant in
Wood Dale, a western suburb of Chicago, still in Cook County.
Joe "Gags" was assigned to go out and buy gas at this station and
get to know this guy. Then they would consider an approach to
him if he was put on the jury. Joe Gagliano was a strong "made"
guy on the west side.

This all bumped along for a couple of weeks. Then Hump decided that things were too busy in headquarters with all the other
business of the mob being transacted there. Besides, as the jurors
were selected, he would have to have a place to approach them. So
he discussed with his driver-bodyguard-appointment secretary,
Hy Godfrey, where they might find another place to handle the
business of fixing the Accardo jury. Thank God, he discussed it
with Hy. When he assigned Hy to go out and find an appropriate
spot for this, we were able to get to the mob headquarters, a place
we ordinarily stayed away from to keep them unaware that we
knew its location. We put what the Bureau calls a "fisur," a physical surveillance, on Godfrey. Ralph Hill and I tailed Hy Godfrey
until he finally found the spot, the Lake Shore Drive Motel, on
North Lake Shore Drive. After I made contact with the manager
on this case, I made arrangements for my sister to spend her
honeymoon night there.

In any event, after we spotted Hy talking to the registration
clerk and then watched him leave, we contacted the manager. We
found that Hy had registered for the best suite in the house for the
next month under a fictitious name, and had paid in advance. That
captured the manager's attention. He knew immediately who we
were talking about, even though we were unaware of the name Hy
might have used.

Ralph and I immediately made a phone call back to the office.
We contacted Ray Connelly and he contacted our "sound men,"
our technicians trained to plant hidden mikes, bugs. We were able
to penetrate the suite that Hump would now use as his headquarters to fix the jurors in the Accardo trial. When Ralph Hill and
I led the sound men into the suite, it was no time before we were
set up with a bug, just awaiting the arrival of Hump and his crew
of jury fixers.

The information we might obtain from bugs like the one at mob headquarters and in the motel would be inadmissible in court as evidence. In 1960 we had no statute authorizing us to do what we did. So as we listened to Hump preparing his crew to make their approaches to the people on the list, we could only note the identity of those prospective jurors and wait to see who got picked.

We had an unwritten rule in the FBI at this time that we did not share our information with anybody outside the FBI. Even the United States Attorney's Office or the Justice Department, to whom we ostensibly reported, since the FBI is under the jurisdiction of the Justice Department. If there was not a "need to know," it was our rule that we didn't share that information with anybody else, so as not to compromise the bug. In this case there were two things going for us in this respect. One, Dick Ogilvie had impressed us so much that John Roberts had no misgivings about approaching him with our knowledge of what was up. Two, he was "need to know," at least in our opinion. So John and I talked to Dick Ogilvie, the prosecutor.

"Dick, there is something you ought to know. The mob has got the fix in. They've got an in to several of the jurors on the jury list, and when and if one or more of those jurors is picked, they're going to approach them."

"Are you sure? How do you guys know that?" Dick was astounded.

"We got it from a little birdie," John Roberts said.

That was enough for Dick Ogilvie. He got the point. I would later confide everything to Dick without any worry about its splashing back. I don't recall that we spelled it out for him on this early occasion of our close relationship, before he went to bigger and bigger jobs in public office, but he knew where we were coming from.

Dick was up to the task. He went to the judge and told him the FBI believed there was tampering with the jury panel. The judge was Julius Hoffman, later to be of Chicago Seven fame, when Abbie Hoffman, David Dellinger, Jerry Rubin and others were prosecuted before him by the other best prosecutor ever to try federal cases in Chicago, Tom Foran. Judge Hoffman wondered why we just didn't wait for an approach and then swoop down on the approacher. We had considered that *ab initio*, from the beginning. But it might compromise our source at mob headquarters, and we couldn't risk that. We were getting reams of intelligence about mob operations, and we couldn't do anything to jeopardize that bug. So Judge Hoffman, with the counsel of Dick Ogilvie, John Roberts and me, did the next best thing.

On the day the jury was to be impaneled, he pulled a switch. He had the jury panel for the Accardo trial switched with that of another trial about to commence in federal court. Wow, did that fire up the old Hump. All that work, months and months of it, all the conniving and the contacts made by dozens of "made" guys, all down the drain! Judge Hoffman explained that it was just a normal precaution in such an important trial as this, mentioning that it had been done in another income tax fraud case—that of Al Capone some thirty years ago. This threw Hump and his pals off the scent. They accepted that, and our bug continued its life just as before. Not the one in the motel, which went out of business when Hump angrily deserted the suite, but the one in mob headquarters, which continued on and on for five more years.

31 Accardo Meets His Adversary. Loses. Then Wins.

"Some trick you guys pulled with the jury."

The speaker was Tony Accardo.

I was standing at a urinal in the men's room on an upper floor of the old federal courthouse in Chicago, where the Accardo tax fraud trial was being held, the same courthouse where Al Capone had been convicted on much the same charge, before it was torn down to be the site of the current federal building, in the Loop.

I had been tending to my business and hadn't noticed the man who slipped up to the next urinal. It was my first face-to-face meeting, if you will, with Joe Batters.

I smiled, said nothing. But as we moved over to the basin to wash our hands, I said to him: "Kind of punky, getting you after all this time on a rap such as this."

"You haven't got me yet," Tony said as he prepared to walk out.

"Well, whatever happens, happens," I said.

That was my first meeting with Tony Accardo. I'm not even sure he knew my name. He knew I was with "the G," as mobsters referred to us, because he had seen me caucusing with Dick Ogilvie and the other government people attending the trial.

On another day during the trial, he was standing during another recess in the hall outside Judge Hoffman's courtroom. With him was Jackie Cerone, his ever-present pal. I smiled at Joe.

"What have you got to smile about?" J.B. asked, in a pleasant tone.

"Just that it's a nice day, I guess."

"Every day that we can smell the fresh air, I guess it's a nice day," Tony rejoined.

"Well, good luck," I said as I walked on by.

I could be pleasant because the trial was going well, or at least that was the perception of Dick Ogilvie and the rest of us. Dick had presented our witnesses, i.e., those who had to stick to their stories that they had purchased Foxhead 400 beer without ever being contacted by Accardo, thereby nullifying his claim on his tax return that he used his Mercedes car as a salesman.

One of the first government witnesses at the trial described how Accardo got this "job" with Premium Beer Sales. He testified that officials of the company had met with Jack Cerone, Murray Humphreys, Eugene Bernstein (Accardo's tax attorney) and Sidney R. Korshak, another attorney often used by mob figures in deals like this one. The meeting took place at the Armory Lounge, later to be distinguished as Sam Giancana's headquarters in Forest Park. There Bernstein suggested, according to the witness, that "Accardo could sell a great amount of beer." He said that "certain people associated with Accardo would 'push' the sale of beer." Witnesses also testified that the Foxhead Brewery had agreed to reimburse Premium Beer Sales for Accardo's salary. At this point, Accardo's attorneys, Walsh and Stanford Clinton, made motions alluding to the vast newspaper coverage of the trial, which they claimed made the trial prejudicial.

Then the bookkeeper for Premium Beer Sales testified. She said that she had never observed Tony Accardo on the premises of Premium Beer Sales. She had prepared his weekly salary check by filling in only the amount and then giving it to Dominic Volpe to fill in the name of the payee. She assumed Volpe delivered the check weekly to Accardo.

After six weeks it was then the turn of the defense. They presented a parade of Accardo's friends and associates, much to the delight of the press and ourselves. Each day, "Little Al," our mike, would alert us to what testimony Hump was dredging up, most of it perjurious. If Little Al had been monitoring the strategy of the defense while either Accardo or his attorneys were present, we would have been precluded from monitoring it, because that would be a clear violation of the law and the canons of legal ethics. But neither the defendant nor his attorneys were privy to these conversations. These were between Hump and the witnesses whose testimony he was suborning. If such conversations had been picked up by a bug that was authorized by a statute, such as often happened in later years, we could have used it to prosecute Humphreys. We could use the information to do two things only. We could alert Dick Ogilvie as to what was coming, then give him the information he could use to destroy the credibility of each witness when he took the stand on cross-examination. We also did one other thing. We alerted Sandy Smith, the *Tribune* reporter, about each witness and furnished Sandy with the mob background or anything else which would discredit him in the minds of his readers. As a result, Sandy was able to fascinate his readers each morning with the shady story of just who every defense witness was. We were perhaps stepping up to the thin line of legal ethics by doing this, but we did not cross it.

One of the witnesses was Irving Singer, owner of the Black Angus Restaurant at 7127 North Western, long a hangout of many mobsters. At one time Singer had "fronted" for the mob in some of their strip joints. He testified that "Mr. Accardo came to my place and told me he was selling beer. He asked me to place an order. I told him I would be more than willing to and gave him an order for five cases."

Another witness, believe it or not, was Carmen Fanelli, the owner of record and liquor licensee at the Armory Lounge, Giancana's headquarters. He testified that Accardo had solicited him to sell Foxhead 400 beer. Another witness was Ben "Foggie" Fillichio, Tony's longtime friend whom Sandy described the next day in the *Tribune* as "a mob gambling boss and convicted moonshiner." Fillichio owned the big liquor and beer retail chain Austin Liquors, and testified that he not only bought beer from Accardo but had seen Accardo driving his "red sports car" at the time. He also testified on cross that he had been arrested on several occasions and had also been deep-sea fishing with his "old friend" Accardo. Tom Lechos, owner of Tom's Steak House in Melrose Park, testified that he too bought beer from Tony. So did Lewis Ganzer, the owner of the oft-raided Mannheim Road Tavern, and Joe Nicoletti, the president of a tavern association. On and on they came. Steve DeKosta, my old adversary who owned the Tradewinds, a prime mob hangout on Rush Street; Al Pilotto, who would later become the capo in charge of the southern suburbs for the mob and would also be indicted with Tony years later in Florida; Bernie Glickman, the fight promoter who managed Sonny Liston and other world's boxing champions; Frank Campagna, Joe Costello and John Maculuso, all tavern keepers who had been primed by Hump. All testified that Accardo sold them beer while using the now well-known "little red Mercedes."

Ogilvie and Tony's attorneys, Maurice Walsh and Stanford Clinton, gave their final summations to the jury, and the jury went out to consider their verdict. As we left the courtroom that day, I had my third conversation with Tony. This would be as brief, and about as pleasant, as the first two. As we waited by the elevators to go down to the ground floor of the courthouse, I impulsively reached out my hand and, as he responded in kind, I smiled and said, "Let the best man win." He smiled and replied, "I'll go for that."

Looking back later on, I believe these three cordial contacts with Accardo served me well when I needed something many years later. I think Tony got the idea that I was not some wild fanatic, that though I wasn't going to flip over onto his "pad," I wasn't some hostile hardnose who was going after him one way or the other, ethical or no. The pleasant contacts probably served as a foundation for what was to come. On the other hand, these friendly contacts also gave me the idea that what John Roberts had reported about Accardo was accurate. He was pleasant and cordial. He was approachable. Just as I was not some wild-eyed fanatic in Joe's eyes, I felt that he was not either. I contrasted that with my feelings about almost all other people in his milieu. Hump was like Tony, Jackie was, Butch was, Ralph Pierce was, Les Kruse was and a few others were; but by and large, they were it. The rest of the hundreds of mobsters I would confront through the twenty-three years I worked exclusively on organized crime matters were not. Some were just plain thugs whose *modus operandi* was to act tough when approached. Others just didn't have the confidence in themselves to respond in a friendly fashion, not knowing what might come next. By and large, almost all mobsters are unfriendly when contacted by law enforcement people, or at least keep us at arm's length.

When the jury came in, it was bad news for Tony Accardo. He was found guilty on three counts. Later Judge Hoffman would sentence him to six years in prison, two years on each count. Tony was also assessed a fine of $15,000. Maury Walsh immediately announced he would appeal, and Accardo was allowed to remain free on bail. This is in contrast to the procedure these days. When a mobster of any stature is arrested today, he is generally sent to the MCC, the Metropolitan Correctional Center, in the Loop, while he awaits his trial and during his trial. Then, if convicted, he is returned to the MCC while awaiting the sentence which will send him off to prison. Unlike Accardo in 1960, a ranking member of the Outfit these days will be held in confinement from the time he is arrested. Since this was not the case with Accardo in 1960, he was still free to claim he had never spent a night in jail.

The mob put together a great effort to make sure Tony's appeal would be successful. John D'Arco and Pat Marcy, the major functionaries in the Regular Democratic Organization of the First Ward, came to mob headquarters on Michigan Avenue before our hidden mike, Little Al. Al was present when D'Arco and Marcy conferred with Hump. I would later testify before the U.S. Senate Permanent Subcommittee on Investigations that these figures in the First Ward were "the conduit through which the orders passed from the mob to those public officials who were corrupted." We listened as D'Arco, especially, the alderman and ward committeeman of the First Ward, conferred with Murray Humphreys about his relationship with two judges of the appellate court where the appeal would be heard. He thought that he might be able to influence them to reverse Accardo's conviction. Hump ordered him and Marcy to make this their top priority. Unfortunately, Little Al was unable to give us any further information about this situation. In the spring of 1962 the Circuit Court of Appeals for the Seventh District overthrew the verdict in the Accardo case and remanded the case for a new trial. They cited the great publicity which had attended the trial, saying it had made it prejudicial for Tony to obtain a fair trial under those circumstances. They also ruled that the W-2 form, the withholding form, was improperly used and could not be used as part of the evidence in the new trial.

As a result, and due in large measure to Richard B. Ogilvie's having moved on from the prosecutor's job, Tony was retried in the early fall of 1962, without the W-2 form, and on October 3, 1962, the jury returned its verdict of not guilty. Tony had walked again.

I was not there that day and, in any event, was in no mood to congratulate him.

32 The McClellan Committee

At about the same time that Tony Accardo was undergoing his trial in Chicago, he was also going through another ordeal. This was the era of another crime-investigating committee of Congress. Tony had withstood the pressure of the Kefauver Committee at the beginning of the decade of the Fifties. Now it was the McClellan Committee that required his presence near the end of the decade.

This time the FBI was in a position to give the committee some assistance. John Roberts and I were able to lead the committee investigators directly to Accardo; therefore, it didn't take several months to serve the subpoena calling for his appearance. Just about everybody of any stature in the Chicago Outfit was brought before the committee. Jackie Cerone, Sam Giancana, Joey Aiuppa, Ross Prio and Caesar DiVarco were there. So were Johnny Lardino, an official of the mob-influenced Hotel and Restaurant Workers Union, and Abe Teitelbaum, who represented the mob-influenced Chicago Restaurant Association. The committee charged that all were involved in an effort to control the restaurant business in Chicago, especially the north side, through domination of the various unions which served the restaurants. The committee was especially interested in the testimony of those two great Chicago police officers, Joe Morris and Bill Duffy, who testified about their investigations of the situation while the Scotland Yard Unit was still functioning. They especially keyed on the attempt by two mobsters, "Needle Nose" Labriola and Jimmy Weinberg, to intimidate Teitelbaum by threatening to push him out his high-rise office building window with the "blessings of Tony Accardo."

This, of course, was a nice introduction to the appearance of Tony Accardo, and he did not disappoint. He was the focal point of the nationwide television coverage, as he gave his name and address, then took the Fifth 172 times. By now the "open door" doctrine had set in and he took no chances by answering even those questions, such as any involvement in narcotics, which he had answered at the Kefauver Committee hearing. The questions were put to him by Bobby Kennedy, the chief counsel to the Committee, which his older brother served on as a Senator.

The McClellan Committee, just like everybody else, never laid a glove on Accardo. It was just another inconvenience for him. Just like so many other situations, these investigations were a big nuisance, and probably caused him to lose some sleep. Maybe even to send him out to the woods to "chop, chop, chop," as he advised Gus Alex to do to fight stress. When push came to shove, the McClellan Committee was not much of a problem for Tony. Just another bump in the road. Certainly not a roadblock.

The questions put to him were all pertinent, since they had been prepared by the committee investigators after consultation with guys like John Roberts. But since Tony had the recourse to the Fifth Amendment, they did not serve to puncture Tony's defense.

On the other hand, the committee did a fine job of alerting the public to Tony's stature in the mob and to the overall menace of organized crime in general. Such hearings, in my opinion, serve a fine purpose and are well worth the time, energy and expense involved. If the public is sanguine about the threat presented by the mob, law enforcement and legislative bodies are bound to be as well. That is not the climate in which mobdom flourishes. Tony Accardo counseled his people at all times to "keep your head down," meaning that anytime the public gets aroused, it is bad news for the mob. They should endeavor at all times to keep the lowest profile possible—to kill "only their own," and only when it is imperative to establish and maintain discipline and order.

Therefore, when committees like Kefauver, McClellan and, as we shall see later, the Senate Permanent Subcommittee on Investigations (the so-called Rackets Committee) come to town, it bodes ill for people like Joe Batters, even if no conviction is handed down.

Tony handled the McClellan Committee with dispatch and aplomb, however, and then went right on with his business. Such things were all in a day's work for him at this period of his life. Obstacles, not dead ends.

33 More Exposure of Tony

It was just prior to this time that my friend Sandy Smith did a series of stories in the Chicago *Tribune* on Local 110 of the Motion Picture Operators Union, giving heavy play to his thesis that it had been a longtime mob union and that it was now under the dominion of Tony Accardo.

Sandy gave great emphasis to the fact that Anthony Ross Accardo, Tony's elder son, had been given a very nice situation as a new member of the union. Apparently Sandy's sources inside Local 110 were disgruntled members who had been shoved aside in spite of their seniority, while many relatives and friends of mobsters, such as young Accardo, were given choice jobs. Tony's son, for example, was assigned to the Mercury Theatre in suburban Elmwood Park, less than a mile from the Accardo residence. And his partner in the projection booth, now that the "bolsheviks" had won the concession that there must be two operators in each booth, was none other than John Sortino, the brother of Frank "Strongy" Ferraro, true name Sortino, the underboss to Giancana. Other, more senior, projectionists had applied for the job at the Mercury but had been passed over by Clarence Jalas, the president of Local 110, who was under the strong influence of the mob.

Smith reported that many of the mobsters' relatives were given the choice assignments by Jalas. John Accardo, Tony's kid brother, also had a cushy job, at Arlington Park racetrack at a whopping $600 per week, one of the very top-paying jobs in the local. Hump's brother was a member of Local 110, as were Joey Aiuppa's relative, Sam; Willie Bioff's brother, Herman; Nick Circella's brothers, Angelo and Augie; "Cherry Nose" Gioe's brother, Anthony; Charles and Nick Giancana, relatives of Sam; the list went on and on.

Then, in October of 1959, Tony got some more ink. He and

Clarice took a European trip with Anthony and Mrs. DeGrazia. Which might not seem particularly noteworthy except that Anthony DeGrazia was then a lieutenant in the Chicago Police Department. While still in Europe, Lt. DeGrazia was suspended by the embarrassed police commissioner, Timothy J. O'Connor, for "bringing the police department into disrepute."

The press caught up with the travelers in Zurich. Lt. DeGrazia admitted, since it was so obvious, that he and his wife were good friends of the Accardos and had been since childhood. He saw nothing wrong, he said, with travelling with Accardo, and he would continue his vacation with him. He denied that he had been hired to "bodyguard" Accardo. He seemed unconcerned about being suspended since he had thirty-seven years on the force, was sixty-two years old and his pension was fully vested. Tony likewise seemed unconcerned. He refused to testify later before the Civil Service Commission hearing, which eventually resulted in Lt. DeGrazia's dismissal from the CPD. Tony was finding that he was as much, if not more, in the spotlight as before, when he was heavily engaged in the day-to-day operations of the Outfit.

Even the IRS would not let up on Tony at this time. On December 2, 1959, a lien was filed against him seeking $195,669 in back taxes on his share of profits from the old Erie and Buffalo policy wheel he had sanctioned Giancana to take from the leaders in the black belt. That went back to 1950. In reporting this the Chicago *Tribune* noted that "the millions rolling in from the rackets touched Tony Accardo with gold. He acquired stocks, bonds, hotels, restaurants, auto agencies, liquor firms, appliance companies and a sprawling stone house in River Forest, where even the plumbing was gold-plated."

It was about this time that we followed Tony Accardo and Murray Humphreys downtown. Imagine our surprise when, in the middle of the afternoon, they skipped into the old Roosevelt Theater, then located on State Street across from Marshall Field's, where "Skate on State" is now located. I couldn't resist taking a seat in the row right behind them and eavesdropping on their conversation. I got a huge kick out of the whole thing, because the movie was the one starring Rod Steiger and Fay Spain entitled *Al Capone*.

I have to say that Tony and Hump didn't think all that much of the story line. Frequently, I heard Tony say, as he nudged Hump, "No, no." All in all, it didn't give us anything of any intelligence value, but it was intriguing to know that the two guys in front of me had played such a huge role in the real life story of Al

Capone's gang and that they knew a lot more about the subject matter of the movie than did the screenwriters and producers. Sometimes even a G-man gets to have some fun.

34 "Little Al" and the Commission

In the spring and summer of 1959, we started something that would have a terrific impact on Tony Accardo and his people.

J. Edgar Hoover, albeit belatedly, had brought the FBI into an all-out, no-holds-barred investigation of the organized crime groups all over the country. As Ross Spencer had told me, Hoover expected those of us assigned to the Top Hoodlum Program in Chicago and New York to carry the ball, since it was in those two cities where he perceived the biggest mob power lay. He was well advised.

Now he was pressuring his supervisors at the Seat of Government in Washington to put like pressure on the supervisors of the THP in the field to show results. Those supervisors were, in kind, putting great pressure on us street agents or, as we are known officially, us field agents.

One of the things Mr. Hoover was most adamant about was that he wanted "elsurs," electronic surveillances, of strategic places where the mob discussed their business. In other words, he wanted hidden microphones, bugs. There are actually two types of "elsurs": bugs (hidden mikes inside the premises) and taps (on telephones). The latter, taps, were of some use but not much, because mobsters at the time were alert to such tactics. They talked on phones, but not on phones from their homes or their hangouts, and when they did, they were most circumspect, talking mostly in code. But we had never before—nor had any other law enforcement agency—ever penetrated a strategic mob location in order to place a bug in it. Therefore, the mobsters were free with their conversations "inside."

Mr. Hoover felt that we had planted elsurs successfully with the CP-USA and had terminated that menace, so why couldn't the same tactic be used against the menace of organized crime?

Some of the big problems, other than the obvious ones, were the conditions that Mr. Hoover attached to our mission. When those of us on S-1, Security Squad Number One, had penetrated Communist Party headquarters in Chicago, we were very much aware that we had the authority to do so. The FBI had specifically been given this authority, spelled out in no uncertain terms, by more than one U.S. Attorney General. "To protect the national security," was the wording they used.

But did this apply to organized crime? Was the mob a threat to the "national security"? Mr. Hoover believed it was, so he took it upon himself to tell us so. However, at the same time he also made it clear that we were not to carry any document identifying us as FBI agents when we penetrated. And we were not to identify ourselves if caught, either by the mob or by the police, as we were breaking and entering. If we were subsequently so identified, we were branded as "rogue agents," working outside the scope of our authority, and thrown to the wolves, open to prosecution or worse.

These instructions turned off a lot of agents on the THP, probably for good reason. If we were apprehended by the police, we could be prosecuted, under these conditions, for breaking and entering, then discharged from the FBI, disbarred from the practice of law therefore, and never again be able to get another decent job, certainly not in law enforcement. Add to that the jeopardy attached to the risk that we could be shot as we broke and entered by anyone lawfully guarding the inside of the premises. It was not something most people would want to undertake, FBI agent or not.

However, I was not as smart as most FBI agents. If you don't believe me, consider that when I was fifteen, I entered my first Golden Gloves boxing tournament and thereafter had sixty-five amateur fights. That is dumb. And now I was the agent who volunteered to be the "case agent," the lead agent, on our first penetration—the first one, in fact, by any FBI field division.

It was now a year and a half or so since the THP was put into operation. We had stumbled and bumbled along. I had finished reading the CAPGA files and then gone over to the public library and perused the records of the Kefauver Committee from the early Fifties. I had set out on my investigation of my first assigned target, Gus Alex, the boss of the Loop, and then my second target,

Hump. At the same time, I spent part of my investigative time working with my partners, John Roberts on Accardo, and Ralph Hill on Giancana.

I guess one of the reasons I was more "gung ho," as we used to say in the Marine Corps, may have been that in the early days of the THP, I had gotten personal with the mobsters—or rather, to be accurate, they had gotten personal with me. When they used to make me on a surveillance, a "fisur" as it was officially termed in the Bureau, a physical surveillance (as contrasted to an elsur or a "misur," a microphone surveillance), they called Jeannie. They asked her in obscene language who I might be sleeping with that night. On occasions they would tell her she would never see me again, they had killed me. Then they started following my kids to school in the mornings. Jeannie had not informed me of this, since she did not want to hinder my work, knowing that I would stay home more at night rather than responsibly do my job. But when they came to the door one day and tried to get into the house by posing as insurance company officers, Jeannie, who handled such matters, realized that I had not requested them to come by the house as they claimed. She slammed the door in their faces; she let me in at last on what had been going on, feeling now that she was in over her head. I solved the problem by going to Hump, the elder statesman of the mob, and making an agreement, what we would call the "family pact." They would thereafter stay away from our families and we would not harass theirs. The sins of the fathers would not be visited onto the sons and daughters—the hoods were still fair game and so were we, but not the kids and wives on either side.

For this and other reasons, I felt something more than just professional duty as I went about my job. The mob had chosen to get up close and personal, and I guess my instinctive nature as an old fighter accepted that challenge. I don't recall now that I gave it a lot of consideration. I just went to Ross Spencer and volunteered to lead the penetration of the mob headquarters so that our "sound men," our technicians who knew how to do this job from years against the CP-USA, could plant the hidden elsur.

By this time, a year and a half after we started our attack on the mob, we had located the mob headquarters. We had followed just about every upper-echelon leader of the Outfit to the corner of Rush and Ontario, where they entered a building on Ontario. For a while we were perplexed, since we couldn't find anything at that location which appeared to be a location for meetings. Then one day, as I waited for Hump to arrive, I found that he didn't remain long at that location. Inside there was a service entrance, a long corridor which led to an adjacent building, now called the Briskin Building, which fronts on Michigan Avenue, right in the heart of the Magnificent Mile: 620 North Michigan. (I have taken the television program *American Justice* on the Arts and Entertainment Network through the steps we went through to penetrate this building in order to plant our mike. The program, narrated by the renowned Chicago television anchorman, Bill Kurtis, aired on January 11, 1995. I have done the same for other shows and the location has become somewhat famous. It was torn down in 1995 in line with some renewal.)

The mob was using a large custom tailor shop on the second floor of the building as their central headquarters. It was called Celano's Custom Tailors and was run by Jimmy Celano, a close associate of most of the top Outfit guys, who depended on their patronage to sell his expensive custom-made suits and overcoats, even shirts. Jimmy had a private office on the south side of his large shop, which he turned over every morning and every afternoon to the boys. In the office he had a desk and chair, a large sofa, one easy chair and a bar stocked with beer, wine and liquor. Also contained therein was a safe.

To make a long story short, I spent a couple weeks in the spring of 1959 making the arrangements to gain a key to the building and determine what problems we might have with security. I then sent this "survey," as we called it, to S.O.G. for Mr. Hoover's approval. Needless to say, he was elated that somebody was finally following his instructions to accomplish this, or so we were informed by Spencer.

In addition to the usual concerns we had with our entry, there were two unusual ones. First, we were led to believe that there might be a guard with a shotgun inside the tailor shop in the evening and night hours, the hours when we would have to make our move. If he shot us, he could legitimately claim he perceived us to be thieves breaking and entering. Second, as I surveyed, we found that at night the Chicago police were on the rooftops with rifles, not only on 620 North Michigan but across the street and down the block, on patrol looking for a crew of burglars who were, in fact, hitting the many shops on the Magnificent Mile. If they spotted us moving into the building or around the tailor shop with its large windows facing out on Michigan Avenue, we would be fair game and, under Mr. Hoover's instructions, unable to identify ourselves as good guys. It would be our tough luck under either of those scenarios.

We did it anyway. It took at least six penetrations, all early in the morning on Sundays when the tailor shop was closed for business, but we accomplished it. We planted the bug, which was about the size of a pineapple, a World War II mike, which we had to wire not only out of the shop, but out of the building, so that it could be monitored in our office several miles away at 536 South Clark, in the far southwest part of the Loop. We secured the mike behind the radiator in the private office of Jimmy Celano and activated it for the first time on July 29, 1959, my wife Jeannie's birthday, as a present for her, since I'd be home on Saturday nights–Sunday mornings now. (If that was a present.) It remained active—and productive beyond what we had imagined—for the next six years. It would prove well worth the risk, everything Mr. Hoover had expected it to be, and more. We gave the mike the acronym "Little Al" as its code name. After all, he would live his life in the presence of the successors to Al Capone.

Arguably the best overhear we would have from Little Al came on September 8, 1959, just weeks after we had planted the mike. Tony Accardo and Sam Giancana met at Celano's that day and carried on a far-reaching discussion of their main concerns of the day.

In the fall of 1959, Giancana was still in his early days as the boss of the Chicago Outfit. He had been in charge for two years now, always under the guidance of Joe Batters. Here he had just returned from his first solo meeting with the Commission.

J.B. had been the Chicago *representato* on the Commission for some fifteen years and knew most of the current members. Obviously, Giancana had no problem explaining to Joe what the agenda of the Commission on this occasion had been. You can imagine my interest and curiosity as I listened to their unguarded conversation. By this time Ralph Hill and a new agent, Marshall "Maz" Rutland, had become my partners on this project. It was our job to monitor the conversations, analyze and interpret them, send the transcriptions we typed to Washington and then discreetly to cover any logical leads—discreetly, so as not to jeopardize Little Al in any way. We always sat on the information rather than take any chance we might compromise our great new source. No other field office in the Bureau had a source such as Little Al, and we took great pains to protect him. (I received scores of commendations, incentive awards, quality raises and other awards as the years went by, but if I deserved any of them, it was the one I got for being the lead agent on the installation of Little Al. That award I prized more than any other in my thirty-year career in the FBI. Mr. Hoover was very generous to me on that occasion and I have always appreciated that.)

Before they got to the Commission meeting, however, Giancana and Accardo began their several-hour meeting by discussing the politicians they felt they should back in the elections that fall. As was usually the case, they supported Democrats more than Republicans, although Peter Granata, the Republican Ward Committeeman in the First Ward, was always one of their favorites. Paul Ross on the north side was another. And there were many Democrats they worked against, like Dan Ward who would demonstrate why when he became the Cook County State's Attorney and hired Ross Spencer as his Chief Investigator. Dick Ogilvie, who would soon start his public career, would prove to be anathema to the mob, although he would make one major mistake in his long career.

Then they discussed a public official, a law enforcement official, who they felt was "under the wing" of "the G," the FBI. We realized that we would have to build support for this guy, since the Outfit would now come after him.

Giancana told Accardo that Joe Bonanno had moved from his home in New York to Tucson, Arizona, where he had "planted a flag." He retained his control of his LCN family in Brooklyn, where he had been since 1931. Accardo was furious at what he perceived to be Bonanno's moving in on open territory in Arizona.

Then the mob boss and the *consiglieri* proceeded to discuss the Commission meeting from which Giancana had just returned.

It is difficult to understand just how excited we were when we taped this conversation and then played it back, word for word, many times in order to gain the full impact of what was discussed. Understand that even though the Commission, their ruling body, had been in existence since 1931, nobody in all of law enforcement, local or federal, had ever heard of it before. Not the great local police officers like Ralph Salerno of the NYPD or Bill Duffy of the CPD. Not the great federal officials like Bobby Kennedy, then of the McClellan Commission, or even J. Edgar Hoover. Now we were getting it firsthand, just as if we were in Jimmy Celano's private office with Little Al, Tony Accardo and Sam Giancana.

I have gone into great detail in my autobiography, *Roemer: Man Against the Mob*, about this conversation and there is no purpose in detailing it once more here. Suffice it to say that we learned a great deal that morning and afternoon. Not only did we learn that there was such a thing as the Commission, but who the current members were, who were the bosses of the twelve La Cosa Nostra families at the time. As a matter of fact, the Philadelphia office and the Pittsburgh offices of the Bureau had yet to identify the leaders identified by Giancana in his meeting with Accardo.

In any event, Little Al, who had already furnished several most interesting conversations by September 8, had now given us a real bombshell. We tipped our hats to Accardo and Giancana and thanked them for making heroes of us in the eyes of our supervisors in Chicago and back in Washington. Mr. Hoover recognized more and more how wise he had been to push us in the effort to install our listening devices in mob headquarters.

Of course, now we were pressured to penetrate other mob locations. The Bureau in Washington, the S.O.G., couldn't get enough now that they had a taste of what Little Al was producing—they had developed a sweet tooth of sorts. They pushed other FBI offices to emulate our success as well. Our squad, C-1, the Top Hood Squad in Chicago, had become the best THP squad in the Bureau by any standard, but there were other offices who were in close competition like New York, Detroit, Newark and Philadelphia, which were working hard to catch up. We knew that we had to keep up the pace to stay ahead of them.

We were successful in these other operations, but I guess we never did place an elsur as valuable as Little Al. We came close from time to time. Al remained in place until July 11, 1965, and alerted us to just about everything Tony Accardo and his guys were doing or were about to do. It was just too bad that Al's information was inadmissible. Not only could we have used it to prosecute so many of the top leaders who met almost daily at Celano's, but the concomitant public exposure would have greatly enlightened the country, especially about Tony Accardo.

35 Police Corruption in Chicago

It was at this time that the Summerdale police scandal would tax Tony Accardo's patience. He had been successful during the last decades in corrupting scores, maybe hundreds, of Chicago police officers and sheriff's deputies, to say nothing of their superiors. Now it was all tumbling down. Several police officers in what was then called the Summerdale District, the 40th District, now called Foster Avenue, since that's the street it is located on, had actually been working in tandem with a young burglar named Richie Morrison to rob stores in that district, on the far north side of Chicago. Now the "babbling burglar," as he became known, had snitched on his police pals. They were being prosecuted by no friend of the mob at that time, State's Attorney Ben Adamowski. When we heard on Little Al that Accardo, Hump, Giancana and the rest of the mob leadership wanted to protect the police by getting to Morrison, we alerted Adamowski, who was already wary about protecting Morrison, although he always assumed that it should be from the police. He was surprised that the mob wanted to quiet Morrison. Why would they want to suppress this scandal? Weren't the police their enemy? Not in the perception of the Outfit. Tony Accardo had spent decades putting his corrupted officials in high places in the CPD. Now the public was demanding a major overhaul of the department. That could sweep many of the mob's people out of their commands. As we heard on Little Al, Tony was especially concerned that Joe Morris and Bill Duffy, who were as capable as they were incorruptible, might be returned to the investigation of the Outfit as they had been before Mayor Daley ordered their Scotland Yard Unit disbanded.

Mayor Daley created a special committee to investigate the situation and to recommend a new police commissioner. Again, it was Little Al who alerted us to the fact that one of the most prominent members of the committee, a guy who would later serve on the police board and as a member of the Cook County Board of Commissioners, would agree to meet surreptitiously with the three top Accardo people in a car near O'Hare Airport. This guy had been close to Hump for years and agreed to a sit-down with Hump, underboss Frank Ferraro and boss Sam Giancana. He was later immortalized in Chicago when a popular street in the city was named after him. Streets have been renamed for such worthy people as my friends Jack Brickhouse and Irv Kupcinet, and it is in poor taste, in my opinion, that one should have been named for this guy. But that's Chicago.

In any event, the chairman of the committee whose charge was to find a new police chief, Orlando W. Wilson, wound up getting the job himself. The title was even changed as if that would cleanse the stench. One of the first things I did was to tell my boss, the Special Agent in Charge of the Chicago Office, that when he sat down with the new superintendent, he should inform him that he had two most honorable and capable organized crime investigators in his department and that if he desired to win the respect of those of us in federal law enforcement, it would be a good idea to promote those two guys and give them authority over his organized crime investigation function. I could not give this advice to Wilson myself, of course, since I was just a street agent. Always would be. I have never had an audience with the police superintendent, although the present one, Matt Rodriguez, was a friend when he worked organized crime matters years ago under a fine lieutenant, Ed Berry.

The two guys I had in mind were Joe Morris and Bill Duffy. Wilson did have the good sense to reorganize the CPD and to create what he called the Bureau of Inspectional Services, and he put Morris in charge of that. Under the BIS was the Intelligence Unit, the organized crime unit which replaced, to some degree, the old Scotland Yard. Morris promptly appointed Bill Duffy to this spot. The worst fears of Accardo and his pals were realized. Not only did the reorganization give rise to a new unit to investigate them, but the two most capable, honest officers in the department were put in charge of it. Bill Duffy got to be as good a friend as I ever had. As sharp and as trustworthy as any person I ever had the privilege of working with—in any agency. We exchanged information on an unlimited basis as the years would go by, until another administration would "chase" him, "dump Duffy." Tony Accardo would suffer now with Duffy on his tail, but would win the battle about two decades later.

In order to give some perspective, after Bobby Kennedy came into office in 1961 as Attorney General, he came to Chicago and got an earful about what we had been doing in the three years or so since Mr. Hoover had unleashed us. Bobby, who would soon be instrumental in having us change our program's name from the Top Hoodlum Program to the Criminal Intelligence Program, the CIP, asked us on the occasion of his first visit to give him a detailed rundown on the Outfit and the alliance between crime and politics. John Roberts led us off in that all-day session by informing Bob about Tony Accardo. We considered him the number one target for the new CIP, just as Joe Batters had been under the THP. Ralph Hill then detailed Sam Giancana, and I told Bobby about Gussie Alex and Hump. Four or five other fine C-1 agents gave talks about their targets; Marshall Rutland about the underboss, Frank "Strongy" Ferraro, for one. Then I came back once more to talk about police corruption. By this time we had placed three additional important bugs. One was in the headquarters of the Regular Democratic Organization of the First Ward, the stomping ground of those two rascals, Pat Marcy and John D'Arco. What I gave Bob from that bug, code-named "Shade," since it existed right across the street in the shade of City Hall and was as shady as you could get in that office, was that Marcy was conspiring to kill a Chicago police officer. Marcy had already made two separate arrangements with vice officers in the Central Police District to neutralize this officer, both of which proved to be unsuccessful. The officer continued to work hard and honestly at his job of ridding the Loop of prostitution. In this third conversation, the three decided the thing to do was to kill him. I remember Bobby saying to me after we played the tape from that conversation: "Wow, I guess that removes any gloss a person might have about honest police officers and honest public officials."

Whenever Bobby Kennedy would come to town after that, he would call ahead to one of us street agents, not infrequently me, and request us to pick him up and debrief him on our investigations of Accardo, Giancana and Hump especially. Those three guys were his favorite targets, in Chicago certainly. He always turned to me and asked what was going on with my special interest and, naturally, his: the alliance between the mob and the Chicago politicians. I always anticipated his request and made certain I outlined all that had become current since our last talk. Of course, all of this would have been sent to him via Mr. Hoover by what we called our "daily summary airtel," a communication sent by the fastest mail from Chicago to Washington. It was a bitch sending that out every day when I wanted to spend most of my time on the street instead of in the office, but I got it out daily. Most of the information in it came from our elsurs.

One day I got a call from Bob. "Bill," he said, "I'd like you to put together all you guys know about corruption in the Chicago Police Department. I have a special reason." That was good enough for me! He didn't have to spell it out.

Following is a summary of my report to Bobby Kennedy in response to his request:

An informant advised that the Central Police District, which encompasses the Loop, is one of the worst in the city. The Syndicate (I'm surprised now that I used that name for the Outfit) makes monthly payoffs to a central fund which is distributed to various members of the district force, ranging from Captain _____ down to certain sergeants. Payoffs total as high as $4,200, which was the amount paid in February 1963. Gus Alex, who controls gambling in the First Ward, was cautioned by Captain _____ to be extremely careful in view of Wilson's desire for strict law enforcement. Favorable treatment was promised but agreement was reached to the effect that Captain _____ would conduct raids and enforce laws pertaining to strip joints on occasions in order that his reputation not be tarnished and in order that his superiors would consider he was performing his functions efficiently and honestly. This is why raids have been made on occasion but strip operations continue to flourish.

An informant advised that during the late fall and early winter of 1960, Murray Humphreys instructed his associate in the Outfit, namely Gus Alex, to maintain contact with a member of the Intelligence Unit of the Chicago Police Department, who at the time was furnishing information to Alex regarding investigations of Chicago hoodlums by the Intelligence Unit. On several occasions Alex was able to obtain information from this police source, which included the lines of information, the makes of the automobiles being utilized by the Intelligence Unit, the locations of meeting places of the hoodlums known to the Unit, and the identity of the hoodlums who had been observed by the unit to be in contact with each other. The hoodlums were able to have these reports destroyed.

An informant advised that Humphreys and his associates, notably Ralph Pierce, were apparently able to corrupt Captain _____ during the time he was a lieutenant and acting captain in the Summerdale District on the North Side. The subject later was placed in charge of a unit of the Bureau of Inspectional Services and at one time was Chief of Detectives of the Chicago Police Department. The subject meets every month, between the first and fifth, with Humphreys. The meet in March 1963 was in the Roosevelt Club, a coffee shop in the 800 block of West Roosevelt Road. Sometimes it takes place in the Bismarck Hotel. Sole purpose of this meet is to chat and make a drop. This captain was originally sponsored by Jake Arvey (a high-powered Chicago politician).

An informant has advised that he has operated a gambling house on the South Side of Chicago with the knowledge and consent of the Fifth Police District. This informant's gambling operation, a small one, pays about $500 a month to the district. All other gambling operations there make similar payments, the larger ones paying up to $1,000 a month.

An informant advised in late 1960 that Humphreys was very satisfied that State's Attorney Dan Ward accepted Lieutenant _____ on his staff of investigators. Humphreys enjoyed a relationship with the Lieutenant _____'s father and uncle, Chicago police captains, and was pleased to form a similarly pleasant relationship with Lieutenant _____.

An informant advised that Ross Prio (a capo in charge of the North Side of Chicago) was reportedly acquainted with Captain _____, who at one time was in charge of the Intelligence Unit of the Chicago Police Department (not Bill Duffy). The subject reportedly accepted money in the past from Prio, Jimmy Allegretti and others and once accepted a loan of $1,400 from Allegretti just prior to the time he was promoted to captain.

An informant advised that Humphreys and his associates were able to corrupt Captain _____ several years ago, prior to the time he was placed in charge of

a South Side District. When a captain in charge of the
district covering the First Ward announced his retirement, Humphreys wanted this captain to replace him
and asked Alderman John D'Arco to determine
whether the subject wanted the position. At first it did
not appear that he wanted it, but he subsequently
changed his mind. D'Arco then contacted Mayor Daley
and advised him that he wanted this captain to command his district. The appointment was then announced by Commissioner O'Connor.

An informant advised that Captain _____, one of
Chicago's highest police officials at the time of the
Summerdale scandal, received payoffs for a substantial number of years and once was in command of a
First Ward district. Humphreys was quite concerned
when he learned from D'Arco that information had
been received by the department from a federal law
enforcement agency that the possibility existed that
Captain _____ was a homosexual. D'Arco was given
orders by Humphreys to do what he could to protect
Captain _____ so that he did not lose his newly acquired position in the Wilson administration.

An informant advised in February 1962 that two
detectives, who are now with the Intelligence Unit of
the department, are handling policy payoffs and other
gambling payoffs. This informant advised that Jimmy
Allegretti will take care of the police district in which
a madam or prostitute operates for a ten- to twenty-
five percent payoff of the establishment's take. If a hotel or tavern in the North Clark Street area uses
B-girls or prostitutes, they have to pay Allegretti or
his men $200 a month for the privilege and part of
the money goes for police protection.

An informant advised on January 21, 1961, that
during the past eight years the estimated Outfit payoff
to police in one district was a half-million dollars. The
money was left in numbered envelopes for the various
police officers to pick up at a certain location. The envelopes were numbered to indicate the specific police-
man to receive it. One Julie Epstein always dropped
the envelopes at a certain restaurant. Epstein is a
trusted aide of Gussie Alex and his associates who formerly operated the gambling activities of the J and J

Picnic Grove. Policemen receiving envelopes included six captains (one a high-ranking staff official), one lieutenant, one sergeant and one patrolman.

An informant advised that Sergeant _____ is on the payroll of the English brothers, who are pleased with his services. (Chuckie and Sam English were high-ranking Outfit members.) He performs favors without even being asked. They frequently meet at 5th Jacks, a known hoodlum hangout on the west side. Information indicates that in March 1963, just before the murder of Alderman Benjamin Lewis, Sergeant _____ was in close touch with him and they were "doing a lot of business." The sergeant has been a protector of organized crime interests in the Fillmore area (on the West Side) and receives a cut from various gambling activities and from prostitution. Once when he received instructions from the Syndicate to keep an individual from running a competitive policy wheel in the Twenty-Fourth Ward, he stopped it within a week's time.

An informant advised during the fall of 1960 that Sam Giancana was making grandiose plans for the replacement of individuals holding politically appointed state jobs, particularly with the state police since the incumbent Republican administration was defeated. It was indicated that Frank LaPorte, a Syndicate representative in Southern Cook County, was well situated with the state police administration in that area, particularly with Captain _____ of the Blue Island state police district. It was indicated that Captain _____ received a considerable amount of money on a monthly basis for his services to LaPorte, Giancana and others. Another state police captain, covering the northwest section of the state, was also placed on the payroll and performed services for Joe Amato and Willie "Potatoes" Daddano, hirelings of Giancana and LaPorte. In the fall of 1960, LaPorte found it necessary to pay off all the way down the line, from captains to patrolmen. Although this cut considerably into the profits, it was a necessary evil. (Another captain) received $1,850 per month from Eddy Vogel, LaPorte and Robert Ansani, who were Giancana's representatives in gambling enterprises in Cicero. LaPorte estimated that extra income could be derived by sharing the payoff Captain _____ was getting from overweight trucking operations in Northern Illinois, which amounted to a quarter-million dollars per year. Captain _____ later transferred one lieutenant because he believed he was not getting his share of the payoffs collected by the lieutenant.

An informant advised that when Rocco Potenza reported to Giancana that he was getting "rough treatment" from a committeeman in Wheeling Township, who was supposed to be on the syndicate's payroll, Giancana recommended that the committeeman be taken out of office.

In my report to Bobby Kennedy I named forty-nine police officers. Four were state policemen, two were Cook County deputy sheriffs and the others were with the Chicago Police Department. I made sure that the officers named were the subjects of reliable information, mostly from our bugs in mob meeting places like Celano's and the First Ward. I did not want to hinder the careers of honest police people by trusting information that was shaky.

Soon Kennedy released the report to the Chicago Police Department and, as might have been expected, it was quickly leaked to the press. Mayor Daley was highly critical. "I would be surprised if it (the report) had any validity," he announced. "If it is what they say it is, I have too many things to do of a constructive nature rather than read this. It is a vicious document." Wow! The mayor wouldn't even take the time to read what the Attorney General of the United States had sent him. Does that say something? Police Superintendent Wilson took much the same stance. Not much was ever done about the contents of the report, although two of those named in the report were later disciplined. One of those named was mightily defended by Wilson. I have not described every allegation in the report, but one was of a man on Wilson's own staff at police headquarters who had been observed with some of the top hoodlums on the near north side. Wilson went all out, publicly and privately, for his man.

You might think that my report might have been the basis, at the very least, of transfers of those named from the districts where they had been corrupted and where they allegedly were providing favorable treatment to the mob. In fact, the report, which I had expected to be furnished to the department regardless of its being leaked to the media, caused a tidal wave from the press but nothing inside the department. The officers were not transferred.

Things under O.W. Wilson changed a lot as far as cosmetics

were concerned, however. And if he did nothing else but put Joe Morris and Bill Duffy in place where they could develop intelligence about the Outfit, he did something well worthwhile. The traffic division was much more efficient under the new superintendent. But the problem of corruption in the department remained. It was really not addressed. That was a barrier even Morris and Duffy could not jump over. As long as corruption existed, they had little chance to develop informants inside the mob. What knowledgeable hood would furnish information to the Chicago Police Department, knowing it would be recorded and shared with those corrupt officers who might betray them? Many corrupt officers would certainly use the information to further line their pockets by sharing it with the subjects of our investigations.

That, then, was the state of the alliance between the mob and the police as Tony Accardo was trying to keep everything on an even keel.

36 The Personal Family of Accardo

Tony Accardo put on one of the social highlights of the year in Chicagoland when his youngest daughter, Linda Lee, married Michael Palermo in April of 1961. The guest list was impressive. Any mobster of stature anywhere in the country attended. The crowd at the church was predominantly a mink-clad and bejeweled one, mostly elderly women. The reception which followed at the Villa Venice, near Wheeling, became what may have been the social function of the year. About 1,000 people attended the reception. Jack Cerone showed up in his flashy gray Chesterfield coat and topped it off with a gray derby. Joe Batters looked just like what he was, the handsome father of the bride in a cutaway coat, striped trousers and ascot. Linda Lee wore the traditional white, and was a lovely bride.

Although many members of the press and several law enforcement agencies sent their people to get photos and a list of the guests, I was not one of them. I guess my philosophy was always in keeping with the "family pact." Let the families alone when they are enjoying themselves in a non-mob-related function. I know there is a legitimate reason to determine just who is who in the structure of the Outfit, but I felt always that I'd just as soon let somebody else handle that. I wouldn't want mobsters hanging around the perimeter of any family function of mine, that's for sure. Neither Linda Lee nor Michael had any mob function. Mike was the nephew of a pal of Accardo's, Nick Palermo, a Melrose Park plumber.

Anybody who was anybody in the Chicago mob attended with their wives, their children and some with their girlfriends. Cerone. Paul Ricca. Murray Humphreys. Gussie Alex. Frank Ferraro. Sam Giancana. Fiore Buccieri. Caesar DiVarco. Dominick DiBella. Charley "Specs" Di Caro. Jimmy "The Bomber" Catuara. Jimmy "Monk" Allegretti. Joey Glimco. Louie Briatta. James "Cowboy" Mirro. Francis Curry. Sam "Rip" Alex. Sam Battaglia. Felix Alderisio. Chuckie Nicoletti. Eddy Vogel. Dominic Brancato. Lenny Patrick. James Caruso. Ralph Pierce. Skid Caruso. Les Kruse. Hy Godfrey. Dominic Blasi. Chuckie and Sam English. Sam Pardy. Joey Aiuppa. Joe Amato. Willie Daddano. Donald Angelini. Rocky Infelice. Dominic Cortina. Bill McGuire. Bill Kaplan. Pat Marcy. John D'Arco. Joe Laino. Johnny Roselli. Tony Pinelli. Johnny Lardino. John Matassa. Toots Palermo. Dominic Senese. Al Pilotto. Frank LaPorte. Vince Solano. Joe Lombardo. Tony Spilotro. Bobby Ansani. Angelo Volpe. Dominic Nuccio. Nathan "Butch" Ladon. Davey Yaras. Ross Prio. Rocco Fischetti. Joe Fischetti. Joe Ferriola. Lou Lederer. Frank Aulelli. Rocco Potenzo. Vince Inserro. Pat Manno. Johnny Formosa. Al Tocco. Frank Buccieri. Marshall Caifano. Rocco Prano. James Torello. Rocco DeGrazia.

If you weren't invited to this affair, you had better be worried. Your star wasn't on the ascendancy in the Outfit.

Not that these were the only hoods in attendance. All the members of the Commission were invited. Joe Bonanno was the only one who was not. Joe Batters had no love for Joe Bonanno, the boss of Brooklyn, who now lived in Tucson and ran his fiefdom by remote control, attempting in Accardo's mind to "plant a flag" in Arizona at the same time. But Carlo Gambino, Joe Columbo, Joe Profaci and Vito Genovese, the other New York Commissioners, were there. So were Joe Zerelli from Detroit and Angelo Bruno from Philadelphia. Raymond Patriarca from New England

John Scalise from Cleveland and John La Rocca from Pittsburgh. All Commissioners in 1961. Also coming in were Moe Dalitz from Las Vegas, Meyer Lansky and Frank Costello from New York, Santo Trafficante from Tampa, Carlos Marcello from New Orleans, Russell Buffalino from Scranton, Frank Bompensiero from San Diego and Nick LaCata from Los Angeles, Peanuts Smaldone from Denver, Nick and Carl Civella from Kansas City, Frank Balestreri from Milwaukee, Joe Sica from the San Fernando Valley, Vincent Alo (Jimmy Blue Eyes) from New York and Funzi Tieri of New York.

Joe Bonanno had put on a similar display in New York when his son Salvatore (Bill) married Rosali Profaci. This one in Chicago rivaled Bonanno's, which probably didn't escape the notice of Joe Batters. He was just vain enough to want to outdo Bonanno.

It certainly was a beautiful affair, probably Clarice's proudest moment. Marie Judith, Tony and Clarice's older daughter, had been married the year before. Marie was the bridesmaid to Linda Lee, and both daughters were lovely representatives of their family. Joe and Clarice had every reason to be happy with the way their four children had turned out. None had ever given them any reason not to be proud of them. Anthony Ross would be married to a former Miss Utah in the Miss America pageant. Neither he nor young Joseph has ever followed in their father's footsteps. Joseph left Chicago at an early age and has stayed away from the mob fringe. The only reason to look askance at Anthony Ross is his favored treatment in Local 110. He is now independently wealthy after hitting the Illinois State Lottery in the early Nineties for a couple million.

Marie attended Michigan State University in East Lansing, Michigan, and married a star Spartan football player, Palmer Pyle, of a high society family in Winnetka, the brother of Mike Pyle, one of the best Chicago Bears linemen of all time. They would have a son, Eric, and a daughter, Cheryl. Marie later divorced Pyle and married Ernie Kumerow, who became the president of the Laborer's Union in Chicago. He would adopt Eric and Cheryl and give them his last name. Eric Kumerow, as he was known, grew up to be one hell of a football player, taking after his heritage. He had the genes. First he starred at Oak Park-River Forest High School and then at Ohio State, where he teamed with Chris Spielman to give the Buckeyes just about the best linebacker corps in the college game.

In 1988 he was scheduled to graduate from OSU and eligible to

be drafted into the National Football League. At the time I was
working as a consultant to the NFL Director of Security, Warren R. Welsh, a former FBI agent. While in that capacity, I heard
a rumor. The league was considering whether it might blacklist
Eric Kumerow because of the identity of his grandfather. Not for
any other reason. The sins of the father might be visited on the
son—in this case, on the grandson. In the spirit of the family pact
I thought that would be all wrong. I gave my opinion, which I
thought might bear some weight, due to my particular background. On December 18, 1987, several months before the draft, I
wrote the following letter to Warren Welsh. (Since I believe it
conveys my true feelings about the situation and about Tony Accardo, I'll quote it here. I hope Antoinette Giancana will not be too
offended.)

Mr. Warren R. Welsh
Director of Security
National Football League
410 Park Ave.
New York, N.Y. 10022

Dear Warren:

   I know that George has given you the downside as to
this young man (Eric Kumerow). That he is Tony Accardo's grandson. But let me tell you this. I am probably the only law enforcement agent who got to know
Accardo. I'll not go into what you already know about
him, that's all very obvious. But there are two strik-
ing things about the man, perhaps three, that teams
thinking of drafting Kumerow should be aware of.
   Accardo has kept the Chicago outfit out of drugs.
Whereas other families of organized crime around the
country have in recent years failed to resist the big
temptation, because of the vast amounts of money involved, to deal narcotics, Chicago has not. In fact, involvement in narcotics in any way continues to be
reason for severe disciplinary action from the leadership should any member be caught. I know the FBI
won't tell you this, for the reason that a great deal of
their appropriation is now for the fight against drugs,
but it's true. And you won't read that in the newspapers. The point is, Accardo is the guy who has led

the fight inside the outfit to stay out of drugs in spite of tremendous pressure to get involved. I believe he deserves a lot of credit for that and the sad fact is, he probably won't get it except from me.

I have listened to Joe (he is called Joe Batters by his associates) on scores of occasions on our microphones during the late Fifties thru early and mid-Sixties. His has always been the voice of reason in the outfit. While others have advocated quick violence, Accardo would counsel caution and patience, looking toward a resolution by other means. He was always a calming influence on the rest of his people . . .

There is (another) factor which might be of more importance than any other in evaluating Kumerow's situation. Accardo has always been as fine a family man as there is in any strata of society. We've had many presidents who don't have the family values of Accardo. He has always been a completely faithful husband, a real oddity in his milieu. He has kept his sons out of the outfit. They have never been involved, even in the slightest, in mob business. I got to know one, although not well, when he was involved in a travel agency. He was a gentleman and a credit to any family. I have never met Accardo's daughter, Kumerow's mother, but I have every reason to believe she would be in the same mold as her brother and, for that matter, the rest of the family.

I guess what I am saying, Warren, is that I can understand the potential for a bad press in relation to Kumerow. But I don't think it has hurt the Ohio State program and, even tho' he has been a real name in Chicago high school and in college, it hasn't seemed to crop up to the disadvantage of his schools or the boy. And I feel virtually certain that the boy would never do anything to the detriment of his team, such as shaving points or dumping a game. In fact, I would strongly feel that if anybody would caution him to be the cleanest player in the NFL, it would be his grandfather. And it would be his grandfather who would take every measure in his power to insure that unclean influences were kept from the kid. I'm sure he has already. If I know Tony Accardo, that would be precisely the one thing that might lead him to violence.

I know the family relationship will come up as teams evaluate Kumerow. I only hope that my observations above might balance those evaluations in the cause of justice to the boy.

Fraternally,
Bill

cc: Paul Brown

I don't know if my letter had any real effect. I'm not even sure the NFL would have put a blacklist on young Eric, even if I had not written my letter to Welsh. But in any event, Eric Kumerow was drafted in 1988 in the first round. He was the sixteenth player selected, by the Miami Dolphins, coached by perhaps the most respected coach in the game, Don Shula. Eric's college teammate Spielman, who had gotten more glory at OSU, wasn't drafted until the second round. While Spielman went on to star with the Detroit Lions, even making the All-Pro team in 1994, Eric wasn't so fortunate. He suffered a serious injury early in his career. Even though he was later signed by his hometown Chicago Bears, he could never overcome that injury and left the game of football before he could make the mark I believe he was destined to make. It is too bad. The last I heard, he was operating a landscaping business in the western suburbs of Chicago. God bless him.

The reference to George in the first paragraph of my letter is to George Mandich, the NFL security representative in Chicago, a former FBI agent in Chicago and a good pal. George informed me that he had filed a report with the NFL regarding Eric Kumerow's parentage, along with a rundown on Accardo.

37 Luck and Exposure

Tony Accardo was lucky. Actually, I think the nickname Charley Luciano had, Lucky, should apply even more so to Tony. There haven't been many people in his tradition who remained as fortunate as Joe Batters. To do all the terrible things he did and never, ever to be punished for them, never even to spend one night in jail, seems incredible. To have killed so many, and to have so many others killed, and never get convicted for anything.

Tony's luck continued to hold in May of 1962, when he got off the hook once more. The tax court stated that the IRS effort to collect taxes from him for his share of the old Erie-Buffalo policy wheel was not viable. Their reasoning was something else. The court held that the wheel was really owned by Sam Purdy and Pat Manno and that Accardo had been hired "for the purpose of handling all promotional and public relations matters" for the racket "and further to act as consultant on such matters as may arise in the conduct of the business." If one reads the court's opinion, it is very clear that what the court was talking about was "protection." Tony didn't own Erie-Buffalo, he just made sure the mob got it and that it stayed in their control. Therefore, the court was saying, he didn't owe taxes on its income. Tony had put Purdy and Manno in as his fronts, to act in his behalf, and the income had been shared with him. But he didn't owe taxes on the profits. Nice work, if you can get it.

It was at this time that the second Foxhead 400 beer trial for tax fraud was in court. This time Tony's defense lasted just over two hours. He hardly bothered to put on a defense at all. There were none of the witnesses who had appeared at the first, claiming that they were sold beer by Tony or Jackie Cerone. The jury stayed out for a short time and came back with their acquittal. The government's years of effort to prove Tony's tax fraud had been wasted.

Virgil Peterson of the Crime Commission put it best. "I think it's a miscarriage of justice, but then he's been involved in so many other miscarriages of justice that this is just another notch in his gun. He can still look down on the government and law enforcement officials with contempt, just as he has for thirty years. Frankly, I'm not surprised at the outcome; this is the way these important cases seem to be turning out. It's getting more and more difficult to get a conviction that will run the gamut of the Appeals Courts." Then Pete added, "The irony of the second trial is that in the first trial he had all those phony defense witnesses that turned out sour and he was convicted. This time he put on no defense and is found not guilty."

Tony celebrated his victory by traveling to Hot Springs, Arkansas, with his constant companion Jackie Cerone and two other mob bosses, Sam "Teets" Battaglia and Ralph Pierce. Clarice, who had been in London, cut short her trip and joined the group there. Tony was never long out of her presence. Everything was fine, except that Pierce ran his golf cart into a tree and had to be hospitalized for a time. One of his people, Bill McGuire, had to fly to Hot Springs and escort him back to Chicago when he was well enough to travel.

In November the *Saturday Evening Post* ran a story about Tony by the finest investigative reporter of the day—and maybe any other day—Sandy Smith, who had been tracking Accardo for decades. The story was entitled "The Charmed Life of Tony Accardo." Sandy contrasted the fate of the two witnesses for Tony, Tom Lechos and Joe Nicoletti, who were spending their days in prison for perjuring themselves on behalf of Tony at his first tax fraud trial, with that of the defendant Tony Accardo, who was enjoying golf in Hot Springs and the good life.

Because of the publicity he was receiving, in 1963 Tony decided that his life was just too ostentatious. He was sticking out like a sore thumb, and he seemed to be disrespecting the authorities and the public. Joe decided he was too high-profile, and made arrangements to get out of that palatial palace, the twenty-two-room mansion which had become the showplace of the western suburbs of Chicagoland. First, he planned an auction of his household goods. He had intended to keep it quiet, but when Sandy Smith learned of it—from the little birdie who twirped in his ear now and again—he wrote an article about it, and Tony realized that it would be chaos. He cancelled the auction but did put the house up for sale. When it sold, for almost a million, he contracted with a guy named Sam Panveno, who called himself Van Corbin, to build another house in affluent River Forest, this one not nearly as large or obtrusive as the former. He moved in 1963 to 1407 North Ashland, a couple blocks southwest of North Avenue and Harlem Avenue. This was the house which was alluded to in the first chapter of this book, the burglary of which led to the torture and murder of eleven people.

In December 1963, shortly after he moved onto Ashland Avenue, he ran into some little problem with the police. Not to worry. He was stopped by the Oak Park Police, the suburb adjacent to River Forest, for doing forty in a thirty-mile-per-hour zone. He was happy to pay the $15 fine without fuss or argument.

Then Sandy Smith brought Joe some more unwanted attention. That same little birdie (who wore a Notre Dame ring on his right claw) sang a short little song to Sandy, and Sandy did it up in an article in the *Trib*. Sandy wrote that all mob contracts (killings) at this time were being approved by a "council" composed of Accardo, Giancana, Paul Ricca and Murray Humphreys. The story was based on our knowledge that whenever Giancana, as the day-to-day boss, decided that somebody had to be disciplined, it was necessary for him to first clear it with Joe Batters. Joe would then consult, sometimes down in the basement of his home on Ashland, where he had a large office with a huge desk and a conference table seating up to thirty conferees, with the wise old heads, Paul "The Waiter" Ricca and Hump. It was our intention just to let Tony know that, although he had moved from the lap of luxury into more modest digs, we hadn't lost track of him. Although he might not be in prison, where we wanted him to be, we were going to keep the spotlight on him. Sandy was not solely our tool in this regard. Our relationship with him was a two-way street. He had helped us when we started the Top Hood Program, and now that we had put Little Al and Shade and a couple of their brothers in place, we could pay back the debt we owed him. When we came across information that would be of interest to the public, and which would not compromise our source or our investigations in any way, we shared that information with Sandy in particular, but also with other fine media people in Chicago at the time, like Art Petacque of the *Sun Times*, Bob Weidrich of the *Trib*, and later with fine reporters like John O'Brien of the *Trib*; always Kup, the columnist with the *Sun Times*; and the O'Connors, Matt and Phil. Public exposure of the activity and personalities of mobsters is of considerable benefit to law enforcement because it influences legislators to pass bills and appropriate money, enabling police agencies to function efficiently. Since Tony Accardo had now slipped behind Giancana's shadow, with respect to the daily work of the Outfit, we recognized that he was still the power behind the throne. So we continued to leak information about him to those people in the media who had the background and knowledge to write an appropriate story. John Drummond of WBBM-TV and Chuck Goudie of Channel Seven also became favorites of the public, who thirsted for knowledge about mobsters. We tried to help quench that thirst.

It was at just about this time that Little Al let us in on another conversation. Gus Alex, code-named Slim in the mob, and my main target, had become very nervous due to the pressure we continually exerted on him. No hood enjoys being under the gun, so to speak. As it is, so many wind up as "trunk music," in the vernacular of the mob, or in the ground. That is one risk. The other, more prevalent if not as deadly, is law enforcement. Today more than ever, top mobsters constantly are winding up their lives in a federal prison. These two worries put stress on a guy. Most of them handle it. Some better than others, but most of them don't die of heart attacks or commit suicide. Gussie was one of the few who let the pressure get to him. Before 1957, when he had ascended to become the boss of the Loop, Gussie really enjoyed life. But when J. Edgar Hoover brought his FBI into the fight and we zeroed in on Slim as one of our top ten targets in Chicago, Gus didn't enjoy it anymore. I was on his tail almost constantly, and it got to him. He even put himself in a mental institution for a time, at Silver Hills in New Canaan, Connecticut, the same place where Ted Kennedy's wife, Joan, spent time. I remember Joe Batters conferring one day with Alex in front of Little Al in the tailor shop. "Slim, take it easy. Go away to the mountains like I do and chop wood. When I chop wood, I chop and chop and chop, and I don't think of nothin' until it's all chopped. Then I come back all cleaned out and I can go back to work again." It was a conversation we in the Bureau found ultimately gratifying. It meant that our work *was* making a difference.

Tony and Clarice liked to relax when they could, too. They soon discovered an area they liked even better than Florida, where they had kept their winter home in Surfside, or Bimini or Hot Springs. It was Palm Springs, California, in the Coachella Valley. They found they enjoyed the mountains and the sunshine even more than the ocean. They enjoyed the warmth in winter and could stand the heat of the summer better in Palm Springs than they could in Chicago. They began to spend more and more time there.

Then, in July 1965, Sandy Smith, assisted once more by the little birdies, did a huge exposé of the mob control of Las Vegas, for the Chicago *Sun-Times*, where he was now working. He focused on the *sine qua non* of the mob in Vegas, their ability to skim, the reason they were so interested in the first place. Sandy wrote that the mob was skimming six million dollars a year from the casinos they controlled. When Sandy reported that one of the prime recipients was Tony Accardo, the regulatory agency in Vegas, the Nevada Gaming Control Commission and its enforcement arm, the Gaming Control Board, the GCB, focused their attention on Tony. Now another agency would poke their noses into the affairs of Joe Batters. No rest for the wicked.

38 Las Vegas Redux

The following is from an FBI report by John Roberts, dated August 31, 1962, and captioned "Interstate Transportation of Stolen Funds from Nevada Gambling Casinos, Chicago field office file number 92-1238."

"The organized criminal element in Chicago area, headed by Tony Accardo, Gus Alex, Frank Ferraro, Sam Giancana, Murray Humphreys and Ross Prio, have been successful in obtaining interest and/or control in gambling casinos in Las Vegas, Nevada, namely the Desert Inn, the Stardust and the Riviera. Chicago group has dealt with John Drew, Stardust Hotel, Charles "Babe" Baron and John Roselli as entries into Las Vegas affairs. Eugene C. James (deceased) negotiated with Teamsters Funds for Murray Humphreys et al. in establishing control in those above-mentioned hotels. Nick

Civella, Kansas City hoodlum, used in these negotiations. Civella to get $6,000 per month for his part and James to get $1,000 per month. Accardo ably assisted Giancana in closing deal with Las Vegas people, who were led by Moe Dalitz and Morris Kleinman. Louis Lederer also utilized by Chicago group. Also utilizes Sidney Korshak as front and legal counsel."

This report featured much of the information we were receiving from Little Al, making it available to Agent Roberts, who was then disseminating it in the form of his report to the Las Vegas division. Las Vegas had not even been a field division when Mr. Hoover initiated the THP. It had been a "resident agency" reporting to the Salt Lake City Division. Now, however, it had more than enough work to be staffed by dozens of agents.

In the details of his report, John Roberts reported: "(Little Al) advised that the groundwork for these negotiations was laid a number of years ago by Tony Accardo and Paul De Lucia (Ricca's true name)."

John's report also reflected that the Chicago mob had utilized the services of Lou Lederer and Sidney R. Korshak. Lou would become a good friend of mine as the years rolled by. He was a Jewish man who had converted to Catholicism and sent his son to Notre Dame. When New York mob boss Frank Costello was shot in 1957, the police had found records of the Tropicana Hotel in his pockets. They were in the handwriting of Lederer, who was then fronting for the New York mob at the Trop. He later became the owner of record of a casino in Teheran, Iran, after Sam Giancana bribed the Shah for the right to open that casino. Korshak would be the mob's attorney for many years, up to the present time, although he is ill and now spends most of his time in Palm Springs. I remember one time when he placed Dinah Shore, a client of his, in a Las Vegas hotel other than one of those controlled by the Outfit. Hump really gave it to him then, as he told Gussie Alex in front of Al. "I told him who brought him up and when we told him to do something, he was to do it," Hump told Alex. I had several confrontations with Korshak, who was especially close to Alex.

Roberts' report also reflected that "there was no question as to who was dictating the terms regarding the negotiations in Las Vegas (the Stardust-Riviera-Desert Inn deal) and that the Chicago group was definitely the dominant factor." Also Hump, at one point, said that Moe Dalitz "did not have any authority and was not to be worried about." Maybe not by Hump and his pals, like Tony Accardo, but certainly by anyone else desiring to do business in Las Vegas.

John made clear in his report that the "names of the Chicago mobsters would never appear anywhere" indicating that they had any financial interest in the Stardust, Riviera or Desert Inn.

None of the books of these hotels would ever show that any monies from their profits went to the Outfit. Instead, the report showed, the Outfit obtained their income from "skimming" the tables and machines. Skimming is that procedure whereby money is taken en route from the tables to the counting room, or in the counting room itself, before the official count. In each casino there are dealers and stickmen, the lowest echelon of gaming employees. Then a pit boss who supervises the dealers (at the blackjack tables) and the stickmen (at the craps tables) in each of several "pits." Above him or her is a floorman, who has authority over several pit bosses. And over him is a shift manager, who is in charge of the casino during one of the three eight-hour shifts, twenty-four hours a day. Over the shift manager is the casino manager. Working along with the casino employees is the security staff. In order for the skim to operate, several of these employees, including the security people, must be involved. Skimming, at that time in Las Vegas, amounted to millions and millions of dollars per year.

I recently prepared a history of gaming in Las Vegas—"From Capo to Corporate"—for the autumn 1994 edition of the *Illinois Police and Sheriff's News*, the official publication of the Combined Counties Police Association of Illinois. It gives a crisp rundown on Las Vegas from the time gaming started there until the date of the publication. (See Appendix C.)

In 1983 we initiated the "VEGMON" caper—"Vegas money." The Las Vegas division had placed a bug in the executive offices of the Fremont Hotel. It was determined that the mob had set up a courier system whereby the skim was carried by messenger from Vegas to those mobs who had hidden "points" in certain mobbed-up hotels, including: the Stardust, Riviera, Desert Inn, Fremont, Marina, Hacienda; and later, the Sundance belonged to Chicago; the Tropicana belonged to Kansas City, answering to Chicago; the Dunes belonged to St. Louis, answering to Chicago; the Aladdin belonged to Detroit; the Sands, Circus Circus, the Frontier and the Flamingo belonged to New York. None of these hotels is mobbed-up today. All are now owned by legitimate interests, almost all by corporations. The deal, as the bug in the Fremont indicated, was for the skim from all of the above hotels to be taken weekly by courier to those mobs above who owned the "rights" to the points. In other words, if Detroit had ten points in the Aladdin, then they were entitled to ten percent of the skim from that hotel.

We found the prime courier to be Ida Devine, the wife of Irving "Niggy" Devine, a supplier of meat to various hotels and restaurants in Vegas. She traveled regularly by train to take the skim to those mobsters who were entitled to it. We followed her. When she came into Chicago, she was met by either George Bieber or Mike Brodkin, the partners in the notorious "B and B" law firm, which represented so many of the gamblers and hoods in Chicago. Bieber was especially close to Felix "Milwaukee Phil" Alderisio, the mob hitter, and Brodkin was socially and professionally close to Hump and to Gussie.

Either of those two "lawyers" would then escort Ida to the Ambassador East Hotel, where she spent the night after dining at the famous Chicago dining room, the Pump Room, located at the hotel. Never, when she left, did she carry the attaché case, probably packed with thousand-dollar bills, which she carried whenever she arrived at Union Station. She was escorted back to Union Station by either of the "B and B boys," en route sometimes to Miami to visit Lansky, sometimes to New York to visit Costello, sometimes to Cleveland to visit John Scalisi and sometimes to Detroit to visit Joe Zerelli.

For years the Chicago Outfit had been represented in the West by Johnny Roselli. Al Capone had sent him to Los Angeles to oversee his interests there. When Bugsy Siegel began construction of the Flamingo in 1943 and completed it in 1946, Roselli's responsibilities for the Chicago mob were expanded to include Nevada. In the late Fifties, Accardo had counseled Giancana that another strong hand was needed there. By 1971 Tony "The Ant" Spilotro had been sent there, until in 1986, when he was "put in the ground," killed by burying him alive in a northern Indiana cornfield. Donald Angelini would replace Spilotro until he was convicted in San Diego in 1992. All "Mr. Outsides" whose job was to enforce the edicts of Accardo and Giancana in the Sin Capital.

The biggest contribution the Chicago mob made to the casinos, however, came from their "bank." In 1959 the Teamsters had set up their pension fund; from then on, the Chicago Outfit influenced loans from it to the high-risk hotel-casinos in Nevada. Nick Pileggi, a good friend and author of *Wiseguy*,

which became the movie entitled *Goodfellas*, told me that
when he first conceived of writing his latest book, *Casino*,
which is now also a movie, he was thinking of New York. "Lansky, Bugsy, Costello. They were the people I conjectured about
then. But as I got into it, I soon discovered that it was Tony Accardo and the Chicago mob who really made Las Vegas what it
became." I agree, with the caveat that it was the Chicago mob
under the direction of Accardo, but implemented by guys like
Hump, Korshak, Roselli, Giancana, Caifano, Angelini, Lefty
Rosenthal, Tony "The Ant" Spilotro and the people Tony counseled, not so much by his efforts on the scene itself. I don't
know that Tony spent a lot of time in Vegas. He was most interested in keeping a low profile as much as possible, and probably didn't feel he had to be on the scene to direct his interests
there. I also don't believe Clarice felt that the ambience of Las
Vegas, especially in the Fifties and Sixties, was what she was
interested in.

One thing is certain. Las Vegas was always a risky spot in the
desert for those people whom the mob sent out there to handle
their lucrative business. Witness Johnny Roselli, who ended up
in a drum at the bottom of the ocean off the coast of Florida. Or
Marshall Caifano, who was sent to prison and who ultimately
was given the most menial tasks in the mob as punishment. Or
Tony "The Ant" Spilotro, who was found in the bottom of a
grave in a cornfield in northern Indiana. The coroner could not
determine whether he had died from suffocation because he
had swallowed his own blood from the beating in the face he
took, or because he had been buried alive. Whatever the case,
Tony Accardo had to make some tough decisions about how to
handle them.

39 Giancana

In the Sixties we had some more success in our penetration of strategic mob places, especially at Giancana's headquarters at the Armory Lounge. In the mornings and afternoons Giancana trekked the ten or twelve miles from his house at 1147 South Wenonah, at the corner of Fillmore, in Oak Park, to meet with his underlings on Michigan Avenue, on the near north side of Chicago, but his evening meets were regularly held at the Armory Lounge, near his home.

We decided to bug it. This time my partners, Joe Shea, Ralph Hill and Marshall Rutland, would have the ticket. I helped, but it was their assignment. They were perhaps the sharpest agents I ever had the honor of working with. What they did to gain entry to the Armory was to wait until the janitor there got off work at about 2:00 one morning. They grabbed him and shoved a "wanted flyer," a poster of a fugitive wanted by the FBI, in front of him. The picture resembled the janitor. "We have to take you downtown," they told him. When they did, they told him to empty his pockets, including the keys to the Armory, so they could take him to be fingerprinted and photographed. While he was out of the room, copies of the keys were made. Thereafter, we had access to the Armory. Ralph was the first one in on those entries as we again made a penetration under the same circumstance that Mr. Hoover had ordered for the entries into the tailor shop and the First Ward.

We knew that "Mo," the mob code name for Giancana, had a back room on the north side of the restaurant-bar, which he had exclusive access to. That's where he held his meetings, and that's where we put our mike. We code-named it, for obvious reasons, "Mo." After several penetrations, we finally got it operational on August 8, 1961. From that day on, except on a few days when thunderstorms knocked "Mo" out and we had to go in and fix him back up, we had Giancana in our pocket. We knew his every move—when he was in town, at least—whether he was talking in front of Al or Mo.

I remember one of the more interesting times. A thug named Rocky DeGrazia, with the help of two others, had beaten up one of our finest agents. Three of us were sent out to teach Rocky that this was unacceptable, and we did. I then sent word to Giancana through a contact I made with Ralph Pierce, the boss of the South Side for the Outfit. I told Ralph to inform Giancana that we had engaged in "retribution in kind" after DeGrazia had initiated the action, and that would forever be our response to any such incident. Frankly, I would have enjoyed telling that to Giancana himself, but I didn't want him to realize we knew where he headquartered. We wanted him to believe he was perfectly secure. It was the same procedure we used at the tailor shop and every other location which we had penetrated with a mike. Ralph Pierce took my message to Giancana immediately. Giancana, who by that time had had other up close and personal confrontations with me, exploded. He referred to me using obscenities I won't repeat here, then said: "I've had enough of that guy. I'm putting up a fund of $100,000 to figure out how to get that guy!"

Not to worry. When Tony Accardo was informed of Giancana's plan, he immediately vetoed it. "That would be counterproductive," he told Giancana. "The whole FBI would come down on us from all over the country if we hit one of them. Call it off. Now."

It may be that episodes like that concentrate my mind on why I have always had a much higher regard for Tony Accardo than I did for Sam Giancana.

I guess the reason Giancana was quick to want to chop me was the nature of our relationship. The first time I ever met him, we tangled. Verbally, not physically, but somewhat forcibly nevertheless—and we did touch each other, not either of us to harm the other, but to reinforce our points.

On July 12, 1961, just a month or so before we planted Mo, Giancana had arrived at O'Hare Airport in Chicago with his mistress at the time, Phyllis McGuire. At this point we had made no effort to do anything which might damage her career or that of her sisters. They were major stars in the entertainment world at this time. We had, however, devised a strategy to elicit her cooperation. We planned to serve a subpoena on her, calling for her appearance the next day before the federal grand jury in Chicago. But while serving the subpoena on her privately, in a room at O'Hare for which

I had made arrangements, she would be advised by the two agents who would interview her, Vince Inserra and Johnny Bassett, that if she agreed to cooperate with us in the future by informing us about Giancana's activities, we would withdraw the subpoena. There were five of us assigned to this project. In addition to Bassett and Inserra, Harold Sell, our current supervisor, would be present to observe, and Ralph Hill would conduct an interview of Giancana, who would be arriving on the plane with McGuire from Phoenix. I would assist Ralph and, in addition, use my presence to prevent Giancana from interfering with the interview which would simultaneously be taking place with Phyllis. It was expected that, as a Marine Corps boxing champ and a Notre Dame heavyweight champ, I might be able to handle the likes of the punk that Giancana was.

That is the background for the FD 302, the interview form dated July 18, 1961, that Ralph Hill and I dictated the next day and sent to Mr. Hoover. I should tell you up front that it does not tell the whole story of what happened that evening. But here it is, verbatim, for the first time anywhere.

FEDERAL BUREAU OF INVESTIGATION
Date *July 18, 1961*

SAMUEL GIANCANA was interviewed at the O'Hare International Airport, commencing at 7:10 p.m. as he departed from American Airlines Flight 66, arriving from Phoenix, Arizona. GIANCANA was a passenger on this flight under the name of MOONEY CECOLA.

GIANCANA was approached by the Bureau Agents as he departed from the Airline. He brushed off the attempts of the Agents to identify themselves and stated that he was well aware of the fact that the Agents were representatives of the FBI. He stated that he had absolutely nothing to say to the Agents. From the very outset and throughout the interview, GIANCANA was alternately obscene, abusive and sarcastic. At no time did he exhibit a friendly or cooperative attitude.

He asked relative to the reason for the interview and at this point was questioned concerning his knowledge of the wire tapping of the hotel room of DAN ROWAN in Las Vegas. GIANCANA replied that he had absolutely no comment and had absolutely nothing to say. He refused to admit that he is acquainted with the identity of ROWAN and repeatedly refused any comment concerning that situation. When asked whether he was acquainted with ROBERT MAHEU, GIANCANA very belligerently refused to make any comment or to indicate in any manner that he was aware of the identity of MAHEU.

GIANCANA became very abusive and obscene and very heatedly advised that he was well aware of the FBI's investigations of him. He stated that he is aware of the identity of SA RALPH HILL and aware of the fact that SA HILL has talked to numerous girlfriends, relatives and other associates of his.

At this point, GIANCANA requested the Agents to move away from him and leave him alone. It was pointed out to him that he was in the public waiting room of American Airlines and that the Agents had every right to be situated where they were. It was pointed out to GIANCANA that he was not under arrest and that the FBI had no interest in detaining him. It was made clear to him that he had every opportunity to leave his present location and that the FBI had absolutely no objections to him reboarding his airplane en route to New York. It was pointed out to him that as far as the Agents were concerned there was absolutely no reason for his presence in Chicago and there was no objection to him leaving without plans to return.

At this point in the conversation, GIANCANA created a disturbance by accusing passengers who had disembarked from American Airlines Flight 66 of being FBI Agents.

At this point, GIANCANA requested the identity of SA WILLIAM F. ROEMER, JR., and when told, advised he was well aware of SA ROEMER's identity. When it was pointed out to him that this seemed to be unusual, since SA ROEMER has not been concerned with investigations of GIANCANA, GIANCANA replied that he was aware of this and was also aware of the individuals whom SA ROEMER had been investigating. He also advised that he is aware of the fact that SA ROEMER is a "member of the Bar."

At this point, GIANCANA became very curious concerning PHYLISS MC GUIRE. He attempted to locate her but was unable to do so. He thereupon became very abusive and obscene, commenting that it is a sad situation when the government interferes with the normal relationship between a man and his girlfriend. He accused the Agents of taking Miss MC GUIRE away from him without her consent. He was advised that Miss MC GUIRE made absolutely no objection to leaving him and conversing with other Agents.

At this point, GIANCANA asked the Agents if they had ascertained how many men he had killed. GIANCANA was asked if he could furnish the Agents information in that regard and said that he could not remember; however, he thought he might have to be responsible for a killing shortly, looking at the Agents while making the threat. He was asked if that remark was a threat to the Agents and denied making any threats and said that it was not a threat.

GIANCANA referred again to investigations being conducted regarding his activities and made a remark "my sister-in-law told me all about you, HILL, and about the threats which you made if she refused to furnish information. She also told me that you told her that I had killed thirteen men." The Agent emphatically denied the above remark by GIANCANA and asked him if he was referring to an interview conducted of Mrs. ROSE FLOOD, a sister-in-law of GIANCANA. GIANCANA shrugged his shoulders and merely replied, "don't worry, I have it all down in writing."

At that point, GIANCANA then presented his ticket, and announced in a loud voice in the presence of everyone in the waiting room of American Airlines that he was "going to get the hell out of here and go to Cuba." GIANCANA thereupon reboarded American Airlines Flight 66 en route to New York City.

After approximately five minutes, when it apparently became obvious to GIANCANA that Miss MC GUIRE was not aboard the airline and apparently did not intend to board, GIANCANA again disembarked from the airline. He approached the Agents, again in the waiting room of American Airlines and in a loud voice again became very abusive and obscene concerning his inconveniences and the fact that Miss MC GUIRE had separated herself from him. He stated that the United States Government had lost all its fineness and that "American citizens might as well be in Russia" due to the treatment which he was receiving. It was again pointed out to GIANCANA that the Agents had no desire that he remain in Chicago and would be very happy if he remained on Flight 66 en route to New York City. It was again pointed out to him that he was not under arrest and the FBI had no interest in detaining him and he was free to come and go as he pleased.

GIANCANA again remarked, "This country is getting just like Russia where a man is not free to escort a young lady where he pleases. Why don't you investigate these dope fiends." He was asked if that remark implied that he had information relating to narcotics and his reply to that question was "Why aren't you investigating the Communists." GIANCANA was asked if he was dissatisfied with this country and replied, "I love this country and I would sacrifice my life for it." He said, "I proved this not long ago." He was asked to clarify the last remark and he refused to comment.

GIANCANA then sarcastically asked the Agents if they had found out that he owned 25 per cent of Marshall Fields, 20 per cent of Carsons, and 20 per cent of Goldblatts Department store to which the Agents asked if this were a statement on his part and he replied, "Yes, I own all of these places," again in a sarcastic manner. He was asked if he had any interest in Las Vegas, Nevada, and he stated that "I own 99 per cent of Las Vegas." GIANCANA then sneeringly asked what the Agents desired to know and invited a question about his activities. The question then put to him was if he would confirm the allegations that he was the head of organized criminal activity in Chicago. He replied, "I'm not the head of anything and I don't know what you are talking about." After making this remark, GIANCANA uttered a few more obscenities.

GIANCANA then stated, "If you want to talk to me, give me a subpoena and I will appear before the Grand Jury and answer any and every question put to me." He was asked if he meant by this that he would answer every question truthfully or if this meant that he would stand on his Constitutional guarantee of the 5th Amendment. He replied, "That all depends on the question."

GIANCANA advised the Agents that he was aware of the fact that the FBI would make every attempt to "frame" him into the penitentiary, at which point the Agents advised GIANCANA the FBI conducts its investigations in an impersonal, unbiased manner and that the history of this organization is not that of "framing" anyone and this is certainly not the intention or the purpose of this investigation. GIANCANA then referred to his prison sentences, stating, "If I go to the penitentiary this time, I'll go like a man just like I did the other time and you know what I'm talking about." The Agents stated that they did not know what he was talking about and he replied, "I went like a man then even though I was a victim of circumstances." He was asked how he was a victim of circumstances in the instances where he had been given jail terms and he refused to comment further about how he was victimized.

GIANCANA was asked if he was acquainted with JOHN D'ARCO, an Alderman of the First Ward of Chicago. At this point, GIANCANA said who's D'ARCO. It was pointed out to GIANCANA that Mr. D'ARCO had commented at one time recently that he was acquainted with Mr. GIANCANA and knew him well. At that point, GIANCANA directed an obscene remark to Mr. D'ARCO and requested the Agents to pass on the obscenity to Mr. D'ARCO. He was asked if he knew MURRAY HUMPHREYS and he stated he did not know MURRAY

HUMPHREYS. He was asked if he knew GUS ALEX and he replied, "No, I don't know GUS ALEX. Do you think I know everyone in the world?"

GIANCANA then indicated that he was aware that the Agents intended to report the results of this interview of him to their "boss," who in turn would report the results to their "super boss," who would thereupon report to his "super super boss." He was asked to whom he was referring to as "boss," "super boss," and "super super boss" and he said, "You know who I mean, I mean the KENNEDYs." He then said, "I know all about the KENNEDYs and PHYLISS (McGUIRE) knows a lot more about the KENNEDYs and one of these days we are going to tell all." When asked for clarification of his comments in this regard, GIANCANA uttered an obscenity and refused further comment.

GIANCANA then made a reference to ADLAI STEVENSON and vaguely criticized his conduct in office and the manner in which he has involved the United States in the Cuban situation. When asked for clarification in this regard, GIANCANA stated that he has knowledge that STEVENSON directed *that mess in Cuba* and stated that STEVENSON is a "book worm" who has no common sense.

GIANCANA then advised that the United States Government is not as smart as it would like to think it is. He stated that he knows that the United States Government made a deal with FIDEL CASTRO during the BATISTA Regime to furnish support to CASTRO and assist him in his ascent to power in Cuba on the condition that when CASTRO came into power he would eliminate gambling in Cuba. GIANCANA stated, "now that deal has boomeranged on you, hasn't it." When it was mentioned to GIANCANA that at least one good effect of the above situation might have taken place in that his interests in Cuba were destroyed, GIANCANA then became very emotional and abusive and commented that he had never been in Cuba and had no interest in Cuba. When asked whether the individuals who ran gambling in Cuba during the BATISTA Regime were subordinates, GIANCANA refused to comment.

At this point, GIANCANA advised that it is his firm belief that he is being "persecuted" due to the fact that he is a member of the Italian nationality. When it was pointed out to him that the investigations by the FBI of MURRAY HUMPHREYS and GUS ALEX have been pursued just as vigorously as the investigation of him and that HUMPHREYS and ALEX are not Italians, GIANCANA then uttered a string of obscenities and indicated that by far the majority of the individuals investigated by the United States Government were of Italian descent. He pointed out that it was his opinion that the FBI "not only prosecutes but persecutes Italians." When asked for specifics concerning what he intended to indicate by this comment, GIANCANA again referred to the fact that he was not being allowed to associate with his girlfriends in a normal fashion. It was pointed out to GIANCANA again that Miss MC GUIRE accompanied other Agents for a purpose of interview entirely under her own volition.

On more than one occasion during the interview, GIANCANA advised that he did not intend to "take this thing sitting down." He very heatedly stated: "I'm going to light a fire under you guys and don't forget that." When asked for clarification of his comments, GIANCANA refused any further comment. When asked how he enjoyed his recent visit to Florida, GIANCANA very sarcastically said, "Yes, I have been to Florida and I own the Fontainbleau, The Americana, and The Diplomat." When asked whether it was true that he owned the Eden Roc, GIANCANA sarcastically affirmed the Eden Roc also.

When requested whether he would desire that the Agents telephonically contact one BUTCH BLASI in order to provide him transportation from the airport, GIANCANA replied, "Yes, call Butch and tell him to bring two shotguns with him." When asked whether he intended that remark as a threat to the Agents, GIANCANA replied that he did not.

GIANCANA facetiously referred to the fact that in
Russia if you commit a crime they merely shoot you
rather than send you to prison. His next comment was
that "I think I will kill myself. Why don't you give me a
pistol so I can do this?" GIANCANA made remarks
throughout the interview to the effect that he was going to kill himself. Regarding his general health, GIAN-
CANA remarked that he "had a cancer"; however, he
did not elaborate on this and stated, "If you want to find
out any more about my health, see my doctor." When
asked as to the identity of the doctor, he refused to disclose his identity.

On frequent intervals during the conversation with
GIANCANA, it was pointed out to him that he was not
under arrest and that the FBI had no intention of
detaining him. It was pointed out to him that the FBI
did not desire to harass him or any of his associates
and that he was entirely free to leave the area at his
desire. It was also pointed out to him that he was
under absolutely no obligation to converse with the
Agents and that his Constitutional privileges were
fully guaranteed.

GIANCANA frequently during the conversation proclaimed in a loud voice scattered with obscenities "get
away from me, you (obscene), and quit bothering me. I
don't want to talk to you." At each such instance, it was
pointed out to GIANCANA that he was free to leave at
any time, that he was in a public place and that he was
not by any means being detained.

The conversation was terminated upon the appearance of Miss PHYLISS MC GUIRE whom GIANCANA
had previously referred to during the conversation as
"the Mrs." He was asked if he was married to Miss MC
GUIRE and he said sarcastically, "I married her a long
time ago." Upon Miss MC GUIRE's appearance, GIAN-
CANA stated to her in a loud and clear voice, "Why
didn't you tell them to go to hell like I did."
GIANCANA, accompanied by Miss MC GUIRE, then left
the interviewing Agents.

On 7/12/61 at O'Hare Airport   File # CG 139-105
                    Chicago, Illinois   CG 92-349

by SAs RALPH R. HILL and WILLIAM F.
ROEMER JR. Date dictated 7/13/61

That pretty much captures what happened that evening. I say
pretty much because Ralph and I didn't put down *everything* that
happened in our 302. The reason we didn't—and I thank Ralph for
it—was because if we did, I would have been in deep trouble. I hate
to have to admit I was devious in our report to Mr. Hoover, but it
must be understood that Mr. Hoover, believe it or not, was a stickler
for civil rights. We were constantly cautioned not to violate the civil
rights even of mobsters. The part we did not include is as follows.

Giancana had called me many obscene names, not just four-
letter ones, but others I had come to recognize from my Marine
Corps days. Finally I lost my cool.

"Take a look at this piece of garbage!" I shouted to passengers
at the "H" concourse at O'Hare who were arriving or leaving the
airport. "This piece of scum! You people are lucky you're just
passing through Chicago. But we have to live with this slime. This
is Sam Giancana, the boss of the underworld here. Take a good
look at this jerk!"

Then Sam really lost it. He replied in kind, moving up close to
me, pounding his dirty little finger into my chest. "You lit a fire
tonight, Roemer, that will never go out. We'll get you if it's the
last thing we ever do!"

That exchange set the stage for numerous other confrontations
with Tony Accardo's man. Any contacts I ever had with Joe Batters were civil. Only the very last one of some fifty with Giancana
would be.

Soon we forced Tony Accardo to make another choice. We lock-
stepped his guy Giancana, staying right in step with him as he
moved around the city during the summer of 1963. Even if he
went golfing, we stayed with him. I was in charge of the surveillances on the street that summer, and we had many angry words
with each other. Even when he urinated in public restrooms, I was
right there in the next urinal. And, unlike the time I was in a similar situation with Joe Batters, those pit stops were not friendly, to
say the least. Then Giancana started aiming his cameras at us. The
other agents on the tail were smart; I was not. "Screw you," I
shouted, "take my picture. Show it to all your guys. Screw you!"

Giancana, at least in this instance, was smarter than me. He took those pictures to court. He submitted to Judge Richard Austin that we were violating his civil rights by hounding him so close. He showed Judge Austin—no friend of ours—the pictures, and his attorney put my boss, Marlin Johnson, on the stand. "Is this Roemer, does he work for you? Did you send him out to do this? Was he authorized?" Johnson had been instructed by Bobby Kennedy, the Attorney General, who had jurisdiction over the FBI, not to respond to questions, since it was RFK's theory that the judicial had no supervisory jurisdiction over the executive branch of the government. Johnson was held in contempt and fined, his voting privileges stripped from him. He let me know in subtle ways that he was not my biggest fan.

Giancana had done something no other plaintiff had ever done. Judge Austin, in his supreme wisdom, granted the injunction, instructing us to stay a block from Giancana at all times. That made it very difficult to effectively stay with him. He lost us quickly and often after that.

Tony Accardo at this time had let Giancana have his head. What was there to lose? I don't believe he thought Giancana had a prayer of winning—none of us did—but when he did, Giancana became cocky as hell. He had, after all, done something no other mobster anywhere at any time had done. He had taken on the FBI and won. Now he became, at least in his own mind, his own man. To hell, he thought, with Tony Accardo. "I'm the boss of this Outfit, fuck anybody else." That is the impression we got from listening to his victory dance in front of Mo. Giancana, never a blushing violet, was bursting his buttons. Oh, how he gloated. And oh, how I was embarrassed. If I hadn't been so proud, if I had handled the situation a little more tactfully, if I had ducked, like my smarter fellow agents, when he aimed his camera at me, then maybe it wouldn't have come down to this. My star wasn't shining brightly in the front office, in Harold Sell's office on C-1, or back in Washington, let me tell you that. I know there was scuttlebutt that I would be transferred and maybe not just off the squad, maybe to Butte on a disciplinary. As tough as Mr. Hoover was in those days, it would not have been surprising. The FBI was embarrassed and that was the cardinal sin in Mr. Hoover's FBI. "Don't ever do anything to embarrass the Bureau!" That was his dictate. I sure had. On the other hand, my motto in life is "Keep Punchin' and Keep the Faith!" I resolved to remember it that summer. It was several weeks before I became convinced that I would be left to do the job I relished—to battle the Chicago mob. But it was touch and go for a while that summer. I never received a letter of censure, but if ever I deserved one, it was for my performance on "lockstep" in the summer of 1963.

There was one incident that summer, however, that I did enjoy. Marshall Rutland and I were lockstepping Giancana as best we could one Saturday night, and although we didn't want to, we followed him to the Armory Lounge. We were amazed he would take us there, since he had always made a great effort to make sure we did not discover his headquarters. Maz and I soon found out why—he had loaded the place with his men and they came after the two of us when we entered. We shouted back and forth for a couple hours with the toughest guys in the Outfit. Killers.

When we had talked our way out of there, I got into my car and Maz into his, and we sat waiting for Giancana to leave. That was when Chuckie English ran up to me. Chuckie was, with Butch Blasi, the closest to Giancana, his pal. Chuckie had a message for me: "Sam says to tell you, if Kennedy wants to sit down with him, he knows who to go through." I immediately put two and two together and said, "Frank Sinatra?" English hesitated. He had not been instructed to identify the intermediary with John Kennedy— or did he mean Bobby? Then he said simply, "You said it." I got on the radio, told Maz about it and then we waited until the Armory closed and followed Giancana when he left to travel the mile or so to his house.

All well and good, I did a report on the evening and went home myself. Then a couple of days later, I transcribed a conversation we had picked up on another installation we had made, on which I had served as the case agent. This one was on the condo of Murray Humphreys on the fifty-first floor of Marina City, the high-rise apartment building on the north side of the Chicago River, just north of the Loop:

"So help me, God, I'm about to jump out your fucking window!" It was Giancana's underboss, Frank "Strongy" Ferraro, talking before the bug we had code-named "Plumb."

"What's wrong?" asked Hump.

"That fucking Giancana, wait until you hear what he's done now. I tell you, those guys are driving him goofy. He's not making good decisions."

"What happened?" Hump asked again.

"Saturday night, Roemer and Rutland, they're on Giancana. He takes them to the Armory. They get in a fucking shouting match with Roemer and Rutland. Whole bunch of our guys and Roemer and Rutland. When it's all over, Giancana sends Charley McCarthy out to see Roemer. What do you think he told Roemer?"

"What?" Hump asked, obviously not understanding most of this.

"Charley McCarthy told Roemer that Mo told him to tell Kennedy that if he wants to talk, he's to go through Sinatra!"

"For Christ sakes, that's a cardinal rule!" Hump yelled. "You don't give up a legit guy! He tells Roemer that Sinatra is our guy to Kennedy?"

"More or less, for Christ's sake," Ferraro replied. "I'm so fucking mad, I could jump out your fucking window!"

Ferraro's reference to "Charley McCarthy" was to English, who was considered to be Giancana's puppet.

The pair then discussed what they should do about this violation of mob rules in disclosing the identity of a most important contact.

"We got to do something about this," the underboss, Giancana's top aide, stated. "The 'G' is driving this man goofy. He's not right. He's making mistakes. He don't belong in that spot if the pressure gets to him like this."

Hump was in complete agreement. "I think this has got to be brought to the attention of Joe and Paul. They've got to know the condition of the man's mind."

That was exactly what we believe took place. Ferraro, instead of jumping out Hump's fifty-first-floor window, went with Hump to see Tony Accardo and Paul Ricca. They gave J.B. the benefit of their information and let him decide what to do about "the condition of the man's mind."

That was the beginning of the end for Giancana. When Ferraro and Humphreys furnished Accardo, and perhaps Ricca, with the circumstances of what Ferraro had learned—from Butch Blasi, incidentally—Joe Batters began to have doubts about the man he had put in place when he stepped aside. Joe had instructed one and all to keep their heads down. Now Giancana, like Capone, had gotten much too overconfident, too arrogant, too big.

We were now about to force Accardo's hand. Soon he would have no choice.

40 One More— And Then None

Tony Accardo continued to be pleased with the manner in which the "connection guys" were doing their business.

At this time Hump was in charge, as he had been since Greasy Thumb Guzik died in 1956 at St. Hubert's Olde English Grill. By the early Sixties, he was in full stride, heading what we always called the Corruption Squad because that seemed to better define their function to corrupt those public officials, like judges, cops, labor leaders and even legitimate businessmen, who could be influenced to provide favorable treatment to the mob.

Hump had a great crew of people. His top aide in the connection guys was Gussie Alex. Along with Gussie, he had Giancana's underboss, Frank "Strongy" Ferraro, Ralph Pierce, Les Kruse and Hy Godfrey. Alex was the boss of the Loop, in addition to his duties on the connection squad; Pierce had the south side, and Kruse had Lake County, the county north of Cook. They were all sharp guys, very capable of doing what they did.

Accardo depended on them. No family of organized crime can function without corrupting those people they need to protect them from enforcement of the laws and to facilitate their illicit endeavors. Although not technically a member of the connection guys, Giancana worked on this area also. As the boss, he had the authority to make deals and to dispense money.

At about this time, Little Al let us in on quite a little situation. Ben Adamowski was running for reelection as the Cook County State's Attorney, the top prosecutor on a local level of the laws, such as those against gambling and loan-sharking. The position was, therefore, of prime interest to the Outfit. Adamowski was the incumbent. While in office, such as during the Summerdale scandal, when he had developed and protected Richie Morrison, the "babbling burglar," as a witness, the Outfit had had no use for him

235

and had fought him. But now he was running against Dan Ward, a highly qualified man whom the Outfit perceived would be more trouble for them than Adamowski.

Hump put Gussie in charge of this caper. One day Mike Brodkin and Slim, as Alex was code-named in the Outfit, conferred at Celano's. Brodkin, the mouthpiece of the mob, who, with his partner George Bieber, was, in our opinion, merely an extension of the connection guys. They were involved in corruption of judges and cops almost to the extent that Hump and his pals were. Most FBI agents and other law enforcement agents felt that the B and B boys, as they were known, personified criminal defense attorneys, the operational word in their description being "criminal," that they, many times, are nothing but part and parcel of the group of people they represent. I personally never felt that way. I recognize that even the most heinous criminal is entitled to the best defense he can get. Some courts feel otherwise, and when it can be demonstrated that the defense team is, in fact, working hand in glove with its client, the defense will be disciplined. Witness the flamboyant New York attorney Bruce Cutler, who has handled the defense of mobsters all over the country, such as in Chicago and San Diego. He revels in the fact that he "brucified" government witnesses. The New York office of the FBI placed a bug in the headquarters of John Gotti in the Eighties and Cutler was frequently overheard conferring there with Gotti when Gotti was the boss of the Gambino family of La Cosa Nostra—just as Brodkin had done at Celano's, the mob headquarters in Chicago. When Gotti was indicted in New York, he called on Cutler to defend him. The FBI in New York objected, citing the conversations on the bug at Gotti's headquarters, the Ravenite Social Club on Mulberry Street, in the Little Italy section of lower Manhattan. When the judge assigned to the Gotti case reviewed the transcripts of those conversations, he ruled that Cutler should be precluded from defending Gotti.

We had the same situation. Here was Mike Brodkin conspiring with Gus Alex to bribe a prosecutor, Adamowski. Brodkin had a contact with a person very close to Adamowski, who could possibly act in Adamowski's behalf. Alex—while Little Al behind the radiator was all ears—instructed Brodkin to sit down with this friend of Adamowski and deliver to him an envelope containing $20,000. Alex told Brodkin that he was to tell this man that "this is from Sam."

A couple days later, Brodkin reappeared before Little Al and again conferred with Alex. He told him that the man had refused to accept the envelope. When Alex became surprised, Brodkin told him the man had wanted more information on precisely what conditions were to be set, not just that "it was from Sam" Giancana.

I want to make it clear that we heard nothing further about this situation. If there was any further discussion, it did not take place within earshot of Little Al. Therefore, there is no indication that Adamowski ever accepted any money, did anything on behalf of the Outfit or even knew about the above situation, only that the Outfit would have liked to corrupt him. It is merely an example of the methods used by these connection guys.

No report of the activities of the connection guys would be complete, however, without reference to the masters of that game, the functionaries of the Regular Democratic Organization of the First Ward. I testified before the U.S. Senate Permanent Subcommittee on Investigations that this organization was "the conduit through which the orders of the Chicago mob were passed to those public officials who were corrupt." My testimony was in 1983, but it could have been 1893 or 1923 or 1943 or 1973. This was the ward of Hinky Dink Kenna and Bathhouse John Coughlin. It was as corrupt in 1963 as it had been in the days of The Hink and The Bath.

The alderman and ward committeeman was John D'Arco. He was just a figurehead, however. The real power behind the throne in the First Ward was Pasquale Marchone, better known as Pat Marcy. Marcy was a "made" guy, an actual member of the Chicago Outfit, who had been placed inside the headquarters of the Regular Democratic Organization of the First Ward as D'Arco's "administrative assistant." That was his title, but it was not his function. D'Arco marched to *Marcy's* orders.

At this time we had three great elsurs in place: Little Al in the general headquarters of the mob; Mo in the headquarters of the mob boss, Giancana; Plumb in the residence of Murray Humphreys, the leader of the connection guys. We felt we needed at least one more bug to perfect out coverage of the Chicago mob. We had become the best Criminal Intelligence Program Squad in the entire FBI—at least this is what we were being told by the supervisors back at Seat of Government in Washington. We were receiving so much information from these three bugs, we couldn't transcribe it all. There were only three agents doing that job— Ralph Hill, Marshall Rutland and myself. We had to be very selective about what we took off our tapes and made a matter of record, especially since we had other duties at the same time. We spent much of our time, maybe most of our time, out on the street investigating our targets. And we had about twenty targets assigned to each of us at this time, twenty subjects to be reported on regularly.

Our tremendous workload notwithstanding, we did feel that there was one more penetration just crying to be consummated. Hill, Rutland and I knew full well that we couldn't consider that we had blanketed the Chicago Outfit with listening devices, the ultimate method of determining what they were doing, until we had one inside the headquarters of the First Ward. (I should say that when I refer to "First Ward," I refer to the Democratic headquarters. There was also a Republican headquarters of the First Ward, headed by a guy not much better than D'Arco or Marcy, Pete Granata, but there was nowhere near the ability of that organization to corrupt, and Granata was not utilized nearly as much in this regard.) The headquarters of the First Ward at this time, and until the ward was recognized and stripped of much of its power in 1992, was located in suite 2306 at 100 North LaSalle, right across the street from City Hall. It was a corner suite. D'Arco had the corner, and to the north of his office in the same suite was the office of Pat Marcy. From the outset, knowing what we had learned from Little Al, we realized that if we could put a bug in the First Ward offices, it would be far and away the best if we could locate it in Pat's office, not John's. D'Arco did the work of the First Ward, the legitimate work. He then went on to do whatever Pat instructed him to do, whatever Pat was instructed *ab initio* by his superiors in the Outfit: Hump, Alex, Ferraro, Pierce, Kruse and Giancana.

Just as I had been given the responsibility to plan the penetration of Celano's and Murray Humphreys' residence in Marina City, and as Hill had been given the job to get us inside the Armory Lounge, now Maz Rutland was given the ticket on the First Ward. He was to do the survey which was required before the implementation of all elsurs. To show Mr. Hoover that 1) the installation would be worthwhile, 2) the plan we had devised would do the job, and 3) we would not "embarrass the Bureau" by getting caught.

I took some time off my lead role in analyzing and transcribing Little Al and Plumb, my cases, and from my twenty targets, to assist Maz. In fact, I came up with a way to get in during non-business hours, past the guards who patrolled the lobby and up the elevator to the twenty-third floor. Our work would take three or four such penetrations, all, of course, long after Marcy, D'Arco and the other employees had left the premises. For security reasons, I cannot go into what it entailed, but we did it. Maz led us into the First Ward offices and we accomplished our purpose. We put "Shade," as we code-named this bug, inside the baseboard of the office of Pat Marcy.

From the first day we had no trouble justifying Maz's survey. The source rivaled the information we were receiving from Shade's brothers in the three other vital locations. Shade may have been a kid brother in age, but he quickly became a key member of our family of microphones.

Little Al was giving us mob activity and corruption. So was Mo. But primarily they were focused on mob activity, the day to day machinations of the Outfit. Whom they were planning to murder. Where they were getting their income, whether from their gambling joints in Chicago or from their interests in Las Vegas. *Secondarily*, their interest was corruption. Plumb was giving us both, too. But Shade was giving us corruption, corruption, corruption, pure and simple. Or rather, not so pure and not so simple. Even some of the crooked cops and corrupt politicians showed up on Shade. Cops never turned up on Al, Mo or Plumb. Politicians almost never did.

Now that we had the coverage at the First Ward, we felt we had the mob almost blanketed. Almost. There were two spots we never did penetrate. We were never able to install a device at Meo's Norwood House, in the alcove where Accardo, Ricca and Cerone conferred so often. And we were never able to penetrate any of the homes of Joe Batters. We had a device, Plumb, at Hump's, and we had another in the Lake Shore Drive condo of Gussie Alex, which agents Bob Cook and John Parish had installed during the period of time when they were the case agents on Gussie while I concentrated on Hump. However, the device on Gussie was never of much value. It did keep Bob and John aware of his coming and goings but Gussie, unlike Hump, never—and I mean never—conducted any of his business from his residence. He never discussed anything of any concern to us with his second wife Suzanne, whom he called "Shatzie," German, as I understand it, for sweetheart. She had been a Playboy Club bunny and hooked up with Gus after his first wife, a beautiful and very popular Chicago fashion model, left him.

We had great coverage of the Outfit from July 29, 1959, all the way into the mid-Sixties. We pretty much knew on a consistent basis just what Tony Accardo's guys were up to. We were able to learn of their plans as they formulated them and then work secretly to thwart them. We knew who Accardo's corrupted judges were, who the corrupt police captains and many of the CPD officers were, who the labor leaders were under their influence and/or control, what they were doing in Las Vegas, where the skim produced so much of their income in those days, who their bookmakers and loan sharks were and where they were operating. It was really a glory time for us in the Chicago Division of the FBI.

Then it all came crashing down. After we had put in two or three of our bugs, the other divisions of the FBI began to catch up with us. They emulated our success, and in some cities they almost caught up to us. Then the Washington Field Office, in the District of Columbia, put a bug in a location where they began to get some information of value. One of the people who was heard frequently on that elsur was Bobby Baker, who had been the chief aide of Senator Lyndon B. Johnson. The WFO began to develop a lot of information about the machinations of Baker, who was later convicted, while he was practically the alter ego of Johnson. Then, while in the presidency, LBJ got wind of this mike and became, as I understand it, considerably alarmed. How could he order that the bug be removed? He simply ordered that *all* our electronic surveillances be removed, reasoning that they were violating the civil rights of the targets. That the targets were the top mobsters in the country made little difference to him. Of course, we had to comply with his order. On July 11, 1965, six years almost to the day after we completed the installation of Little Al, we had to turn them all off. In fact, we were ordered to go in and remove the mikes altogether, which we felt was as risky as going in in the first place.

We were devastated. All that hard work was one thing, but now we would go back to the dark ages. Removing the bugs put us in a really tough spot. We were so much better off now than we had been in 1959, when we knew so little about who the mobsters were and how they operated. This felt like falling head over heels in love with a girl and then losing her. We went from being kings of the hill to paupers literally overnight. I had gotten dozens of commendations from J. Edgar Hoover for our work on installing the mikes and for the pieces of great information we had picked up. Now we were back to ground zero. We had feasted at the table of plenty and now we were about to go hungry. July 11, 1965, was one of the worst days of my life, I tell you that!

41 Back Close

Tony Accardo was now faced with one of the most important decisions he was faced with during his tenure as *consiglieri* of the Chicago family of La Cosa Nostra.

LCN was now the official terminology which the FBI used in referring to the mobs across the country. It was what almost all the mobs called themselves, although the Chicago mob was singular in refraining from its popular usage. They simply referred to themselves as belonging to "the Outfit" when they had talked so freely in front of the hidden mikes. A New York office agent by the name of Jimmy Flynn, working with Jim Mansfield, Jack Danahy, Jim Mulroy, Warren Donovan, Pat Collins, Pat Monihan, Frank Gerrity, Guy Berado and many of the other fine NYO agents, had developed Joe Valachi as the first "made" guy of the LCN to become a fully cooperative witness. Valachi had opened up many eyes as he talked so freely and openly to Flynn, then before the McClellan Committee and Bobby Kennedy in 1963, about the so-called "La Cosa Nostra."

Bobby had moved on after his brother was killed and there was a new Attorney General. The Justice Department decided to try another new strategy on the mob, one that had never been attempted before. The guinea pig would be the guy who took such great pleasure in rubbing our noses in it. Giancana.

This pleased me no end, of course. It was a strategy that could very easily backfire, and Giancana would have another victory to crow about. But it was worth the shot.

The U.S. Attorney's Office in Chicago, headed by Ed Hanrahan and represented by Dave Schippers and Sam Betar, two of Ed's top aides, offered Giancana immunity. Immunity? When we learned of this tactic through our liaison with the U.S. Attorney's Office, our agent Christy Malone, we were perplexed. Offer immunity to Sam Giancana? Complete forgiveness for all his crimes? For his thirteen murders and the many more he had ordered after getting the OK from Tony Accardo? Why?

When we heard the reason, we fell right in with this thinking. If Giancana could not be prosecuted for any of his crimes because he had now been granted immunity, then he did not have the right to resort to the Fifth Amendment, the right not to self-incriminate. Without this right, he had to testify or be held in contempt and sent to jail. But what if he did testify? Then he had choices. He could tell the truth and walk free—until Tony Accardo ordered him killed for violating the oath of *omerta*. Or he could lie on the stand. We would then have to prove he had perjured himself. It would be up to the FBI to provide the evidence that he had lied, that he had not told the truth. That would be difficult. Remember, we couldn't introduce the information from our hidden mikes to do that—that information wasn't evidence. We went right along with what the Justice Department wanted to do, however. Anything ethical and legal to get this guy.

Giancana was granted immunity in May 1965 by Judge William Campbell, one of the top judges ever. Judge Campbell told Giancana that even if he was illegally parked outside the Federal Building at that very moment and was ticketed, he was immune. He sent Giancana back before the federal grand jury, where Giancana still refused to testify. We sighed with relief. He had walked right into our trap. He was taken back before Judge Campbell and ordered to be held in the county jail until he agreed to testify or until the term of the grand jury expired. He stayed until May of 1966, a year, when the grand jury's term ended.

We didn't know it then, but a couple of years after that, I developed an informant who had discussed this situation with Giancana. He was a source who was very close to Sam. Giancana had told him he had no recourse but to refuse to talk. He had seriously considered testifying by lying, expecting that we could not prove his perjury. But there was one guy who countermanded that, one guy who had the power to order Giancana to do just what he did. That man, of course, was Joe Batters.

I believe, as did my source, who was close not only to Giancana but also to Accardo—one of the three best informants I ever developed—that Accardo had become very upset with the way things were going.

Joe Batters might have allowed Giancana to lie before the grand jury. But my source and I agreed there was one big reason he ordered Giancana to keep silent. He was tired of Giancana. He was tired of seeing him keeping his high profile. He had ordered him to "keep his head down," but this did not seem to be in Giancana's nature. He could no more refrain from gloating when he won a round in this fight against "the G" than he could refuse to fly all around the country with Phyllis McGuire and be seen at the appearances of the McGuire Sisters, or bed with Judy Campbell Exner when she was bedding John Kennedy in the White House, or take Marilyn Monroe to the Cal Neva Lodge in Lake Tahoe, where he and Frank Sinatra had her, or take on the FBI by bringing them to court to win an injunction against them. Giancana in the Sixties had become what John Gotti would become in the Eighties and early Nineties: the most widely recognized mobster in the country.

Joe Batters had been there when Capone carried on with such a high profile. Now Sam Giancana was doing the same, only this time Giancana was *his* responsibility. Giancana was the guy he was supposed to be controlling. If ever there was a mobster out of control, it was Sam Giancana.

For this reason, I believe, as does my informant close to Giancana and Accardo, that Accardo may not have planned it, but when the opportunity presented itself, he was not at all unhappy to see Giancana taken down. He therefore commanded Giancana to take the course of action he did. To put himself in the can. It was the easy way out for J.B. It would have been very difficult to supplant Giancana with another. The Chicago Outfit was a tightly structured, monolithic, highly disciplined organization, thanks especially to Accardo, who had so much respect for his underlings. Every "made" guy respected Joe Batters, who had put it all together. Every made guy had heard the old Ricca saying about Accardo having more brains at breakfast than Capone had all day long. There was none of them who doubted that the same comparison, more or less, could be made with Giancana, nor did we doubt it. Not that Giancana was anybody's dummy. He was a sharp guy who had matured a lot in his job. He was tough and arrogant, but reasonably intelligent. I'll give that to the Mafia Princess. But his high-flying ways were dumb. He had gotten away with it for years, calling me names on many occasions, sometimes in public, and treating all of my fellow agents with the same kind of contempt, although they were smart enough never to allow it to get out of hand as I had.

When Giancana went to jail in May of 1965, Tony Accardo had his decision to make. He decided then to name an acting boss under his dominion and not to resume control as the boss. He would be there to guide the new boss but not to make a decision as to whether Giancana should resume his position when he returned from jail. It was obvious all along that, since the grand jury's term would expire in May 1966, Giancana's absence would not last too long. In the meantime, Giancana's troubles were also Tony's. Because, no matter what, the jailing of the boss meant that Tony would have to become much more involved in the everyday machinations of the Outfit than he wanted to be. Under Giancana, especially as Giancana matured and became more experienced in his job, Tony had been able to move further and further away from everyday oversight. Now events brought him back into a more active leadership once again, not to where he would have to shoulder all the burdens of the routine problems as he had from 1943 to 1957, but more so than he had done in the early Sixties. Clarice didn't like it and neither did he. But he had a responsibility. He could not walk away. I don't know who or what faction of the mob could have enforced that responsibility, but it was there, and most importantly, Tony recognized it. He had to step up once again.

42 A Word Good as Gold

It was at this time that I had my next talk with Tony Accardo. We fully recognized that the problem we now had could only be solved by one guy. I could have gone to Hump and he might have helped, as he had with the "family pact," but Hump did not have the authority that Joe Batters had.

In the mid-Sixties we had lost most of our top agents to advancement, as promotions are called in the Bureau. Ralph Hill had gone on to become the supervisor of the Organized Crime Squad in Miami, his hometown. Maz Rutland was back in Washington as a supervisor. John Roberts had become a supervisor of another squad in Chicago. All but one of the original ten agents assigned in 1957 to the Top Hoodlum Program, the first wave, had gone up—and off our squad. So had most of the seventy agents who had bulked up the squad when Bobby Kennedy took over as A.G., the second wave. After all, C-1 had become the most highly recognized organized crime squad in the Bureau, and anybody who had spent any time on it at all and who was interested in advancement just had to say the word and he was up and out. Since I was in my official "office of preference," close to South Bend, my hometown, where my mom, dad, brothers and sisters were still living, and was excited to be fighting my enemies in the Chicago mob, I was not interested in advancement. My sons, Bill and Bob, were fine athletes who were comfortably situated at Thornridge High School, then one of the most competitive high schools in the country, with almost 5,000 students. Bill was excelling in track and Bob would be all-state in football and baseball on his way to becoming the captain of the Notre Dame baseball team after going there on a football scholarship. (He later played pro baseball in the Pittsburgh Pirates farm system after he graduated from ND.) They were another reason why I did not seek a transfer to Washington or anyplace else.

My partner for the next ten years or so was Johnny Bassett, a great guy and a fine agent. John had developed Bernie Glickman into what we call a PCI, a potential criminal informant. Bernie was then a fight manager, and in his stable were some world champs like Sonny Liston, Virgil Akins and Ernie Terrell. John Bassett had been a contender for the professional light-heavyweight championship as a fighter before he became an FBI agent, and he and Bernie had developed a rapport. Bernie, who had been one of the "phony witnesses" for Tony Accardo when Tony had been tried for using his red Mercedes as a tax deduction, also owned the Hickory Pit restaurant and had perjured himself by testifying for Joe Batters, saying that he had purchased Foxhead 400 beer from Accardo. He and Joe Batters were close pals. They had breakfast every Sunday morning at Joe's Ashland Avenue house.

Bernie had a problem. The New York mob was trying to steal his heavyweight champ, Terrell. One Sunday morning when Bernie was breakfasting with Tony Accardo, he brought it up, and Tony responded by sending Phil Alderisio, the mob hitter, to New York with Bernie to face down the guy giving him the trouble, Frank "Funzi" Tieri, who was soon to become a member of the Commission as the boss of one of the five New York families of the LCN. However, for reasons we have never understood, "Milwaukee Phil" took Tieri's side of the argument in New York. He even roughed up Bernie.

Since Bernie had a relationship with Johnny Bassett, he now came to John. I got involved with the situation since John and I were partners and since, as the former Marine Corps and four-time Notre Dame boxing champ, I knew a little about the fight game. Bassett and I hammered out an agreement with Bernie. He would testify before the grand jury against Alderisio and Tieri, along with some lesser fry. He would also give us details about the mob's involvement in the fight game all over the country, a heavy involvement at that time. It was a nice deal. But Bernie would not give up Tony Accardo. Try as we might, we could not get Bernie to agree to testify against Joe Batters. Joe was his pal. He had done him a favor by sending Alderisio with him when he went to do battle with Tieri and the New York mob, or at least that was Accardo's intention, and Bernie would not betray him by testifying that Accardo was in any way involved. This was typical in that Joe Batters was so highly respected by those who came in contact with him that they were not easily convinced to betray him.

When we realized how adamant Bernie was, we agreed to leave Joe out of it. We prepared an FD 209, the informant report, and an FD 302, an investigative memo, from the 209 and left all references to Joe Batters out of it.

Then we took Bernie to Ed Hanrahan, the United States Attorney for the Northern District of Illinois, on the fifteenth floor of the Federal Building at 219 South Dearborn. We gave our reports to Ed and told him we had not included any information about Accardo because of our agreement with Bernie. It was the only way, we told him, we could get the others.

We thought Ed had understood. When he took Bernie Glickman before the grand jury and led him through our 302, he had just what he wanted. Bernie was a fine witness. But then Ed went a step further. He questioned Bernie about the involvement of Accardo. Bernie perjured himself, denying that Tony had been involved in any way. As a result, none of his information was any good, the whole testimony was tainted. Ed Hanrahan threw him out, told Bassett and me: "Take him out of here. The case is down the drain. Finished. Kaput. Put him on the street!" Put him on the street? He'd be dead before he got to State and Madison! The mob had a contract out on him to have him killed.

Here's what happened. We had sequestered Bernie under the ruse of his being a colonel in the army at Camp Sheridan, the army base located north of Chicago. While there, Bernie had contacted the Chicago *Tribune* reporter, our pal Sandy Smith, to collaborate with Sandy to write a book about his experiences when this was all over. But now Art Petacque, Sandy's competition on the *Sun Times*, had broken the story about Bernie's expected testimony in that rival paper. Sandy, therefore, felt freed up to write about what he had learned firsthand from Bernie, a better story, since it was right from the horse's mouth.

When the fact of Bernie's cooperation with us thereby became a matter of public knowledge, Tony Accardo put out a contract on his old pal's life. He was to be located and killed before he could testify. Alderisio, who was given the contract, since he was the mob killer, had more reason to find and whack Bernie than he had ever had, of course. He was the guy who would go down if he didn't get to Bernie first.

So when Hanrahan ordered us to "put this guy on the street, we're finished with him," that made Bernie fair game, a ready target for Alderisio, the guy who was most experienced in this sort of thing.

John and I hustled into the front office of the FBI in Chicago to plead with our boss Marlin Johnson to let us keep Bernie under wraps, under our protection, in spite of Hanrahan's wishes. Marlin called Washington. He was told that Bernie was no longer any responsibility of the FBI, that when he testified, he was now the responsibility of the Justice Department and that he was to be left in their custody—in other words, in the custody of Hanrahan, the U.S. Attorney. Marlin then called Hanrahan, who told Marlin to have Bernie thrown out on the street! Marlin then turned to us. "Do as you are told. The man is out of our hands."

We would be sending Bernie to his immediate death. He wouldn't last long on the streets of Chicago by himself, not with Milwaukee Phil and his crew hunting like mad for him. There were just two things I could do. First, I contacted Bill Duffy, our pal in the Chicago Police Department, who was now a deputy superintendent. I asked Bill to put Bernie under the protection of his people. Bill, the great guy that he was, did just that, keeping Bernie under guard for the night in the Pick-Congress Hotel.

Then I set out to do the other thing I felt I could do.

Ralph Pierce was a guy I could talk to in the Outfit. He was the boss of the south side of Chicago for the Outfit and was also a member of Hump's connection guys. He had been around in the mob since the early days of Frank Nitti, maybe even during the latter days of Al Capone, and was always very close to Hump. He and I frequented the same restaurant during the lunch hours, Morrie Norman's basement dining spot in the Pittsfield Building at

55 East Washington, in the Loop. Ralph used it for his message drop. We were cordial whenever we ran into each other there.

I used Ralph to get to Joe Batters. I thought of just talking to Hump again, as I had for what became the "family pact," but for this I felt I needed to go to the very top. That meant the *consiglieri*, the chairman of the board. I couldn't find Ralph at Morrie's but did run him down at the parking lot behind Old St. Mary's Church at Van Buren and Wabash.

"Ralph, I need to see Accardo immediately," I said to him. "It's a matter of life and death, it really is. I think if I can properly explain everything to him, we can save a life here—a life I think Joe will feel should be saved if he knows the whole story. It's Bernie Glickman's. I want you to set it up."

"Bill, I can do that," Ralph replied. "But there can't be any tricks. If there are, if you're pulling something here, I'm fucked. I have to trust you on this."

"You have my word, Ralph. I'll come alone, unarmed, anyplace, anytime you say. He can have all the guys he wants with him and if I don't keep my word that it's for our mutual interest, then I'm fair game. Tell him I think you guys know I'm good for what I say. Trust me.

"I'll go back to my office while you set this up. I'll hang in there all night if I have to. You call me when you get it done. 431-1333. Give me a time and a place, that's all, you don't even have to say who's calling. I'll know what it means."

Ralph Pierce got back to me about three hours later. He had gone out to River Forest from the Loop and explained what little he knew to J.B. It was the first time an FBI agent had ever requested a sit-down with Tony, and even though he had been informed it was about Bernie Glickman, I suspect he was curious.

"In the Sears parking lot at North and Harlem at midnight," Ralph said when he called me at the FBI office. I thanked him and we hung up. North and Harlem was about a forty-minute drive, as I recall, at that time of night from our office in the Loop. I drove out as I had promised Pierce, alone and unarmed.

I parked my Bureau car in the Sears and Roebuck parking lot and got out. It was just before midnight and it was very quiet. I strolled around the lot for about ten minutes looking for Accardo. Finally Ralph stepped out of a Sears doorway. I had not spotted him but obviously he had been observing me when I arrived and waited. I suppose he was confident that I had kept my word and that there was no tail car. I'm sure that Joe and Ralph must have had some thought in their minds that I was setting Joe up for an arrest. On the other hand, I knew they would probably trust me. I had heard them talk about me dozens of times on Little Al, Plumb, Mo and Shade. I was aware that they considered me a reasonably "stand-up guy," an agent who would do his best to put them away but would not frame them or use unethical or illegal practices to do so. They were fighters and I was a fighter, and although I guess we didn't abide fully by the Marquis of Queensbury rules, especially during their harassment of Jeannie, we respected each other and did not throw low punches at each other.

"Walk west for a couple of blocks," Ralph said. Then he walked the other way.

I did as I was told. It was very quiet in this neighborhood at this hour. The Sears store had been closed for three or four hours, I guess, and the residential neighborhood west of Harlem Avenue on which it was located was very dark and quiet.

I hadn't walked more than three blocks west of Harlem when a man stepped out from behind a tree where he had been standing for how long I don't know. We were now in Elmwood Park, a suburb of Chicago. I recognized him immediately. My first thought was that he, too, had come alone, not that it mattered to me. We shook hands.

I needed to make sure Joe was up to no tricks himself. After all, what I was doing was not in Mr. Hoover's FBI manual of rules and regulations. I was supposed to be following the instructions of my boss, Marlin Johnson, putting Bernie Glickman on the street. Although I had informed my immediate supervisor, Vince Inserra, what I was up to and obtained his tacit understanding, he had not authorized me to do what I was doing. He didn't object but he didn't say go to it, either. So I did not want any record to be made of what I was up to that night. I didn't want Tony Accardo recording our conversation. He probably wouldn't have realized he could blackmail me with it, but I sure didn't want it coming out to my superiors, and especially to the Justice Department. They were finished with Bernie—Hanrahan had made that explicit—but at the same time could have raised holy hell with me for going to the Man in the Outfit to save Bernie's life. I suspect they might even have desired that Bernie be busted up so that we could make an obstruction of justice case against the perpetrators and trace it all the way up to Batters—a plan that was anything but certain.

"Joe, I have to search you," I said. "What I want to talk to you about might tend to compromise me, and I want to make sure you're not wired."

With that, I stepped up to him and began by removing his hat.

Wow! That did it. Immediately six guys jumped out of two cars parked on the curb. I should have spotted them, I guess, but it didn't matter. They all came running toward us. I thought I recognized the first guy as Jackie Cerone, Joe's confidant, the guy who had hit Big Jim Martin with the load of old buckshot and the guy who had gone down to Florida to hit Frankie the X—and who had bragged on the mike down there of other killings, too.

Joe waved them back. "Hold on, I think it's OK," he said. A couple went back to their cars, the others remained in the immediate vicinity. I finished my pat-down of Accardo and was satisfied he was up to no tricks.

He scowled and said, very seriously, "This is a switch. I trust you, I don't worry about you being wired, but you don't trust me. I'm the guy who should think *you'd* be wired."

He was right, of course. He trusted me and I hadn't him. I was just a bit embarrassed.

"How do you want to handle this?" I asked. "You want to go someplace?" I knew his home on Ashland Avenue was just a mile or so away.

"No, let's just take a walk here."

We walked north on one of the side streets west of Harlem, just north of the Mercury Theater, where his brother John was a projectionist. We then turned around and retraced our steps. It was quiet and we were not disturbed. The only sounds were our voices and a dog barking somewhere close by. The two cars of Joe's bodyguards followed us, one car with three hoods to our front and one to the rear.

After just a few pleasantries, talking about the full moon that was out that night, appropriately, I got to the object of our sit-down. "Joe, you know Bernie Glickman testified today before the grand jury. Our agreement with him was that he would testify about Philly and the New York people, including Funzi, but not about you. His deal from the very beginning was that he wouldn't bring you into it. As you can imagine, we wanted you in it. Badly. And so did Hanrahan and the entire FBI and the Justice Department. But Bernie wouldn't budge from that agreement. Today he goes before the grand jury. He tells all about how Philly double-crossed him. I think you know he did, Joe. From what I understand, Philly didn't do what you ordered him to do. He double-crossed you, too. So if I were you, I'd want to talk to Philly Alderisio pretty carefully, Joe. But that's not why I'm here."

Here I paused to let what I had said so far sink in. Then I continued: "After Bernie had completely implicated Philly and Funzi and the others, a very good catch for us, he was then asked in the grand jury about you. He lied, to protect you. He said he had never come to you, that you were no part of this. After he said that, Hanrahan had no more use for him. He had impeached himself. He destroyed his credibility about all the rest he had testified about. The case against everybody is out, kaput. Finished."

"Where is he now?" Accardo asked.

"I'm not going to tell you that, Joe," I said, "but he's in a safe place."

After a while, as we walked, Joe asked, "What is it you want from me?"

That is what I had come for. I put it on the line. "I want your word that he won't be harmed. Call off the contract."

Joe showed some anger in his voice for the second time. "You believe what you read in the papers, huh, Roemer. Is there a contract?"

"We won't debate that, Joe," I replied. "I don't expect you to acknowledge any contract. What I'm asking is for you to give me your word, which I can then pass on to Bernie, that your people will not hurt him. Listen, Joe, he's in bad shape. It really got to him. He needs a lot of help. He not only needs peace of mind to restore his sanity, he needs a lot of medical attention. And rest."

I remember Accardo's words to this day: "Roemer, I thought *we* were supposed to be the bad guys. It seems to me here *you* are the fuckin' bad guys."

He had me there. It seemed the treatment Bernie had received in our custody had made him somewhat unstable, especially during the last twenty-four hours after he read in the newspapers that the mob was out to kill him and after the understanding that he would not be testifying against Accardo had gone down the drain. He had not expected to be thrown out onto the street without any money, except for less than $100 which Hanrahan would give him as "witness fees." I suppose it would shake a guy up to know that the worst killer in Chicago with a huge crew and all the resources of the Outfit was out to find him, hunt him down and kill him. They might even torture him first, for sport. So J.B. had a point when he offered his opinion of what kind of people we were. (Years later the Witness Protection Program was instituted and the U.S. Marshals who handle it do a fine job. But even if the WPP was in existence then, Bernie would not have been in it. Ed Hanrahan had seen to that, not that I feel that Ed is at fault. That is, I give him the benefit of the doubt. It may even have been my fault—maybe I hadn't explained the situation properly and thoroughly enough. There are those that feel that Ed Hanrahan was trying to do what Dick Ogilvie had done—to convict Accardo as a springboard to the governor's office. But that is crass, and not very good faith.)

Silence prevailed for two or three minutes. At this point I became a little concerned. I really needed to get Joe Batters to give me his word—which I would readily accept, knowing him as I did—that his people would not kill Bernie. He had the ultimate power in the Outfit. He was the Man. Even if I had gotten to Hump, he would have had to get to Joe and convince him. Hump or anybody else. All Batters had to do was snap his fingers, either way, and the matter was resolved. But what if he refused to call off the hit? What would I do then? Morally, I felt very strongly that I owed it to Bernie to protect him. How could we accomplish that if we didn't get this contract called off?

So I piped up again. "Joe, this guy is in such bad shape. He's just about to snap. But the big reason is his overriding loyalty to you. If he had testified, instead of lying about it to the grand jury, that he came to you and you gave him Philly, then he'd be sitting pretty somewhere, in good health, protected and cared for for the rest of his life. It was his loyalty to you that got him where he is tonight. That's what I want you to understand. He's your friend, your people. If it wasn't for that gunsel, Philly, who beat the hell out of him and double-crossed him—and you too, Joe—he never would have come to us in the first place. It was Philly who made him come over to us, and then it was his loyalty to you that put him in the no-man's-land he's in today."

I think it was that series of facts, spoken as forcibly as I could muster, which finally got to him. We walked for another couple minutes in silence. I was on pins and needles. Finally he turned to me and said: "OK, he won't get hurt."

I could have let it rest, and I took a chance of insulting him again when I faced him, looked him in the eye and said, "I've got your word on that?"

"You've got my word."

"That's good enough for me," I said, "and I'm sure it will be enough for Bernie, too."

Then Joe started walking again. "Tell me what you're talking about with Philly."

"Why I say he double-crossed you and Bernie both?" I asked. Joe nodded.

"Because you sent him to New York with Bernie to be on his side. To straighten out those New York wise guys. And he did just the opposite. He took their side and beat the hell out of Bernie. There may be an explanation for that, but if there is, I don't see it. If I were you, I'd call Alderisio in and find out what his side is. And I'd talk to Bernie about it. If you call off the contract on him, I imagine he'd be glad to give you his whole side of the story."

Joe said nothing. Our business was over. We had some casual conversation about his son, Anthony Ross, whom I had met. As I recall, he asked me about how my family was. I wasn't sure whether he was referring to the "family pact" or not, so I just told him they were fine and asked him about his family, knowing what a family man he was.

Then he suddenly reached out his hand, shook mine, and jumped into one of the two cars encompassing us. He was gone.

I got home at about four in the morning. Jeannie woke long enough to ask if I had had a nice day. I told her it had been interesting.

The next day I informed Johnny Bassett and Vince Inserra of the results of my "midnight walk" with Accardo, then I called Bill Duffy to alert his men that we were on our way to the Pick-Congress Hotel, where the CPD had Bernie under their wing. When we got there, we thanked the policemen for their good work and for their cooperation with us. Then I let Johnny fill Bernie in about the results of the walk with The Man.

"Joe said it was all right?" he asked, incredulously.

We assured him that that was what he had said. Then we told him Joe was curious about Alderisio. We suggested that we could take him right out to River Forest to Accardo's house on Ashland Avenue. Since he knew Clarice well, he could probably wait for Joe even if he wasn't home. We did just that.

What Accardo did then was right in character for him. It's part of why I have some grudging respect for him. He had given me his word that the contract would be called off, and it was. But then he took Bernie to his personal physician. The physician put Bernie in St. Luke-Presbyterian Hospital, just off the Eisenhower Expressway on the west side, and treated him while Bernie recuperated from his ordeal. Bernie later told John that Accardo had paid all the bills.

Bernie settled in southern California and lived a good life for the next twenty years. In 1986 he died of natural causes. He was never bothered, certainly not by the likes of Alderisio. He was under the protection of The Man, whose word was as good as gold.

43 Changes and Killings

Tony Accardo wasn't too happy when the incarceration of Sam Giancana in May of 1965 forced him back into a much more active leadership of the Outfit. During the year Giancana was in prison, there were three major problems Tony had to deal with. On September 11, Manny Skar was murdered with his blessings. Manny had had juice problems and something had to be done about him. He was well liked by most of the people who knew him, including me, but he was so delinquent in his payments on his loan that something had to be done. It got beyond the point where if Manny could be allowed to get away with it, other such debtors would be affected by his bad example. So Manny, the owner of the Sahara, a very nice restaurant on Mannheim Road, was chopped. He was taken in his garage at his high-rise building at 3800 Lake Shore Drive. Manny was living very well there, but he could not be allowed to continue to do so when he wasn't paying his juice payments. It was as simple as that.

Then Angelo Boscarino got in trouble. He had been involved in a hijacking of $380,000 worth of silver bullion. He didn't want to pay the street tax, his commission to the Outfit for allowing him to operate as a burglar in Chicago. As an example to others, Boscarino's throat was slashed, he was beaten, and on November 14 his dead body was thrown out on the street at 4214 West 24th Place. Accardo had had no other recourse. Another example had to be set.

And on February 28, 1966, another of the silver bullion hijackers, another guy who didn't feel the street tax was fair, was shot *eleven* times. He was Leonard Centrone and his body was found behind a factory on George Street in Melrose Park. Joe Batters felt that these guys had to be taught a lesson, and the fact that Boscarino and Centrone were Italian added to the importance of their crime in not paying as required. They, of all people, should have recognized the seriousness of their failure to divvy up.

It was shortly after this that Van Corbin got his. We never nailed down exactly why this contractor of Tony Accardo's new home on Ashland Avenue in River Forest got it. It may have been just coincidental that I had recently contacted him in order to obtain the blueprints to Joe's new home. I was, of course, interested in penetrating the house before LBJ put the stop to our work in this area in July 1965. I'm not sure exactly when I made contact with Corbin, but it was undoubtedly prior to July of 1965. If Accardo had him whacked because he hadn't satisfied Tony that he had turned me down, as he had, I'm not sure why Tony waited over a year before he had him done in. We could not be sure that is the reason Corbin got it. He could have aroused the ire of the Outfit in some other manner. It may have been purely coincidental that he was the guy who had built Joe's new house.

When Memorial Day of 1966 rolled around, Giancana was released upon the expiration of the term of the federal grand jury. Almost immediately he sat down with Accardo. The meet probably took place at the Armory Lounge, or perhaps at Celano's Custom Tailors on Michigan Avenue. We can't be sure, because we didn't have it covered. LBJ had pulled our teeth.

At the time I had no source who could tell me what occurred at this meeting. However, sometime thereafter, I was able to develop one of the best CTE's ever. A CTE is what we called our very best informants, a criminal top echelon informant, called just a TE today. The title can be given only to those who are fully developed mobsters in high positions. Obviously, we didn't have many of them! At one time, however, I had *three* in the top tier of the Outfit. This one, whom I code-named Romano, was very tight with all of the top people in the mob, he being one himself. Jeannie and I came to enjoy his company very much and when he died recently, we were very saddened. He is in our daily litany. Romano told me later that the sit-down between Giancana and Accardo in June of 1966 was vituperous. That wasn't his word but it conveys the nature of the meet. Giancana was as adamant as ever that he was coming back to run the Outfit. Joe, on the other hand, had already made up his mind. He had been very disappointed with the high-profile style of Giancana, which he blamed for much of the trouble now facing the mob. Accardo felt that Giancana had gotten the G very upset and that they were honing in on the mobsters, not just professionally but for personal reasons. Although he understood that Giancana was our prime target, he felt that by making the mob boss our priority, we were in effect going after all Outfit members. Which was true. Accardo, after conferring long and hard with his mentor Paul Ricca, had made up his mind. He was not going to be dissuaded by Giancana now. He told Sam he had to go. Romano later told me that Giancana told him afterward that he initially felt he should defy Accardo, but after thinking about it, realized that he could not win that battle. He, therefore, decided to give it up and leave Chicago. He was driven to St. Louis by Butch Blasi, his driver-bodyguard-secretary-confidant, where he hooked up with another guy who would become one of my three best CTE's, Dick Cain. (Dick was not even a PCI, a potential criminal informant, of mine at the time, but later he, too, would become a full-fledged CTE, a double agent of mine inside the mob.) Giancana and Cain flew off to Mexico City, where they took up residence, and for the next decade or so they established and ran a gambling empire of their own outside the United States, mainly in the Caribbean, but also including a casino in Teheran after they bribed the Shah of Iran to allow it.

Giancana had now been deposed by Accardo, who already had a replacement in mind. He was Sam "Teets" Battaglia, the fishing companion of Accardo in Bimini and elsewhere. Joe had three main fishing companions when he took off for his frequent forays for fish: Jackie Cerone, Joey Aiuppa and Sam Battaglia. Keep them all in mind.

In all my years in Chicago, I never met Sam Battaglia. It was a surprise to all of us when Romano identified him as the new boss and when we began to get it from other sources. Although I had never met him and had very little to do with his investigation up to this point, I had been inside his house. He lived on Ridgeland, on the north side of Oak Park near Harlem and North avenues, not too far from Accardo's Ashland Avenue abode. When the McClellan Committee met in Chicago in the early Fifties, they wanted Battaglia as one of their witnesses and had asked the FBI to locate him and lead their investigators to him so he could be served the subpoena commanding his appearance. But we couldn't find Sam. We knew he had a luxurious 400-acre stockbreeding farm in Pingree Grove, southwest of Elgin in Kane County, some fifty miles west of Chicago, but we couldn't find him there either. He had, like so many of his pals, taken off to avoid the subpoena. So the committee got an idea. They asked me to implement it. It went against my grain. I feel strongly about the "family pact." But I got my marching orders. A subpoena was issued by the committee for a daughter of Battaglia, Joanna. I went to his home at 1114 North Ridgeland in Oak Park and was admitted by Battaglia's gracious wife, Angie. I was as much a gentleman as I could be, given the circumstances, and she was gracious, too. I recall seeing several trophies in their living room, trophies won by Rich and Sam, the sons of Battaglia, who were fine athletes at Oak Park-River Forest High School and in Pony League. I explained to Mrs. Battaglia that I had a subpoena for her daughter, but before she should get excited, she should know that we would exchange it when and if her husband made himself available for service of his subpoena. If he did not, we would have to have the daughter honor the subpoena by appearing before the committee in public session, but it was up to him. We wanted him, not his daughter. As I say, this was not my idea and I was very uncomfortable with it and with my role in it. But I had my orders and I have found that there are times in one's career when there is no choice but to follow orders. We located the daughter at her place of employment, Vignola's furniture store on North Avenue, almost at Harlem. It was not long thereafter that Battaglia showed up and accepted his subpoena. The committee then canceled the one for his daughter. I guess there are times when "The G" can get somewhat nasty when it perceives that that is the only way to get the job done.

That was my only exposure to Battaglia, and as I say, I never met him. Other agents were assigned to him, and when he was designated by Accardo to step up and become the boss, they, of course, continued that assignment.

They did a fine job, because Battaglia didn't last more than a year or so. He went away in May 1967, convicted of bribing officials of Northbrook, a northwestern suburb of Chicago. His role as Accardo's new appointee lasted just that one year and then he was gone. He was released after six years only because he was dying of stomach cancer. Prison doctors had performed surgery on him and found incurable and inoperable cancer. He died just eleven days after his release in the fall of 1973.

Now Accardo needed yet another boss. First Giancana had gotten his when we invoked the unique contempt situation. Then Battaglia was put away.

Who would Joe Batters come up with now? We were very interested, to say the least. We tried hard to get inside—inside his mind and inside his organization. The big problem we had then, as I have made clear, is we didn't have the ability to penetrate their meeting places any longer. We had been deep inside but now we were outside—and not really able to look in.

This is when Mr. Hoover put pressure on us to resort to what I

came to call the second part of the "one-two punch." The first part
had been our ability to place hidden mikes inside strategic spots
where the mob openly discussed their business. The other punch
was the one we had to resort to now: the CTE. The double agent.
The mobster who could be "flipped" or "turned," who would continue to function inside the mob but now as a fully developed informant for us, telling us all the secrets he became privy to as a
full-fledged "made guy." If one believes that this is an easy task,
then one does not understand the nature of the problem. At the
time, in the mid to late Sixties, prior to the time I developed "Romano," the Bureau had developed just two such people, and those
were not developed by us in Chicago. One was Jimmy Flynn's Joe
Valachi, who had gotten himself in trouble in prison when he
killed a guy he thought was out to kill him on orders of the mob.
That made him vulnerable to the approach of Agent Flynn. The
other guy was Jimmy "The Weasel" Frattiano, who had likewise
gotten crosswise with his people in the mob, this time in San Francisco. Agent Jim Ahearn there was able to "flip" Frattiano. I got to
know Jimmy Frattiano years later.

That, then, was the kind of thing we were looking for—
somebody in Joe Batters' army who had had a falling-out with
them and who could be persuaded to "turn," come over to us. Actually, we wanted something a little better than Valachi or Frattiano. We wanted somebody who had a reason to flip, but we
wanted him to stay inside the mob so that he could give us correct,
up-to-date, daily information about what the mob was doing. Nobody like this had ever come over to us before, anywhere.

In order to facilitate the development of this kind of source, the
Bureau instituted the TECIP, the Top Echelon Criminal Informant
Program. Before long, I was designated the coordinator of the
TECIP. My job was not only to develop my own sources, but to
supervise the development of such informants by other agents. In
1966 we were a long way from any success under the TECIP—in
Chicago or in any other FBI office in the country. But it was our
only recourse now, the only way we could get our ears inside the
mob, thanks to LBJ.

Eventually, however, we did it. It's immodest of me, but our
three best, in my not-so-meek opinion, were mine: "Romano,"
"Sporting Goods" and Dick Cain. I can identify Dick because he
wanted me to, if he was ever killed. He wanted me to tell that "I
was one of you guys, that I doubled for you." Dick was killed by
the mob, but not because they found him out. He got crosswise
with one of his associates inside the mob. Romano and Sporting

Goods have died of natural causes; I still don't feel I should identify them by their real names. But you have been reading about them herein. In the years after their coming over to us, they kept us well advised about the activity of Tony Accardo and his people.

44 Another Change— and More Killings

Tony Accardo was obviously not impressed by what I had to say about Felix "Milwaukee Phil" Alderisio double-crossing him in New York. Tony replaced Sam Battaglia with Philly. Maybe Philly convinced Tony that he did the right thing when he turned against Bernie Glickman. Maybe Tony had known all along. Or maybe he just didn't care what I thought.

I was surprised when I learned of this development. I had had little contact with Philly Alderisio. The investigation of him was assigned to other agents, not particularly to me, although, of course, he had come up in many of my investigations.

I also had a thing about Philly. I couldn't prove it—and Jeannie could not identify him from his photo—but I suspected he was behind the mob's harassment of her, which led to the family pact, and their following Bill and Bob to school. The reason was that they seemed to call on the nights when I worked with Ralph Hill in surveillance of Philly's hangout, the Tradewinds nightclub on Rush Street. Ralph had developed the car hiker there as a PCI, a potential criminal informant, to keep us advised of who was inside on the nights we staked out the place in the early days of the Top Hoodlum Program—when we had little going for us before Little Al and his brothers. I never trusted the guy. I thought he was giving us a little bit while he gave them a lot, telling them when we came around so they did not transact any particular mob activity that night. If my suspicion is correct, they were well aware that I was out that night and not home when they called Jeannie. I sure wouldn't put that kind of thing past Philly. It was part of the reason he was not my favorite guy.

What surprised me about his elevation to boss under Joe Batters was that I didn't perceive him to be Joe's kind of guy either. He was a brutal killer. That was his expertise. He excelled in shooting people in the back or slashing their throats after sneaking up on them. None of the mob killers ever gave their victims an equal chance, of course. They killed from ambush, never by giving the victim the chance, like in the movies about the old West, to draw with them. Since that was Philly's claim to fame, not his brains, we were caught off guard when Accardo put him in charge of the day-to-day routine of the Outfit. Of course, Joe stayed on as the *consiglieri*. He was needed now more than ever.

Philly Alderisio turned out to be a halfway decent boss, though not for long did he hold the title. And surprisingly, his reign was relatively nonviolent. You'd think that due to his quick trigger, he'd rule with a lot of mayhem. During the two years that Philly was the boss, there were few gangland killings. The only two which were of particular consequence were the killings of Allen Rosenberg and Boodie Cowan in the spring and summer of 1967. Rosenberg was a pal of Philly, so there is little doubt that his was either sanctioned or perpetrated by Alderisio. His hands were handcuffed while he sat in the front of his rented Cadillac, and he was shot seven times. Cowan was a juice collector for the mob. He became trunk music after being shot just once, behind his left ear, up close with a .32. He lived in Lincolnwood, a northern suburb, but he was found in the trunk of his car at 418 South Kilpatrick, on the south side of Chicago.

Then we got Philly. Actually it was a cheap pinch. We got him for conspiracy to defraud the Parkway Bank in Harwood Heights, a Chicago suburb, of $78,935. The Chicago newspapers made it their front-page headline story. In fact, the Chicago *Sun Times* of Monday, July 28, 1969, featured a photo almost across the top of their front page of three FBI agents leading Alderisio into the rear entrance of the Chicago Police Department lockup after his arrest. The guy on Philly's left was me. We had pinched him in his home at 505 Berkley in Riverside, a southwestern suburb, and while there, we found a huge gun collection; when we notified ATF of this, Philly had more troubles.

As we took Philly downtown to the FBI office in the Loop, he and I got into it just a little. He accused me of "bad-mouthing" him "all over Chicago, telling people what a murderer I am." Then he got off on complaining that I had informed Joe Batters that he had "double-crossed him." I didn't let him rile me up, not as I had with Giancana.

I merely expressed my opinion to him that "if you aren't what I say you are, you won't have to worry. But I think you got more to think about now than Roemer 'bad-mouthing you all over Chicago.' "

Alderisio shut up.

He soon would be gone. He was found guilty and sentenced to Marion, at that time the toughest prison in the country for guys like him, where he would join Battaglia. One day while Philly was out in the exercise yard, he dropped dead of a heart attack. He would kill no more.

Now Accardo had another spot to fill. This time his choice wouldn't surprise me at all.

45
A Sharp Guy, and Then Attrition

The next guy in line to become Tony Accardo's caretaker boss had everything it took to command the Outfit, to lead his troops and to operate in the Accardo manner. He was a man in Accardo's image, his protégé, a guy Tony had groomed just for this spot at the right time: Jackie Cerone.

Cerone's nickname in the press was "Jackie the Lackey." Don't believe it. He is nobody's lackey. The reason he was dubbed that was that he was constantly seen in public with Joe. Cerone, born in 1914, was eight years younger than Batters, but he had been at his side since Jackie was about twenty-one. Now he was a very young fifty-six. Jackie was in great physical and mental shape. He jogged every morning near his home in Elmwood Park, not far from where I took my midnight walk with Accardo. Then he did his mob business at Rocky's, his hangout in Melrose Park. Following that, almost every mid-afternoon he traveled to the Regency Health Club in the Regency Hyatt O'Hare, where he lifted weights. My kind of guy, from that perspective, at least. I followed much the same physical routine, then and now.

Jackie was also one of the most erudite guys in the Outfit.

Maybe Hump and Donald Angelini read bestsellers, maybe Rocco Infelice. But not many. (I know the other guys read my stuff, but I believe that is only to see how I depict them, to see if I get them right. Knowing that, I try especially hard.)

Since Jackie was the personification of what a mob boss should be, we tried particularly hard to get him. We gave Giancana our best shot because we disliked him so—or at least I did. Battaglia was capable and, with Joe the power behind his throne, he did a good job and we wanted very much to down him. Alderisio was noted more for his brutality than for his intellect, and we endeavored to get that killer as soon as we could. Now we had a real problem. Accardo had put on top the guy who could lead the mob for years into bigger and better things, who could be the best, maybe, since Joe himself. His experience ran the gamut of the qualifications it takes to be a mob boss. He had done it all. He had killed, he had corrupted, he had led his own crew, the Elmwood Park street crew, in gambling and juice, and he had done it all showing great leadership. Next to Joe Batters himself, Jackie Cerone was the most qualified mob boss in their history. Capone and Nitti and Giancana were more infamous, according to the popular history of the Chicago family of La Cosa Nostra, but if Jack Cerone had been left in power for anywhere near as long as, say, Giancana or Nitti, he would be at least as recognized as they were—and more so.

Fortunately, we had an ace FBI agent on our C-1 squad in Paul Frankfurt. Paul was one of the nicest guys and best agents I ever was privileged to know. For one reason or another, I never worked really closely with Paul, but when I was around him in the squad room, I always enjoyed his company. He is a class act. He worked a lot by himself, without partnering up. One of the guys he was targeting was a bookmaker named Lou Bombacino, not a big guy in the Outfit but "made." Paul got to know Lou. Then Lou got in trouble with his people. He was working under Frank Aurielli for Donald Angelini, Joe Ferriola and Dominick "Large" Cortina. I had gotten to know Donald Angelini very well, posing as a degenerate sports bettor at a handicapping-bookmaking establishment in the days before J. Edgar Hoover died and undercover work became a big staple in our array of operations. His establishment was called the Angel-Kaplan Sports Service and was located on the north side of the Loop on Clark Street, behind where the Sherman Hotel was then and the State of Illinois (Thompson) Building is now. Donald was Angel in Angel-Kaplan. Donald and Bill Kaplan knew I was an FBI agent—I didn't pretend not to be—but they also took me to be an avid sports bettor in the days before such gambling became a federal crime in 1961, the year the gambling laws were passed under Bobby Kennedy, when he first became Attorney General.

Now Lou Bombacino got in trouble with Ferriola, Aurielli, Angelini and Cortina. They had a dispute about his handling of their bookmaking operations. They took the dispute to the boss, Cerone. (This was just what Tony Accardo wanted to avoid—these mundane, day-to-day ordinary problems of the Outfit. How wise he was.) Jackie ruled on the dispute in favor of four of his top guys, Donald, Aurielli, Joe and "Large."

This pissed Lou off to no end. He called the guy who had been courting him, Paul Frankfurt. Paul recognized immediately the potential of what he had. He jumped at the opportunity.

Soon about eight of us were in on the action. We took Lou out to a safe house, a farm near Elgin, where we debriefed him under Paul's supervision. And we guarded him. As soon as Cerone and the others realized that Bombacino was missing from his regular haunts and his house, they began looking for him. Cerone went to Accardo with the problem and Joe immediately instructed him not only to locate Lou, but to whack him immediately when he was found. Joe and Jack realized what it meant when a disgruntled "made" guy suddenly was nowhere to be found.

That summer of 1970 was a great time in my life. The farm near Elgin had a lake on its property, and every day when I was on duty—twenty-four hours on and twenty-four off—I worked off the great Italian meal Lou had prepared for us by jogging around that lake in the fresh country air. Lou turned out to be a really entertaining guy and we all came to enjoy his company, all of which—the fresh air, the great food, the exercise and the company—combined to make that summer a fine time. Then Lou was ready. We brought him to the Federal Building in the Loop to testify before the grand jury. It was an ITAR case—Interstate Transportation in Aid of Racketeering, gambling and loan-sharking, juice being the racketeering. At the trial Jackie Cerone and his four sharp, capable, top guys were convicted and sent to prison. I took on the task of arresting Donald. I liked Donald after all the hours I had spent talking to him at Angel-Kaplan, and I wanted to make sure it was handled without any rough stuff. Not that any agent would have chosen this method, but I wanted to make sure. Donald didn't deserve tough treatment. He was in the wrong, he was a "made" guy, but he is one of the very few that were "made" without making their bones by killing somebody. Donald got "made" because of his intellect and, especially, his expertise in gambling. He is a very unusual Outfit guy. As I write this, he is in a halfway house in Chicago, having recently been released from prison on yet another conviction, this one in San Diego. Donald never became an informant of mine, but he was a guy I could always talk to.

When I say I wanted to insure that Donald was not handled badly, I should explain. He wouldn't have been. All FBI agents, almost without exception, act appropriately under sometimes extremely difficult circumstances. But I do recall the arrest of Hump. It was my case; I had worked it all alone. I respected Hump, but since he was my target, I worked hard to put him away. I built a case that I felt was bullshit, but it was my opportunity to get Hump and put him in prison. It was my job and I wanted him badly. The case was for contempt of a grand jury—for evading my attempts to serve a subpoena on him when I could prove that he knew he was aware I was trying to do that. I don't know that such has ever been done before or since. It was like the singular effort we made against Giancana. In 1965 I had built this case alone and by myself, but when it came time to arrest Hump, I let three other guys handle it. I liked Hump and didn't want to be there when we took him down. The other three agents handled it as well as possible, but Hump, who did not recognize that they had the right to search his premises "incidental to the arrest," thought they needed a search warrant to do so. So he pulled a gun on them and made to resist them. The agents subdued him, took him into the Loop from his Marina City condo and booked him. When he was released late in the afternoon, he returned home, where, a couple of hours later, his brother, Ernie, who was called Jack Wright in the mob, found him on the floor, dead of a heart attack. That bothered me because, as I say, I liked Murray Humphreys. Later I was confronted by one of his pals who told me that if I had been there, Hump would have respected what I told him about our ability to search incidental to the arrest without a warrant and would not have overly excited himself so. This guy thought Hump might still be alive if I had been there. At the age of sixty-five or so, it had been too much for him.

That was the kind of thing I did not want to happen to another guy I had some feeling for, Donald Angelini. We became friends when I frequented his office, and I didn't want anything untoward to happen to him—even though I knew almost all agents were better equipped to do the job than I was.

In any event, we got Jackie Cerone long before he was able

even to get his feet wet. The best guy available to Tony Accardo was now . . . no longer available.

Joe Batters had run out of guys like Jackie Cerone, guys who had the experience and the capability to do the job, handle the daily affairs of the Chicago mob. Even with Joe behind them making the major decisions, attrition had taken its toll. Who was there now who could step in and fill Jackie Cerone's shoes? Nobody— or was there?

46 Accardo Walks Again

Tony Accardo was having other troubles besides whom to name as the boss of the Chicago mob. In September 1968, Joe went before one of those infernal grand juries again, only it wasn't a federal grand jury this time. This time the Cook County grand jury was investigating irregularities in the handling of funds for the Veteran's Park District, which covered several western suburbs, like Melrose Park, River Grove, Franklin Park and Northlake. Talk about my case against Hump being bullshit. But, hey, I'm all for it. Get these guys any way you can, whether it be Accardo or Humphreys or Capone or Nitti or any other mob chieftain. If they assume the job, then they assume the risks, no matter how petty they might be. I made up a slogan for my fellow agents many years ago (we didn't have many women in the Bureau in those days): "If you don't get 'em by the balls, get 'em by the scruff of the neck or the seat of the pants. But get 'em!" So I'm always happy when a made guy goes down, no matter for what. As long as it's legal and ethical.

The Cook County grand jury took a page out of our book. It would be the first—but not the last—time Tony Accardo would get the Giancana treatment. Tony was represented by three attorneys, Mike Brodkin, Maurice Walsh and his son Carl. Talk about running the gamut. Brodkin was just a shyster, the worst of the worst of legal "mouthpieces," the reason they put the word *crimi-nal* in the description of criminal defense attorney. Maury Walsh was just about the best—tough, experienced and as capable as any, and his son, Carl, would be the same one day but was still somewhat inexperienced. Tony, therefore, had the best, the average and the worst representing him. On their advice, Accardo took the Fifth. All well and good.

However, the Cook County State's Attorney's office then did what we had done with Giancana. They offered Tony immunity. He now had the same choices as Giancana had in 1965. Refuse to talk and be held in contempt; go to jail like Giancana. Talk and tell the truth and suffer the consequences from the mobsters you so implicate. Or lie and take a chance it can't be proven as perjury, thereby getting sent off to jail. None of these choices, of course, are good ones for a mobster.

In this case, however, the questions did not pertain to mob affairs or to his fellow mobsters. So Tony did what Giancana could not do. Although he volunteered nothing, he did truthfully answer the questions of the prosecutor. Unfortunately, they did not implicate him. He admitted nothing because, frankly, as far as I could see, he was not guilty of anything. I applauded the State's Attorney for taking a shot at Tony but he had little ammunition to work with. Tony walked once again. He had taken the immunity, thereby precluding prosecution for anything he admitted, while not opening himself up for a contempt citation. Unfortunately, what was lacking was any evidence against him. The grand jury did indict Rocco J. Culotta, the former treasurer of the Veteran's Park District, on charges of forgery and official misconduct. Among the charges was that Culotta had used $2,000 in Park District funds to pay the real estate taxes on the home which was beginning to become so infamous, that of Accardo at 1407 North Ashland in River Forest. Tony had surely thought when he sold his twenty-two-room mansion at 915 Franklin that his home would no longer cause a ripple in the public eye. He was finding out he was wrong.

The Accardo Ashland Avenue abode came into the limelight once more in April 1970, when Tony Accardo was indicted on charges of unlawful possession of a Mauser semi-automatic pistol and an H & R Handy Shot pistol, which had been seized when agents of the ATF executed a search warrant on the Accardo residence on April 13. The guns were part of a collection that had been assembled over the years as a hobby of Accardo, but according to the government, they had not been properly registered.

Batters quickly made bond. He did not spend the night in jail—in fact, he obtained the court's permission to go fishing at his favorite fishing hole in Bimini.

Accardo's firearms trial lasted a week. After the U.S. Attorney's office put on the government's case, Maury Walsh called young Joseph Accardo, then age twenty-six, to the stand. Young Joe, hardly ever in the spotlight (he was kept out by his father), testified that the two guns in question were actually his. He swore that his father had given him a fifty-piece gun collection on his twenty-first birthday and that the two guns were part of that collection. He swore that he had personally mounted the fifty guns which the agents had confiscated onto the wall of the house on Ashland.

The jury was out for only twenty minutes, if you can believe that. Not guilty, they said. Again.

Tony was now free to look into the collection of mob members—the made guys—to see who, if any, could succeed to the throne. Who could be trusted to conduct the usual operations and turn over the unusual ones to Accardo as the *consiglieri*.

This is the motley crew that was served up, from which Joe Batters could choose: first there was, as always, Paul Ricca. Paul would be around for just several more months until he died of a heart attack in October 1972. Paul had wanted nothing to do with mob leadership anyway, ever since he got out of prison on his early parole in 1947. He sure didn't know that he was practically on his deathbed. When Paul died, Tony Accardo was quoted as saying he missed "the best friend a man could have." Then there was Joe's friend, Gussie Alex, my target, the boss of the Loop. There was Ross Prio, the boss of the north side. Under him were Vince Solano and Lenny Patrick, who controlled the Rogers Park area. Fiore "Fifi" Buccieri had the west side then. Under him was Joe "Gags" Gagliano, Buccieri's brother Frank, Joe Ferriola, James "Turk" Torello and Angelo "The Hook" LaPietra. Joe "Caesar" DiVarco commanded the Rush Street area on the near north side. Ralph Pierce had the south side. Frank La Porte had the southern suburbs, headquartering in Chicago Heights and living in Flossmoor. Under him were Al Pilotto, Al Tocco, Toots Palermo and Jimmy "The Bomber" Catuara. Les Kruse, the connection guy, had the northern suburbs, Lake County. The newspapers called Les "Killer Kane." He told me a dozen times that he did not deserve that nickname, that he had never killed anybody. I believe that to be true. Joe Amato had DuPage and McHenry counties in the far western suburbs. Dick Cain, aka Ricardo Scalzetti, was Giancana's top aide. As enforcers, Accardo had Tony Spilotro, "The Ant," and Chuckie Nicoletti working for him. And, of course, Alderisio, but he was now in prison. He died there in September 1971, just months away.

By this time Tony had acquired another house—not in Chicago (where he continued to spend most of his time in his Ashland Avenue home) but where he would begin to spend much of the winter season. He was there now, as he contemplated whom he could place to overcome the attrition which had set in. This home was not as nice as Ashland Avenue but it was very nice. It was the house in Indian Wells, California, on Roadrunner Drive. That neighborhood was probably more expensive than 1407 Ashland Avenue. Tony's condo was on the Indian Wells Country Club fairways, completely guarded by walls, gates and guards. If he had had his choice, surely he would have preferred to spend most of his time there.

47 AAA

Tony Accardo found none of the members of the Chicago mob qualified to handle the job of boss, even if he remained the *consiglieri*, giving guidance and approval on the major decisions.

He sat down with Gussie Alex. Slim had taken over the connection guys when Hump died, and had given up the Loop in the process. His pal Frank "Strongy" Ferraro had died of cancer, and Gussie had enough to handle with his corruption duties. Now the Loop was being handled by the west side crew under Fifi Buccieri, Turk Torello, Joe Ferriola, Frank Buccieri and Angelo La Pietra.

Gus, being Greek, could not be "made," but he had done it all. His dad had operated a small restaurant at Wentworth and 26th Street in the Patch, where Italian immigrants had settled around the turn of the century, which was frequented by many of the members of the Capone, and then the Nitti, mob. Gus and Strongy had worked in the restaurant from an early age. Both were sharp guys and came to the attention of the boys. Gus had, therefore, been one of them almost since birth. Gus, born on April Fools' Day in 1916, was ten years younger than Tony, but like Jackie Cerone, who was still in prison, had drawn Joe Batters' attention for decades. Joe proposed to elevate him, but since Gussie was Greek, he would have to be supplemented by someone else who could attend Commission meetings, where no Greek would be welcomed by the La Cosa Nostra bosses from all over the eastern part of the country.

Joe turned his eye to someone else, a mobster who had had a checkered career, but such was the state of the "made" membership in the early Seventies. Joey Aiuppa was no spring chicken. Only a year younger than Joe himself, Aiuppa had started out as a professional fighter, taking the ring name of Joey O'Brien. Then he came into the mob and eventually was given Cicero as his domain. I remember Giancana, when he was boss, telling his underboss Ferraro that Aiuppa might be running to see him, since Giancana had turned him down for something which would have made him some money. Giancana said, "We gave him Cicero, that's a good spot. If he can't make a go of it there, he can't make it anywhere." Now Giancana and Ferraro, for one reason and another, were gone, and Aiuppa was being elevated to the top spot.

Or was he? Gus was disqualified because he was Greek. And O'Brien, as the boys called him, was not as well qualified as any of his predecessors. He wasn't as sharp, respected or even experienced as any of them. He was old enough, had been around long enough, but had been confined to Cicero, a good area for the mob but a small one.

Tony Accardo realized all this. How could he in good conscience—and Joe did have one, of sorts at least—leave his Outfit to these two guys? When he really gave it some thought, he realized he couldn't. Gus was qualified, but all "made" guys would reserve judgment when he gave orders. He wasn't one of them. And O'Brien was not any more respected. He had no leadership qualities at all. Small, dumpy, ugly as sin, no personality—what kind of leadership could he provide?

Like it or not, Joe realized he had to come back all the way, come off the role of *consiglieri* and get more and more involved in the day-to-day action. Like it or not, he found there to be no other tenable way for him to be faithful to the Outfit, in whose service he had spent fifty years, thirty of those in the top job.

Joe Batters dealt himself back in. He would join Alex and Aiuppa, and together they would pull the Outfit back together. It was this trio which now assumed the leadership.

We called it the Triple A: Alex, Aiuppa and Accardo. We also called it the Triumvirate. Or the Committee (as opposed to the Commission). As it turned out, they worked well together.

By this time the proceeds from the skim were becoming smaller and smaller. The mobbed-up casinos in Las Vegas were becoming fewer all the time. Howard Hughes had purchased the Desert Inn, Frontier, Sands and Castaways in 1967, then he purchased the Landmark in 1968. He even attempted to purchase the Stardust, but was blocked by the Securities and Exchange Commission and the Justice Department due to antitrust laws. In 1969 legislation was passed under Governor Paul Laxalt of Nevada allowing publicly traded corporations to own hotel-casinos.

Tony sent Tony "The Ant" Spilotro to Vegas as the Enforcer. He shaped things up by killing five people as soon as he arrived— a move that would concentrate the mind of anyone with any ideas about fooling with the Chicago Outfit. Still, the skim was not what it had been in the glory years of Las Vegas. Gambling and other illicit activities in Chicago were doing well but were not covering for the loss of the skim in Vegas: the street tax, juice, etc. A new income, from "chop shopping," the dismantling of stolen cars and the subsequent sale of their parts, was adding to the coffers but was no panacea.

One problem had to be handled on behalf of Alderisio. Sambo Cesario had to be chopped. When Alderisio went away to prison, a "made" guy, Sambo, had latched onto Nan, Philly's mistress. This was a violation of *omerta*, the code of the LCN. You can't covet another's wife or mistress. Just before he died, Philly sent word back to have Sambo killed. In the matter known as "the hit from the grave," on October 19, 1971, while Sam was sitting with his wife on lawn chairs in front of a building he owned at 1071 West Polk, two masked gunmen carried out Philly's request. They spared Sambo's wife and Nan.

In March of 1972 Chuck Carroll was killed. We never felt that this was an Outfit killing sanctioned by J.B. Chuck had been a longtime lieutenant of Ralph Pierce on the South Side. At this time my CTE, Dick Cain, had been back in town, doubling for me inside the mob while also working for himself there. We had been turning a blind eye on his machinations as he tried to take over gambling in Chicago. What an ambition! The deal was that we would not focus on his activity if he spun off his competitors to us—that is, give us information on their operations. This would not only facilitate his takeover, but would obviously be of great assistance in our investigation of the mob's "lifeblood," as I call it. All was well and good for a while. We didn't follow Cain as he went about his business, and since he was filling me in on the mob and its activity during our weekly meetings every Wednesday afternoon, we were happy for two years. My supervisor, who had OK'd the deal with Dick, thought it was just great. But then somebody bound, gagged and blindfolded Chuck Carroll, then shot him and left him as trunk music in the back of a car at 8119 South Ada in Chicago. That's when we began to look closely at what my CTE was up to. We couldn't condone murders, after all. We told Dick that it was no deal. He was tear ass but I was adamant about it. That was the end of his effort to take over gambling in Chicago. My point is not that Dick Cain was directly involved, just that we didn't feel that Tony Accardo and the Triple A's had had anything to do with the killing of Chuck Carroll.

We did feel they had something to do with the next one, however. On April 14, 1973, a Saturday, Mad Sam DeStefano got his. The king of the juice men was gone, shotgunned by his own brother and by the Enforcer, Tony "The Ant" Spilotro, both of whom were soon to go on trial for the murder of a DeStefano henchman, Leo Foreman. Even though Mad Sam was not "made"—he was too demented for that—the hit had to have been sanctioned by AAA.

Then came one of the worst times of my life. One of my closest friends, believe it or not, was then my CTE Dick Cain. We had had a short tiff when I called off our arrangement with him, but we had reconciled. He came to me on December 17, 1973, the day before our regular Wednesday afternoon meet. He had been followed that day and thought it might be us. It wasn't. Three days later I began my Christmas leave. I was down in our basement in South Holland, the southern suburb of Chicago, shadowboxing when a news flash came over the radio: "Dick Cain, the gangster, was shot and killed this afternoon." Two gunmen had come into the place where he was meeting an associate, Rose's Sandwich Shop, right in the heart of Little Sicily at Grand and Ogdon, where Tony Accardo had been raised. They had lined the diners up against the wall, a lot like Tony had done in the garage on St. Valentine's Day, then they walked up to Dick. They put a shotgun under his chin, blew his brains out the top of his head. So my pal was gone. It was one of the very worst times of my life. Hard to cope with something like that. I have often said I have never had any stress in any respect of my life, but that came close.

The killing of Dick had to have been sanctioned by the Triumvirate. I was initially worried that it had been caused by a leak somewhere, that Tony and his guys had found out Dick was a double agent for me inside their Outfit. I found out otherwise. He had double-crossed Marshall Caifano, a strong Outfit guy, and Caifano laid the facts out to Joe Batters. Joe had approved the hit because of that. *I* didn't learn that; Pete Wacks did. Pete is maybe the best agent in the Bureau today, and he got it from his CTE several years after I had left Chicago. It made me feel a lot easier, since it really bothered me that maybe I had done something which might have led to the uncovering of Dick, and thereby to his death.

Things percolated inside the Outfit from the time Tony Accardo formed his AAA. In fact, 1974 would be a big year for chops. There were ten gangland murders that year. 1975 was a banner year also, including one murder which ranks among the all-time infamous hits in the inglorious history of the Chicago mob. It was one of only nine that year, but it was as mind-grabbing as any but a couple of thousand gangland killings since 1919.

48 We Lose Another

Tony Accardo had a big decision to make in the fall of 1974. Tony openly subscribed to the theory—he might as well have coined it—that "the mob kills only its own." He was of the firm opinion that as long as a large segment of the public believes that the mob is dangerous only to its own people, then the thinking of public officials would be similarly affected. Judges, prosecutors, cops and the like would feel that there was more to be concerned about than just the Outfit, that they had more important things to spend their time and resources on than organized crime. That street crimes and drugs, for instance, constituted much more of a threat to our society than organized crime does. Of course, he had a point, but that philosophy should not be allowed to go overboard. The FBI itself was on the cusp of taking some of its manpower off "traditional organized crime," as it officially called La Cosa Nostra, and placing it in the investigation of "the emerging crime groups," such as the Crips, the Bloods, the Medellin and Cali cartels, the Yahuza and the other drug organizations which were then about to "emerge." Tony Accardo felt that every effort should be made to foster the belief that the Outfit engaged only in "victimless" crimes, such as its lifeblood, gambling, and that the public should not be aroused to feel that this supposition was off base.

Therefore, when Joe Lombardo came to him to request sanction to hit an intended victim, Joe Batters had serious misgivings. At the time, Joe "The Clown" Lombardo was becoming more and more important in the Outfit. (Joe really is no clown. I don't know him well but I have arrested him—in his home, where John Bassett and I waited all day for his return while his good wife cooked us a fine Italian meal—and do know something about him. Lombardo is one of the more intelligent members of the Outfit. He is a killer and a tough guy. But he assumes the same posture as Vincent "Chin" Gigante, the current leader of one of the five New York families of the LCN. "Chin," the guy who shot Frank Costello in his apartment building at 115 Central Park West in New York in 1957, has ascended all the way to the top of his family. But he poses as though he were senile, walking around outside in his pajamas and slippers. This, people like the fine New York FBI agent Doug Lintner believe, is simply a pretext to throw off the public, and law enforcement in particular, to make them believe he is "out of it" and, therefore, of no concern to them. Joe Lombardo, I believe, follows the same strategy. He acts like his nickname. But he is no clown, believe me. And especially in 1974 he was not.) Lombardo was on his way to becoming a capo, and a most important one, in the organization now being led by AAA. He had been given two prime responsibilities. One was to oversee Tony "The Ant" Spilotro, the enforcer in Las Vegas. Las Vegas was, therefore, essentially the domain of Lombardo. Secondly, Lombardo was given responsibility by Accardo over the "bank" of the Chicago Outfit, the Central States Pension Fund of the Teamsters Union. Each of these two responsibilities was of equal

importance to Accardo and the Outfit. Las Vegas, in 1974, three
years after Spilotro had been sent out there to muscle the scores of
people responsible for getting out the skim and getting it to
Chicago, was still a big moneymaker for Chicago. And the pension fund of the Teamsters, the money contributed by hardworking truck drivers, taxicab drivers and warehousemen for their
retirement, was raided continually and heavily by the Chicago
mob for high-risk ventures, some of which paid off and many of
which did not.

One such venture which did not was set way off in Deming,
New Mexico (I have spent much time there—it's not much), the
site of the American Pail Company, a phony enterprise set up by
Lombardo, Spilotro and other mobsters to siphon off money for
their personal use. The FBI came down on this phony company
and indicted Lombardo, Spilotro and, almost as important to the
mob, Allen Dorfman, the son of Paul "Red" Dorfman, the guy
who initially brought Jimmy Hoffa to Hump, who had then facili-
tated Hoffa's route all the way to the presidency of the Teamsters.
As payoff to the Chicago Outfit, Hoffa had placed Red's son Allen
into the spot where he more or less controlled loans that were requested from the Central States Pension Fund. So Allen Dorfman,
one of the defendants in the Deming, New Mexico, case, was just
about as important to Accardo as his fellow defendants Lombardo
and Spilotro.

It was important to Accardo that he not lose these guys, so this
was not just another routine case. If these people went down, it
would be another serious blow to Tony and the Outfit in a time
when it was tough enough to find good people.

There was one huge key to the prosecution of the Deming case,
one which was absolutely essential. This was the testimony of the
prime witness, the *sine qua non* of the case, "that without which is
not." His name was Daniel R. Seifert. Seifert had been a partner in
an unaffiliated company with America Pail, the International
Fiber Glass Company of Elk Grove, a western suburb of Chicago.
His partners had been Milwaukee Phil Alderisio (before he died)
and Irwin Weiner, a bail bondsman closely associated with the
Outfit. The Deming case, which was to begin in January of 1975
and which would accuse the mobsters of defrauding the pension
fund of $1.4 million, would have little chance in court without
Seifert—as we would find out.

Accardo, therefore, had a dilemma. If he failed to allow Lombardo et al. to whack Seifert, and Seifert testified as he had testified before the grand jury, Tony Accardo would lose some of his

best men and the "bank" with them. On the other hand, if he gave Lombardo permission to hit Seifert, who was a private citizen, it went dead bang against Tony's philosophy that the public should be conditioned to believe that the mob only hit its own. The killing of such a person would surely arouse the public, and therefore law enforcement.

Joe Batters gave it his complete attention. This decision was precisely why the Outfit needed him. It needed him to be up on top to use his experience and capability to determine what the course of action should be in major cases. And this was one big major case, believe it! After considerable thought, Tony Accardo gave Joe Lombardo his answer: "Take him out."

On September 27, 1974, twenty-nine-year-old Danny Seifert was conversing with his wife and child at eight in the morning as they were about to enter the plant of another company he operated, Plastic-Matic Products, Inc., in Bensonville, a northwestern suburb of Chicago. He looked up—there, approaching him, were two masked men carrying shotguns. Danny, fine husband and father that he was, thought first of his wife and child. He jumped up and ran, thereby focusing the attention of the gunmen on him alone, but as he approached the front door of his plant, a third gunman stepped out. Danny was blasted to his death. A fourth man then drove the three men away in one car while another followed in the familiar "tail car getaway" scheme—the tail car was used in case there was a car chase, maybe cops. In this case there was none, and the four gunmen made good their getaway. Danny Seifert lay dead on the ground while his wife and child stood watching. They had seen it all.

Tony Accardo was angry as a hornet. It was bad enough that a private citizen had been gunned down in cold blood. That would arouse society. But to do it in the presence of his wife and child! That was a colossal blunder. Tony could understand that Tony Spilotro would stoop to such stupidity. The Ant was the Enforcer, not noted for his brain. (In fact, I later told Spilotro, "We call you Pissant, not for the size of your body but because of the size of your brain." He didn't like that, or me, for that matter. Nor did I care for him.) But Accardo had a hard time reconciling that Joe Lombardo, a much sharper guy than Spilotro, could be so stupid.

Indeed, the Chicago media whooped it up. It was a front-page story, above the fold, and jumped onto inside pages for the next two or three days. Action was demanded. How could gangsters get away with such a brazen act? Tony almost felt he had made the wrong choice. Maybe it would have been better to let these guys go down. Who needed people like that? But Tony had to live with it. It may have been his biggest error—not that Lombardo, Spilotro, Dorfman and the others were convicted. Of course they weren't. Without the testimony of Seifert, the prosecution was almost empty-handed. They put another witness on the stand at the trial, one Harold Lurie, but he turned out to be not a good witness. He had been a good informant for our agents Denny Shanahan, Christy Malone and John Roberts, but he froze on the stand. Without Seifert, we had no case at all. The case went forward anyway, and we lost. The jury, in this case understandably, voted to acquit all the defendants. It was a sad day in my life. A real standup guy like Danny Seifert had lost his life for no good reason, leaving behind him a shocked wife and child. What a waste of a courageous guy. God bless Danny Seifert.

49 A Shot at Accardo

Tony Accardo was soon faced with another crisis. This was what Joe Batters was being paid for. (Since he put the Outfit back on its feet once more, he was being "paid" very well. It is very difficult to try to estimate what the wealth of Joe Batters might have been at this stage in his life; on the other hand, anybody who leaves $275,000 in cash lying around in his basement while he goes off to his other home, as Tony later did, must have a buck or two.) This crisis involved the flamboyant gangster whom Tony Accardo had put in place as the mob boss a couple decades ago and whom he had then forced into "retirement." Sam Giancana.

Here was the problem. When Giancana left Chicago after he "abdicated" his job as boss, he had taken off for Mexico City, then settled in Cuernavaca, where he lived in a mansion rivaling 915 Franklin. Then he and Dick Cain, my pal, traveled the world setting up gambling casinos and cruise ship casinos. Giancana and

Cain were living in the lap of luxury, with millions of dollars flowing in, almost all for Giancana. He split almost none of it with anybody else. He had done it, with only Cain's help, almost by himself. Why, he felt, should he give any portion of it to the Outfit? He was no longer, in his opinion, "made," since Joe Batters had effectively thrown him out. When he was on his way up in the Outfit, working under Joe in the invasion of the black policy racket, for instance, anything he garnered thereby had to go "out west," to the leadership. He retained only a small part for himself. When he was the boss, he got a lot more, but still a split had had to be made with the capos and the soldiers. But to Giancana's thinking, he had been tossed out by Accardo; why should he divvy up with him or with anybody else in the family? He was no longer a part of it. His response, therefore, when Tony sent Butch Blasi to convey to him in Mexico that Accardo wanted a "sit-down" to discuss the situation, was to tell Butch to go to hell. Butch had been the bodyguard-driver-appointment secretary for Tony when he became the boss, then did the same for Giancana in 1957, when Sam succeeded Tony. (Butch was now operating in this capacity for Joey O'Brien.) He was, therefore, very close to Giancana. Tony had picked the right guy for the assignment.

When Butch returned from Mexico, he gave Tony Sam's answer. Tony simmered, but did nothing. Butch went back to work with Aiuppa and nothing was done about it.

In 1973, after Cain had left Giancana in Mexico and was attempting to establish a gambling empire in Chicago, Cain was called before Accardo. (Cain reported on it to me on one of our weekly Wednesday afternoon meetings.) The meeting took place at Meo's, Tony's regular meeting place in the western suburb of Norwood, with Joey Aiuppa and Gus Alex also in attendance, the entire Triple A team. Tony did almost all the talking.

"Cain, your guy thinks he's bigger than we are. How do you feel about that?"

"It's not my business," Cain replied. "That's between you and him. I'm out of it."

Dick said that Tony gave him the icy stare he was famous for. Cain, nobody's patsy, was the first to look away.

"I want you, Cain, to go to Mexico and explain the facts of life to him. I mean the facts of *life*, do you understand what I'm saying?"

I don't think Dick ever did go to Mexico or anyplace else to see Giancana about this. He told me he really didn't want to get involved between two such powerhouses as Accardo and Giancana. But it was his opinion that he knew who would win that war, if it came to that. In one of our very last meetings before he was killed, Dick told me that the impasse continued (this was in December of 1973). He also thought that as long as Giancana remained holed up in his walled-in mansion in Cuernavaca, with the armed servants he had there and the precautions he was naturally taking in view of the situation, it would be difficult for Accardo to prevail. And Dick did not believe that there was any way Giancana, as hardheaded as he was, would cave in. Sam was especially bitter about the treatment he had received at the hands of Accardo and the rest of the Outfit—and he had done the job of building his off-shore gambling empire without any extra help from them. At the same time, Dick realized that Giancana wasn't dealing with some patsy. Tony Accardo was still Joe Batters. Dick was chuckling as he wondered who was going to win that one. I thought I knew.

I guess I fanned the flames in this matter. Being careful not to compromise Dick as my source on this, I ventured out one day. It was about this time that I had been put in charge of the TECIP, the Top Echelon Criminal Informant Program. I had recently transferred, temporarily, as it would turn out, from C-1 to C-10. I was spending almost one hundred percent of my time, thanks to my new supervisor, Bob Dolan, developing informants and supervising the development of informants by the other agents of the two Chicago FBI organized crime squads, C-1 and C-10. Although, in exchange, I no longer tracked long-term targets such as Gus Alex, that was fine with me. I enjoyed the rapport I had developed with a small percentage of the top mobsters in Chicago whom I had developed into CTE's, top echelon informants, and looked forward to the challenge of doing the same with others. My enthusiasm for the job was as high as ever; I was at the top of my game.

In this new capacity, I gave Joe Batters some thought. We knew each other by this time. We had come across each other, one way or another, four times now. It was out of the question that Tony Accardo, The Man, would ever betray his family of La Cosa Nostra by becoming an informant for me. But, gosh, what would be the loss if I spent some time working on him? And it would be fun. That's the kind of million-to-one odds guys like me can't resist.

So one day in 1974 I had set up a surveillance, a "fisur," on Joe. Jackie Cerone was out and back in stride—he picked up Joe about eleven-thirty and then drove to the condo on Bonnie Brae in River Forest, where Paul Ricca was spending the last days of his life. They picked up Paul and then drove to Meo's, their regular lunch spot. Even though I was alone, I had no trouble tailing them without being observed, since I had a very good idea they would follow their regular pattern. I waited outside in my car while they ate.

Jackie dropped off Joe at his home. I waited the couple minutes until Cerone had turned the corner, then walked up and rang the doorbell. I stepped back into the yard, so Joe would be able to see that it was just me.

He opened the door. I almost expected him to invite me in, but he didn't. Instead, he stepped outside, didn't say a word.

I recall the conversation went pretty much like this:

"Hello, Joe. It's been a while and I thought I'd stop by and say hello."

"That's nice," Accardo said, returning my smile.

"I've got something I'd like to chat with you about, Joe, if you've got a moment."

"Well," he said, then hesitated. "Clarice is napping. Maybe I'll put on my coat and we'll take another walk."

That was fine with me. He went back inside, closed the door. He returned about two minutes later.

We walked. I didn't get around to the reason for my visit for about ten minutes as we chatted somewhat like old friends might. Some way or another we got into a discussion about Dick Ogilvie. Dick had been the governor of Illinois until recently, and was, of course, the prosecutor who had convicted Joe in the Foxhead 400 beer sale case about Joe's use of his red Mercedes. Joe knew that Dick and I were close friends, and he was wondering what Dick might be planning to do. I told him he was going into private law practice, and Joe said he thought Dick "would make a million. He's actually not a bad guy."

"There's a few of us around like that," I said, and Joe smiled. We were off to a nice start and I was in no hurry to get to any point. Frankly, I was surprised that we were walking around River Forest at his suggestion. No other mob figure would have taken the chance of being seen—even talking amiably—with the G. It could very easily be misunderstood. (Action Jackson had gotten his because he was seen talking to me on a street corner on the west side. He had never flipped, but the mob put him on a meat hook, stuck a cattle prod into his penis, smashed his kneecaps and let him hang in agony for three days before he expired from the punishment and pain. But Joe Batters was not Action Jackson. He wouldn't have anybody above him to explain to. He could tell it like it was and nobody would consider disbelieving him. He was his own man. *The* Man.)

Then I came to the point. "Joe, the reason I came to you today is to let you know we are aware you are thinking of hitting Mo," I said, using Giancana's code name in the mob to indicate that I knew something about the situation.

Accardo said nothing.

"I don't think that's a good idea, Joe. The reason I don't is that whether you believe it or not, I don't want to see the blame fall on you. I think you know you're the right guy for the job you've got. And we think so, too. You keep the Outfit out of narcotics, you do only what you have to do with the heavy stuff. You're much better there than Mo, for instance. I know you might find that hard to believe, but I think you recognize why I'm saying it. So, with that in mind, I want you to stay right where you are. I'm not saying we aren't out to prosecute you. You know we are. But you also know we're not about to frame you. Haven't so far, won't now. You're fair game, of course. But until we do get you, Joe, it is our feeling that better you than anybody else we can think of, and I'm coming to you now with a little warning. Watch out on the hit on Mo. It'll splash back on you."

There was a lot of hot air in what I told Joe, that's clear. On the other hand, hot air or not, it was friendly advice. It was as good a ruse as any to open the door to Tony Accardo, to do my job as the full-time TECIP agent by approaching anybody who was in a position to do us some good—become a PCI and then, hopefully, a CTE.

Joe said nothing at this juncture, probably a smart move. We walked silently for a half a block or so.

We had circled several blocks around North Avenue and Harlem Avenue and were now approaching Accardo's house. He looked at me and shrugged his shoulders. "Well, whatever," he said. He took my hand and shook it, holding the shake for several seconds. "Roemer," he said, "I appreciate your thoughts. There are worse guys than you around. But I don't think there's any good in your coming around. You do your job and I'll do mine. Whatever is gonna happen will happen. You apparently come to me in a good spirit. OK. But that's it. Good luck to you." Then he dropped my hand, smiled slightly, turned and headed up the large circular driveway that fronts that house. That was it. As I say, it was fun but not productive. I watched him go, then returned to my car, headed south on Harlem through Oak Park to the Eisenhower and returned to the FBI office. What had I gained? Nothing. What had I lost? Nothing.

Later "Romano" told me that at the next meet Accardo had with his capos he advised them of my approach to him. Romano said the Outfit had become very much aware that I was making contact, as I was, with most of their top people, and that it should be kept in mind that while I was "honorable," I was "not to be trusted." "Don't fall for this guy and his good manners. Keep him at arm's length."

I expected as much. As I made my way through the ranks of the top people in the Outfit, those in position to help us by providing information of real value, we fully expected that those who did not succumb to my "charm" would make sure that their superiors and peers were made aware that I had tried and had been rebuffed. Frequently "Romano," "Sporting Goods" and Dick Cain would smile at me during our regular meetings and say something like, "I hear you got tossed by Fifi Buccieri the other day," or "I hear you stopped by Turk Torello's place last week." I therefore knew that those capos had reported to the "west side" that I had approached then in my capacity as the TECIP agent and that there was no sense stopping by again. It was only when my CTEs did not report one of my recent approaches to one of the Outfit members that I felt I had a chance and *did* stop by again. Almost all such approaches were unproductive. But those few that were successful were well worthwhile!

50 Giancana—Downed Again

He knew he was at risk. As soon as he came back to the country, he sat down with Tony Accardo. Not that he softened up or gave anything away. His position was the same. What was his was his and he would share it with nobody, except for a bit to Butch Blasi and Gus Alex, who had helped a little. But he kept 98% of it for himself and that was the problem.

Sam Giancana was nobody's pussy. The longer he had remained on the top job in the Outfit, the tougher and more arrogant he had become. Even when Joe Batters deposed him and he went packing, he had retained his rough edge. Now he was back and he still was tough.

A little different than before, though. I had been out in my radio car the day he returned from Mexico. He had been bribing the guy in the Mexican government who could keep his temporary resident alien status secure. Then the guy had moved up to the presidency. He didn't need Giancana's drop anymore. Therefore, the pressure we had been putting on the State Department to pressure the Mexicans to throw him out finally took effect. Sam was deported—without even his shirt. The Mexicans grabbed him in his pajamas while he was walking in his cactus garden inside the walls of his mansion in Cuernavaca, threw him in their car and took him to their headquarters, where they gave him a shirt and a pair of pants that were three sizes too large. Then they put him on a plane to San Antonio, where our agents served a subpoena on him calling for his appearance before a grand jury in Chicago shortly thereafter. They bought him a plane ticket on American Airlines to Chicago and watched him go. Then they called us and let us know the expected time of his arrival. I was called to go out to O'Hare and greet him.

When Giancana arrived, fortunately with no baggage (he needed his hands to hold up those trousers), I stepped in his way. I fully expected he would snarl the same obscenities at me as he had in this same American Airlines concourse over a decade before. I was fully prepared to respond in kind once again. Even more so, now that I was alone. Harold Sell, my supervisor in 1961, who had kicked me in the shins the last time to restrain my outburst, was not there this day, nor was anybody else from the FBI. I was on my own, and I was going to give a lot more than I would take.

How surprised I was. When I stopped Giancana, he looked at me and said, "Roemer! I should have known!" I took that to mean he blamed me for his deportation. That was fine with me. Then he said, "Look, I'm back. I don't wanna be, you know that. Now I'm not gonna be involved in anything back here. I'm out. So let's forget what has gone before us. If you want an apology, this is it. Let's let bygones be bygones, not be personal again. OK?"

Wow! This was the tough, bellicose mobster of yore? This was not the Sam Giancana I knew. Maybe Toni was right after all. Maybe her father was a pussycat. Hardly! But that was the way he acted that day.

Giancana returned to his residence in Oak Park, which his caretakers had maintained for him at 1147 South Wenonah on the far south side, just a couple blocks east of Harlem Avenue, at Fillmore. As Joe Batters had at his Ashland Avenue digs, Sam Giancana had furnished a lavish basement, and that is where he lived, down there, with his caretaker couple upstairs. I guess I've been on the street outside that house a hundred times.

First, Sam had to appear before the federal grand jury in Chicago pursuant to the subpoena served on him in San Antonio. Jerry Gladden, then a sergeant on the Intelligence Unit of the CPD, and now the fine chief investigator of the Chicago Crime Commission, wanted to go at him about the extent of his knowledge about the shooting six months earlier, on December 20, 1973, of Dick Cain. A subpoena was also served on him commanding an appearance before the Church Committee of the U.S. Senate, which was investigating the Castro-CIA caper, the plot of the CIA when they conspired with Giancana and Johnny Roselli to assassinate Fidel Castro of Cuba. Johnny had wound up dismembered in an oil drum in Biscayne Bay off Miami—drum beat, not trunk music, as it were.

Then Sam, who had dumped Phyllis McGuire for a new love, traveled out to Santa Monica to visit her. While he was there, he got sick. A gallbladder problem. He was flown on an emergency basis to Houston to be treated by the famous surgeon, Dr. Michael E. DeBakey. When he was well enough to travel, he snuck out of Methodist Hospital in Houston to avoid the cops and the press and was flown home. Butch, the loyal old friend, picked him up at O'Hare and took him home.

It was June 18, 1975. Feeling much better after the removal of his gallbladder, Giancana hosted a party that evening for his two closest pals, Butch and Chuckie English, and his family: Giancana's daughter, Francine, and her husband, Jerry DePalma. When it was over, they all departed. Shortly thereafter, however, Francine realized she had forgotten her purse and returned to retrieve it. After a few minutes in the house, she took off once more. As she and Jerry were leaving, they noticed that Butch was also returning. Thinking nothing of it, the DePalmas once more left Giancana, who was feeling good now, at home.

Whoever did it—no one was ever convicted—must have been trusted. There was no sign of any struggle, no sign of any breaking and entering. Giancana must have let him—or them—into his basement and then turned his back as he prepared a late night snack of cici beans and Italian sausage. It was done with the weapon of choice, if it can be done up close and personal, a .22. This one turned out to be a High Standard Duromatic target pistol with a silencer. The caretakers upstairs never heard it. Bang. A shot in the back of the head of the completely unwary mobster, then several more into the throat and head. Giancana had gotten the same chance he had given the thirteen men Ralph Hill had documented he had killed—none.

A few weeks later the gun was found in the grass along Thatcher Avenue in River Forest. Knowing the approximate time of the killing, the police theorized that as the shooter drove north on Thatcher that evening, a squad car, with lights and siren full blast, came south on that main thoroughfare in the village. Presumably any such person might get quite cautious under those circumstances. He might throw the gun out the window, thinking the cops had zeroed in on him.

This, and the fact that Butch was highly trusted by Giancana, focused investigative attention on Blasi. That route on Thatcher Avenue headed towards his home on Park Avenue, near North Avenue in River Forest. Or it might have been the route such a killer might take to go report to Joe Batters that the deed was done, since Accardo's Ashland Avenue abode was just several blocks from the Blasi home. Both were on the north side of River Forest, about five miles from Giancana's house on the south side of Oak Park, the next town.

I had gotten to know Butch very well. His wife Connie, who was one of Clarice Accardo's close friends until Connie died in the mid-Eighties, occasionally fixed us lunch when I was in the neighborhood. She was a sweetheart. I am one of the few—maybe the only one—who didn't right away put the finger on Butch. He had been Accardo's man before he switched to Giancana when Giancana became boss—and then to O'Brien when he became boss. The theory is that if Accardo ordered Butch, due to his easy access to Giancana, to make the hit, Butch would have followed those orders. He would have had to. And indeed Butch was taken before the federal grand jury by Doug Roller, then the Strike Force Attorney in Chicago, and granted immunity when he took the Fifth about any role he might have had. Like Giancana before him, Butch refused to testify regarding any role he might have had in the hit on Giancana. He was sent to the MCC, the Metropolitan Correctional Center in the Loop, where he would spend eighteen months with his mouth shut. When he was released, he never again became involved in mob business.

A couple years ago I tried to contact him in a nursing home in a western suburb of Chicago. The attendant told me he wouldn't know me, that he wasn't lucid. He had an advanced case of

Alzheimer's. He died shortly thereafter, never to be officially connected to one of the most infamous murders in Chicago mob lore. One of the most infamous hits ever ordered by Joe Batters.

51 Jackie Cerone Returns

If Butch Blasi could not be hooked up by investigation to the Giancana hit, then neither could Tony Accardo. We took no part in the investigation. As it turned out, officers of the Intelligence Unit of the Chicago Police Department had conducted a surveillance at the Giancana residence in Oak Park much of the evening of the killing, before the hit took place. They questioned Jerry and Francine DePalma and Chuckie English, all of whom, they were aware, were at the party just prior to the shooting, but to no avail. All denied being there at the time, and since the CPD had seen them leave, they knew that it was true. (Chuckie followed his leader several years later. He could never bring himself to believe that the new leadership was as good as his buddy Giancana's. He would sit around his hangout, Horwarth's, and bad-mouth his current leaders. Joe Batters didn't approve of such stuff, especially when it was being mouthed almost in hearing distance of his home. He gave the nod, and one night as Chuckie was coming out of Horwath's, they took him in the parking lot.)

We took no part in the Giancana investigation because we had no jurisdiction, just as we had had none in almost every one of the thousand such gangland killings which the Chicago Crime Commission had tracked since 1919, when the CCC first started. Unless there was some interstate jurisdiction or the presumption of same, as in the Lindbergh Statute, which gave us the right to investigate kidnappings, then we had no authority to investigate. (Now that has changed in many respects and the FBI many times can come in on such non-interstate cases. But not in 1975, when Giancana was clipped.)

As the investigation wore on without bearing any fruit, the consensus focused on Butch. I guess we'll never really know who did it. I talked to Butch about it, since he was a guy I could talk to, one of the top guys I had approached, but he declined, courteously, to respond to my questions. I guess that's what I expected him to do.

It was about this time that Tony Accardo decided he could once again step aside—not down, aside.

The reason was that the best man for the job had returned. Jackie Cerone had served his sentence in the Bombacino ITAR case and was released, was back in Chicago living in his Elmwood Park home with Clara and his son Jack, the reputable Chicago attorney, who does his father proud.

The only trouble for Joe was that Jackie was not dumb. He was too sharp to want to be in the limelight again as the boss. He had found that there are guys out there who could be flipped, like Lou Bombacino, disgruntled guys who could be wooed by fine FBI agents like Paul Frankfurt and persuaded to see what the FBI considers the light.

Jackie, however, was loyal. In the image of his mentor, Tony Accardo. When Tony sat Jackie down and explained the situation, Jackie understood. Later he would tell "Sporting Goods" about his lecture. And "Sporting Goods" told me.

"Jack, it's your turn," Accardo reportedly said. "Look at me. You think I wanted this? They brought me back twice. I had to. I took the oath. I owed it. How long have I been at this? Twenty-six from seventy-five? What's that? Almost fifty years. How long as top guy? Forty-three from seventy-five. What's that? Thirty-two years. More or less the boss for thirty-two years! And where am I going? You need me, I'm here. I'll go aside to *consiglieri* once more. You got a problem, you come to me. Just like before, when you were boss. Count on it. But you owe. Just like I owe."

Jackie understood. But as "Sporting Goods" let me know later, Jackie held out for one concession. Everybody knew that Joe Aiuppa, aka O'Brien, was not nearly as capable as Jack Cerone. O'Brien was in place as boss now. Joe and Gussie had stepped aside once Aiuppa got some experience. They let him have the job. It was my experience that sometimes Aiuppa's elevator didn't go all the way to the top floor—not that O'Brien's mental capacity was seriously lacking, he just didn't impress me as being in the same class with such guys as Accardo, Cerone, Alex, Hump, et al.—and "Sporting Goods" felt the same way. He believed that Jackie had hoodwinked Aiuppa, letting him think that he, Aiuppa, was the boss while Cerone was just the underboss. That way Aiuppa stayed in the spotlight. Let the soldiers, even the capos, come to him. Let them believe Aiuppa was running the Outfit. Cerone would fulfill his responsibility to the Outfit by fulfilling the wishes of J.B. He would, in fact, be running the show, but out of the spotlight. (Therefore, when I turned one of those capos, he quite accurately informed me that Aiuppa was the boss. Then when I turned in my report—and then leaked it to pals like John O'Brien and John Drummond in the media—it would be Aiuppa who took the heat, not Cerone.) Any tough, major decision would be tossed to Joe Batters, as always. But any tough decision not of such magnitude would be handed up to Cerone, while Aiuppa would see that it was implemented. If somebody had to be put in the ground or made trunk music, it would be Aiuppa who received that order directly from Accardo and who passed it on to the executioners. That would keep the cagy Jackie Cerone out of the line of fire, just as it had Tony Accardo for years, where only inadmissible hearsay evidence could link Accardo and/or Cerone to the crime.

52 Accardo Hits

One of the first decisions that had to be made by the new Aiuppa-Cerone leadership team was what to do with Chris Cardi.

Christopher Joseph Cardi was the nephew of Willie Messino, a prominent "made" guy, although he was never a capo. First, Willie had gone to Pat Marcy and seen that Chris was put "on the job," on the Chicago Police Department. Like Dick Cain and many before him, Cardi had "carried the satchel," become a "bag man" inside the cops, collecting the drop from the mob and distributing it monthly to those captains, commanders, lieutenants, sergeants and patrolmen on the pad. It wasn't a hard job, but the

Outfit needed people in that spot who could be trusted. It was expected that a nephew of Willie Messina would be. Unfortunately, it got to be boring for Chris Cardi. He asked his uncle for permission to quit the job.

When Willie acquiesced, he put Chris in another spot. Now Cardi became a "juicer." Actually, not quite. He became a collector and muscle man for the juice business, the loan shark operation of another prominent Chicago "made" guy, "Joe Gags," before Gagliano passed away. This was still not good enough for Cardi.

Cardi wanted more. More money. He realized it would take him years to be "made" and then become a capo, and even his uncle had never achieved that, nor had Joe Gags, his boss. So Chris went where the money was—into dealing drugs. Oh, boy! This was a direct violation of the strict edict of Tony Accardo. *Nobody* dealt drugs when he was a made guy. Now, Chris Cardi wasn't made, but he was "Outfit"—what the FBI, the CPD and the CCC call "an associate." Not only had he worked for the Outfit under Joe Gags, but he was the nephew of Willie Messina. That is tight.

It might never have gotten to J.B. if Cardi hadn't been caught by the police—dealing heroin, no less. Now it was a matter of public knowledge, and soon everybody would learn of Cardi's pedigree, his connection to the mob and his crime. How could Accardo and his people claim they were only involved in so-called "victimless" crimes? Wasn't pushing heroin about as heinous as you can get?

Joe B. couldn't let this violation go unpunished. An example had to be set. Joe made his decision in two seconds—and then he had another thought. "Let's let this bastard stew in his own juice for a while. Go see Pat, have him get to the judge and have him throw the book at Cardi! Give him every day he can give him. Pat will like that. It'll do what we want. Make the judge look like a hanging judge. Then when we come to him for a pass, he can give it without worrying about criticism. He can just say, 'Look at my record! Didn't I give that gangster Cardi the maximum?' This will shoot two birds at the same time. Then when Cardi serves his full sentence, then you whack him. Not now, then." (I'm not aware that Pat approached the judge in this fashion, but in any event, Cardi went to prison.)

Chris Cardi served his sentence. Then on July 14, 1975, he went inside Jim's Beef Stand at 1620 North River Road in Melrose Park. It was just after midnight. Chris was now forty-three, had a wife and three kids. He had been out of prison three weeks, just enough time for his wife to get used to his return. She and the three kids were with him at the moment, but it didn't matter. This guy was bad. Taking him out in the presence of his family would strengthen even further the example that was to be set. Let the guy stink in the slammer and then when he gets out, blast him.

Two ski-masked gunmen snuck up behind Cardi, his wife and three kids. They used .45s this time. Eight times in the back, naturally. Then for good measure, while the wife and kids screamed, they rolled him over and put one in his face.

Tony Accardo was pleased. "Good job. That will teach anybody wants to go into drugs a good lesson."

I guess so. It would me.

Joe Batters ruled on another one in 1975. This time it was Nick Galanos, who should have known better. He was an independent bookmaker. He paid the street tax as required. That was not his sin. His sin was moving into Forest Park, the western suburb where the Armory Lounge was located. He did it without getting the approval of the mob. Forest Park was mobbed-up. You just don't move into that village without sitting down with the Outfit and making some arrangements. Nick did, though, and on August 30 he paid for it. Again it was done with .45s. Nick got it nine times, first in the back, of course, and then in the chest. He had let the gunmen into his basement, probably thinking they wanted to do business. They did, all right.

Then came another, just two months later to the day. Tony Reitinger was also an independent bookmaker. He had another kind of problem with the Outfit, the usual one for guys who operated on their own. Tony was doing very well. His handle was $30,000 a day on sports betting. He had some very good customers who lost a lot and could afford to pay off. When this was brought to the attention of Joe Batters, he couldn't let a guy who was supposed to be going 50-50 get away with that. "$30,000 a day and we get scratch? Scratch *him*!" Reitinger was thirty-four at the time. His office was his home at 5203 North Magnolia, just above Lawrence Avenue, where he handled most of the action on his private phone, mostly bets this time of the year on college and pro football. But buckets was coming up.

Tony was eating at Mama Luna's Restaurant on Fullerton, waiting for a client. It was a Friday night and Reitinger was looking forward to a big football weekend. It wouldn't happen. Two gunmen, wearing hockey goalie's masks and armed with a shotgun and a .30 caliber carbine, like the one I carried in the Marine Corps in World War II, rushed into Mama Luna's, spotted Tony in a booth, pushed him back as he tried to get out and hit him with two shotgun blasts to his head and four carbine shots into his right side and back. Slam-dunk.

A couple months later, in January 1976, Tony was presented with a tough one. This was family. Blood family. Frank DeLegge, Jr., was a bad guy. He was a burglar and a thief, one of the main targets of the FBI's Top Jewel Thief Program, staffed by three of the best agents we ever had, two guys named Tom Green and one Ray Stratton. Frank lived in Melrose Park. He had recently been released on a case in which I had been involved. It was a bank robbery, something I wasn't usually concerned with, since it was not organized crime, but this one had had mob overtones. In 1963 the Franklin Park Bank, in Franklin Park, was robbed. One of the Tom Greens and Ray Stratton solved it immediately, because Guy Mendola, who was one of their 137s, their informants, took part in the robbery. At the time Willie "Potatoes" Daddano was the "made" guy who liaisoned with the burglars and robbers to make sure they paid their street tax to the mob. He suspected foul play. The case had been solved too quickly. Green and Stratton weren't that good! So Daddano reached out for Dick Cain, who at the time was not doubling inside the mob for me—he was doubling for the Outfit inside the Cook County Sheriff's Office as their Chief Investigator! A "made" guy, true name Ricardo Scalzitti, and he was one of the top officials of the Cook County Sheriff's Office, and to make it more unbelievable, the sheriff at the time was Dick Ogilvie, the best sheriff ever, the public official I respected most. We all make mistakes, and that was perhaps the only one Ogilvie ever made. Unless you consider the increase in state income tax he passed as Governor a mistake. The voters did, and they elected a much lesser guy when it came time for Dick to run for re-election. In any event, Daddano went to Cain. Actually, he called him in Paris, where Dick was vacationing. Daddano wanted all the bank robbers put on the lie box, the lie detector. Cain couldn't do it himself, so he assigned one of his subordinates in the S.O., Bill Witsman, who was also a capable lie box operator, to meet with Daddano in a motel in the western suburbs and administer the tests to the robbers lined up by Potatoes. He did, and he fingered Mendola. Daddano went to Giancana, the boss in 1963, and Sam went to Batters, and the next day Mendola was chopped.

The other robbers went to prison, including among them Frank DeLegge, Jr. Also included were Dick Cain and Potatoes Daddano! Green and Stratton, thanks to the ingenious U.S. Attorney we had at the time, Tom Foran, brought in Dick and Potatoes on a conspiracy rap and had them sent away—Cain for ten years and Potatoes for fifteen.

But now DeLegge had gotten sideways with the Outfit because he brought trouble. Aiuppa wanted him whacked, so he went to Accardo. This was a real problem for Joe because Frank DeLegge, Jr., was a son-in-law of Nick Palermo, the plumber in Melrose Park whose nephew just happened to be married to one of Tony's daughters, and who was one of Joe's best friends. It was not a thing to be taken lightly, this thing of chopping Nick's son-in-law.

But business of the La Cosa Nostra family came before business of the blood family. Anytime. Just to prove it, not only was DeLegge killed, his hit was assigned to Tony Spilotro, who usually served up his hits rather half-baked. What do I mean by that? First, DeLegge's throat was slashed from ear to ear, just as the seven Ashland Avenue burglars' throats were slashed, then his body was thrown out into the Chicago winter, into a ditch near the Tri-State highway near Elmhurst, where it was found by a young boy—imagine his surprise—frozen stiff. Treatment like that was generally reserved for only the worst offenders of mob edicts. Business first, as they say.

In March 1977, Aiuppa was still the boss when he came to Accardo once again. Even Romano could not definitely tell me the reason for this hit. The rumormill had it that this guy had gone up to Milwaukee and killed the underboss up there, then the underboss' driver came into Chicago and had paid him off in kind. It sounded a little exotic but not unlikely. For years one of the two mob hitters had been Chuckie Nicoletti, the partner of Milwaukee Phil Alderisio for years. Together they had engaged on some of the top hits in Chicago. (Maybe even the Giancana hit. Who knows? Maybe Butch went into that basement first and then let Chuckie in. Chuckie sure had the wherewithal to do a job like that.) For some reason, Chuckie was now in a problem himself. I didn't know Chuckie well. I only had one sit-down with him, years before at the Cal-Lex Social Club at California and Lexington, his hangout on the west side. Vinnie Inserra and I had attempted to turn him without success.

It was March 29, 1977. Chuckie was sitting in the front seat of his Olds, parked in the lot of the Golden Horns Restaurant on North Avenue in Northlake, a western suburb. Chuckie was sixty now, still living at 1638 North 196th Avenue in the blue-collar western suburb of Melrose Park. Somebody must have been talking to Chuckie from the backseat. In any event, the job was done in the usual manner, into the back of the head. Three shots from a .38. Those who took Chuckie to Northlake Community Hospital forgot one thing—to turn off the engine to that Olds. It caught fire when it overheated and burned, not that Chuckie was concerned. He died six hours later in the hospital. Retribution! How many guys had Chuckie plugged in the back of the head? Twenty? Maybe more.

Tony Accardo was then presented another problem. (I believe, in this chapter especially, I'm making it very clear that Tony Accardo was not "Saint Accardo," as Antoinette Giancana believes I feel. He was one bad guy. He couldn't order all these killings, some of them very brutal, without being such a poor example of a human being.) Tony had to determine whether Maishe Baer should go down. Maishe, true name Morris Saletko, was the owner of a large deli-type restaurant in the Loop located near City Hall. At his restaurant, Maishe operated a bookmaking office, was a juicer and even a fence. He had recently returned from prison after being involved in a million-dollar silver hijacking. Maishe was one of those guys who felt he could short the Outfit on his street tax. Another example had to be set. Accardo was especially wary about sanctioning a hit on this guy, however, because he was well known. Many of the pols from City Hall frequented his Loop restaurant and he was well connected. But perhaps especially *because* he was well connected, the bottom line was that he could not be allowed to thumb his nose at the mob.

So Tony reluctantly gave Aiuppa the OK to have it done. Maishe got it while he was parked in his '77 Olds on July 13, 1977, in the Brickyard Shopping Center at Narragansett and Diversey on the northwest side of Chicago. He was found shot in the left side of his face and head.

If approving the hit on Maishe Baer was difficult, the next one brought to Joe Batters for his OK was even more so. The mob had a solid rule: they don't hit cops. In every case such a hit causes a counter-action; all of law enforcement has a huge reason to be angry and to put all of its resources into the investigation to find the culprit and to retaliate. But here was a most unusual case. Mark Thanasouras had been a watch commander at Summerdale in Rogers Park, now Foster Avenue. I recall spending an evening with him, having dinner in the showroom of the old Edgewater Beach Hotel, way up on the north side near the lake. Then he became the commander of the Austin Police District on the west side. He did a very unusual thing when he took over Austin by wiretapping all the book joints. That might seem to be a smart thing—find out where all the mob's wirerooms were and raid them. But Mark didn't want to raid them, he wanted to find them all and then shake them down, and that's what he did. Then he spread his wings a little, organizing a large crew of his officers to shake down all the tavern owners. We got him for that and he went away from 1966 to 1970. He got out a little early by testifying about four other corrupt police captains. Quite a guy! Mark was now working as a bartender out in Lake Bluff at the L & L Club Number Two. Nobody would hire him in law enforcement—not so much, it's sad to say, because he violated the law, but because he squealed on his fellow captains. He had known what they were doing because he was doing it too, following their example. But in the polite circles of the police community, you don't snitch.

It was July 22, 1977. Mark was taking his girlfriend home, walking her to 5507 North Campbell, on the north side. It was five-fifteen on a Friday afternoon in this peaceful neighborhood, and Mark took it: shotgun blasts in the head and abdomen. Joe Batters had had him hit. He couldn't let a fink live, even if he had been a cop.

By this time Joe was hardened when it came to sanctioning gangland slayings. By then he had approved one of the most infamous hits of all time, ranking right up there with his participation in the St. Valentine's Day murder and the job on Sam Giancana. This was the hit on Jimmy Hoffa. Of course, it hadn't been up to Joe alone. This was so big it had to be sanctioned by the Commission. But Joe had cast his vote as a participating member at the time, in July 1975.

James Riddle Hoffa had been groomed for his job after Paul Dorfman recommended him to Hump. The Chicago mob, with its control of several Chicago locals, was instrumental in facilitating the rise of Jimmy to the presidency of the International Brotherhood of Teamsters. Now they were in position to command that Jimmy do what they requested of him. I remember Hump saying on Little Al, "I never met a guy like Jimmy. When we ask for something, he just does it. He goes boom, boom, boom." But Jimmy proved to be a tough guy, too. He went boom, boom, boom for the mob all right, but once in a while he didn't jump as high as they asked. He'd occasionally have a problem with their "requests" and say no. Still, while he was president of the Teamsters, he was very good for the mobs—not only in Chicago but in New York, New Jersey and, especially, in Detroit. The mobs were very happy with Jimmy. Then he went away to prison, and the mob had to come up with somebody new. Jimmy recommended Frank Fitzsimmons and the mob followed that advice. Fitz, by contrast, wasn't tough at all. He granted each and every "request" of the mobs which had control of him, and the mobs began to consider that he was a much better IBT president than Jimmy Hoffa had ever been.

When Jimmy got out, he signed his acceptance of his parole with the stipulation that he would never again become involved with labor unions. That stipulation had been slipped into his parole papers under the influence of Fitzsimmons, who was fat and happy in Jimmy's old job. Fitz had become very close to the Nixon administration and had been able to influence the terms of the parole. Jimmy apparently hadn't read his parole papers closely when he signed them, and when that stipulation was brought to his attention, he blew up. Notwithstanding the agreement, Jimmy began to make moves to regain his lost presidency. Fitz didn't care for that. He went to Aiuppa and Cerone, to Fat Tony Salerno in New York, to Tony Provenzano in New Jersey, and to the guy closest to him, Tony Giacalone, in Detroit. (When Fitz was coming up in 1969 and 1970, he frequented the Market Vending Company in Detroit. It was owned by Maxie Stern, the leading figure in the Detroit "Jewish Mafia," which controlled gambling in certain areas of Detroit. Bob Fitzpatrick, as fine an agent as ever worked in the FBI, frequently surveilled Stern and Fitz at the Market Vending Company and often observed Fitzsimmons conversing with Giacalone there. He also saw him with Black Tony Termaine, another top Detroit mobster, and Pete Licavoli, a Detroit capo.) Actually, Fitz's connection to the Detroit mob was the stepson of Jimmy Hoffa, Chuckie O'Brien. O'Brien was the actual conduit between Fitzsimmons and the mob, according to what I learned from Bob Fitzpatrick.

When Fitzsimmons asked the mob to help him fend off Hoffa, they took it to the Commission, since so many mobs had their fingers in the Teamster pie. The Commission voted to return the favor to Fitz by taking Hoffa out. In fact, Fitzsimmons had dinner at Larco's Restaurant just days before Hoffa was hit. This restaurant on Six Mile Road in Detroit was a favorite of Pete Vitale and Raphael "Jimmy" Quasarano, reputed hit men for the Detroit Outfit, who became the prime suspects in the Hoffa hit. They met Fitz at Larco's that evening.

As is well known, Hoffa had expected to meet with Giacalone at the Red Fox restaurant. When Giacalone didn't show up after Jimmy had waited for some time, Jimmy called his wife Jo, wondering what had happened to Tony. Finally, it seems, Chuckie O'Brien showed up, and Jimmy, who had no reason not to trust his stepson, got into his car. Hoffa was never seen again.

The FBI investigated the killing of Hoffa—an investigation that is ongoing, in fact, since the case has never been solved. We called the investigation by the code name "Hofex," short for "Hoffa Execution." My part in the investigation in 1975 was to canvass my informants, like "Romano," "Sporting Goods" and a new one I had now developed as a CTE, to determine what they knew.

Years later, after I had retired, I got a call from the producer of *Larry King Live*. A guy had written a piece for *Playboy* magazine for which he was paid some $50,000, as I recall. He was Lake Hadley, a private investigator in Las Vegas. He had been retained by *Playboy* to check out the story of a convict who claimed that he had helped bury the body of Jimmy Hoffa in the end zone of the New York Giants Stadium in the Meadowlands in New Jersey. That was all news to me. So I called Jim Fox, an old pal of mine, who was then the FBI agent in charge of the New York office. He put me in touch with his deputy, Jim Esposito, who, in Detroit, had been assigned as the case agent on the Hofex case. He told me the FBI still believed in what we felt was the burial ground for Hoffa back in 1975, that Hoffa's body had been thrown into a vat of boiling zinc in a fender factory in Detroit. Esposito assured me that they had questioned the source of the Meadowlands information, the convict, three years prior to this. At the time he had claimed that Hoffa's body had been buried in a shopping mall in New Jersey. They had determined, Esposito said, that the convict was not credible. They checked out his new story and found it to be lacking.

Apparently the shopping mall burial ground was not sexy enough for *Playboy*, so this convict had come up with the end zone story. I flew to Washington, where Larry King does his show on CNN, and debated Lake Hadley on the program. Although we are fairly certain his story lacks credibility, the case remains unsolved to this day.

These were the problems Tony Accardo faced in the mid-Seventies. He continued to be The Man in the Chicago family of La Cosa Nostra—the Outfit, as he referred to it. Joe was at the height of his powers in those days. He was strong mentally, emotionally and physically, and respected by all who worked under him—and against him. Though times were tough, *he* was in his prime.

53 Accurate Reports on the Outfit

It was about this time that an "intelligence analysis" was done by the Chicago Strike Force, that group of Justice Department attorneys who had been assigned the prosecution of organized crime in Chicago. It was done for Gerald Shur, then the Attorney-in-Charge of the Intelligence and Special Service Unit of the Justice Department in Washington, after consultation with me and several other FBI agents, DEA agents, ATF agents and IRS agents in Chicago.

The report was focused on what it called "the Chicago Syndicate." A portion of it reads: "The Chicago Syndicate is the best known, most well established organized crime group in the Chicago area, with a famous heritage from the Al Capone era. Although most members have Italian ethnic origins, the group is seldom called La Cosa Nostra by state or federal officers here. The Chicago Syndicate differs from its Eastern counterparts in that it does not have the initiation rites or formal membership common to the LCN. While there is an inner circle of Italians from which the boss must rise, non-Italians play strong roles in this organization . . . There are several area bosses or capos who control the illegal financial operations of the geographic sections of the Chicago area. In reference to these geographic divisions, the boss would control the gambling (bookmaking), juice and business extortion of the area. He is also responsible for any public official kickbacks necessary to maintain the operations. The area boss answers to the syndicate boss and delivers a portion of the profits to him. It is believed that 'the west side,' the term for the Syndicate hierarchy, ultimately receives payment for all organized illegal activity in the metropolitan area, whether through direct payment, or as a kickback in exchange for allowing others to operate independently of the mob (street tax)."

The report went on to identify the illegal activity of the "Syndicate," the name most used in those days by the media when describing what the "made" members referred to as the Outfit. Since they themselves do not refer to their organization as "the Syndicate," we in the FBI do not. But, picking it up from the media, other federal agencies and local law enforcement did use this terminology in referring to the Outfit.

The report identified gambling in all forms as the "traditional stronghold of organized crime throughout the country, and Chicago is no exception." It identified "sports betting on horses, football and other sporting events," as "the forte of the Syndicate and is believed to be their principal source of revenue. The bookmaking generates the juice or usury loans made by the Syndicate." The report identified that the clientele for this form of gambling is "predominantly white." Then it went on to say that other "common forms of gambling—bolita, policy, and numbers—are more common to the black and Latino neighborhoods."

The report then stated that "Organized crime has infiltrated Chicago labor unions more heavily than in any other city in the country. The Syndicate profits in three ways from the liaison. First, the union can employ mob members and associates as organizers and business agents. Secondly, the Syndicate can control and manipulate unions' funds, such as pension and health funds, and skim money off through quasi-legal means. Finally, the mob through the union can manipulate legitimate businesses by threatening union problems."

The report contained a section captioned "Syndicate Leaders." The first name mentioned was Anthony Joseph Accardo. He was identified as "holding the ultimate control of Syndicate organization . . . Accardo, at age 70, is available for purposes of consultation, policy matters, and major personnel problems. He is not employed and has no financial holdings of record. For these reasons, Accardo is well insulated from criminal prosecution."

The report then listed the top men under "the ultimate control of Accardo . . ." Joseph John Aiuppa. Aka Joey O'Brien: "The operating boss. He controls the day to day business of the mob in general . . ." Gus Alex, "the highest placed non-Italian in the Chicago Syndicate. He is useful to the Syndicate for his political influence. Described by the FBI as an exceptionally intelligent man, Alex is considered the strategist of the organization. Before his rise to this position, Alex controlled the downtown 'Loop' area.

"There are four capos who answer to Joey Aiuppa and among these the city is geographically divided. They are James Torello, Al Pilotto, Vincent Solano, and Jackie Cerone.

"Torello had nine known active lieutenants to handle his responsibilities on the west side of Chicago:

> Joe Ferriola
> Angelo La Pietra
> Donald Angelini
> Dominic Cortina
> Bill McGuire
> Joe Spadavecchio
> Frank Buccieri
> Arnold Garas
> James Inendino

"Al Pilotto had the following lieutenants to handle his responsibilities in the southern suburbs of Chicago:

> Dominick 'Toots' Palermo
> Edward 'Tarpy' Arambasich
> John Arambasich
> John Costello
> Sam Aprile

"Vincent Solano had the following lieutenants to handle his responsibilities on the north side of Chicago:

> Caesar DiVarco
> Mike Glitta
> Lenny Yaras"

John Phillip "Jackie" Cerone was described as "an enigma for law enforcement officials.

"Cerone was known to be operating boss of the Syndicate until his conviction and imprisonment for gambling in 1970. After his release in 1973, Cerone appeared to retire from the Syndicate operation for a few years. It now seems he has returned to the organization and is a frequent companion of Anthony Accardo.

"Cerone is described by the FBI as a troubleshooter for the mob. He is well respected for his intelligence and organizational ability and could have returned to the top spot when released from prison if he had wished. In contrast, the Illinois

Bureau of Investigation does not list Cerone on their organizational chart and considers him in retirement.

"DEA finds Cerone the highest level link of the organization to the narcotics traffic in Chicago. They report he meets frequently with Aiuppa and Accardo and has met with 'capo di tutti capi' Carmine Galante (a New York boss).

"The following subjects are also of note in the Chicago Syndicate: Charles 'Chuck' Nicoletti is the top hitman or enforcer for the Syndicate. He is believed to supervise the activity of other enforcers, including Tony Spilotro and Frank 'The German' Schweihs. Anthony John 'Tony' Spilotro supervises the Chicago Syndicate's investments in Las Vegas. Spilotro is believed to report directly to the LCN Commission and take orders from them. He is a known Chicago syndicate hitman, answering to Nicoletti, but Spilotro is the more powerful, flamboyant and aggressive of the two. Dominic 'Butch' Blasi could be called an expediter for Joey Aiuppa, acting as his personal secretary and chauffeur. He had been in this capacity since 1950, working for Accardo and Giancana. It is the opinion of the Strike Force, the FBI and the Cook County State's Attorney that Blasi killed Giancana in 1975, having been seen with him just minutes before Giancana's death. Marshall Caifano at age 65 has been a powerful member of the Syndicate for most of his life."

The report went on to include other prominent members and then had this to say under the caption "Future Leadership Changes": "Joey Aiuppa's health problems and age suggest that an organization change will occur in the Chicago Syndicate in the next few years. The two prime contenders for the position are Jackie Cerone and James 'Turk' Torello. Cerone, with his experience and reputation, is a likely choice for the present time. However, at age 62, Cerone would probably be considered too old for the spot in a few years. Conversely, Torello's relative youth (he is 46) may preclude him from the top spot at this time, despite his strong organization."

The report, before going on to deal with other organized crime groups in Chicago (the emerging crime groups known as the Herrera Family, from Mexico, and the Black P Stone Nation), concluded that those Syndicate members "who deal in drugs do so without Syndicate backing. Their involvement appears to be principally at the financial level, with little involvement with the actual narcotics."

The final paragraph was captioned "Report Sources": "Information for this report was supplied through reports and interviews with the following agencies: FBI, DEA, ATF, IBI (Illinois Bureau of Investigation) and Strike Force Attorneys. In instances of minor variations, usually FBI data is presented, unless otherwise noted."

I recall that when I read this report in March of 1977, I was struck that it made no mention of Joe Lombardo. I felt that Lombardo, not Nicoletti, should have been described as the capo in charge of Spilotro, and as the important liaison between the "Syndicate" and the Teamster Pension Fund. Very important roles, thereby making him too important not to be identified in this report. I also had no indication that any mob leader was involved in narcotics, certainly not Jackie Cerone. I recognized that this information came from the DEA. At the time I was the official FBI liaison with the Chicago office of the DEA, and I knew they were fine, capable, hardworking individual agents. But I also suspected that in order to justify their activities, they felt they should find some connection between the major organized crime group, the Chicago family of La Cosa Nostra, and narcotics trafficking. I'm not saying they were intentionally inaccurate in connecting Cerone to the narcotics traffic, but knowing what I did about Jackie Cerone, I felt that there was possibly only one other person who would keep himself more distant from narcotics. That would be his mentor, Tony Accardo.

With these minor exceptions, I feel, as I did then, that the author of the report, Denise Bonitsky, the Intelligence Analyst for the Chicago Strike Force, did an outstanding job of putting the report together. She had impressed me a lot when she came down from her fifteenth floor to our ninth floor of the Federal Building to interview me and a couple other Bureau agents. The report, I believe, was well researched and well written. It certainly captured the essence of what the Outfit was all about at the time, in March of 1977.

Speaking of reports, there was another one done at precisely this time, the spring of 1977, one which was not official but which carried the same weight with me. It was the May 16, 1977, cover story of *Time* magazine, written by Sandy Smith, my old friend who was now a senior correspondent with *Time*. Since I for some years had been one of his prime sources—and had been, anonymously as always, since I was an FBI agent, a source for this article, I had a special personal interest in it. Accompanying the article was a chart of the current makeup of the Commission, the ruling body of La Cosa Nostra, including a photo of Tony Accardo as the Chicago representative on the Commission. The other commissioners in 1977, as identified by this article, which was entitled "The Mafia: Big, Bad and Booming," were Aniello Dellacroce, Carmine Galante, Funzi Tieri, Tony "Ducks" Corallo and Dominick DeBella from New York; Tony Accardo from Chicago; Angelo Bruno from Philadelphia; Carlos Marcello from New Orleans; and Joe Bonanno from Tucson. The chart also indicated that Tony Spilotro controlled Las Vegas, that Mike Rizzitello was the boss in Los Angeles, that Jimmy "The Weasel" Frattiano was then in San Francisco, that New York controlled Atlantic City and that Las Vegas and Miami were "open cities."

The *Time* article, which is very well documented and researched, estimated that "the Mafia takes in at least $48 *billion* in annual gross revenues and nets an incredible $25 billion. Exxon, the largest industrial corporation in the U.S., reported sales of $51 billion and net profits of $2.6 billion in 1976 . . . Chicago authorities estimate that because of mob operations, the average citizen pays an additional 2¢ on the dollar for almost everything he purchases on the legal market—the passed-along business costs of extra theft insurance, additional security forces and outright extortion. Organized crime flourishes in part because of a peculiar moral obtuseness—or anger at tax-happy authorities—on the part of many Americans. Extraordinary numbers of otherwise honest people see little harm in patronizing discount cigarette vendors and neighborhood bookmakers, in buying 'hot' merchandise at bargain prices, even in using the expensive and illegal services of loan sharks. Abetting this ethical blind spot are the romanticized accounts of the Mafia in novels and movies. In addition, dramatic changes in American moral attitudes—the new sexual permissiveness, relaxed concern over marijuana and cocaine, and the drive to legalize gambling—create an ever-increasing appetite for organized crime's services. Last week, for example, two organized crime figures and seven associates were indicted in Detroit on charges of luring rich businessmen to sex and gambling parties and then extorting large sums of money from them—in one case $200,000 . . . While law enforcement officials know the identity of the major mobsters and the nature of their crimes, turning up enough hard evidence to put them in prison is often impossible. The Mafia reputation for vengeance frightens many victims, witnesses and potential informers into not cooperating with authorities. To make matters even easier for the mob, the growing public concern over street violence has prompted city and state police to concentrate less of their limited resources on organized crime. The government has also lost two of its best weapons: virtually unrestrained bugging and wiretapping which once provided 80% of the information about mob activity, and easy access to hoodlums' tax returns.

"For all its impact on American life, the Mafia is a remarkably small organization. As reckoned by the FBI, the Mafia numbers about 5,000 'made men,' or members. All are of Italian ancestry, often with roots in Sicily. The Mafia is by far the best organized criminal group in the U.S. and the only one with a national structure of 26 cities—five of them in New York City—of 20 to 1,000 'button men,' or soldiers.

"The familiar Mafia lore that has become commonplace knowledge through movies and fiction is essentially true. All the made men are bound by a loyalty oath of blood and fire . . .

"In Chicago, the 250-member mob, known as the Outfit, is still nominally in the hands of Anthony 'Big Tuna' Accardo, 71. He spends most of his time at his $126,000 condominium in Palm Springs, leaving day to day operation in the hands of his Underboss, Joseph Aiuppa, 69. But Aiuppa's grip is shaky—some authorities say he has no executive ability—and career young thugs are on the warpath against the old guard. So far, they have not gone after Accardo or Aiuppa but have settled for promotion by gunfire to the Outfit's middle and upper echelons.

"A few of the war's 21 victims in the past three and a half years have been police informants and potential prosecution witnesses. But most have been mobsters. Among those killed were Sam Giancana, who abdicated as the Outfit's leader in 1965, and Richard Cain, an ex-cop who served as the top aide to Giancana. The latest to die was Chuckie Nicoletti, 62. He caught three .38 caliber slugs in the head on March 29 while sitting in his blue Oldsmobile outside the Golden Horns Restaurant in suburban Northlake . . ."

The article then spent some time on Tony "The Ant" Spilotro, the Chicago mob's boss over Las Vegas. It noted that "Nevada authorities are investigating this swaggering, street-wise punk for his alleged involvement in skimming millions from the slot machines of the Stardust casino." In another place the piece stated that "Spilotro watches over the Chicago mob's investments in Las Vegas casinos and controls loan-sharking, narcotics and prostitution along the Strip. Says a Justice Department official: 'Spilotro has become the most powerful man in Las Vegas, next to Moe Dalitz. Spilotro takes a cut of all illegal activities of any consequence.' "

This article was as good as any ever done on "the Mafia." I would not have called the mob that, since it is misleading in that there is a Sicilian organization known by that name which is separate and distinct from La Cosa Nostra and since the American mobsters call themselves La Cosa Nostra, not the Mafia. Other than that, I felt that this article captured the essence of what the LCN was across the country, just as Denise Bonitsky's official document had focused on the Chicago mob.

That period was a tough time for us in law enforcement. We had lost our Little Als and had not yet acclimated ourselves to the new statutes allowing us, under strict conditions, to bug. For example, the RICO, or Racketeering Act, had been enacted in 1970 and would give us a vital weapon in the fight against organized crime. But in 1977 we had not yet realized the strengths of these acts and had not yet begun to fully take advantage of what they gave us. Now, with probable cause to believe that a crime was being committed, we could again penetrate mob hangouts, and the evidence thereby obtained could be used in court against the defendants. The problem, of course, was probable cause. We had to develop specific information that the mobsters involved in this specific location would, in fact, discuss the future commission of crimes within our jurisdiction. In order to do that, we had to have concrete information, not supposition. We had to prepare an affidavit based on a live informant's information that such was the case. In other words, we practically had to have a live informant inside the targeted location before we could swear in our affidavit that crimes were being plotted there. In practice it was a Catch-22; if we had such an informant, we didn't really need the bug, and if we had the bug, we didn't need the informant. This is overstatement, because one supplemented the other as evidence when the case went to trial, but the difficulty of establishing both is daunting.

As for our ignorance with respect to RICO, we should have had our asses kicked. It was passed in 1970, yet by 1977 it had not really been utilized. For some reason we did not recognize what a great weapon we now had at our disposal. We did, however, come to understand that the RICO act, the Racketeering Act, was a potent weapon in our arsenal.

It wasn't much longer before we began to fully utilize both the eavesdropping power given us in 1968 by the Omnibus Crime Control and Organized Crime Act, especially its Title III, which addresses the power to eavesdrop and wiretap, and the RICO Act of 1970. When the Justice Department finally made us aware of the potential of these two statutes, we came into a new age in our fight against Tony Accardo and his people.

*   *   *

Another fine author wrote a fine summary of the status of the mob in 1977. This was Bill Brashler, who that year had written the biography of Giancana, entitled *The Don*, and who, like Sandy Smith, had good sources and contacts, including me, in law enforcement. Brashler wrote the cover story for *Chicago* magazine in its issue of November 1977. It was entitled "The Outfit, 1977: A Progress Report." Brashler identified Tony Accardo "at 71, still chairman of the board." He wrote: "For the past twelve years the mob had been dominated by the thinking of Tony Accardo and the late Paul Ricca. They believed in not hurting themselves, in operating as quickly and quietly as possible in taking care of business. The antics of Sam Giancana—the court suits, the night-clubbing, the tirades, the entertainers—brought nothing but attention and heat, and business suffered from it. Accardo and Ricca never forgave Mooney for that; the mob yearned for the day he'd lose his hold and finally they put him to sleep."

Bill also did a chart of the mob to accompany his story. At the top he had "Tony Accardo, the Chairman." Others featured were "Jackie Cerone, the Underboss/senior advisor; Gus Alex, senior diplomat/near north; Joey Aiuppa, Operating Director; Vince Solano, Underboss, north side; Jimmy Torello, comptroller/gambling chief; and Al Pilotto, Underboss/far south."

In the article Brashler identified Jack Cerone as "a close associate of Accardo and for years considered his natural successor. Cerone never really wanted the job. Contrary to a persistent report, Cerone is not about to oversee new mob narcotics efforts. Informed Federal investigators strongly dispute any new Chicago dope move (it has never been an active mob concession here) and cite no evidence for a report Cerone met with New York's Carmine Galante for the purpose of pursuing narcotics sales in Chicago." I wonder what little birdie put him right on that?

54 Transferred

It was at this point in time that I chose to move on, to leave Tony Accardo to his own devices—well, not exactly. There were many fine agents who were being groomed to take over from the first wave of Top Hoodlum agents in Chicago and now even from the second wave. The old Top Hoodlum Program had become the Criminal Intelligence Program under Bobby Kennedy and was now known as the Organized Crime Program.

Jeannie and I went out to Tucson to visit our elder son Bill, who was hired in August of 1975 to be the sports director and sports anchor on the evening news of KOLD-TV, the CBS affiliate in Tucson. We had now visited him twice a year for three years, and we had fallen in love with Tucson. Jeannie wanted to move there. I didn't, but only because I was in love with Chicago and the work I was doing there. (Jackie Cerone, in a motion he filed in the Cook County Circuit Court in 1981, would call me "the nemesis of organized crime in Chicago." I liked to think that that was pretty much true, whether it actually was or not. I used to walk into City Hall, tongue firmly in cheek, saying to myself, "Watch out, you crooks, here comes Roemer!" A little much, but that's what I was in those days.) I didn't want to leave Chicago, warts and all, for Tucson, beauty and all. Since Jeannie did, I gave it a lot of thought. Then I found that the FBI in Tucson was about to go all-out in an intensified effort to get Joe Bonanno, who was running his Bonanno family in Brooklyn by remote control from Tucson. I, therefore, felt able to do what Jeannie wanted us to do, move to Tucson in the cactus desert, with the sunshine, the fresh air and the mountains, and still, perhaps, come up against a strong mobster, a member of the Commission since it was formed in 1931, one of the legendary mob bosses. I made some inquiries and found out from Bud Gaskill, the SAC in Phoenix to which office the Tuscon

FBI reports, that if Washington would approve my transfer, he would assign me to organized crime investigations in Tucson, including the case on Bonanno. I put in my request and when it was approved, we moved to Tucson in May 1978.

If Tony Accardo noticed my departure, I'm sure he didn't sigh in relief. And it was certain he would continue to go about his business as The Man of the Chicago Outfit, while plenty of better FBI agents than I continued to focus on him.

55 The Picture and a Big Hit

Two of the fine agents who had been groomed to take the Organized Crime Program to new heights were just about to do so. They were the new wave which had begun to recognize what old-school agents such as myself had not—the potential of Title III and RICO.

Title III of the Omnibus Crime Control and Organized Crime Act of 1968 had given us the legal right to eavesdrop, to penetrate mob meeting spots and listen to what was being discussed. LBJ had taken our Little Al away from us, but now Congress had given us something even better. Now we had the ability to break and enter under court order, and to use any information we gathered from the hidden mikes as evidence in court against them. The procedure was that when any of them came up to be prosecuted, we had to have what is called an "elsur hearing," a hearing in a courtroom in a federal building with their attorneys present to listen to every word disclosing what we had picked up on our elsurs of them, on our electronic surveillances. As a result, the mobsters were now keenly aware of our surveillance techniques. The members of the criminal defense bar brought the new statute to the attention of their mob clients hard and fast, and they were cautioned to be very careful of what they said and where they said it. Now, although we could go in and penetrate as we had in 1959, the mob knew that we would be coming. You gain some and you lose some.

Some of us older guys had moved along. Some of us had retired at the minimum retirement age of fifty, some of us had advanced to bigger (and better?) positions inside the FBI, some had resigned and taken better paying jobs in private industry. One had requested an office of preference transfer to Tucson. Those we left behind on C-1 and C-10 were well prepared to exceed even what we might have accomplished.

I have described all the minute machinations of how these agents did the job of "Pendorf" in *The Enforcer* (published by Donald I. Fine, Inc., in 1994). Suffice it to say that Pete Wacks and Art Pfizenmayer did us proud. Joe Batters must have been pulling his hair out. What they did was to penetrate the headquarters of Al Dorfman, the key to Accardo's bank, the Central States Pension Fund of the Teamsters Union. This was the fund which loaned so many hundreds of millions of dollars to the mob's high-risk investments, mainly its casinos in Las Vegas—the Stardust, the Desert Inn, Circus Circus, Caesar's Palace, the Dunes, the Hacienda, the Tropicana, the Aladdin and the Fremont—and to several other high-risk enterprises like the American Pail Company in Deming, New Mexico.

It was, of course, Al Dorfman who had been placed in position by Jimmy Hoffa as a payback to Chicago's mobsters for facilitating his ascendancy into the executive offices of the Teamsters Union.

Dorfman's offices were in the International Tower on Bryn Mawr Avenue, alongside the Kennedy Expressway, near O'Hare Airport in Chicago. (Every time I take the CTA train from O'Hare into the Loop and approach the Cumberland Avenue stop, I gaze out to my right and see the International Tower building and think of what a great job Pete and Art and the others did there. I think, too, of the time I served a subpoena there on Dorfman, only to return to my car and find that, in my hurry to intercept Dorfman, I had locked my keys inside. Imagine how humbled I was when I chose to go back into Dorfman's office in the International Tower and request that he allow his chauffeur to drive me back to Avis at O'Hare, where I had rented my car, to get a new key. This was after I had retired and was working as an investigative attorney defending news organizations against libel suits brought by organized crime figures. Still bumbling and stumbling, as always.)

What Pete and Art did ranks right up there with the best FBI work of all time. They dubbed this operation "PENDORF" for

Penetration of Dorfman, and eventually obtained enough information of an evidentiary nature not only to sink Dorfman and the president of the Teamsters, Roy Williams, but Joe Lombardo, the mob's man over Dorfman and over Spilotro in Las Vegas. The PENDORF operation started in late 1978 and finally culminated with the convictions in late 1982.

The upshot of it was that Tony Accardo had another decision to make. Allen Dorfman had been a gold mine of information with respect to the mob's interests, especially in the Teamsters but also in Las Vegas. If Dorfman wanted to sing, he could obliterate the vast income the mob was generating in those areas—and Al Dorfman, as J.B. was painfully aware, was no hardened mobster. He had already served a long sentence after a conviction in New York and he wanted no more hard time like that. In January 1983, Dorfman was awaiting sentencing.

I can't tell you how close the Bureau was to flipping Dorfman. I wasn't involved, but I knew enough to know that the information Tony Accardo was getting didn't make him happy. He gave the nod. He was now very used to taking a life with just the snap of his fingers. If he shook his head from side to side, the guy lived. If he nodded up and down, the guy was dead. It was that simple. He would sit and listen when first Giancana, then Battaglia, then Alderisio, then Cerone and now Aiuppa or Cerone brought in a request. And when he granted it—which he usually did—his organization had more than enough manpower and gunpower to accomplish what he asked for. How many people in our history have had that kind of power? Not many. Knowing Joe, I imagine that the first few decisions might have bothered him. He did have a good side. In 1977, Joe was endorsing the contracts on so many, it had gotten to him. He had suffered a mild heart attack and was confined for a short time at St. Mary's of Nazareth Hospital. But he had snapped back quickly. I doubt that in 1983 he was losing any sleep after condemning a man to death.

By 1983 Joe was spending most of his time on Roadrunner Drive in Indian Wells, watching the golfers on the fairway in front of his condo. No longer was he making such decisions at his desk or alongside his conference table in the basement of 1407 Ashland Avenue. When in Chicago, he was living in a smaller place, another condo on Harlem Avenue. The Accardos had moved for a short time to 1417 Bonnie Brae, near where Paul Ricca had lived, and were now nearby at 1020 North Harlem Avenue. Still in River Forest, not far from Horwath's, where Chuckie English had gone down.

It was shortly before this that the police had been given a rare opportunity to take a good look at the mob's hierarchy. Federal agents—not the FBI but, as I recall, the IRS—raided the home of capo Joe "Caesar" DiVarco, the boss of the Outfit's Rush Street, near the north side area. They couldn't believe it—or at least I wouldn't have—but there on DiVarco's wall what did they find but a beautiful color photograph of the top leadership of the Chicago Outfit! My lord! The agents leaked the photo to the two Chicago daily newspapers, the *Tribune* and the *Sun Times*, and its resultant publication caused quite a stir. It was a real coup. Here was a graphic illustration of the top guys in the Chicago mob, all smiling brightly as if on their best behavior at a private party. Which, after all, is just what it was.

The party had been for Dominic DiBella, one of those who were called "The Three Doms," namely Dominick DiBella, Dominic Brancato and Dominick Nuccio, who had ruled an area on the north side. DiBella was dying of cancer and was being feted at a restaurant on the northwest side of Chicago, called The Sicilian. Vince Solano was being inducted as his replacement. Butch Blasi had been asked to bring a camera and he had snapped the picture, which had turned out very nicely, like most things Butch did.

There they were. Accardo was up front, of course, but Aiuppa was at the head of the table. Cerone and Lombardo stood in the back. Di Varco, Pilotto, Solano, DiBella, Amato, and Torello were there. The boss, the underboss, all the capos, the entire top leadership. Wow! If you didn't know better, you'd think they were a bunch of old geezers sitting around swapping stories. Actually, I guess some of them were just that.

On January 20, 1983, Al Dorfman was walking in the parking lot of the Hyatt Hotel in Lincolnwood, a northwestern suburb, with a pal, the same Irwin Weiner who had been indicted in the Deming, New Mexico, case but who had walked when Danny Seifert was gunned down. Joe Batters' nod was climaxed when eight shots were pumped into Dorfman. Some believe that Weiner set Dorfman up.

If Wacks and Pfizenmayer had come close to flipping Dorfman, they would be unsuccessful now. On Accardo's orders, the mob had flipped him first.

56 Tony Walks Again!

Joe was sipping his coffee on the morning of June 4, 1981. He and Clarice were reading the Chicago papers, the *Sun Times* and the *Trib*. Jackie was scheduled to pick him up shortly and Joe would ride in a cart with Cerone while Cerone tried to break par, which he did once in a blue moon, at Riverwoods, the country club they belonged to in the northwestern suburbs. The condo in which they were staying at 1020 North Harlem was nice. It wasn't 915 Franklin and it wasn't 1407 Ashland, but it wasn't exactly shabby either. Noisy, maybe, on that busy thoroughfare edging River Forest, Oak Park, Elmwood Park and other nice western suburbs.

It looked like a nice early June day in Chicagoland. (Chicago winters end about that time, or just a bit before. One day it's snowing and the next day summer arrives without any real spring. Then in July it gets hot and very humid.)

All of a sudden they were shattered out of their peace. The FBI was at the door! God damn, what now? Joe had made every effort he could to insulate himself from this kind of thing. There were a couple of layers between him and mob activity now. Anybody who might know he still had a role would have nothing but hearsay, and nobody but two guys he trusted with his life, Jackie Cerone and Joe Aiuppa, could testify that he was involved when he gave the nod. Maybe a third, Gussie Alex. But he trusted these men as much as he had trusted Paul Ricca or Machine Gun Jack McGurn—as much as anybody in his life. They would not give him up under any circumstances. Nevertheless, at age seventy-five Joe had been indicted once again.

The agents had a warrant, told him only that it had been issued in Miami. In Miami? He hadn't been there for years! Only to pass through on his way to Bimini to fish. What could somebody have possibly said he did in Miami? The arresting FBI agents didn't know Joe, hadn't even spoken to him before. Their manual of rules and regulations, which they had been issued at the FBI Academy in Quantico, Virginia, specified that it is not mandated that a subject be furnished with the reasons for his arrest. He is allowed to dress appropriately, then he is to be handcuffed and immediately taken downtown to the Federal Building, where he is fingerprinted and photographed, mugged as we call it. Then, and only then, is he allowed to make his phone call, to his lawyer if that is his choice, which it almost always is. Then he is taken before the U.S. Magistrate, still in the Federal Building, and allowed, sometimes, to make bail. It is then that the subject learns the nature of the charge against him. Had I been there that morning, I would have allowed Tony to call his lawyer from his home and then escorted him, uncuffed, from his home in a fashion that the neighbors didn't get their rocks off gawking as the guy was pushed into a Bureau car, which then roared away, siren sounding, lights flashing. That's the way I handled arrests, like that of Donald Angelini. Guys I had a little respect for. Not the way, however, I handled the arrest of Philly Alderisio. A guy I had no respect for.

When Joe sat down with his lawyer Carl Walsh (now that Carl's dad, Maury, had died and Stanford Clinton was no longer available), he found that he was one of sixteen defendants in the case. What the hell was it all about? What could he have done in Florida to warrant an arrest? Carl would tell him later. Now one of the other guys in the picture at Dominick DiBella's "last supper" was led in—Al Pilotto, the capo in charge of the southern suburbs, one of Tony's top guys. Al was also the president of a local of the Laborers Union. Another capo, Vince Solano, headed another Chicago local of the Laborers. Angelo Fosco, a guy close to Tony Accardo for decades, was the international president of that union—not a local, the whole union. That's the union Frankie "The X" Exposito was involved in as an officer when Jackie Cerone, Turk Torello and Fifi Buccieri had gone down to Miami to try to hit him.

Tony's bail was set at $100,000, of which $50,000 was on his own recognizance and the rest in cash. Tony was given the requisite $5,000, the 10% of the $50,000, and he walked out in a blaze of flashbulbs as the media had their field day. "The Big Tuna" was once more in the public spotlight. As much as he had tried, as much as he thought he had insulated himself, he was still, midway into the seventh decade of his life, fair game to the paparazzi.

Accardo was being charged with RICO. The government

charged that he was part of an enterprise that had engaged in a pattern of racketeering, involving a scheme designed to strip more than two million dollars from the Laborers Union through a series of kickbacks from the Union's health care, dental care and vision care programs.

A week later Tony was back before the magistrate requesting permission to travel from Chicago, where the glare of publicity was so strong. Although late June is not the time to be in the heat of either Palm Springs or Miami, that's where he wanted to go. To his condo in Indian Wells, protected by walls and guards, and to Miami, where he could plan his defense after getting some sense of what the hell this was all about.

Among the other fifteen defendants, he was to discover, was another big-time mob guy—Santo Traficante, the boss of the Tampa family of La Cosa Nostra. Some believe that he was on the Commission, but he was never a member to my knowledge. He was never quite that big. His family in Tampa was relatively small and ineffective, and although Traficante got a lot of publicity from his involvement with Giancana and Roselli in the CIA-Castro Caper, he was never a Tony Accardo.

The next month, in July 1981, something happened to Al Pilotto. He was playing golf out in his territory, the southern suburbs, when a gunman jumped out of the rough, where he had been waiting in ambush, and put three shots into Pilotto's body. Although he was seriously wounded, Pilotto survived to stand trial in Miami. There were a couple of theories about the shooting which were leaked to the press. One was that the Ferriola faction of the mob wanted in on Pilotto's territory in the southern suburbs. When he resisted, they threw some fear into him in order to force him to relinquish some of his territory. The other story was that his own men sent a message because they were afraid Pilotto was caving in to Ferriola in his quest to take over the southern suburbs. I believe both are wrong. Shortly after Pilotto was hit, I came to Chicago. As I did then, and still do, I first reached out for an old friend, one of my former CTEs. I had been retired in 1981 for a year but was now working as an investigative attorney defending news organizations. At the time I was working for the Sacramento *Bee*, looking for Tony Accardo and Gus Alex to serve subpoenas on them commanding their appearance before the court to tell what they knew about the plaintiff in the case, a Palm Springs car dealer close to both Accardo and Alex. (The case was settled in favor of the Sacramento *Bee* when the plaintiff in Palm Springs dropped the case, three weeks after Accardo and Alex learned of my desire to deposition them in the case.) I asked my CTE, a top guy in the Outfit, about the Pilotto situation, and this is what he told me. Joe Batters had become a little "queasy" about Al Pilotto, his capo and his fellow defendant. He wanted Al to know there were worse things than a stretch in the pen. So he gave him a little shot just to "concentrate his mind." So he would not think to co-operate with the government in return for leniency.

As it turned out, the government's case against Tony in Miami was not a strong one. There was very little evidence to show that Tony had been linked to the kickbacks from the union's health funds. There were two principal witnesses against Tony who had some information which could be construed to put Tony in on the payoffs, but their testimony was somewhat convoluted. It was not actually firsthand. They had been told that Accardo got part of the kickbacks somewhere well up the line from the principals. It was a very complex trial, lasting for many weeks, and it took the jury a week and a half to deliberate. Six of the defendants, including the frail Al Pilotto, were convicted. Two were acquitted. One of these was Tony Accardo.

The Man had skated one more time! What did it take to get this guy? He was the proverbial cat with nine lives. If this kept up, it would indeed be nine times he had walked out of a courtroom after being found not guilty. Give the government credit for trying, for not letting the guy rest on his many laurels. Nobody had ever seen any envelope being passed to him—in Miami or Chicago or Palm Springs or anyplace else. The government must have known that, but any shot at Tony Accardo, "The Man," was worth taking. Maybe they would get lucky. What a feather in the cap of a U.S. Attorney that would be! But not this time. Once more the big tuna had slipped off the hook!

57 Accardo Wins Again

Tony Accardo was now going to have a good reason to have a keen dislike for Bill Roemer. The year was 1983. Not only had Allen Dorfman been killed, but now there was another shooting. Another that had obviously been sanctioned by Joe Batters.

For years Ken Eto, an Asian-American, had been in charge of the bolito gambling in Chicago for the Outfit. He had been indicted and Joe Aiuppa had been led to believe that Eto, like Dorfman, might not desire to spend a big portion of his latter life in prison. He might, therefore, be susceptible to an approach by the FBI before he was sentenced. If he whispered the right words into the agents' ears, it would mean some leniency for him. He wouldn't have to spend so much of the rest of his life in confinement, maybe instead in the Witness Protection Program. So Aiuppa went to Accardo and got yet another nod.

Eto operated on the north side of Chicago, where Vince Solano was the capo in charge. On February 10, 1983, Eto was instructed by Solano to drive to the parking lot of an American Legion Hall on the northwest side of Chicago, where he was to meet with Jaspar Campise and John Gattuso.

Eto later testified about what happened. After shaking hands with Gattuso and Campise, Eto got into his car behind the steering wheel, with Campise beside him and Gattuso, a sheriff's deputy, behind him in the backseat. He was told to drive to a restaurant at the corner of Grand and Harlem Avenue, where the men planned to have dinner. When they got to the parking lot of the restaurant, "That was when John Gattuso shot me three times in the head." Three shots in the head. From the backseat! Point blank! The gunmen, having every reason to believe that Eto was dead, ran off. Eto, however, somehow found his way to a hospital and, after being treated for the three shots into his head, called the FBI. They

314

came right away. It turned out that Gattuso's gun had a faulty silencer attached. The muzzle velocity of the bullets from the .22 caliber pistol was reduced enough so that Eto was able to live to talk about the incident. He became, in fact, a good witness. Joey Aiuppa and Jackie Cerone and several others would find that out as the years passed. Much to their regret.

In the meantime, Tony Accardo had to figure out what to do with the two mob guys (Gattuso was "made," even though he was a deputy sheriff) who couldn't do their job any better than that. Joe didn't have to think about that much. The press was crucifying the mob and, of course, the FBI was debriefing Ken Eto, who was in their protective custody away from any attempt Batters might make to locate him and shut him up. When Aiuppa voted to have Gattuso and Campise put away to make an example out of such bungling, Joe agreed wholeheartedly.

In July it was done. They became trunk music, stuffed in the truck of Gattuso's car, which was found in Naperville, a nice, quiet, upscale western suburb.

Somewhat as a result of the Dorfman and Eto hits in early 1983, the U.S. Senate Permanent Subcommittee on Investigations, which had begun hearings on organized crime in the tradition of the Kefauver and McClellan committees, decided to focus on Chicago. They put Cass Weiland, their Chief Counsel, in charge. Weiland came to Chicago and conferred with Ed Hagerty, the SAC of the Chicago FBI, and other law enforcement chiefs. He then approached the Chicago Crime Commission, where Pat Healy was the executive director in the tradition of the most capable directors before him, like Virgil Peterson. Weiland put a request to Healy to have the Crime Commission serve as the focal point of the Chicago hearings which would take place in order to alert the general public about the current and continuing menace of organized crime in the Windy City. Healy took the request to CCC president Gail Melick and the CCC board, and it was decided to expend the funds necessary for this purpose. It was understood that an airing of the terrible problems presented by the Chicago mob must be brought to the attention of the general public in the city and that the time was ripe.

As a result, I got a call in Tucson. Pat Healy was asking if I would be interested in presenting the facts of the situation in Chicago to the committee as a special consultant to the Crime Commission. He asked me to leave Tucson for the month of February and spend it in Chicago. That did not particularly appeal to me for obvious reasons. But the chance to acquaint the public in

Chicago with the menace presented by the Outfit did, so I accepted the invitation of the Chicago Crime Commission and, with the exception of weekends, I spent February of 1983 living at the Union League Club and spending my days in the offices of the Chicago Crime Commission in Suite 605 at 79 West Monroe, in the heart of the Loop. I spent the month interviewing law enforcement people to bring myself up to date on current conditions; I had, after all, left Chicago in 1978.

When the committee held their hearings in the Federal Building on March 4, I was one of the key witnesses before it. The hearing was chaired by Senator William V. Roth, Jr., and attended by such members of the committee as Senators Sam Nunn, Warren Rudman and Charles Percy.

I spoke for an hour or so and then entered into the public record about seventy pages of a statement I had prepared. My testimony and my statement focused on three areas: the history of the Chicago mob, much as I am presenting it here; the story of the alliance between crime and politics in Chicago, always my special investigative interest in the years I was in the FBI in Chicago; and the current structure of the Chicago Mob as of the date of the hearing in 1983.

As can be expected, it was Tony Accardo I focused on. I gave heavy emphasis to his role in the mob under Capone, under Nitti, as the boss from 1943 to 1957 and again in the early Seventies and as "the Man," the Chairman, since 1943, forty years up until then, in 1983. Bill Lambie, who was then with the Attorney General's Office and a former FBI agent and special investigator for the Crime Commission, had prepared, with my assistance, a chart of the Chicago mob as of 1983. Naturally, right at the top we had Tony Accardo. I used the chart during my testimony, in which I stated: "Tony Accardo has been the most capable leader in the history of the Chicago group." Under the caption "Current Status and Structure of Organized Crime in Chicago," my testimony continued: "Tony Accardo is still called upon when matters of high policy are to be determined, and for this reason he still maintains a Chicago-area condo. After all, he is the best leader the Chicago mob ever had, and his experience goes back to the days when he was a muscle man for Capone in the Twenties. He is truly the elder statesman of the mob."

Later in my statement, in the portion devoted to Jackie Cerone, I presented this: "The day to day details, the ordinary problems, are decided by Cerone. And when a major problem presents itself, such as what to do with a Dorfman or an Eto, it is Cerone who will present the case with the pros and cons, together with a recommendation, so that Accardo can understand the magnitude of the problem and then approve or disapprove Cerone's recommendation. Knowing, however, that Cerone is the protégé of Accardo, who has been his almost inseparable companion for decades, it would be hard to believe that Accardo overruled him very often."

These statements and others focused the attention of the Committee on Tony Accardo. My testimony was buttressed by the testimony of Ed Hegarty, the FBI boss at the time.

Shortly thereafter, Cass Weiland, the Chief Counsel for the Senate Committee, approached me and told me that they had decided to subpoena Tony Accardo to Washington and grill him on the basis of my testimony. That was a good feeling.

Now Tony Accardo was set to be grilled by the very best. In that sense it would be nothing new to him, but this particular interrogation would be quite difficult for him if what Cass had in mind came to fruition. At this stage of the life of Joe Batters, he didn't need this. At seventy-seven he was not up to a great deal of strife and excitement. But more than that, what Cass had in mind, and what would be approved by the senators on the committee, was to bring Tony into Washington, swear him in, put him under oath and then question him about my assertions. Then, and this is the crucial part, if he took the Fifth Amendment and refused to answer the questions, he would be given that cursed immunity! If he lied, he could be prosecuted for perjury. If he violated his oath of *omerta* and answered the crucial questions about people like Jackie Cerone, Joey Aiuppa and, particularly, his fellow members of the Commission, like the New York bosses, then one can imagine the consequences. It was the seldom-used tactic that we had forced on Sam Giancana and Butch Blasi which had sent them to jail. Joe Batters would suffer greatly if that happened to him now. He had had a heart attack and at his age was hardly the bear of a man he had been during his glory days.

Tony had also had a bout with lung cancer about this time. Although he had beat it, this, coupled with the heart attack he had suffered, had drained the Man's strength. He continued to be in frequent contact for major decisions, as he was throughout his life, since that took only a few minutes of his time and none of his strength. But he didn't have the stamina now, and when I saw him on television, that much was apparent. He walked with a cane—one with a big tuna on the handle—a gift he accepted good-naturedly.

On November 18, 1983, some eight months after my testimony,

Tony responded to a subpoena which had been served on him and appeared in Washington before the panel of senators who were members of the Senate Permanent Subcommittee on Investigations. The panel threw forty questions at him, mostly based on my allegations to the committee in March. At this point, I should say that I had mixed feelings about the situation. We had failed to get the Man when he was at full strength, and now there was something a little less important about getting him. Cass Weiland, I feel, understood my feelings. He had sent me a photo of several people around Al Capone in the late Twenties. One, he had been told, was Accardo. Could I verify that? I think my response reflected my feelings, which were thereby communicated to Cass. I told him I was very dubious about it being Accardo in the photo. My response was less than enthusiastic. I could have taken it to a CTE of mine who had been associated with Joe Batters shortly after the photo was taken, but I didn't suggest it. I really wasn't all that shot in the tail with going after Tony at this stage of his life. There were other, stronger fish to fry. On the other hand, as long as Joe continued to be the Chairman, I suppose he was fair game.

On February 23, 1984, the full Senate voted to cite Accardo for civil contempt of Congress after he refused to answer questions other than by taking the Fifth. Carl Walsh, Accardo's lifetime attorney, appealed the ruling. He claimed that my statements about Joe had been based on "illegal wiretapping" and submitted a motion calling for my appearance so that I could be questioned about this. Obviously, he was referring to the information I had received from Little Al, Mo, Plumb and Shade.

In defense of Walsh's motion, Senate attorney Michael Davidson told Chief U.S. District Judge Aubrey Robinson in Washington that a check of all Justice Department agencies, the CIA, the Cook County State's Attorney's office and even the California Attorney General's Office, revealed that only the FBI conducted wiretaps of Accardo. Davidson told the judge that the FBI had secret microphones planted at two locations frequented by Accardo. Court records showed that the bugs were at the Armory Lounge, 7427 West Roosevelt Road in Forest Park, and in the second floor offices of a custom tailor at 620 North Michigan Avenue in Chicago. (These were "Mo" and "Little Al.") According to Davidson, his check revealed that Accardo's conversations were taped on thirty-eight occasions at the tailor's shop and on nine occasions at the lounge. Davidson's position was "we don't want past history" from Accardo.

Carl Walsh argued with this. "It is unbelievable" that his client had not been the subject of any other electronic surveillance.

I'll quote thereafter from an article in the Chicago *Tribune* of March 31, 1984, under the caption "Judge Tells Accardo To Answer Questions." Speaking of Walsh, the article states: "He charged that former Chicago FBI agent William Roemer had testified before the panel that he had engaged in illegal wiretaps until he retired in 1978." (That was erroneous. I never said the bugs were illegal or that they extended past 1965.) Walsh continued, according to the article: "Since Roemer was involved in investigating so-called mob activities in Chicago, we want to question him and look at the transcripts of the conversations in which Mr. Accardo was overheard. In that way we can find out if the committee based its questions on any illegal surveillance." The article went on: "Judge Robinson noted in court that it would be difficult to determine, even by questioning Roemer, if any of the senators' questions were a direct result of wiretaps. 'There could have been other types of surveillance, plus the use of informants,' he said." Judge Robinson then ordered Accardo to answer the questions of the committee. "In his two-page order, the judge denied Walsh's motion to question Roemer and to see the wiretap transcripts."

And so it was that on June 21, 1984, some fifteen months after it had started, Tony appeared once more in Washington. The Arizona *Daily Star*, as did practically every newspaper and television station in the country, covered his appearance. Astoundingly, Tony had really taken the bull by the horns. I'll quote the Associated Press story in *The Star*: "Insisting that he has 'never been a boss' of the Chicago mob, Anthony "Big Tuna" Accardo told Senate investigators yesterday that he was friendly with other reputed crime czars but never discussed business with them. 'I have no control over anybody,' the 78-year-old, frequently hospitalized Accardo said during a court-ordered appearance before the Permanent Subcommittee on Investigations.

"Testifying under a grant of immunity from prosecution, he said . . . that his only knowledge of organized crime came from newspapers.

"Holding a walking cane with a carved tuna handle, the witness said his illegal gambling activities (in the Owl Club) and 'selling beer' brought him homes in River Forest, Illinois, and Palm Springs, California, and bank accounts totaling $700,000.

"He said he met legendary Chicago mobster Al 'Scarface' Capone at the racetrack but denied allegations that he was once Capone's bodyguard and had inherited his criminal empire.

"Accardo said he also had social contacts with reputed Chicago organized crime figures Joseph Aiuppa, John Phillip Cerone and the late Sam Giancana, whose daughter, Antoinette, discussed Accardo in her recent book, *Mafia Princess*.

"Accardo denied her assertion that he continued to receive a cut of the mob's earnings after he retired from day to day leadership in the 1970s.

"Accardo said that although he and Aiuppa had been close friends for years, they had never once discussed crime."

The Chicago *Tribune* also covered the appearance of Accardo. In their article, the *Trib* stated that "Accardo denied that he was a member of any organized crime group or that he has ever killed or ordered the murder of anyone. 'I only know about that from the newspapers,' he said.

"He drew laughter by telling senators that he didn't know what Joe Aiuppa did for a living."

One line of questioning by Senator William Roth, R-Del., subcommittee chairman, dealt with Accardo's role as a top crime boss:

ROTH:	Isn't it true that you have stepped down as boss of the Chicago crime family?
ACCARDO:	I've never been boss.
ROTH:	When you hold an annual Fourth of July party at your home in River Forest, Aiuppa and Cerone would be there. Weren't these people perceived as members of an organized crime family?
ACCARDO:	I have no knowledge of a crime family in Chicago.

The article in the *Tribune* continued: "Asked whether he had ever done anything illegal, Accardo first said no and then, after consulting with his lawyer, responded that his only criminal activity had been gambling. 'You never worked at any time?' he was asked by Roth. 'We sold beer at one time,' Accardo replied. Asked if taxes had been paid on the $700,000 as his net worth, Accardo replied: 'All taxes have been paid,' raising his voice.

"Other assets listed by Accardo were a $150,000 condominium in River Forest, and a $110,000 condominium in Palm Springs."

I waited for the other shoe to drop. Tony had obviously taken a big risk. There was all kinds of information available, and not just from our "illegal" wiretaps, to prove his perjury. To prove he had lied when he said he knew nothing about the mob and had had no part in it. And, incidentally, our bugging was never "illegal." As I reported above, we had the authority of J. Edgar Hoover in every operation, and he had the authority to command us by reason of the authority he had received from more than one Attorney General to wiretap and eavesdrop "to protect the national security." Now if his extension of what is involved in "national security" did not extend to organized crime investigations, no one had ever let him know about it. Therefore, we were not operating "illegally" and the bugs were not illegal. The information garnered through them was *inadmissible* but not *illegal.* There is a vast distinction between the two terms.

We waited to see what action the Senate would take on the obvious, brazen perjury of Accardo. As I say, I was not enthused about going after Accardo at this stage of his life and in his career. On the other hand, as long as he kept himself directly in the line of fire by acting as the "chairman" and sanctioning hits like those on Dorfman and Eto, then I did have an interest. So now I waited, too.

I waited. And waited. And I am still waiting.

Nothing happened. Joe Batters had gone to Washington, had limped in on his Big Tuna cane, had looked the senators in the eyes—and never blinked. They did. For reasons I still don't understand, the Senate backed down. They had challenged him by granting him immunity, and then when he accepted that challenge by brazenly lying about his involvement in organized crime, they let him get away with it, never taking any steps to indict him for his obvious perjury. Perjury which, to my thinking, would have been so easy to prove, with or without the "illegal" wiretapping. By 1984 we had live informants who could testify, in addition to "legal" eavesdropping (not wiretapping, a misnomer, since wiretapping refers only to tapping telephones, not to hidden microphones inside a premises).

I was not consulted, since there was no reason I should have been unless the Senate had decided they wanted to take on this fight. They might have contacted me to determine what sources other than the "illegal wiretapping" formed the basis for my testimony. But I was never contacted by anyone from the committee in this matter. I was contacted on numerous occasions by investigators from the committee about other investigations of theirs, and even about the continuation of this one which concerned the mob's dominance over Ed Hanley and his Hotel Employees and Restaurant Employees International Union.

Not that it mattered to me. It was not my fight. I'm sure Tony was upset with me and my testimony. It must have worried him and caused him some sleepless nights as he and his attorneys attempted to determine the best method to handle the situation. I'm sure I was not his favorite person after that, not somebody he considered a friend by any means. I was now just a private citizen and had no official function any longer. I could afford to let Tony's wins roll off my back. Let the guy continue to brag that he had never spent a night in jail. It wasn't my fight. Not any longer.

58 Unions

Tony had attempted to duck the committee all the way from the time I testified in March until he finally was hauled to Washington in November. He had undergone lung cancer surgery in August of 1983 and he used this, coupled with a heart condition, to excuse himself. But the chairman of the committee, Senator Roth, required his attorney, Carl Walsh, to file weekly reports regarding his condition. The senator had become very skeptical when Tony had entered a North Side hospital on September 16, the very day that committee investigators came to Chicago to serve him with a subpoena. The senators kept the pressure on Walsh and Accardo to appear, a prelude as no one could have anticipated it, to the Senate's final capitulation.

Actually, the Senate hearings had focused on something, regardless of Tony's victory, which should be given attention. The mob's involvement in labor unions. Such involvement was, after all, the reason for the hearings, not only in Chicago but all over the country in 1983. This was the ostensible reason that Tony Accardo was required to testify.

Eventually the committee would take testimony indicating that the Chicago Outfit had infiltrated at least seven unions in the Chicago area.

First, the two First Ward politicians, the "made" guys John D'Arco and Pat Marcy, sent notification that they would invoke the Fifth Amendment if they were called to testify. They would decline to answer any and all questions. As a result the senators excused them. Nice.

Jeffrey Kent, chief of the Cook County State's Attorney's office (headed then by Richard M. Daley, who became mayor of Chicago), was the prime witness before the committee in its investigation of mobbed-up unions. He testified that Vince Solano, the Chicago mob's North Side boss, had been president of Local 1 of the Laborers International Union. "He controls the gambling, extortion and prostitution in this area," Kent said. Then Kent named Local 450 of the Hotel, Motel, Club, Cafeteria, Restaurant Employees and Bartenders Union as "the local chartered in 1935 by Joseph Aiuppa . . . a Chicago underworld boss. Today the secretary-treasurer of Local 450 is Anthony Spano, who oversees day to day operations for Aiuppa."

Actually, I had testified to this effect before this committee as well. After I concluded my prepared testimony, I was questioned by Cass Weiland, the committee's chief counsel.

MR. WEILAND: One more question, Mr. Roemer, before you go. The subcommittee has been involved in a long, in-depth investigation of the Hotel and Restaurant Workers Union.

ROEMER: I am aware of that.

MR. WEILAND: We have hearings scheduled for later this month and also in April. I would ask you, based upon your long experience with the FBI in Chicago, whether you can comment on testimony the subcommittee has received in the past which indicates there is a very close link between organized crime—and I mean Chicago organized crime—and the leadership of the Hotel and Restaurant Workers Union?

ROEMER: Yes. When I was here in Chicago, Mr. Weiland, we saw the rise of Ed Hanley. You are familiar with Ed Hanley. He is the international president of the union that you speak of. He was brought to the attention of Joey Aiuppa. Ed Hanley at that particular time, and we are now talking about 1960, give or take two or three years, came to the attention of and became associated with Joey Aiuppa. Joey Aiuppa, then not a top boss of organized crime as he is today,

but in charge of the Cicero area of organized
crime and very active in the affairs of the Hotel,
Restaurant and Bartenders Union, brought Ed
Hanley into the union. I understand that Aiuppa
has had a very close relationship and influence
over Hanley since that period of time, up until
the present time, although I haven't researched
that in the past few months.

Next Jeffrey Kent testified that the Projectionists Union "is an
exceptionally violent union, noted for the arson and bombing of
nonunion movie theaters and at one time its membership read like
a 'Who's Who' of organized crime."

Kent identified a relatively new union which he said was dominated by organized crime, the International Union of Dolls, Toys,
Playthings, Novelties and Allied Products. He identified a
lieutenant of Angelo LaPietra, the capo on the near south side of
Chicago, as a business agent for this union. This was new to me.

Then another, the Construction Trades Industry Laborers International. Employees of the department of Streets and Sanitation in
Chicago belonged to that union, Local 1001. He identified Tony
Accardo's son-in-law, Marie's husband Ernest Kumerow, as the
president of Local 1001.

Kent talked about Local 703 of the Teamsters Union, the National Production Workers Local. He spotlighted Joseph V.
Senese, the son of "current mob figure" Dominic Senese, as the
president of Local 703. Dominic Senese, of course, was a brother-
in-law of Tony Accardo. Not too many years later, Dominic and
another son were shot in two separate incidents. Tony must have
had a tough time OK'ing those hits, over which he certainly had
approval. Dominic Senese, about a year after he was shot, stopped
by my table at Harry Caray's Restaurant on the near north side to
say hello. His face was badly disfigured from the bullets which
had paralyzed portions of it. Gruesome!

Kent also identified Al Pilotto, the capo in charge of the southern suburbs of Chicago, as the president of a local of the Laborers.
Pilotto later testified that he never belonged to any organized
crime group. Pilotto admitted "often" having dinner and drinks
with Accardo, Aiuppa, Jack Cerone and Tony Spilotro, but said he
never knew "what kind of work they do."

Kent made a good witness.

Actually, the committee could have questioned several other labor unions in Chicago. While I was in Chicago, we had ongoing

active investigations of others, such as Local 46 of the Laundry, Cleaning and Dye House workers, which Gus Zapas, a well-known Chicago hood, controlled under the influence of Gus Alex. Also Local 593 of the Hotel, Motel Service Workers, Drug Store, Sports Events and Industrial Catering Employees. And Locals 705, 710, 714, and 727 of the Teamsters. Also Local 136 of the Machinery Movers. These investigations were primarily conducted by our Labor Squad, not C-1, or C-10, the Organized Crime Squads. Fine agents like Ed Bloom, Bill Downey, Mike Dyer, Joe Servel, Lamont Pugh, Bobby Tompkins (who had been with us early on C-1) and especially Len Treviranus, all working under supervisor Leo Pedrotty, did an excellent job in their field of expertise. I enjoyed working with every one of those guys.

The "$700,000 net worth" that Tony Accardo claimed before the committee would have been a lot less if the mob's income from their involvement with unions had been sharply curtailed. Actually, I'd love to have just a small corner of the pot where Tony kept his real money. $700,000, in my estimation, was just walking-around money for him.

59 The Mob Losses in Las Vegas

The "west side" would soon take another shot. A mammoth one. I had retired from the Bureau in 1980 after we indicted Joe Bonanno in Tucson for obstruction of a federal grand jury in San Jose, which was hearing evidence against his two sons. We had used Title IIIs on the public telephones he utilized to oversee his LCN family in Brooklyn by remote control from Tucson, and had picked up his garbage twice a week. His garbage, we found, contained notes of his daily agenda. Now I was frequently back in Chicago as a private citizen working on libel cases.

It was during this time that Joe Batters had a most serious setback. The Chicago mob for years had been able to skim their casinos in Las Vegas, thereby bringing untold wealth to Accardo and those he now shared it with, such as Cerone, Aiuppa and, probably, Gussie Alex too.

It happened that we had a great agent in Kansas City, one Bill Ouseley. Two, in fact, since Lee Flosi was also there at the time. Both worked for a fine supervisor in Gary Hart.

They put some bugs in KC and soon developed two of the best cases in the history of the FBI. They were called Strawman I and Strawman II.

Strawman I focused on the Tropicana Hotel in Vegas. It was controlled for the KC mob, which was headed by Nick and Carl Civella and Carl DeLuna, and a guy named Joe Agosto. Joe ostensibly was nothing but the Entertainment Director of the Trop, but he actually was the boss there. This is important to the situation with Joe Batters, because the Kansas City mob is a subsidiary of the Chicago mob. Every family of La Cosa Nostra west of Chicago belongs to Chicago. Not only is every such family represented on the Commission by the *representato* from Chicago, but the Outfit takes a hunk of their income and oversees their activity. Such families are worked independently from Chicago, but when crunch comes to crunch, Chicago steps in. And God help them if they should try to cheat Chicago when the monthly cut is due.

Ouseley and company got some real good poop from their elsurs, enough so that they were eventually able to indict, and then convict, just about every mobster of any real stature in Kansas City. This directly affected Accardo because it immediately put a huge crimp in the income of the KC family, thereby seriously decreasing their cut to Chicago every month.

That was nothing, however, compared to what would happen next. Strawman II, which had commenced in 1978 and was still ongoing in the mid-Eighties, focused on the four Chicago-controlled Las Vegas casinos, those under the Argent umbrella that were controlled by fronts in Las Vegas like Lefty Rosenthal, Allen Glick and Al Sachs. These were the Stardust, Hacienda and Marina Hotel-Casinos, all three on the Strip, and the Fremont, one of the best hotels downtown in Glitter Gulch on Fremont Street.

Of the three fronts in these hotels, Lefty Rosenthal was perhaps the most interesting. Lefty, true name Frank, had come out of the west side of Chicago. I had first met him when he was working for Donald Angelini and Bill Kaplan at Angel-Kaplan Sports Service on North Clark Street, on the north side of the Loop, when I had infiltrated the sports handicapping-bookmaking office there as a degenerate baseball bettor. Lefty, as a young guy, was answering the phone, taking bets and giving out handicapping odds on football, basketball, baseball and lesser sports about the time that sports betting became a much bigger income producer for the mob than horse racing, its hard-rock gambling producer in earlier years. Lefty then moved on to Florida, where he got into trouble fixing college basketball games.

In the late Sixties, Rosenthal moved on to Vegas, having been sent there by the Outfit to oversee their interests in the casinos, particularly the Stardust. When Tony "The Ant" Spilotro came along to oversee Chicago's concerns as The Enforcer, he and Rosenthal became closely aligned, both professionally, as the mob's guys in charge of Vegas, and socially.

Based on the FBI's knowledge of all this, which was then passed on to the Gaming Control Board, Lefty was barred from the casinos. He not only lost his ability to work in the casinos but also his wife. He had married Geri, a showgirl in Vegas. But his good pal from the west side of Chicago, with whom he had been working under orders of the Outfit, had hoodwinked him. Spilotro took up with Geri. One morning she came home all doped up after an all-night session with The Ant—whom I always called the Pissant, even to his face—and got into a beef with Lefty, who was fed up with her trysts with the "little guy." He was frustrated because he couldn't get the powers in Chicago to force Spilotro to live up to the code of *omerta* by not screwing his wife. Lefty charged at Geri, and she pulled a gun on him—one that had been given to her by her "sponsor" Spilotro. Neighbors called the police, but it wasn't until Nancy Spilotro, The Ant's wife, arrived in her pajamas that the tussle was untangled.

But it was not over. Geri requested that the police take her to the bank where Rosenthal kept a safety deposit box with hundreds of thousands of dollars in cash and jewels, in Geri's name no less! While the police kept Lefty from interfering with Geri's right to her own box, leaving Rosenthal in a rage, Geri rifled the box of all its contents and then took off for California.

That was bad enough, but worse was to come. Shortly thereafter, in 1982, Lefty had left his kids—he got custody in a divorce from Geri—and was dining at Tony Roma's in Vegas, as he did almost nightly. When he exited from the restaurant, got into his car and turned the ignition, the car exploded. Rosenthal was blown clear, escaping serious injury. It was bad enough. He had been warned by Spilotro to stop making waves.

Then came the Kansas City Strawman cases, where Rosenthal came under close scrutiny. In the end he skated after doing some nifty footwork in talking to the FBI. He did not become an informant or a witness in the case, but neither was he indicted. Lefty is one cagy fellow.

Today Rosenthal is safely ensconced in Boca Raton, Florida, where he moved from Orange County, California, in 1987. For a short time he provided handicapping service to anybody who wanted to pay ten dollars for it. Then, in 1990, a nephew bought Croc's, a nice nightspot in Boca Raton, for about a million bucks and, so the story goes, installed Lefty as the manager, a job he continues to hold at the time of this writing. He lives in a four-hundred-thousand-dollar house and drives a new Mercedes-Benz. It seems some of the skim from the Stardust may have stuck to Lefty. Maybe not. Maybe he made some good investments or struck gold someplace. (If you care to learn a lot more about him and Spilotro, see my last book, *The Enforcer*, the biography of Spilotro, published by Donald I. Fine, Inc., in 1994.)

One of the things the "new wave" of agents had done during the Strawman investigations was to penetrate the home of a Chicago cop while he and his family were sleeping. Wow! Talk about guts! The house was to be the scene, the next day, of a meeting of the top leaders of the Chicago mob at the time—Cerone, Aiuppa and La-Pietra, the south side capo and the top leaders of the Kansas City mob, the Civellas, who had come into Chicago to try to buy the Stardust from the Outfit. This offer was refused because at the time, in 1978, it was a gold mine for Chicago. The agents were successful in their efforts, since Ed Tickel, the master of bugging, was on the job. The next day they recorded the entire hours-long discussion. It became a prime piece of the evidence in Strawman II.

Thanks to the great work by Ouseley and his crew in Kansas City, indictments were returned on Jackie Cerone and Joey Aiuppa for openers. Also on LaPietra, Frank Balistrieri, boss of the Milwaukee family of the LCN, and his two sons, Milton Rockman, a top mobster in Cleveland, and just about everybody in KC. It was quite a haul. On January 20, 1986, the jury returned, and almost all were convicted. All but the Balistrieri sons. Their father pleaded guilty in return for their severance from the case before the trial began.

Tony Accardo, having lost so much from the Tropicana when the Strawman I case came down, would lose a lot more—including his two top guys, Cerone and Aiuppa. For good. Aiuppa was bad enough. But Jackie was not only Accardo's top guy, he was also his best friend, his protégé and constant companion. The guy he leaned on most. It must have been a terrible loss for Joe at this time of his life, for both professional and personal reasons.

As I write this, Jackie and Joey are still in prison, and probably will be for the rest of their lives. Jackie is at Bastrup near Austin, Texas, and Joe is in Minnesota. I have been in touch with Jackie on occasion, and just recently he called and asked me to visit him. He sent me an application so that I can be included on his permanent visitation list. I heard subsequently that he was amazed to see that I owned only two cars (the application is quite thorough)—one a 1964 Pontiac Tempest, thirty-one years old, and my newest one, a 1972 Olds 88, only twenty-three. I have heard he commented, "You can see Roemer is one guy never on the take!"

60 Accardo Promotes Another

In early 1986, the Outfit needed a new boss. The Man, Accardo, was physically a lot less than he had been, and the pool of good talent in the ranks had really been hit by attrition. The two titans of the mob under Joe, Jackie Cerone and Joe Aiuppa, were gone. Joe Lombardo, Angelo LaPietra and Al Pilotto, all tough capos who would have been expected to step up to fill the void left by Cerone and Aiuppa, were also in prison, Lombardo and LaPietra as a result of the Pendorf and Strawman cases, and Pilotto in the Laborers Union trial in Miami, from which Tony had been lucky enough to walk away.

Fortunately for Batters, however, there was one pretty sharp, experienced capo around yet. His name was Joe Ferriola.

Joe Negall, as he was known in the Outfit, came out of what had been the most ruthless, most productive street crew of the Chicago Outfit, the westsiders. It had been under the rule of Fifi Buccieri until he died, then under Turk Torello. Then Turk died and Negall took over. When he did, he assumed control of gambling all over the Chicagoland area. Nobody had been allowed to do that before. That was what Dick Cain had tried before we put a stop to it when we suspected him of killing Chuck Carroll. Joe Ferriola was a most capable guy, which was lucky for Joe B. He had one guy left in his army.

I had had just one meeting with Negall. When the mob learned that I was being transferred to Tucson at my request in 1978, and that I was being invited to a wedding of the daughter of one of their associates, they reached out to me. It was a very coincidental situation. Our son, Bob, had gone to Thornridge High School in our neighborhood in the southern suburbs. At the very same time there was another star athlete in a Chicago area high school. He was almost a twin of Bob in terms of his career path. He was also All-State in football and baseball. He also got tons of football and many baseball scholarship offers. He played for the Austin Boys Club, in a summer baseball league in high school, while Bob played for the Berkeley Braves, the team I managed. We competed against—and beat—the Austin Boys Club a couple times for the Chicago city title. So Bob and the other guy got to know each other pretty well. The other guy then took a scholarship to Michigan, where he monogrammed his freshman year and captained the Wolverines in his senior year. Each year Notre Dame, which Bob attended, and Michigan played each other and the two boys got to know each other even better. His parents and Jeannie and I even became friends. Now Bob and the other guy graduate. They both sign with the Pittsburgh Pirates. They both are assigned to Niagara Falls in the New York–Pennsylvania League. They become roommates. I go to Niagara Falls for a month while they are there, spending most of my annual leave from the FBI there in 1973. I get to know the other guy well. Just one heck of a great young man! I also get to know his parents even better than before.

Both boys leave organized baseball after a while. Bob goes back to South Bend, among all my relatives and his. He gets started in the insurance business with Colonial Life and Accident. Jeannie and I travel to South Bend frequently to watch Notre Dame football and spend other time with him. The other guy, back in Chicago, travels there also and bunks in with Bob. We continue to see him. In Chicago he and I frequently play handball against each other at the University of Illinois-Chicago where I had a locker for years in the athletic staff locker room with the great coaches there, like Bill Fudala, my weekly sparring partner, Tommy Russo and Bobby Beck.

Now the other guy falls in love with a beautiful brunette from Chicago. He introduces Jeannie and me to her. I don't catch her last name.

A couple months go by. Then one day I'm talking to Bill McGuire. Bill had been a Chicago police officer, then had quit the job and gone with Ralph Pierce and become a gambling boss under Ralph on the south side. Ralph was the boss there until he died in June of 1976. Then Bill McGuire went with Fifi, Turk and Negall. On the west side. Not really a mobster, but a gambling boss. Bill was never involved in the heavy stuff. He never broke any legs. He worked in the joints, but never as a collector or anything like that. He thrived because he was sharp, much better upstairs in the brains department than most—almost all.

I got to know Bill when he was with Ralph. We lunched regularly at Morrie Norman's, which was Ralph's message drop (where I had tried to find Ralph on the day I wanted to meet with Tony Accardo to negotiate the contract off Bernie Glickman).

Bill and I got to be good friends. I could talk to him. Now it's 1978. The mob has become aware that I have asked to be transferred in the FBI to Tucson.

I run into Bill at Morrie's. Ralph has died now, so has Les Kruse, another street boss I used to run into at Morrie's. Hy Godfrey, the counterpart to Butch Blasi as the "secretary" to the connection guys, has moved to San Diego. Morrie has died. As a result, I don't go there much by 1978. But one day, for old times' sake, I do—and I see Bill McGuire.

What does he tell me? That the beautiful brunette the "other guy" is about to marry is his daughter! Holy cow! Our son, Bob, was to be in the wedding party as an usher. Bill asked me if we planned to accept the invitation we had received. Actually, we had planned to, but now there was a problem—what appeared to be a big one. Bill had invited just about anybody who was anybody in the Outfit to his daughter's wedding. Ferriola would be there. Blasi is invited. Donald Angelini. Dominic Cortina. Just about everybody listed on the chart I helped Bill Lambie prepare and would use during my testimony later on before the Senate.

I told Bill it wouldn't bother me if it didn't bother them. Bill said it would not. He had already checked it out. They all knew I was about to leave the Chicago FBI and would no longer be a thorn in their side, and so they all agreed it would be good to slap me on the back and say God Bless. Maybe good riddance, too.

I checked it out with Jeannie. She liked the couple and saw no problem, so we went and we had a hell of a time. We spent a lot of it with Donald Angelini, whom I had twice arrested, and "Large" Cortina and their wives, both very gracious, attractive ladies. Then I was introduced for the first—and only—time to Joe Ferriola, aka Joe Negall. We stood at the bar of the country club where the reception was held and had a lengthy conversation about nothing more important, as I recall, than the weather and the beautiful bride.

Joe Negall had impressed me back in 1978. When I went back to the FBI office the following Monday and told everybody on the 16 and 18 Squads (the old C-1 and C-10 Squads), the "new wave" of young agents, about my Saturday night with the "made" guys, I made sure to caution them to expect to see a lot more of Joe Ferriola, Joe Negall. To be sure to keep an eye open for him. I didn't have to tell them my thoughts about Angelini and Cortina. All knew we had to be aware of their capabilities.

In 1986 I had a CTE there when Tony Accardo made Joe Ferriola the boss. Most of the same guys with whom I had quaffed a couple at the McGuire wedding were at Joe's elevation, especially Donald, Large and Gussie. (I have spent a lot of time reporting on this meeting in my last book, *The Enforcer*, the bio of Tony Spilotro.) As explained therein, the primary topic after Joe Ferriola had been promoted was what should be done with Spilotro. He had gotten way out of control with Lombardo, his capo, in prison from Pendorf, and when Cerone and Aiuppa became preoccupied, as they had to be, with their trial in Strawman II in Kansas City. Accardo had recognized what Spilotro was up to, and ordered that straightened out. The situation in Las Vegas should be a priority of the new Ferriola regime.

Soon it was done. Two guys, Sam "Wings" Carlisi and John "No Nose" DiFronzo, were up-and-coming guys on their way to the top. Sam had a driver, a la Butch Blasi, working for him named Jim Marcello. Sam was ordered by Joe Ferriola to summon Spilotro back to Chicago from Las Vegas. Marcello carried the order. Spilotro was lured out to northern Indiana. The next thing the world knew, his and his brother's bodies were found in a shallow grave in a cornfield. Business as usual for the Chicago Outfit.

Tony Accardo liked the new guy Ferriola. He missed Jackie in particular, because of his companionship and his capability, and O'Brien also, because he always carried out his orders promptly and with some efficiency. But this new guy? He was all right.

The only problem for Tony Accardo was that this guy would not last long, though nobody knew it at the time. We didn't get him, but his heart couldn't take it. He died in mid-March 1989. One of my CTEs, with whom I still stay in touch, attended the funeral service at Salerno's Galewood Chapel on Harlem Avenue, near North Avenue, where I had had my "midnight walk" with Accardo years before. My CTE chided me at the time. (He had come to recognize my great faith in the Lord and the hereafter.) He smiled ruefully as he handed me the prayer card that had been distributed to the attendees at Joe Ferriola's wake. I quote from it: "Oh gentlest heart of Jesus . . . be not severe in Thy judgment, but let some drops of Thy Precious Blood fall upon the devouring flames, and do Thou O Merciful Savior send Thy angels to conduct Thy departed servant to a place of refreshment, light and peace. Amen."

I include this in all solemnity and reverence, and I add my prayers for Joe Ferriola. We all need as much mercy from the Lord as we can get, and Joe was no exception to this. I believe the above is a fine petition, particularly for those in Joe's position.

Joe was sixty-one years old when he died in Houston, where he had been attended by the famous Dr. Michael DeBakey, just as Sam Giancana had been. He had had two heart transplants and left behind a wife and five children. His problems were now behind him and I did wish him to rest in peace.

Now, however, Joe Batters had to find a successor. The obvious choice was between Ferriola's top twosome, Wings and No Nose.

61 Even Now Number Two on the Fortune 50

In the fall of 1986, *Fortune* magazine spent a great deal of time and effort researching the nature of organized crime and its leaders across the country. I was one of the prime sources for this project, which became its cover story in its November 10, 1986, issue. Had the survey been conducted several years earlier, or at any time during the Forties through about 1980, I would have counseled *Fortune* to name Tony Accardo at the top of their list of the most powerful mobsters in the country. As it was, in 1986, Accardo was ranked only second in the country in "wealth, power and influence."

Fortune's cover for that issue was entitled "50 Biggest Mafia Bosses: The Crime Business. Who runs it, how they manage it, who profits—and loses." It featured a photo of the only mobster they considered more important than Joe Batters, Fat Tony Salerno, the boss of the Genovese Family of New York.

The author of the piece, which took up about ten pages of *Fortune*'s issue, was Roy Rowan, a most respected journalist-researcher. He was assisted, although the issue does not give him credit, by Sandy Smith, then a senior correspondent for *Time* magazine. Sandy had set up a meeting in Tucson between me and Roy Rowan, and we spent considerable time putting our heads together for the purposes of his article.

I was, of course, far from being the only "expert" Rowan and Smith consulted. I know that they also visited such stars in our world of O.C. investigation as Jack Danahy and Ralph Salerno in New York City, Jim Mulroy in New Jersey, Bill Duffy in Chicago and Jack Barron in Los Angeles. Danahy and Mulroy had been supervisors of the Organized Crime Program in New York, while Barron was the supervisor in Los Angeles for years. Salerno was the supervisor of detectives on the Intelligence Unit of the New York Police Department. Bill Duffy was the Deputy Superintendent of the Chicago Police Department and its expert on organized crime. Those people were all close friends of mine, and therefore I know of their involvement. I know that Roy and Sandy also consulted many other experts in the field across the country. In fact, the article states that "for this story *Fortune* interviewed FBI agents, leaders of federal organized-crime strike forces, and local officials across the U.S."

In order to get a good overview of what organized crime is all about, *Fortune*'s piece may be the best place to start. It began: "Crime pays. Annual gross income from the rackets will probably exceed $50 billion this year. That makes the mob's business greater than all U.S. iron, steel, copper and aluminum manufacturing combined, or about 1.1% of the GNP. These figures, compiled for the President's Commission on Organized Crime, include only revenues from traditional mob businesses, such as narcotics, loan-sharking, illegal gambling, and prostitution. They do not include billions more brought in from the mob's diversification into such legitimate enterprises as entertainment, construction, trucking, and food and liquor wholesaling.

"The organization chart of a crime family or syndicate mirrors the management structure of a corporation. At the top of the pyramid is a boss, or chief executive. Below him are an underboss (chief operating officer) and a consigliere (general counsel). Then follow ranks of capos (vice presidents) and soldiers (lower-level employees who carry out the bosses' orders).

"The crime industry is organized geographically. Though the mob's grasp reaches most major cities—Seattle is an exception—two-thirds of the Mafia's membership is concentrated in New York and Chicago. The Commission adjudicates territorial disputes, settles business conflicts, and even passes on execution sentences.

"Five sometimes-warring Mafia families control New York City—the Genoveses, Gambinos, Lucheses, Bonannos and Columbos. Induction into these families involves a swearing-in ritual that calls for the taking of a secret oath and the giving of a drop of blood. In Chicago a single Mafia organization called the Outfit runs matters with less friction. There the initiation rite is consummated like a business deal, with a handshake. The Chicago Outfit also influences mob activities in Milwaukee, Kansas City, Phoenix, Las Vegas and Los Angeles.

"According to the FBI, there are only about 1,700 sworn, or 'made' Mafia members. For each member, the government figures there are ten 'associates.' Wharton Econometric Forecasting Associates estimates that the average annual income for an individual organized crime member was $222,000 between 1979 and 1981. Of course, the haul for the top 50 crime bosses would be much higher.

"Chicago's boss, Anthony Accardo, 80, boasts that he has never spent a night in jail. Like many a chief executive lately, he was called back from retirement (at the Indian Wells club near Palm Springs) when the organization he had long headed faced a sudden management crisis: the leadership of the Chicago Outfit was packed off to jail early this year. Accardo's renewed position raises him to No. 2 on our list.

"Accardo is reputed to have been a machine-gunner for Al Capone, and he is called 'Joe Batters' by his Mafia cronies because of the baseball bat he formerly used for persuasion. He has always been a master of strategic planning. His formidable Outfit is a racketeering combine that runs everything from diaper services to funeral parlors; its efficiency is envied throughout the Mafia.

"Accardo was the architect of the intricate power plays that made the Outfit the dominant force in the rackets from the Great Lakes to the Pacific over the past decade. Now, with a cadre of couriers winging back and forth from Chicago to California, he functions as the chairman of the board. His operations chief is Joseph Ferriola, 59, a disciplined underboss who is No. 20 on our list.

"Discipline is the Outfit's guiding management principle. The Chicago mob imposes a 'street tax' on all illegal activities and on some legitimate ones as well. Bookies, hookers, narcotics peddlers, even owners of bars, restaurants and parking lots pay from 10% to 50% of their gross revenues.

"The Outfit maintains especially tight discipline over its internal security. Chicago insurance executive Allen Dorfman, a sophisticated money-manager, pioneered the use of union welfare and pension funds to finance an underworld bank in the 1960s. First he funneled loans from the Teamsters' Central States pension fund to several casino-hotels in Las Vegas. Then he showed Accardo and associates how to establish health care organizations in which participating doctors and dentists gave the Outfit kickbacks for processing the Teamster loans and insurance claims after overcharging union patients. Dorfman knew too much about the Outfit's finances. He was gunned down in a suburban Chicago parking lot in 1988.

"Beginning in 1970 (it was actually 1971), strongman Anthony Spilotro was stationed in Las Vegas to monitor casino skimming and to see that the money flowed smoothly back to his bosses in Chicago. Known as 'The Ant' because of his squat, close-to-the-ground appearance, he did not keep an appropriate low business profile, operating out of a Las Vegas hamburger joint called The Food Factory.

"But Spilotro failed to keep the skimming operation well disciplined. Some of the men he supposedly controlled turned up as government witnesses, resulting in the January conviction of Chicago's former ruling duo, Joseph Aiuppa (No. 21) and John Phillip 'Jackie' Cerone (No. 30). Imprisoned with them were seven other gang leaders including Carl DeLuna (No. 33), the Kansas City comptroller, whose meticulously kept financial records were uncovered by the FBI.

"Last June, Tony Spilotro and his brother Mike were found buried in an Indiana cornfield. Investigations suggested that they had been garroted and may have been buried alive. In any event they were victims of wise-guy rules: They had not prevented the guys from spilling the beans, so they suffered the consequences.

" 'There is no way Spilotro could have been killed without Accardo's approval,' says Patrick Healy, executive director of the Chicago Crime Commission.

"Spilotro's execution may lead to the disintegration of an important peace-keeping pact, hatched by Accardo in 1977, that ceded authority in Las Vegas to the Outfit in Chicago, and gave Atlantic City to New York Mafia families.

"William Roemer, a former FBI agent who spent 23 years tailing Accardo and his cohorts, and now is a consultant to the

Chicago Crime Commission, says the Las Vegas–Atlantic City deal had a grandfather clause. Roemer said that 'according to the 1977 agreement, the Eastern mob could keep what it had in Las Vegas, but it couldn't start anything new there. Spilotro was there to enforce the edict.' "

The article went on to address a power struggle in New York and Las Vegas. It went on to say that "what is happening may be a mild precursor of things to come in Chicago. The aged Accardo has heart disease, and when he dies the Outfit may find itself in turmoil."

The article had a sidebar entitled "The Mob's Outside Consultants." It featured Sidney R. Korshak, for many years the Chicago mob's consultant over their labor affairs and their affairs in Las Vegas and Hollywood. The *Fortune* article went into his activity on behalf of the Chicago Outfit.

"William Roemer, the former FBI agent, described Korshak as 'the most important link between organized crime and legitimate business.'

"Investigators learned that in 1958 he helped Tony Accardo draw up a contract that paid the Chicago mob boss $65,000 a year as an employee of a wholesaler called Premium Beer Sales. An FBI bug planted in a mob hangout revealed that Korshak used the code name 'Mr. Lincoln' in his underworld dealings.

"In 1983 Joseph Hauser, a convicted insurance swindler, testified before a Senate labor investigation (the Senate Permanent Subcommittee on Investigation hearing, detailed earlier) that Accardo had told him on several occasions that 'he had sent Korshak to Los Angeles to represent the mob there.'

"In Chicago, politics and organized crime have always been linked. The FBI has had Pat Marcy, a First Ward Democratic leader, under surveillance since the late 1960s. Former FBI agent Roemer told Senate investigators in 1983 that 'Marcy has been calling the shots of the mob as far as politics is concerned for many, many, many years. He was the conduit through which orders of the Outfit passed to those politicians and public officials under their control.' And he still is."

The feature of the *Fortune* cover story was their list of the "Fortune 50," a take-off on their famous "Fortune 500," listing of the top-ranked legitimate business entities. Tony Accardo, as I say, was ranked number two in the country, second only to Anthony "Fat Tony" Salerno, the boss of the New York Genovese family of the "Mafia." (Incidentally, the reader should again be reminded that "Mafia" is actually a misnomer. In the strict sense of the terminology, "Mafia" refers only to the Sicilian organization. Their American counterparts have titled their organization "La Cosa Nostra." The *Fortune* piece does not refer to La Cosa Nostra, calling it instead the "Mafia." Again, this is probably in keeping with what the press feels their readership will recognize.)

On the Fortune 50 list there are thirteen cities represented and twelve families of organized crime. Ten of the top fifty were from Chicago: Accardo (2), Ferriola (20), Aiuppa (21), Alex (22), Cerone (30), Solano (42), Chris Petti (47), Paul Schiro (45) and Frank Buccieri (50). We have discussed Frank Buccieri; he was the brother of Fifi Buccieri, now deceased, and an underling of Ferriola, who was living in Palm Springs at the time. Schiro was, and is, a resident of Scottsdale, Arizona, and was reputed to be a mob hitman working under Spilotro. Chris Petti was Spilotro's man in San Diego. He is now in prison.

As of the date it was written in 1986, this article was the best available rundown of what organized crime looked like. Rowan and Smith did an excellent job and the piece reflected their research and hard work in interviewing the most knowledgeable experts on organized crime in the country at that time, myself included.

In 1986 Tony Accardo, although considerably past his prime and now suffering from many of the ailments generally associated with his age, eighty, was still, by virtue of his experience and ability, the man in charge of the Chicago family of La Cosa Nostra.

However, from this point forward two things would militate against Tony: time, and the renewed pressure from the "new wave" of fine agents who had been assigned to the Chicago Office of the FBI.

Tony now spent most of his time in Indian Wells at his condo there. He sold his condo on Harlem Avenue and purchased a luxurious guest house on Algonquin Road in affluent Barrington Hills, a northern suburb of Chicago, on the estate of his daughter Marie and her husband Ernie Kumerow, the union leader. He would retain his spot as the consiglieri of the Chicago Outfit and be available whenever an important decision was to be made by Joe Ferriola, and then by his successors.

BOOK FOUR

TURNING POINT

62
The FBI Near the Top of Its Game

The year 1986 was also the year the FBI prepared a "white paper" for the internal use of its organized crime agents, those agents in the FBI who were assigned to investigation of all families of La Cosa Nostra, for background in their ongoing investigations.

Obviously, I am not privileged to fully disclose its contents here. However, I can quote from this primer regarding certain portions of the FBI study without jeopardizing the security of any of the sources who contributed to it. The following is an excerpt.

"The Federal Bureau of Investigation (FBI) views organized crime as consisting of group enterprises operating under some formalized structure and whose essential intent is to obtain income from illegal activities. Violence, the threat of violence and corruption through graft or extortion are their weapons against society."

I recognize this as having been the Bureau's official definition of organized crime in this country. Today the traditional and ethnic organized criminal groups and others, such as the outlaw motorcycle gangs and prison gangs that mimic them, present significant challenges to federal, state and local law enforcement agencies. Organized crime is an insidious cancer that saps the strength of our society, threatens the integrity of government, causes taxes to go up, adds to the cost of the goods we buy and jeopardizes our personal safety and that of our families.

"Labor racketeering, drug trafficking, gambling, loan-sharking, murder, kidnapping, extortion, prostitution and smuggling are the stock in trade of organized crime. But the activities of organized crime are not limited to open acts of criminality. Today, there are few businesses or industries in our communities that are not affected by organized criminal enterprises. The profits generated by illegal organized criminal activities are often funneled through elaborate money laundering schemes into otherwise legitimate business. These businesses have an edge over their competitors which must worry about profit margins, overhead costs and re-paying bank loans. In a very real sense, organized crime touches every citizen in America. It is in recognition of the pervasive threat posed by these groups that the FBI has designated organized crime as a national priority. Director (William) Webster has fur-ther instructed that drug trafficking and labor racketeering receive the highest priority within the organized crime program.

"The FBI has learned that the term 'organized crime' is not syn-onymous with any one group. Instead, many varieties and combi-nations of criminal groups are properly included within its definition. Some of the organized crime groups that the FBI is concerned with are the Outlaw Motorcycle Gangs, the Mexican and Colombian Narcotics Cartels, Prison-Spawned Gangs such as the Mexican Mafia, Nuestra Familia, the Aryan Brotherhood and the Black Guerrilla Family; ethnically oriented groups such as the Japanese Yakuza, the Chinese Triad Societies, the Israeli Mafia and Vietnamese organized crime; and organized crime groups which are considered to be traditional, such as La Cosa Nostra, the Sicilian Mafia, the Camorra and the N'Drangheta.

"Of all the organized crime groups in the United States, La Cosa Nostra, or, as Joe Valachi called it, 'this thing of ours,' is the most notorious. Also known as the LCN and referred to by some as 'the syndicate' or the 'mob,' La Cosa Nostra . . . began in the 1930s and continues to the present day.

"During this period Charles 'Lucky' Luciano established a na-tional Commission to oversee the activities of the various LCN families. The purpose of the Commission is to: 1) resolve inter-family disputes, 2) approve selections for the new family bosses, and 3) set a broad policy for the LCN as a whole. Substantial evidence of a 'Commission' within LCN exists. This body re-solves territorial claims by families, makes policy decisions, and 'confirms' new bosses. While concentrated in the Northeast, members and elements have extended the range of organized crime to the majority of states.

"In the 1930s there were an estimated 5,000 official members of the LCN in the United States. That number has decreased today to approximately 2,000 identified, initiated members in 24 fami-lies nationwide. However, for every initiated LCN member, there are perhaps ten nonmembers whose full-time activity is connected with the LCN and is illegal in nature.

"The organizational structure of the LCN is best described by an insider. Aladena Fratianno, better known as 'Jimmy the Weasel,' is a self-admitted member of the LCN. He has testified for the government in numerous organized crime prosecutions, which resulted in the convictions of LCN members and their associates. Fratianno described an LCN family as controlled by a Boss, who is assisted by an Underboss, a Consiglieri, who acts as an advisor, Capos (captains) and at the lowest level of membership, Soldiers. Each of these members has nonmember associates involved in illegal activity. A 'made' member of the LCN is required to keep secret the business of the organization. The code of silence is known as '*Omerta*,' and the penalty for violating that secrecy is death.

"The FBI is well aware of the threat organized crime poses to the rights and security of Americans. Our Organized Crime Program, therefore, is among our highest priority efforts. The FBI is expending more than 1,500 Special Agent work years this fiscal year to investigate organized crime across the nation. The time and investigative efforts are necessary to implement technical and strategic plans to accomplish the goals pertaining to organized crime, and this includes conscientious prosecution and the collection of intelligence regarding its scope.

"In fiscal year 1984 there were 2,200 convictions in the Organized Crime Program: 159 LCN members and associates were among those convicted. During the first nine months of fiscal year 1985 there were 1,996 convictions and 2,580 indictments.

"The FBI is effective today because it knows more about how organized crime groups work, how they are structured, and where their weaknesses are. The FBI is more effective too because it knows that cooperation in this effort is essential. None of us can do the job alone. The FBI is now participating in joint investigations and joint task forces with an ever-expanding number of federal, state and local agencies. Many of the successes were the product of cooperative efforts. And many of them involved undercover agents from the FBI and other agencies working together to penetrate the inner circles of these criminal associations.

"There are other tools available to the FBI as well. The use of judicially approved electronic surveillance and consensual monitoring, to learn more about the day-to-day operations of organized crime groups, is of paramount importance. The FBI has augmented that with improved expertise in auditing the tangled paper trails created by international money laundering and has learned to use the computer to unravel complex financial transactions.

"A weapon the FBI and federal prosecutors have used with great success is the Racketeer Influenced and Corrupt Organizations Act, or RICO statute. In many respects, this is the most powerful federal statute available. RICO's concept of 'a racketeering enterprise' addresses the central problem of organized crime. RICO's stiff penalties add the needed 'muscle' in organized crime cases."

The document addressed several other methods of dealing with the LCN which, for security reasons, cannot be quoted here. It then concludes:

"All of these techniques and others can be enhanced by the cooperation of the American public, and the understanding that together we can be effective in eliminating the scourge of organized crime."

This paper, prepared by a particularly fine Bureau supervisor named Jack D. Blair, presents well the nature of what the FBI had been fighting.

This was, in a word, the world in which Tony Accardo was living at this stage of his life inside the Chicago family of La Cosa Nostra—and it was what the FBI knew of him and his associates at that time. The FBI was becoming more and more knowledgeable about how the LCN operated and who they were. As important, the Bureau now had the tools with which to fight them. The Bureau had ITAR, Title III of the Omnibus Crime Control and Organized Crime Act, and RICO. In 1987 the Bureau was approaching the top of its game, even as Tony Accardo's game was winding down. But the FBI still had not put him away. He was on the scene, always available when his people needed advice.

63 "Greylord" and "Gambat"

Tony Accardo and his people would be seriously affected by two of the most publicized legal cases in the history of

Chicago. One commenced in 1980 and went all the way through the court system for the next fourteen years, until September 19, 1994. The other directly impacted on Tony and the Outfit from its commencement in the late Eighties into the mid-Nineties.

The first was called Operation Greylord; the other, Operation Gambat. Both also seriously impacted upon the local judicial system. Greylord, since it mostly affected traffic court judges, might not seem to have had a direct effect on the criminal bench; therefore, it would not seem to have a direct effect on the Outfit. That was not really the case, however, since Greylord put a very serious crimp in the efforts of the Outfit's connection guys to obtain commitments from any judges, criminal or civil. It scared the living pants off the judiciary, who had just enough reason to believe that the FBI's infiltration of their fellow judges in traffic court could be effected against any of them. Furthermore, it led to a great distrust on the part of the judges towards anybody who came to them offering an inducement for a fix; such a person might actually be either an undercover FBI agent (like the agent who acted in this capacity in Greylord), or he might be a corrupt attorney carrying a wire for the FBI (as was the case in Gambat).

Operation Greylord commenced in 1980. It can best be described the way former FBI Director William Sessions described it when he awarded the Lou Peters Award, the award given annually by the Society of Former FBI Agents to a private citizen who best exemplifies the work of the FBI. I quote Director Sessions at the convention of the Society of Former FBI Agents in 1989:

"Nine years ago, the FBI began an undercover operation within the largest big-city judicial system of the nation. Three years later, when Operation Greylord was made public, cynics in Chicago laughed and said the FBI was wasting its time—they said we could never crack the system—never get indictments—never get convictions.

"Today, no one is laughing: 15 Cook County judges have been convicted; 46 lawyers have been convicted; 8 policemen, 10 deputy sheriffs, and 4 court clerks have been convicted. And the investigation is still ongoing . . .

"In 1980, just after the FBI opened its Greylord investigation, we learned of a young assistant state's attorney who was so disgusted with the corruption he had observed in the Cook County judicial system that he was seriously considering leaving the practice of law. His name was Terry Hake.

"We approached Terry and asked him to help us. We told him that we could not give him promises or guarantees of a secure future. We told him that his cooperation might well jeopardize his personal and professional friendships—and might well destroy his promising legal career in Chicago.

"But Terry said 'yes'—he would help. He wore a wire for three-and-a-half years—first pretending to be a corrupt prosecutor in a narcotics court, then a corrupt defense lawyer who became adept at fixing cases. In fact, while he was undercover, Terry Hake recorded over 1,300 hours of conversations.

"When Terry finally took off the wire in 1983, the FBI recognized Terry's work in the strongest way it could: SAC Ed Hagerty of the Chicago Field Office met with Terry and swore him in as a Special Agent of the FBI—a position Terry cemented when he graduated on June 5, 1984, with New Agent Class #84-6.

"Meantime, Special Agent Hake was assigned to a white-collar crime squad in the Chicago field office, where he worked primarily on the prosecution of the many subjects developed by Operation Greylord. He followed up new leads; he conducted surveillances; he reviewed and analyzed documents; and he conducted hundreds of interviews that, ultimately, resulted in many successful prosecutions.

"At the same time, he laboriously reviewed the transcripts of his own tapes. He consulted with agents and prosecutors on documents, on Chicago court procedures, and on investigative issues. And he testified—did he ever testify! Terry Hake took the witness stand during five major trials, undergoing what prosecutors described as 'the most brutal and grueling cross-examination of an agent they had ever witnessed.' You, of all people, can appreciate Terry's ordeal as he went up against the attacks of Chicago's most prominent defense lawyers.

"It goes without saying that Terry Hake's undercover work took a tremendous toll on Terry's personal life. On the one hand, he had put his life on the line—suffering threats from a variety of sources. On the other hand, he had put his reputation on the line—and I know that he will always bear scars from the attacks he endured here.

"Terry, you were not given a new undercover name; you were not moved to another town; you didn't work with strangers. You remained Terry Hake . . . in Chicago . . . playing the part of a crook in his own backyard. You lost the respect of your friends. You were vilified. You had no place where someone—anyone— knew you to be a man of integrity. And when the truth came out—even when Terry's role as an undercover agent was understood—many of Terry's friends and associates in the legal community felt he had betrayed the profession.

"I think these are the circumstances that try men's souls the most: to be faithful to your principles; to be brave; to be right—yet to be scorned by the people you hold in highest regard. Terry Hake is a special man with a special kind of fortitude. He is a man who has made a difference. He is a man who has set a shining standard of ethical conviction and action in the profession of law.

"Terry, we all salute you. We all honor you. It gives me deep pleasure to present you today with the society's highest accolade—The Louis E. Peters Memorial Service Award."

The supervising judge, the chief judge, of the Traffic Court in the Seventies was Richard LeFevour. I was a friend of Judge LeFevour and had a high regard for him. Usually FBI agents have a real problem with parking in Chicago. It is not always easy to find a parking place near where every investigation is conducted. Police have little problem in this regard, since they use placards on the inside of their windshields which identify them as police officers, resulting in immunity from ticketing by their fellow officers. We had no such immunity—in fact, many Chicago police officers relish ticketing a car which they can identify as being an FBI car. The reason is that the FBI is charged with the responsibility of investigating violations of civil rights statutes. If a local police officer is suspected of violating the rights of a citizen, he can be, and usually is, investigated. Sometimes he is prosecuted. The Rodney King case in Los Angeles is a prime example. The LAPD police officers who were charged with police brutality in the local case were, in my opinion, properly acquitted. But what happened next? They were indicted in federal court and charged with violating King's civil rights. Some of the officers were convicted and are serving time today. This, quite naturally, riles local police against the arm of the federal government which is responsible for their investigation, namely the FBI.

I recall one time in Chicago, 1973. It was Friday the 13th, in which month I can't remember. Four of us were returning to the Chicago FBI office from the west side, on the Eisenhower Expressway. We were stopped for a red light at Wells Street when a car plowed into our rear. When the police arrived to investigate and ticket the driver of the car who had rammed us, who was obviously at fault, since we were stopped at the red light, the driver said to the officers: "Wow, it's Friday the 13th and I have the bad luck to smash into the rear of a car loaded with FBI agents!"

Here's what the cop said in reply: "I only wish it had been the other way around!" When I subsequently questioned him as to why he felt he'd rather ticket FBI agents than this guy who was obviously at fault, he told me he had been assigned to the Austin District when the FBI had conducted a well-publicized investigation of officers from that CPD district and some of his pals had been convicted. He held this against the FBI. Actually, if he had known the background of the FBI agent he was talking to, he wouldn't have been so unhappy to cite the other guy. I had been assigned to the Austin Police District case at its very outset. It involved the allegation that many tavern owners in the Austin area on the far west side of Chicago were being shaken down by police officers for some $50 a week. When they had a problem, they could call those particular police officers, who would respond posthaste. The key element of the case was extortion, and extortion gave us jurisdiction. If the tavern owner was *voluntarily* giving the payment to the officers in return for special treatment, that would be a state violation, but not one over which we would have any jurisdiction. However, if the police officer had approached the tavern keeper and demanded such a payoff, then that was extortion and we had jurisdiction. A fine line but a very important distinction. I was assigned to interview one of the key witnesses, the president of the Tavern Keepers Association in Austin. I queried him in depth about this point after he had brought the complaint to the United States Attorney's office. When I sent my report upstairs to the USA, the assistant was angered. I reported that I did not see this as extortion, that the tavern keepers were very pleased with this arrangement, at least as far as I could see, and we had no jurisdiction to pursue the case on a federal level. This assistant immediately contacted my supervisor, demanding that I be taken off the case and the interview reconducted by other agents. When my supervisor called me in, I didn't appreciate the way it had been handled, but I was very happy to be taken off the case. I felt strongly that the CPD officers assigned to the Austin District were violating no federal laws and that it was a very picky case, even if they were accepting $50 a week in order to give quick service to tavern owners who might have a problem in their establishments with such as rowdy imbibers. Nonetheless, the case went forward under the push of this assistant United States Attorney, and the FBI agents who were thereafter assigned to the case were much more enthusiastic in pursuing it than I had been. As a result, dozens of Chicago police officers were convicted and sent to prison, the public believing that they were major criminals and that it was a disgrace comparable to the Summerdale police scandal, where officers in that police district were robbing and burglarizing. The assistant USA got much favorable press and the agents received incentive awards for their work. I had washed my hands of the case—or, actually, had had my hands washed of it—and did not feel it was one of the finest hours of the FBI or the Justice Department.

Right on this point, when I transferred to Tucson in 1978, I volunteered to be assigned all civil rights investigations of the local police in Arizona. The first one I had involved Skip Woodward, a police officer for the Tucson PD. He had gone to question a black man in a car whom he suspected of having been involved in a serious crime on the east side of Tucson. But when Woodward approached the man, the man made a move towards his glove compartment. Officer Woodward, making a quick decision on the spot, perceived that he was reaching for a gun. He shot the man, seriously wounding him. When the man had recovered, he claimed that he had had his car radio turned up to loud rap music and couldn't hear what Officer Woodward was yelling at him. So, he said, he was reaching for his car radio to turn it off so that he could hear better. The case had become a cause celebre in Tucson and the NAACP and the ACLU had made it a loud cause of theirs, so much so that Bates Butler, who was running the Tucson office of the United States Attorney's Office, under the renowned Mike Hawkins in Phoenix, requested us to investigate under the civil rights statute. I volunteered and investigated. I did it in a most impartial manner, no doubt angering Woodward and his partner no end. But I did it with my underlying philosophy that law enforcement officers, and especially local police officers, who get down in the muck a lot more than FBI agents do, deserve all the consideration, respect and understanding that we can give them. So when I gave my report to Butler, it was with the recommendation that it was a righteous shooting and that, while it was not certain that the suspect was reaching for his glove compartment (no gun was found there), even if he had been reaching for his car radio, Officer Woodward legitimately, ethically and legally, could perceive that his life was in danger, thereby giving him the right to do what he did. I reported that. It was unfortunate, but it was not a violation of the law; it was no crime on Officer Woodward's part. Bates Butler agreed with me and no charges were ever filed against Officer Woodward.

Imagine my surprise three or four years later when I was asked to be the keynote speaker at the awards banquet for the "Officer of the Year in Southern Arizona." Guess who won the award from the Tucson PD? Yep, Skip Woodward. Well deserved! Now every year that I am invited to be the keynote speaker at the graduation of the new recruits from the Tucson Police Department Academy, I feel greatly honored. I know what local police must endure, the hard work it is, the great job they do. It is a humbling experience for me to be asked to address them as if I were of their caliber.

I have deviated a bit from the focus of this chapter, but I wanted to take this opportunity to honor local police. We owe them so much!

Judge LeFevour, my friend in Traffic Court, had been contacted by agent Ray Shryock, then a "relief supervisor," soon to become my close pal and my supervisor when I was on C-10. The arrangement with Judge LeFevour was that when any FBI agent received a parking ticket on official business, not a speeding ticket, which was another matter, not given any consideration, he or she could bring it to Ray, together with the circumstances of its receipt. Then Ray would take it to Judge LeFevour and have it dismissed, if appropriate. When Ray was unavailable and tickets had piled up, I was the one who took them to the judge. So we became good friends. I found that he and my brother Chuck had been classmates at Campion, the Catholic boarding school in Prairie Du Chien, Wisconsin. I gained respect and affection for Judge LeFevour.

At this time Terry Hake had gotten his undercover act in full sway. This fine young agent posed as an attorney in Chicago and, together with the support of other Chicago agents, went about finding out how money-hungry Chicago area judges really were. Unfortunately, it was very easy to find judges to bribe. What Hake had brought to the attention of his superiors in the FBI was very true. Many Chicago area judges had their hands out.

The Greylord investigation got under way in 1978. By 1983 the first indictments resulted in convictions. Judge LeFevour was himself convicted. Judge John Devine went down. In 1985 several more, including heretofore respected judges, like Marty Hogan and Reginald Holzer. Judge Hogan was the son of a friend of mine and Judge Holzer had been a protégé of the great Governor Ogilvie.

Then, in 1988, an even closer-to-home conviction. Judge J.J. McDonnell was a friend. He had been a Notre Dame football player. A nice guy with a very amiable personality. He, too, got caught in the Greylord sting.

I guess the final conviction in Greylord told the story best. Lucius Robinson had been the bailiff of a judge for many years. One of the allegations against him was that he was the conduit of a bribe of $25,000 passed to him by "The Dean of Corruption," attorney Dean Wolfson, to acquit Jack Farmer, the head of a drug ring in Chicago who was charged with murder. Farmer beat the rap. (I had tried when I was in Chicago to turn Wolfson, but without success. He was reputed to be a master fixer for the Outfit.) Now, in 1994, Robinson pleaded guilty to lying to the grand jury when he was charged with passing hundreds of bribes, yes, hundreds, to corrupt judges in the Criminal Courts Building.

When it was over, Greylord had resulted in: 100 individuals convicted of corruption in the Cook County judicial system—there were only three acquittals, two judges and a lawyer; twenty judges were convicted; fifty-eight lawyers were indicted and only one acquitted; eight police officers convicted; eight deputy sheriffs convicted; seven others convicted.

You might wonder how this affected Tony Accardo. It did, quite a bit. Now "made" guys no longer had an easy path to freedom when they got caught red-handed. The job of Pat Marcy, John D'Arco and the connection guys under Gus Alex was now made much more difficult. Let's just say it reaffirmed their faith in the justice system. If they got caught, the case could no longer be so easily fixed. The judges were much more wary. They didn't fix cases nearly so readily. There has never been a scandal on the *federal* bench in the Northern District of Illinois, but now all state and local judges were much more suspicious of anyone who came to them with an offer. Things changed in Chicago starting in 1983.

Then came an even more serious situation for Tony Accardo and his minions: Operation Gambat. This operation first burst on the public scene when a busboy in Counsellor's Row Restaurant found a hidden video camera and mike in a bench, directed at Booth Number 1 in the restaurant. The eatery was located right across the street from City Hall—and the offices of the Regular Democratic Organization of the First Ward. (The spot where we in the first wave of organized crime investigations had placed a hidden mike in Pat Marcy's office.) After we were forced by President Johnson to remove the mikes, Pat, John D'Arco and the then-current alderman of the First Ward, Fred Roti, were very circumspect in their conversations. Now, every day for lunch they came down, right next door to Booth 1. Anybody who wanted to discuss business with Pat, John or Fred came to them in the open—at the restaurant across from City Hall and adjacent to 100 North La Salle. The conversations were whispered and the envelopes got passed under the table.

Now the "third tier" of FBI agents caught on, thanks to some help from the inside, which we will soon learn about. I call them the "third tier" because all of our charter members of the old Top Hood Squad had long gone, the "second wave" had succeeded us, and now, time flies so fast, there were a handful of "second wavers" still around, like Pete Wacks, Jim Wagner and Jack O'Rourke, but most of the agents on the squad were newcomers. Still fine agents and still, obviously, tops at the game.

When the busboy found the mike and the video camera, the owners of the restaurant alerted the press to what they perceived as an invasion of their privacy. The media immediately dubbed the operation "Operation Kaffee Klatsch," whereas the official name inside the FBI was Operation Gambat.

Gambat was short for the "gambling attorney" who was working secretly behind the scenes for the third tier. He was a far cry from the clean-cut Terry Hake, an actual FBI agent working undercover. This attorney had, in fact, been dirty. He had participated on many occasions as the middleman between the mob and the crooked judges in the criminal courts system— judges who could, and did, fix murder cases. Some defendants were even "made" guys who had committed hits for Tony Accardo's Outfit, like Tony Spilotro and Fred Aleman. The cases were fixed so that the murderers were let free to go back into society and be available to Accardo and his people to perform their "heavy work" once again. Obviously, it was vital to Tony that the connection guys be able to fix the cases where the mob was actually involved, where the defendants in some cases were "made" guys.

The name of this attorney was Robert Cooley. He had a bad gambling habit. He had lost heavily and was deep in debt to his bookie and to his juice guy.

This operation was a joint affair between the IRS and the FBI. A wire was put on Cooley, who was known to frequent Counsellor's Row as the conduit between Marcy and the judges, between Roti and the judges, between D'Arco and the judges, between D'Arco's son and the judges, even between D'Arco's son-in-law and the judges. Cooley's wire was a gold mine. Bulwarked by his testimony, Operation Gambat had the perfect one-two punch. The admissibility of the information from the wire and the testimony of a credible witness deeply involved to support the wire is a combination that is virtually unbeatable.

As a result of Gambat, Tony Accardo's people were deeply wounded. For decades Pat Marcy and John D'Arco, Sr., had been to Accardo what Hinky Dink and Bathhouse John were to Colosimo, Capone and Nitti. Since 1950—some forty years— John D'Arco had been there. They were themselves a great one-two punch for Accardo and for Greasy Thumb, Hump and Gussie, the first, second and third waves of the connection guys.

First young John D'Arco, old John's son, and his brother-in-law, Pat DeLeo, would go down, along with the judge they had corrupted. John, Jr., was a state legislator, a senator in the General Assembly in Springfield, the state capital. Wonder how he got there? John, Sr.'s daughter was married to a lawyer named Pat DeLeo. He fell right into the family business, along with Fred Roti, the alderman who had replaced D'Arco, Sr., after the old man stumbled a bit when I surprised him conferring in a private dining room in the mid-Sixties with Sam Giancana, when Giancana was the boss. (D'Arco had promised me on that occasion that "the FBI cannot embarrass me in this town, this is Chicago!" He stepped down the next day.) Accardo and Giancana had allowed D'Arco to remain as the ward committeeman in charge of the patronage, the city jobs dispensed by the ward, probably the most important post in any ward in those days before the system was changed.

Young D'Arco, DeLeo and Roti were all convicted. They went away to prison. Then it was Marcy's turn. He was indicted and brought to court, but during his trial he suffered a heart attack. He died shortly thereafter.

Then Mayor Daley stepped in, as a result of the investigations. With the assistance of three trusted aldermen, he reshaped the First Ward. He gave the 42nd Ward, the ward adjacent to the north of the First, the strategic area known as the Loop, which had been part of the First Ward since The Hink and The Bath. The successors to the notorious Kenna, Coughlin, D'Arco and Marcy slunk away—they even had to move their offices across the street from City Hall into The Patch. (Today Ted Mazola, the First Ward alderman, could not be the power that Hinky Dink and his successors had been, even if he wanted to, which he doesn't.)

When the dust had settled on Greylord and Gambat, the strength of the ability of Tony Accardo and his guys to corrupt had been most seriously curtailed. This was an awful development for

Joe Batters. Corruption goes hand in glove with organized crime. The mob which can't corrupt can't operate.

In October 1994, John D'Arco, Sr., would join his pal Pat Marcy. I quote from the obituary of D'Arco in the Chicago *Sun Times* of October 31, 1994, written by the fine reporter Chuck Neubauer:

"Two years ago, federal prosecutors in Operation Gambat alleged in a motion that Mr. D'Arco was involved in a plan to fix the notorious 1977 murder trial of reputed mob hit man Harry Aleman. But Mr. D'Arco was not indicted.

" 'He was mob controlled. There is no question about it,' said William Roemer, Jr., a retired FBI agent and author of books about the Chicago mob. 'He served as a conduit for the mob in carrying orders to the politicians who were under the control of the mob,' said Roemer, who directed the planting of an electronic listening device in the 1st Ward headquarters in 1962.

"The same year Roemer helped undermine Mr. D'Arco's position with mob boss Sam Giancana by interrupting a private luncheon between the two during which D'Arco was pleading to be allowed to remain alderman.

"Mr. D'Arco, who earlier told the FBI he was not under Giancana's control, got rattled when Roemer came in. Much to Giancana's annoyance, Mr. D'Arco jumped up and shook the agent's hand.

"The next day, Mr. D'Arco announced he was giving up the alderman's job he had for 12 years.

"Roemer said Mr. D'Arco's ties to Giancana had become too public for him to stay in the City Council. But Roemer said Mr. D'Arco kept the more powerful committeeman's job and his share of Anco, Inc., an insurance brokerage that served as the 1st Ward's 'money machine.'

" 'You couldn't do anything in the 1st Ward without going through D'Arco,' said Roemer.

"Both Mr. D'Arco's son, former state Sen. John D'Arco, Jr., and his son-in-law, Pat DeLeo, went to prison as a result of Operation Gambat, as did the ward's alderman, Fred Roti."

How would you like to be remembered with an obit like that? Actually, I felt somewhat embarrassed to be quoted as I was. Even though D'Arco didn't deserve much in memory, it's hard to see it come to that.

In any event, the powerful First Ward bosses were a thing of the past and the connection guys were, too—almost. Guzik, Humphreys, Pierce, Ferraro and Kruse were all gone. Only one guy remained to provide the favorable treatment from public officials which Joe Batters and his mob needed. Gus Alex.

64 Beginning of the End?

It was just about this time that I addressed a group of some two hundred law enforcement officers in Chicago. Speaking as I sometimes do in the vernacular of the fight game, of which I was a part at one time, I told them that it was my opinion that we were then in the eleventh round of a fifteen-round world's championship fight. I said that the mob had won the early rounds and that we were now winning the later rounds. We were winning, but if we did not keep our priorities in the fight, we could still lose. I compared our fight with the heavyweight championship fight between Billy Conn and Joe Louis. Conn won almost all the rounds but Louis rallied and knocked Conn out in the thirteenth round.

This was the situation as I saw it in the mid to late Eighties, not only in Chicago but throughout the country. Tony Accardo, weakened now by the infirmities of old age, was not the warhorse he had once been. It was difficult for him to grasp the reins of the Chicago Outfit and pull it all back together. Not that he was not in there punching or that he was at all out of it, but his age, the problems which came with it, and the recent assaults against him by the federal government had combined to take their toll. He continued to be a force. Perhaps more importantly, our efforts had taken their toll on his organization. And the situation in Chicago was far from being unique. The third tier of FBI agents in Chicago was not unparalleled. Its counterparts in FBI offices around the country were working just as hard and just as efficiently.

The Commission was presiding over a situation where the structure was not wrecked but it sure was weakened. Joe Batters no longer attended Commission meetings. Another Joe, Ferriola, was now the *representato* for Chicago. But Accardo continued to be the power behind the throne, advising Ferriola as he left for Commission meetings as to what he might expect and how he should react. When Ferriola returned from these meetings, which were infrequent, he cut Tony in on the agenda and the decisions which had been made. As always, what happened in the other families of La Cosa Nostra and their cities was of considerable interest to Chicago, although not necessarily of vital impact. Since the FBI and the Justice Department were *federal* agencies, however, their techniques and their investigations in all parts of the country were of prime interest to Chicago. Many times those initiatives were commenced in Chicago, as they had been in the past, but in some instances they were begun in other cities. It was of vital concern to the Outfit as to what was going on elsewhere.

In New York, especially, there was considerable mob activity and counteractive FBI and Justice Department activity. For some years "Big Paulie" Castellano had been the boss of perhaps the most powerful of the five New York families represented on the Commission, the Gambino family. But in December 1985, Big Paulie was no more. He was gunned down with his bodyguard, Tommy Biloti, on the sidewalk outside a popular Manhattan restaurant, Sparks Steak House. The guy who had had him killed was assuming power—a loud, boisterous successor to the laid-back Castellano, a guy named John Gotti. Gotti was a forceful influence in the Commission and one that Accardo cautioned Ferriola to keep at arm's length.

The other New York families were being run by Fat Tony Salerno, who was a very effective leader of his Luchese family; John Francese of the Colombos; Vincent "Chin" Gigante of the Genovese family; and Phil Rastelli of the Bonanno family. Batters' old adversary on the Commission was still alive and functioning, but Joe Bonanno, after I had helped convict him in 1980, was no longer involved. He was about to be released from prison but would return to his Tucson home, about five miles from mine, and write his memoirs, entitled *Man of Honor*. He is still alive at ninety as I write this.

The murder of Big Paulie Castellano in New York underscored the situation in La Cosa Nostra at the time. The scene was changing, along with its cast of characters. This was true for five big reasons.

One was the continued inability of mob families, except in Chicago, to live harmoniously. Castellano had been killed and so had the boss of the Philadelphia family, Angelo Bruno. In fact, several top guys in Philly and other cities were killed.

Two, the federal government had really fine-tuned its investigative and prosecutorial techniques. The third tier had improved on the work of the second wave and on the efforts of those of us who had stumbled and bumbled in the first wave when J. Edgar Hoover first brought us into the action against organized crime. This was especially true on the use of the one-two punch, the now-admissible elsurs and our growing ability to turn mobsters into witnesses.

Three, attrition had by now truly taken its toll. There just weren't any Tony Accardos around anymore—and, like Tony, those who were around were aging into a period where they no longer had the inclination, the energy or the ability to lead their families. In the mid-Eighties there were sixty LCN-related prosecutions going on around the country. Two of the most important were outside the realm of Tony Accardo. But they would impact upon him for the reasons we have enumerated.

One was the "Commission Case." The FBI had brought considerable evidence to the office of the U.S. Attorney for Manhattan, and he had taken it by the horns and was utilizing it where it hurt the most: against nine men, including the then-current leaders of the LCN in New York, the five mobsters identified on p. 356. This U.S. Attorney was Rudolph W. Giuliani, and he would use the glory he justifiably gained to follow in the footsteps of earlier USA's, such as Richard B. Ogilvie and Jim Thompson, to go on to higher office—in his case, the mayoralty of New York City.

As is so often the case, Giuliani referred to the leaders of La Cosa Nostra as leaders of the Mafia, again, one supposes, on the assumption that the American public understood this terminology. "This is a great day for law enforcement but a bad day, probably the worst ever, for the Mafia," he said as he announced the indictments. "We can prove that the Mafia is as touchable and convictable as anyone. And without their mystery, they will lose power."

I have another theory for the downturn in the fortunes of the mob. I believe there is a sociological reason for their fall from the heights, based on the "acculturation of Italian immigrants." My theory is that when the Italian people immigrated to the U.S. after the turn of the century, they had moved into communities populated almost exclusively by themselves and did not flow easily into the mainstream of our society. Many took pride in belonging to the secret society of organized crime. It was an honor to belong to the Capone Gang, for instance. But as the decades rolled on, Italians became Italian-Americans and are now freely and happily accepted into all society in this country. The honor and tradition of belonging to La Cosa Nostra is a thing of the past. It is now considered a disgrace within the Italian-American community, whereas decades ago it was with pride that the son of Raymond Patriarca, for instance, the boss of the New England family, would think of his father, even to the extent that Raymond, Jr., would choose to follow in his father's footsteps by becoming the top leader of the Boston family of the LCN. Now that is not true. Now sons of such mob leaders as Jackie Cerone, Vince Solano, Donald Angelini and others are respected members of their communities. They have stepped out of the shadow of their heritage and become successful in the law and business communities by reason of their own abilities and diligence, not on the coattails of their fathers. I dine with young Jack Cerone as an equal, discussing, not mob business, but current affairs and personalities of the free world, not the underworld.

I take some of the thoughts I have in this regard from conversations I have had with Joe Bonanno in Chicago and in Tucson. This legendary mob boss became a "wise guy," as they call mobsters in New York, about the same time as Batters did in the mid-Twenties. In 1931 Bonanno became a charter member of La Cosa Nostra as it was formed and a charter member of the Commission, which was set up simultaneously. He was given a big hunk of Brooklyn as one of the five New York families. He stayed in this capacity, although in the Seventies he ran his empire in the East from Arizona, until I helped convict him in 1980. I've had several talks with Bonanno, lasting probably twelve to fifteen hours. I know he feels that the membership of La Cosa Nostra is nowhere as "honorable" as it was when he was climbing inside it and into the Seventies. So I guess I am influenced by what Bonanno feels. For instance, I talked to him once when there had been allegations that Carmine Galante, who had taken over the Bonanno family after Joe bowed out of the leadership, had allowed his soldiers to engage in home video pornography. Joe was absolutely aghast. *Never* would this guy have allowed that, this man who has a plenary indulgence from a pope framed and hanging in his vestibule of his home, a promise by a pope that he will ascend directly and immediately to heaven. (I wish I had one of those!)

A fifth reason for the decline of the LCN in general around the country in the mid-Eighties, I believe, was their entry into narcotics trafficking. This became somewhat common in the eastern part of the country, but not in Chicago. Not immediately, anyway. Narcotics literally polluted the membership. Instead of taking pride in their activity, the traditional functions of the mob, they now became engaged in what is perhaps the most insidious crime in our society. No longer could they consider themselves any better than the motorcycle gangs or the prison gangs, the Asian gangs. What difference was there now in belonging to the "honored society," which they had loudly proclaimed for decades, when they were now no better than the "emerging crime groups," as we officially call them, when the LCN was competing for turf and business with these people? How were they any better?

As I say, however, this was not true in Chicago. There the Outfit continued to enforce its ban on drug trafficking. As long as Tony Accardo was in charge, we knew that the prohibition against dealing drugs was strictly enforced. Witness Chris Cardi!

This ban was not enforced in most of the La Cosa families beginning about this time. I remember going into the Chicago Office of the FBI and discussing this precise topic with Ed Hegarty, then the Special Agent in Charge of the Chicago FBI. Ed had been a clerk in the office which he now headed, when I was a C-1 agent. He had become an agent on the Organized Crime Squad in Philadelphia and then eventually came back to his hometown to head up the FBI operation there. Ed told me then that many LCN families were openly permitting narcotics trafficking, and others, like Philadelphia, were not enforcing the ban but not openly approving it either. "In Philly," he told me, "if a wise guy gets caught dealing drugs, he gets no help. He's on his own. But he is not killed, like in Chicago."

This was a huge deviation from 1931 when La Cosa Nostra was set up. Then drugs were included in the oath of *omerta*. Nobody in the "honored society" dealt drugs, period.

This, in my opinion, thinned the hot blood of La Cosa Nostra and was a clear indication of their decline in honor—whatever honor they had, that is.

The Chicago Outfit and the New York families, in particular, worked together. I'm not saying there wasn't discord between them, and jealousy, but especially in their influence over trade unions this was true. And nowhere was it truer than in the Teamsters Union. Chicago was the dominant influence over the Teamsters, but New York and the DeCalvacante family in New Jersey had a lot of influence there, especially in the days when the presidents were Hoffa and Fitzsimmons. Other unions, like the Laborers, the Longshoremen and the Hotel Employees and Restaurant Employees unions, are under the mutual influence of the LCN in Chicago and New York as well.

In New York City, for instance, the President's Commission on Organized Crime found that "a builder cannot construct a building from the ground up without dealing with a union that is controlled by organized crime." The President's Commission found that "the cost of building construction in NYC includes a 20 percent surplus charge for the mob." Think about that! The Commission found that, of the 50,000 labor locals in the country, with a total of $9 billion in assets, some 400 locals were then heavily influenced or controlled by organized crime syndicates. "Many of these are very major locals embracing thousands of members in strategic cities, enabling gangster domination of the internationals," the President's Commission said in its report.

Therefore, just as the Chicago Outfit was badly hurt by Pendorf, Strawman I and Strawman II, Greylord and Gambat, the New York mobs were seriously wounded with several similar prosecutions, all brought before the U.S. Attorney's Offices there (in Manhattan and Brooklyn) by the FBI. The "Commission Case" and the "Pizza Connection Case" were major blows.

Actually, these cases were preceded by the conviction of "Matty the Horse" Ianniello and eight of his soldiers. Ianniello was a capo, a very strong figure, in the Genovese family. He was convicted of conspiring to skim $2.5 million from Manhattan restaurants and nightclubs.

Then in 1987 the top bosses of the New York families of the LCN were convicted in the now famous "Commission Case." These were the members of the Commission which arbitrated the national affairs of the LCN. The director of the FBI, William Webster, said at the time, "We are now taking out the top players. The ruling body of the most powerful organized crime elements in the U.S. . . . has now been brought to the bar of justice." The prosecution involved the authorization by the Commission of five murders. Included was their decision to cut down the successor to Joe Bonanno, Carmine Galante, in 1979. Two of the defendants were not around to hear their verdicts. One was Castellano; the other, Aniello Dellacroce, underboss of the Gambino family. He died of natural causes.

The other case, "The Pizza Connection" case, extended even into rural Illinois, where a pizza parlor, like so many involved in this case across the country, dealt drugs. The case began in 1984 when the Justice Department indicted thirty-one people in the operation of this international drug ring. It was charged that in over five years the ring had brought into this country 1,650 pounds of heroin, with a street value of $1.6 billion, then sold the drugs through pizza parlors in the Northeast and Midwest. Actually, the case had begun when I was still an agent in Chicago, when the New York Office found that the "Catalano faction" of the Bonanno family, led by Salvatore Catalano, was "deeply involved in massive heroin importation and distribution in the United States," as charged in the indictment later. "Although Catalano's organization was located in New York City, the investigation by the FBI revealed that Catalano's heroin business was tied directly to organized criminal groups in Sicily, the rest of Italy, Switzerland, France and Brazil," an FBI affidavit read. This FBI affidavit stated that the Catalano group generated "prodigious amounts of cash." In the period from 1980 to 1982, more than $25 million in cash was wired from New York to other countries, such as Bermuda and Switzerland.

More than 300 drug-related telephone conversations, often in code or Sicilian or Italian, were monitored. As a matter of fact, international cooperation resulted in the arrest of 159 organized crime figures in Italy alone. In one aspect of the investigation, FBI agents seized thirty-six pounds of heroin at the port of Newark, N.J., hidden in the beams of wooden pallets used to ship cargo of tiles from Italy to Buffalo, New York.

As I say, there was a Midwest connection in this investigation. Pietro Alfano of Oregon, Illinois, sixty-five miles from Chicago, dealt drugs from his pizza parlor. More than that, the affidavit charged that he was the "main connection point in the United States regarding narcotics importation." It took 341 pages to contain all the charges the FBI made in its affidavit in this case.

The convictions in the Matty "The Horse" Case, the Commission Case and the Pizza Connection Case, coupled with the Pendorf, Strawman I and Strawman II cases, were crippling blows to La Cosa Nostra in the two stronghold cities. They were convictions J. Edgar Hoover rightfully had expected when he established the Top Hood Program in 1957.

We had turned the game around all over the country. In Boston, Gennaro J. Anguilo and several of his top men in the Patriarca Family would go down, charged with several murders, loansharking, obstruction of justice and gambling. This was a prelude to the later convictions of just about every other top dog in New England, including Raymond Patriarca, Jr., the New England LCN boss. In Cleveland, the acting boss there, Angelo Lonardo, was convicted of RICO and narcotics violations. This would prove to be a most significant situation well outside Cleveland when this conviction caused Lonardo to "flip" and then testify against many of the people with whom he had conspired in other cities, including testimony at the sentencing hearing in Strawman II against Jackie Cerone, Joey Aiuppa and Angelo LaPietra, a prime example of how the LCN was nationally interconnected. He was a major witness in Strawman II. In Denver, the boss there, Gene Smalldone, was convicted of income tax evasion, extortion and firearms violations. In Kansas City, we had the Strawman I and Strawman II convictions of the entire top tier of leadership of the LCN. In Milwaukee, Frank Balistrieri, the boss, went down in the Strawman II case. And in Philadelphia, Nicodemo "Little Nicky" Scarfo, the boss who had taken over after Angelo Bruno was killed, would soon wind up in prison for the rest of his life.

It had taken a long time, almost three decades, to round the corner, but I think the third tier finally achieved what those of us in the first wave of FBI agents had started. "To make sense" of organized crime. J. Edgar Hoover, who had died in May of 1972, must have smiled in pride as he looked down to see what his guys were achieving. Most of them he had not appointed; they had come into the Bureau after he left, but some were his, and in any case, they were all building on the foundation he had constructed. I am happy for this man who, long after his death, has become so unjustly maligned now that he is not around to defend himself; this man who, for one thing, is alleged to have been blackmailed by Meyer Lansky, who, it is alleged, had a photo of Hoover with his chief assistant, Clyde Tolson, in such a compromising position that he "went soft" on organized crime. I've got the scars on my butt to prove that such a belief is absolutely absurd. He brought us in, late, it is true, but when he brought us in, we built the ground floor of what was swiftly becoming a high-rise of accomplishment against the mobs. Those of us in the first wave had built the foundation, the basement and the first floors. The second wave of agents built the middle floors and now the third tier was building towards the penthouse. We weren't there yet, there were still rounds to be fought, but the view to the stars and the moon was closer than ever.

65 Less Las Vegas

As the FBI and the Justice Department were having their successes in Chicago, Kansas City and New York, another development was taking place which would have another prime effect on Tony Accardo and the mob he still controlled with the ultimate authority, the final veto power.

For thirty years one of the major sources of income for J.B. and his people had been their flagship hotel-casino in Las Vegas, the Stardust. Set in the middle of the Strip and built in 1955, it had been the paradise of the visiting low roller, the ultimate "grind joint." "Lefty" Rosenthal had been Accardo's man at the Stardust and he had done a good job there. Millions, maybe billions, of players had put quarters in the slots there and many had bought chips to play at the $2 minimum blackjack tables. Now millions had gotten their "action" by sitting in the sports book, one of Vegas' best, and betting on football, baseball, basketball, boxing, even tennis and golf, watching several games at one time on the big screens. And so millions of dollars had found their way into Tony Accardo's pockets. The $275,000 in $50 and $100 bills bound in wrappers of the Valley Bank of Las Vegas that was found in his Ashland home came from there.

Now, however, the Stardust was about to succumb to the same pressure we had put on the mobs in those cities where the hidden points from the casinos were delivered. Five key employees of the Stardust were indicted by a federal grand jury investigating a scheme to skim between $2.5 million and $5.2 million from gambling operations over five years. The parent corporation of the Stardust, Trans-Sterling, headed by Allen Sachs and Herb Tobman, was also named in the scheme, although Sachs and Tobman themselves were not indicted. The people indicted were instead what the Gaming Control Board, the GCB, in Nevada calls "key employees," most of whom had allegedly been placed in the hotel to control the skim and get it back to Tony and his guys. Most of his employees had worked in mob gambling joints in Chicago, where they had gained the trust of people like Cerone and Aiuppa. Lou Salerno, the director of casino operations, was an example. (Sachs had assumed operating control of the Stardust from another front for Tony and his guys, Allen Glick, on May 16, 1979. Salerno was appointed casino manager the very next day.) Another of the defendants was Fred Pandolfo, the assistant casino manager, whom I had chased in Las Vegas about this same time while attempting to locate and serve a subpoena on the enforcer, Tony "The Ant" Spilotro, the Outfit's man over Las Vegas. The indictees were all charged for failing to answer questions before the grand jury in Vegas, even though they had been given that cursed grant of immunity. The charge carried a penalty of up to five years.

Actually, the indictments were the second in a one-two punch against the Chicago Outfit's operation of the Stardust. The day before, the Gaming Commission had approved a settlement under which Sachs and Tobman surrendered their licenses to operate the Stardust, Fremont and Sundance casinos. They also agreed to pay fines totaling $3 million, which was the largest such assessment in the history of Nevada since gambling was legalized in 1931. Sachs and Tobman were given 130 days to divest themselves of the three hotel-casinos, three of the very nicest in Las Vegas. The Stardust was a venerable old lady of the Strip, while the Fremont shared such a distinction downtown on Fremont Street, also known as Glitter Gulch. The Sundance in 1983 was new. It had been built on land located right in the middle of the Gulch owned by the Godfather of Las Vegas himself, venerable now, Moe Dalitz. Moe had applied for a license to operate the Sundance (for the Chicago mob) but had withdrawn it when he realized that the climate—not only in Nevada but all over the country—had turned cool towards the mob. I would talk to him about this at a meeting we had at the Las Vegas Country Club shortly after this, when he was dying from kidney failure and was on dialysis.

The penalties assessed by the Gaming Commission on Sachs and Tobman were the result of a state investigation into allegations that Sachs and Tobman had allowed $1.5 million to be skimmed from gambling at the Stardust during the years 1982 into early 1983.

The loss of the Stardust was a heavy blow to Tony Accardo and his Outfit. Soon the Stardust would be sold to the reputable Boyd family, who would be surprised at just how profitable the place was. The books had not begun to indicate just how much the Stardust earned each year. Actually, I'm sure they had a good idea. The amount of skim had been so heavy that the profit and loss statement did not present a true picture of the gold mine that the Stardust was. When the Stardust was sold to an honest operation which recorded each penny of its income, the figures leaped well above those of the previous years.

With the Stardust went the Fremont, Sundance, Hacienda and Marina, all hotels which at one time were owned by fronts for Tony and his guys. Soon the Desert Inn and the Riviera would follow. All of these, and others like the Tropicana, the Aladdin, the Dunes, Circus Circus, Caesar's Palace, the Sands, the Frontier, the Flamingo and other Vegas hotel-casinos which were, in one way or another, mobbed-up, were now about to be purchased by legitimate owners, mainly public corporations. When the fronts, like Sachs at the Stardust, could not obtain "suitability" in the eyes of the GCB, permitting them to obtain or retain their required licenses, the curtain came down. The game was over for the mobs in Las Vegas.

66 We Finally Get Gus Alex

Tony Accardo almost popped his buttons with pride, as well he should. His lovely, personable, intelligent granddaughter, Alicia Accardo, was being married to the love of her life. The reception took place in the Hilton Hotel and Towers and was attended by some of the nicest people on earth. Even movie star Robert Conrad came with his wife, Lavelda, all the way from his home in the San Fernando Valley.

Alicia had made a place of her own in the world, having been a script supervisor for Conrad for five years. Knowing Robert as I do, I'm sure he was happy to give Tony's granddaughter a chance to make it on her own. And knowing Tony as I do, I'm sure it was one of the happiest moments of his life. He and Clarice attended the wedding and the reception and both beamed throughout. It was one of the few times Tony spent much time in Chicago in the winter but he wouldn't have missed this event in late November of 1991 for anything.

Another guy who was there was now just about the best friend Joe Batters had. And it would be the last public appearance of this fellow, exactly ten years Joe's junior. He was about to be locked up for the rest of his life—unless he is released in the future because of his physical and mental infirmities. He had been my longtime adversary, my first target some thirty-four years before, when those of us in the first wave of FBI organized crime fighters had initially come to grips with the Outfit. Gus Alex. "Slim," as he was code-named.

I had never been able to put Gussie away. In a mental institution, yes, for a short while, but never in prison. About a year after I first locked horns with Gus, he had put himself in Silver Hill, the place people go to rehabilitate from stress, alcohol or even drugs. Mrs. Ted Kennedy (Joan) spent time there. Gus, unlike his cohorts who didn't like it but could handle it, had succumbed to the stress in 1959 and needed a few months to get himself together after the Top Hoodlum Program commenced and focused on him as one of its subjects.

Silver Hill was just what Gussie needed. He had disregarded the advice of his buddy Tony Accardo, who had advised him to go chop wood. When he came back from the New Canaan, Connecticut, institution, he was revitalized. In 1960 he had put himself back together and for the next three decades he rose in stature and power in the Outfit, even becoming Joe Batters' closest pal after Jackie Cerone went to prison in 1986.

Gussie was, in 1991, the boss of the connection guys, having replaced Hump in 1965, when Hump died on the evening of the day he was arrested on my "bullshit case." Gus and Pat Marcy were handling the great bulk of the connection guys' work as of 1991. But by 1991 Pat was not much use due to his heart condition, and he would not be around much longer.

In December of 1991, at the age of seventy-five, Gussie finally got what all prominent members—save one—get eventually. With that single exception, it is now the rule that a mob capo or boss will enjoy several good years on his way from the middle ranks to the top, but—and it's a big but—at the age of fifty or sixty or more, they will move on to spend the rest of their lives in prison.

When they reach a certain pinnacle, the FBI shifts its focus on them and when we do, we seldom come up empty. Gussie was indicted—finally.

The charge was that Alex had approved extortion schemes of those working under him, threats made to business owners that they would be beaten if they did not fork over thousands of dollars. He was indicted with another longtime adversary of mine, Lenny Patrick. Gussie would never agree to a sit-down with me, but Lenny had. In fact, he had initiated a meeting to discuss a breach of our "family pact." One of our overzealous agents, new on our squad and not yet aware of the "family pact," had gone to the mother of a young man of a high-society family who was engaged to Sharon Patrick, Lenny's beautiful daughter. The agent had informed the mother of the nature of the family her son was marrying into. Shortly thereafter, the son called the wedding off. Lenny was very upset. Understandably. I agreed wholeheartedly with him. It was a big mistake on the young agent's part. I gave Lenny my humblest apologies, not that it could have made Lenny feel much better.

Gussie and Lenny had been indicted in the final stages of their long careers in organized crime. Gus was seventy-five, Lenny seventy-eight. Some people might wonder why the government would be after old geezers like that. Sometimes it is for no other reason than that it may deter others who should know that the FBI and the Justice Department do not let up. Anyone who stays active in the mob stays susceptible to investigation and prosecution, no matter what age.

Gussie had had the Loop under his command for years, in addition to his "connection" duties. Lenny had been convicted of a bank robbery in 1937, became the boss for the Outfit of their street crew in Lawndale and then, when most of his Jewish clients moved from Lawndale on the west side to Rogers Park on the far north side, Lenny moved up there with them and became the street crew boss there. He had been convicted again in 1977 of criminal contempt of court for refusing to testify at a federal trial. He had been out of jail about ten years, and now this new trouble.

I think Bill Braden, the fine reporter for the *Sun Times*, pretty well summed up Gussie's career in an article he wrote on December 22, 1991, just after Alex was indicted:

"Alex is the mob's No. 2 boss under Anthony Accardo, according to organized crime expert William F. Roemer, Jr., a retired FBI agent who now serves as a consultant to the Chicago Crime Commission.

" 'He's a major catch,' Roemer said in a telephone interview from his Arizona home. 'He's been the head of what the mob calls the connection guys. They are a group of about five people who corrupt public officials, labor leaders, judges and cops.

" 'No mob can operate without corrupting public officials,' said Roemer. 'He has been in charge of that important, crucial function of the (Chicago) mob since 1965.'

"Roemer said it has been Alex's job to pass along Accardo's orders to reputed 1st Ward mob superboss Pat Marcy, indicted a year ago in the Operation Gambat investigation of 1st Ward corruption. 'Alex would relay Accardo's orders for corrupted officials to Marcy,' said Roemer.

" 'Accardo, Alex and Marcy are the top three in the Chicago mob,' said Roemer, who has written two books since his 1980 retirement—*War of the Godfathers* and *Roemer: Man Against the Mob*.

" 'Alex rose to prominence as mob boss of the Loop in the '50s and '60s,' said Roemer, 'controlling gambling and prostitution.' During the same period he also was top assistant to Murray Humphreys, then boss of the connection boys. When boss Jackie Cerone went to prison in 1970, Alex joined Accardo and Joseph Aiuppa in a ruling triumvirate. 'It was the first time a non-Italian was made a top leader of the Chicago mob,' said Roemer. 'But he didn't want that kind of limelight. He's very jumpy, one of the most cautious hoods of all time. So, after a year, he wanted out. And he faded into the anonymity of the connection guys,' said Roemer.

"Appearing before the U.S. Senate's racket committee, Alex was described as 'the most vicious and most ruthless Chicago hoodlum.' He was questioned by chief counsel Robert F. Kennedy, who asked:

" 'Could you tell us how much you charge to kill somebody?'

"Alex mopped his face with a handkerchief and read from an index card. He pleaded the Fifth Amendment 40 times."

The article described that "James Ragan, the wire service operator murdered by the mob, told police that Alex had threatened to kill him if he did not turn his wire business over to the mob."

That pretty well sums Gussie up.

As part of the conspiracy that Gus was charged with, Mario Rainone and Nick Gio, allegedly part of Gus' group, were also indicted as the mob enforcers who had carried out Gussie's plans. Rainone, for instance, was charged with throwing a hand grenade onto the roof of the Lake Theater in Oak Park in an attempt to force the owners to give up a percentage of the business. Rainone, a real nice guy, also threatened the owner of a restaurant in the northwest suburban town of Northbrook in 1987, saying that if he did not pay $200,000 to the group, his "entire family would wind up in Mount Carmel Cemetery." He also threatened to "blow away" the children of another restaurant owner. The fine AUSA who would handle the prosecution, Chris Gair, alleged that Patrick personally ordered the beating in 1988 of Alex Tapper, the owner of a construction business. Gio and another, James LaValley, hospitalized Tapper, who has since died.

After their detention hearing, U.S. Magistrate Judge Joan Gottschall ordered Alex and Patrick held in the MCC, the Metropolitan Correctional Center. Alex was thereafter allowed to be confined in his apartment, 31B at 1300 Lake Shore Drive. He was only allowed to leave to visit his doctor and his lawyer and to submit to unannounced visits by FBI agents. He wore a monitoring device on his ankle at all times. Gus had complained that his ulcers (and I know he had them) made it impossible for him to eat the food at the MCC and that all he had been able to consume during his two-day incarceration there was one cup of milk. Gus was also required to surrender his passport and post a $25,000 cash bond and deeds to his two houses, the one on Lake Shore Drive and the other on Galt Ocean Mile in Fort Lauderdale.

Some of the government's case against Alex and Patrick grew out of information provided by LaValley. LaValley became an outstanding witness.

Then Lenny Patrick had decided to seek leniency. He had already flipped once and carried a wire. He had recorded with a body mike hidden under his clothes a conversation he had with Gussie. Gussie, cautious as ever, had set the meeting in as secure a place as he could, in a hallway on an upper floor at Northwestern Hospital on the near north side, after he and Patrick had arrived separately and would leave separately. Gussie, believing his precautions would preclude any surveillance, didn't count on Lenny being wired. His statements on that tape were incriminating, as was the cash from the extortions he had approved, which Patrick delivered to him at the hospital.

Lenny then flipped back. After recording the conversation with Gussie, his cooperation with the FBI was terminated by the FBI when it was learned that Lenny had continued to operate as a mob boss, even though the FBI paid him $7,200 over the two months he had turned. Then Lenny flipped again, back to us. After his indictment he agreed, in exchange for the judge's recommendation for leniency, to testify against Gussie and, as part of his testimony, to support the conversation with Gussie he had picked up on his wire at Northwestern Hospital. The Chicago *Tribune* carried this news at the top of its front page on April 7, 1992. As part of his article, Matt O'Connor quoted me as follows:

"William Roemer, Jr., a retired FBI agent who made a career of investigating the mob, called Patrick 'the most important mobster ever to turn against the Chicago mob. He could be very damaging. He could bring down just about everybody.'

"Roemer said, 'Patrick could not only provide damaging testimony at Alex's trial, but also provide details of Alex's work since 1965' as head of what the FBI calls the corruption squad, the mob faction that corrupts public officials."

The trial was presided over by U.S. District Court Judge James H. Alesia, a fair, intelligent, decisive judge who had been an incorruptible Chicago cop. When it concluded after Patrick's damaging testimony, Judge Alesia sentenced Gussie to fifteen years, eight months in prison and ordered him to pay $823,000 in fines and restitution, in addition to paying $1,400 a month for the cost to the taxpayers of his prison cell. Gus had no chance of parole under the recent federal sentencing guidelines. So, at the age of seventy-six, Gussie faced the rest of life in prison.

Carl Walsh, Gussie's attorney, appealed the verdict and Judge Alesia's stiff sentence in August of 1994. The appeal was denied.

I had not been able to nail Gussie in the twenty-one years I had gone after him. But after reading what the Chief Judge of the United States Court of Appeals for the Seventh Circuit wrote, I would like to think that maybe, after all these years, I did have a small part in the case against Gussie. Because the Chief Judge, Posner, opened his opinion by referring to my testimony before the Senate "linking the defendants in this case to Capone, Nitti, Accardo and other Outfit bosses in an unbroken line of descent." Therefore, although I had nothing to do with the case which finally tripped old Gussie up after all these years, here it was, in the late summer of 1994, that I *did* have something to do with keeping Gussie in jail, which I hope sends a loud signal to any mobster that sooner or later we're going to get you! It might be later, but how would you like to trade places with Gussie Alex at the age of seventy-eight?

Following is the order entered on November 23, 1994:

UNITED STATES DISTRICT COURT
NORTHERN DISTRICT OF ILLINOIS
EASTERN DIVISION

UNITED STATES OF AMERICA) No. 91 CR 727-2
v.   ) Judge James H. Alesia
GUS ALEX   )

ORDER TO DISBURSE FUNDS

This matter having come before the court on the motion of the government, and the Court having been apprised of the circumstances.

IT IS HEREBY ORDERED that the Clerk of the District Court forthwith disburse and transfer funds of Defendant Gus Alex currently on deposit with the Clerk under the following receipt numbers: (1) Receipt Number 366153 dated December 23, 1991, for $25,000; (2) Receipt Number 404241 dated November 17, 1992, for $197,000; and (3) Receipt Number 412021 dated March 19, 1993, for $601,000, to and in satisfaction of the following financial sentencing obligations imposed by the Court:

(1) $154,000 to be paid out in restitution to Myron Freedman & Phillip Freedman, jointly and severally (recipients' addresses are to be separately provided to the Clerk by written communication from the government);

(2) $72,000 to be paid in restitution to William Moss (again, recipient's address is to be separately provided to the Clerk by written communication from the government);

(3) $150,000 to be paid out in restitution to Raymond Hara (again, recipient's address is to be separately provided to the Clerk by written communication from the government);

(4) $250,000 to be transferred to the Crime Victims Fund to cover defendant's fine;

(5) $100 to be transferred to the Crime Victims Fund to cover defendant's special assessment;

(6) $197,000 to be paid to the United States Marshals

Service Asset Forfeiture Fund, to cover defendant's forfeiture judgment.

(7) By agreement of the government and the Defendant Gus Alex, any funds of Defendant Alex remaining on deposit with the Clerk following the above disbursements and transfers, should be returned to Defendant Alex by check made payable to Gus Alex, care of his attorney Carl M. Walsh, 39 S. LaSalle Street, Suite 1400, Chicago, Illinois 60603.

SO ORDERED:
UNITED STATES DISTRICT COURT JUDGE

DATED: *NOV 23 1994*

Two more of Chicago's finest reporters, Rosalind Rossi and Phillip J. O'Connor of the *Sun Times*, put it best: "Star government witness Leonard Patrick helped bag his first mob conviction when Gus Alex fell Thursday.

"Two questions now remain: which mobsters will be in trouble next, and can the mob survive?"

The article went on to wonder which mobsters Lenny would "nail" next. The speculation was that even Tony Accardo would not be immune.

"But," they add, "while the mob has buckled, it remains unbroken. And it will not break anytime soon. The money, estimated to be in the billions by the Chicago Crime Commission, is just too good."

I agreed with Rossi and O'Connor. "Buckled but remaining unbroken." And if I were as articulate, that's what I would have said.

The article's speculation as to "which mobster Lenny would nail next" proved to be unfounded. Lenny would testify in another case, in San Diego, but while on the stand, he perjured himself. He had testified in the case against Gus Alex that he had murdered six men. Although he had testified that they were premeditated and had advised FBI agents during pre-trial interviews in San Diego along the same lines, he changed his story at trial. He testified, for instance, that when he shot Herman Gleck, Gleck had pulled a pistol on him, that he had shot Harry Krotish after Krotish "pulled a pistol on me in the car and I shot him," and that he and his partner, Davey Yaras, killed Davy Zatz after "we were talking there, and that's what happened. He went for his gun and that's it." Patrick summed it up in San Diego by testifying that his six murders were all "spur of the moment killings," when, in fact, he had previously advised the FBI and testified at the Alex trial that they were all premeditated.

This testimony not only got Lenny into big trouble but it destroyed his credibility with respect to using his testimony in future trials. No defense attorney worth his salt would ever overlook it when cross-examining Patrick in any future trial.

In fact, the government moved against Lenny after the San Diego trial, revoking the plea agreement it had reached with him in return for his testimony against Alex, since this agreement did call for his testimony in future trials. Chief Judge John F. Grady then added a year to the sentence Judge Alesia had imposed on Lenny after the Alex trial, making it seven years now that he had to serve. Better than the fifteen years Alex got and which Lenny might have received. At the age of about eighty, however, it might not have made a tremendous difference to Lenny.

67 More of Accardo's Men Go Down

In December of 1991 another one of the top leaders of the Chicago Outfit went on trial in the U.S. District Court of Northern Illinois in Chicago, along with his top henchmen. Ernest Rocco Infelice had been, until he was indicted earlier in the year, the underboss of the Chicago Outfit, the top aide to the boss. Joe Batters was still the consiglieri, the adviser, and the loss of Rocky Infelice would be another major blow to his family.

Rock was a strange breed of cat for a "made" guy. I did have some grudging respect for him, even though I never met him. While almost all his colleagues in crime, even Accardo, were ducking the draft in World War II, Rocky did not. He didn't go out and volunteer but when he was drafted, he went—and he volunteered for the paratroopers. He joined the 101st Airborne, the

"Screaming Eagles," the "Battered Bastards of Bastogne," who fought in the Battle of the Bulge.

When Rocky returned, he had not yet been "made." In fact, it was a long time before he was. He became a burglar, one of the Top Jewel Thieves. Then, of all things, Rocky was convicted of dealing drugs and sent to prison for a stretch.

One would think his dealing drugs as a member of Tony Accardo's Outfit would preclude Rocky from being "made," but it didn't, apparently, because when he got out of prison, he demonstrated to the powers that he was most capable and promised he would thereafter refrain from such bad stuff. Also, being married to the daughter of Tony Capezio didn't hurt.

In the early Eighties I received a visit from Chuckie English, the former lieutenant of Sam Giancana. After Giancana was pushed out by Joe Batters, Chuckie's career in the Outfit had stalled. Now, however, he had regained some stature and was regularly seen at a Texaco station on the west side of Chicago which was then serving as a mob hangout, according to Pete Wacks, the outstanding FBI agent of Pendorf fame.

When Chuckie came out to see me in Arizona, I had been retired from the FBI for a couple years. He asked me about my knowledge of Infelice in relation to the conviction he had in the drug case. I didn't know too much about it, since we in the FBI were not involved (it was a DEA case). But I did mention that I was aware of Rocky's service in the paratroopers, a service I respected as a former Marine. Apparently whatever I had to say about Infelice didn't hurt him. Shortly after English returned to Chicago from Arizona, Infelice was promoted to underboss of the Outfit, the number two spot.

Infelice was subsequently indicted on numerous counts of racketeering under RICO, including the murder of two bookmakers who did not make good on the street tax. Along with Infelice, four of his top lieutenants were indicted: Sal DeLaurentis, Robert Bellavia, Louis Marino and Robert Salerno. The chief witness against Infelice was "B.J." Jahoda. Jahoda had been a member of Infelice's crew, but he had turned and was now testifying as a "CW," a cooperating witness, as it is officially termed, against his former mates. I came to Chicago during the trial and caught some of Jahoda's testimony. He was as good a witness as I've ever seen. Sharp, well dressed, articulate and credible.

Jahoda had carried a wire during conversations with Infelice and others. In fact, one of the exhibits, 446T, which the government produced, was especially interesting to me. This government

exhibit was the tape of a conversation between Jahoda and Infelice. Infelice asked Jahoda: "Have you read Roemer's book?"
(Speaking, I believe, of my first one, *Roemer: Man Against the
Mob*, my autobiography.) When Jahoda indicated that he had not,
Infelice told him, as recorded on the tape and introduced in court:
"He's mostly accurate. He don't lie. You know he was with the G
here for many years. Capable man." That was nice, especially
considering that many of the conversations which were introduced
as government exhibits contained information about whom Infelice and the Chicago Outfit were bribing. For instance, Jahoda related one of his conversations with Infelice: "I was told it (money)
was going straight to the Cook County Sheriff's Department . . . to
Dvorak and to O'Grady." Well, Jimmy O'Grady, a friend of mine,
was the sheriff at the time and James Dvorak was his under-
sheriff—and the Chairman of the Cook County Republican Party
at the same time.

Information from the tape of this conversation was leaked to the
press following the indictment in February 1990, with the result
that one of the finest prosecutors in the United States Attorney's
Office, Jeff Johnson, subsequently resigned.

I got a kick out of one conversation between Jahoda and Infelice. Jahoda, like Infelice, a most unusual mobster, had given an
interview to the Chicago *Tribune* which appeared in the *Trib*'s Du
Page County edition, west of Chicago. Infelice chided Jahoda for
this, complaining to him that "a lot of our guys live in Du Page; I
got more ass-chewings over this!" Jahoda then replied: "I didn't
think three people in our world were going to read that fucking
thing!" I guess that was a good idea of what Jahoda thought about
his fellow Outfit members.

Jahoda also testified that when he was indicted in a gambling
case in 1988, Pat Marcy had made moves on his behalf to fix the
case. Jahoda testified that three local judges were given payoffs of
plane tickets to Hawaii or $10,000 as part of the fix, or at least that
is what he had been told by Infelice.

Another top mob figure, Harry Aleman, the mob hit man who
had taken over the "heavy work" after Milwaukee Phil Alderisio
and Chuckie Nicoletti went down, was also indicted in this case.
He pleaded guilty before the trial and was given twelve years in
prison.

Another interesting overhear on the wire Jahoda was carrying
came in 1989, when Infelice was apparently talking about Mayor
Richard M. Daley of Chicago. The tape recording caught Infelice
calling Daley "rotten" and then, "I still don't trust him. When he

was state's attorney, the old guy (Aiuppa) was supposed to get subpoenaed and everything, and the state, they were going to make a big thing out of it. This guy went to him (meaning Daley, presumably), squashed it right out. It's just like the same story. Money talks and bullshit walks." Indeed, the tape caused a big outcry in City Hall. A spokesman for Mayor Daley called Infelice's comments "an empty boast" by a mobster "trying to impress his friends that he had influence. There's absolutely no truth to it." Another tape, which had previously been played at the detention hearing in early 1990, when Infelice and company were indicted, had Infelice bragging that he had worked behind the scenes for Daley as mayor in 1989 by drying up financial support for one of Daley's opponents, Alderman Eddy Vrdolyak. Vrdolyak, now a popular talk-show host on WJJD radio in Chicago, had been a prominent politician in Chicago, representing the far southeast side in the Tenth Ward.

The trial was marked by some controversy when charges were made by the defense that the government was secretly recording privileged conversations between the defendants and their attorneys in the MCC, where they were confined without bail from early 1990 until late 1991 while awaiting, and then during, the trial. This detention had become standard operating procedure since the mid-Eighties. After indictment of mobsters the government requests during a "detention hearing" that the defendants, being a menace to society, be confined to the Metropolitan Correctional Center while awaiting, and during, their trial. Since 95% of such defendants are convicted, this effectively results in incarceration of such mobsters from the time of their arrest until the completion of their sentences, usually many years in length. This didn't happen to Cerone and Aiuppa, since it was only after their indictments that such procedures became standard. It did happen to Gussie Alex, more or less, since he was released on house arrest while awaiting trial only because of his seemingly perilous physical condition. The reason for this practice is that the government is properly concerned about the danger to society, especially to the witnesses against the mobsters, and also with the possibility that the mobsters may be "flight risks" seeking to flee the jurisdiction.

The judge in this case was Ann C. Williams. She allowed the defendants, who had been confined for nineteen months while awaiting trial, to be released from the MCC for eight hours a day to confer with their attorneys in their law offices—accompanied at all times by agents from the FBI. She did not rule, however, that the tapes had been made by the government. I always believed that this was a nice ploy by the defendants, who probably recorded their own conversations with their attorneys in the MCC and then furnished them to the court with the charge that they were the work of the government. Since this would have been a damaging violation of the canons of legal ethics—and had never, to my knowledge, even been contemplated—I do not believe the government would have been so foolish.

The trial was also marked by the outlandish courtroom behavior of Bruce Cutler, the New York attorney for mobsters such as John Gotti. He represented one of the defendants in this case, Solly De Laurentis. His antics rocked the courtroom as he played to the spectators. The decorum was more or less properly maintained under difficult circumstances by Judge Williams. Cutler's assignment as a member of the defense team of attorneys was to discredit the testimony of Jahoda. Over 200 of Jahoda's tapes were played and analyzed by Jahoda and by a fine IRS agent, Tom Moriarity, who had operated as Jahoda's "control agent" from May 1986 to November of that year, during which time the 5,000 hours of conversations of Jahoda and his pals had been recorded. Jahoda was on the stand on direct and cross-examination for twenty days. Cutler pounded and pounded him, but could not destroy his credibility. I watched Cutler with interest at this trial. I feel his ability is greatly overestimated. He is the hired gun for the mob today, and I hope they continue to rely on him and place their confidence in his histrionics. Most judges can set him down, and most government attorneys are much more effective once the smoke has cleared.

Jahoda testified at length, under both direct and cross, about the killing of Hal Smith. Smith had been an independent bookmaker operating out of Long Grove, a northwestern suburb. He had refused to pay the 50% of his win to the mob. Jahoda said he watched through a window on the fatal night in 1985 when Smith was confronted and killed by Infelice, De Laurentis, Bellavia and Marino.

The jury was out more than a week, then they finally returned with a verdict, finding Rocky Infelice guilty of racketeering and nineteen other charges; they hung, however, on whether he was guilty of killing Hal Smith. Bellavia, Marino and De Laurentis were also convicted of the racketeering spelled out in the RICO charges. De Laurentis was convicted on a separate charge of conspiring to kill Smith. The fifth defendant, Bobby Salerno, a former professional prizefighter, was found not guilty on all counts.

Bobby's son Alex was his attorney and he did a good job for his old man.

The convictions of the underboss and his street crew were one more serious problem for Tony Accardo. At this point, in 1991, Tony was near the end of his rope, but he was still contacted by the mob hierarchy on the most serious decisions.

It was at this point that Joe Batters decided that enough was enough. He felt that the Outfit was generating too much bad publicity; as a result, it was much more difficult to corrupt. Plus, now that the connection guys were having their own problems, as it became known that they were either indicted or about to be, they could hardly be expected to worry about the rest of the mob when they had their own troubles. The mob was suffering from the stigma that it was prone to murder—and not just "their own."

So Tony made one of his last decisions. He commanded the mob to "keep their heads down." It was a command that he had suggested frequently in the past. He had seen so many highfliers like Capone and Giancana go down in flames when they got too big for their britches. He had had to shoot others, like Spilotro, out of the sky for the same reason. Their high profile tempted the FBI agents who targeted them and the federal prosecutors, who used their prosecutions to leapfrog over the bodies of the convicts into higher public office. People like Dan Webb and Jim Thompson spent very little time working on the little guys when they were in the U.S. Attorney's Office, and understandably so. But let a mobster get fame, get attention in the public media, then the reputation of the prosecutor who obtained the conviction flies high in direct relationship to the reputation of the guy he put away. Same with the FBI agent who developed the evidence, the ammunition, that the USA utilized. He gets credit—although only within his bureau—in proportion to the magnitude of the subject. Actually, in this case, it was IRS agent Tom Moriarity who deserved the bulk of the credit.

Bruce Cutler certainly gained a reputation. After the trial Judge Williams, a petite African-American woman, had the last word. She let Cutler know that "this is not New York." She told him that as long as she was "wearing the robe," she would make the rules. When the trial was ended, she held Cutler in contempt. Giancana and Blasi had gotten it, and now Cutler would. His attempts at the "Brucification," as his cross-examinations were known in New York, of Jahoda had apparently impressed nobody in Chicago—not the jury, not his client and certainly not the judge.

The attorney representing Marino attracted my attention, however. He was George Leighton, a man who had gone from being an attorney for Sam Giancana when Giancana took us into court after "lockstep," to become a federal judge in this court, and now was back once again defending mobsters. Strange.

The person who attracted my attention the most, however, was the witness B.J. Jahoda. Having been involved with such witnesses up close and personal, like Lou Bombacino, who was murdered after we had put him in hiding in Arizona, I know what it takes. In order to be in position to obtain the evidence necessary in cases like this one, the witness has to be, *ab initio*, a bad guy. A mobster. And, in most cases, it is leverage that brings them over to the government's side. Usually we promise leniency. These guys know they are caught and about to serve a long sentence. In return for a shorter sentence, they flip. But when they make that decision, they are very much aware of the long history of what happens to many witnesses whose footsteps they decide to follow. Bombacino, Bioff, Danny Seifert and others paid the price. So it takes some kind of courage, a lot of guts, to make the decision. And in this case, Jahoda not only became a witness, but he carried a wire, 200 times! What a chance of getting caught he took. He knew full well that if he were caught, he would suffer the fate of Hal Smith. So my hat goes off to William "B.J." Jahoda, and to the many like him in recent years. How about Sammy "The Bull" Gravano, for example, who looked his boss John Gotti in the eye and shot him down on the witness stand? Several such in Philadelphia. And Boston. And Cleveland. And in Kansas City. And Las Vegas. And New Orleans. And Los Angeles. And San Francisco. And San Diego.

For these reasons Joe Batters had seen enough. He now commanded his people to stay "sub rosa," as his attorneys suggested to him. Under the ground, under the glare of the radar, under the search of the spotlight.

As a result, there has been a dearth of gangland killings in recent years. Nothing like the years when ten or twelve such occurrences were commonplace. Tony wasn't taking any more chances than necessary.

As impressed as I was with the testimony of Jahoda in court, I was not surprised when Bob Fuesel, the executive director of the Chicago Crime Commission, showed me a letter he had received from Jahoda dated May 16, 1992, from a location where Jahoda is, hopefully, in safe hands. Since Jahoda has given Fuesel permission to use his communication in any way Fuesel deems fit, I quote it in its entirety here. I submit it here for the reader's consideration of the intelligence of this government witness who has risked so much at the hands of the people who would surely love to get ahold of him.

May 16th '92
Mr. Robert Fuesel
Executive Director
Chicago Crime Commission

Dear Mr. Fuesel,
Congratulations to you and your executive board for your unanimous stance in opposition to the legalization of casino gambling in Chicago.

As the former boss for one of the Chicago Outfit's biggest and most lucrative illegal gambling operations, I both applaud and endorse your positions even tho I'm certain that none of my erstwhile "colleagues" share that opinion.

In brief, I was "mobbed-up" from 1975 until 1989. During that period I established and supervised countless large-scale bookmaking locations thruout Cook and Lake Counties. I was also the Chicago underworld partner/manager in a long-running scam of rigged casino games during most of that time span.

Criminal investigations for the *IRS* estimate that I've handled at least a quarter of a billion dollars in action for the mob. The actual figure might in fact be twice that amount.

Based on this background, I wish to share with you a few general insights and observations I've gleaned thru my own professional experiences working outside the law.

1.) *The Silent Partner:* During my criminal career, there always existed one solid constant—any new form or expansion of legal gambling always increased our client base.

Simply put, the political dupes or stooges who approved Las Vegas nites, off-track betting, lotteries, etc., became our unwitting and (at least to my knowledge) unpaid front-men and silent partners.

Of most benefit to us in the illegal gambling underworld were:

A.) Agency marketing and media advertising blitzes promoting gambling, coyly, as urgent opportunity or healthy entertainment, and B.) The resultant desensitization within the community from the reality that most forms of gambling, whether ruled by the state, a corporation, or the mob are by their very nature an actual and potentially dangerous vice.

2.) *Crime Inc. Hits Jackpot?:* What a stone-lock score-and-a-half awaits the criminally inclined!

Every made-guy between Cicero, the Chicago suburb, and Sicily, the Mediterranean Island, must surely foster greedy ambitions if casino neon finally and forever dominates the Windy City's nightscape.

And converging from six continents will next be every pimp, burglar, grifter, car thief, booster, arsonist, counterfeiter, whore, dope dealer, con man, hi-jacker, extortionist, and worse making an equally perverse pilgrimage toward those same beguiling neon beacons.

I'm told that the mayor of Chicago says the moral issue of legalizing casino action is a moot point.

He couldn't be more wrong!

The decision on whether not to condone major casino gambling and thus expose the community to the horrific by-products inherent to that mercenary business is precisely the purest of moral questions no matter how the issue is otherwise characterized or camouflaged.

3.) *Gambolling Biz:* Legalized gambling in its many disguises is the fastest growing and most highly promoted con game in this country.

If this dangerous trend continues unabated and revenue growth maintains pace, this new greed of "legit wise-guys" will bust-out many of our middle-class citizens and most of the lower-middle-class within 25 years.

The reason is a simple one: all organized gambling, legal and illegal, is a zero-sum game intentionally designed so that, over time, the player ends up with the zero and the house ends up with the sum.

It was always so and so it will always remain.

Organized gambling creates and manufactures nothing except smoke, false promises, and hard dollars at the expense of the unwary.

And while all forms of organized gambling are parasitic by their very nature, none, not even the Out-fit's, can match or exceed the predatory and rat-hearted level at which many of the major casinos routinely operate.

Please add my name in any way you deem appropriate in your fight against this and any other gambling measure.

Respectfully Yours
William E. Jahoda

I think that gives an understanding of the kind of person B.J. Jahoda is. My hat goes off to him. Would that there were more people like him. Tony Accardo would have torn his own hair out many times!

68 Goodbye

Tony Accardo's swan song, I believe, came in early April 1992, when it became public knowledge that Lenny Patrick was going to sing on Gus Alex in support of the wire he had carried when giving Gussie $11,000 that day at Northwestern Hospital as his cut of an extortion.

Gussie was Tony's last mob pal. Now Gus was in the MCC and about to spend the rest of his life in prison. Lenny had been one of Tony's top guys. Trusted Jackie Cerone had been in prison since January of 1986. Joey Aiuppa had been there since the same time, convicted with Jackie in Strawman II. Paul Ricca had died in 1973. Sam Battaglia had gone to prison in 1967 and died in 1973. Jake Guzik had died in 1956. Pat Marcy died in early 1992. Machine Gun Jack McGurn, "Little New York" Campagna and Tough Tony Capezio were all long gone. So was Al Capone. Other than the members of his close family—Clarice, Marie, Linda Lee and Anthony Ross in particular—Tony now had no close relationships.

In mid-May 1992, Joe Batters finally threw in the towel. His fight was over. He had done it all and now there was nothing left. He had no will to continue the battle. He was taken to St. Mary's of Nazareth Hospital on the west side of Chicago, where he had been before. Again he was under the care of Dr. Motti, his long-time physician. After thirteen days the family asked that all life supports be taken off. At 7:36 PM on Wednesday, May 27, 1992, a nursing coordinator announced that Tony Accardo had died. He was eighty-six. The causes of death, she said, were congestive heart failure, acute respiratory failure, pneumonia and chronic obstructive pulmonary disease.

The wake was held where so many other mob wakes had been held, at Montclair-Lucania Funeral Home at 6901 West Belmont, just three blocks from Harlem Avenue, which seemed to be the street where Joe Batters spent so much time in his glory years. It was fitting. Decades before, the funeral would have been a gala. Witness those of mobsters much less powerful than Joe, like Bugs Moran and Hymie Weiss. This time the only mobster of any notoriety whatsoever who showed up was Joe Amato, one of those pictured in the photo of "The Last Supper," the photo of the top leaders of the Chicago mob who got together to say goodbye to Dominic DiBella when Vince Solano succeeded him.

It seemed as though only relatives were present as the funeral procession of just a few cars made its way from the funeral home south on Harlem Avenue to the Eisenhower and then west to Queen of Heaven Cemetery in the far western suburb of Hillside. There the remains of the great Joe Batters were carried into a mausoleum where there is a private room reserved for the Accardo family containing eight crypts. Nobody noticed that located to the right of the Accardo burial site is the one of perhaps the closest friend Accardo had had in his lifetime, Paul Ricca, inscribed with his true name, DeLucia. And on the other side is the grave of another of Tony's closest pals, Sam Battaglia. There, in Queen of Heaven Cemetery, are the graves of three of the most powerful mobsters ever to tread the streets of Chicago. Tony Accardo, the most important mob boss of all time; Paul Ricca, another of the most important mob leaders; and Sam Battaglia, who, for a short time, also was the boss of the Chicago mob. Side by side by side. Three musketeers in every sense of the word.

While conducting the research for this book, in my files I came across a letter I had written to a former colleague, Jim Mansfield, about Tony Accardo. It contained my thoughts of Tony, I guess, at the time, 1984. I'll quote it here, since it gives an unbiased view of the man long before I decided to write his biography. It was a fair portrait of The Man.

"Bittersweet it will be in Chicago when Tony Accardo leaves the O.C. scene one way or another, because he is the only living link between the LCN today and the Capone era.

"Accardo was a soldier under Capone in the 1920's, a capo under Nitti in the 1930's, the underboss under Ricca in the 1940's, the boss himself from the mid-1940's until 1957, the consiglieri to Giancana, Battaglia, Alderisio and Cerone in the 1960's, a member of the triumvirate which led the Chicago mob in the 1970's and since then the consiglieri again to the present time. A most important Chicago functionary, *the* most important, for parts of seven decades.

"Accardo is undoubtedly the most important O.C. leader in the world today. I have been doing, as you know, extensive work on O.C. in New York, for instance, since I retired and there is no one there today with anywhere near the stature of Accardo.

"The only living LCN leader who can trace his career back as far as Accardo is Joe Bonanno in New York. I've spent many hours with Bonanno, as you know, and would not denigrate him. He became boss of his own LCN family in NYC after the Castellammarese War in 1931, and obviously has been a most important mob figure. However, for all intents and purposes, he left his NY family after we convicted him in 1980, if not before, when he moved to Tucson, away from New York, in the early 1960's. Therefore his role has not come near to equaling Accardo's, and in fact he recently came out of prison, where Accardo never spent any time in his lifetime.

"Nobody in history has ever made the impact in organized crime that Accardo has. Not Capone, due to his short tenure, less than one-sixth that of Accardo, nor the flamboyant and histrionic Giancana, for the same reason, and for the additional reason that he was not the effective leader Accardo was—even though he was under the guidance of Accardo.

"The Chicago LCN would acutely miss Joe Batters when and if he leaves. Conversely, the job of law enforcement would be immeasurably easier.

"I feel that Accardo's ability to remain unincarcerated while serving his organization in the very top positions for so long, with all our powers of law enforcement focused against him, is indicative of his immense performance. He is virtually unique in the annals of O.C. anywhere in the country in this respect. In history, we were able to convict Capone, Ricca, Battaglia, Cerone, Alderisio, Aiuppa and every one of the people who served the Chicago Outfit like Accardo has done—even though there were none who served so high for so long. We didn't get Nitti, but when he was indicted, before his fellow defendants like Ricca were convicted, he cheated the government by committing suicide. We didn't *convict* Giancana, but he was pushed out after he got out of jail when we put him there. Accardo alone, of all bosses, was able to evade successful prosecution. It will be ironic if he is convicted so close to the end of his career for such as contempt of the Senate."

I guess this hurriedly cobbled-up summation of my thoughts, before I gave any thought whatsoever to a biography of Accardo, serves as a good epitaph. At least from the viewpoint of his prime adversary in law enforcement.

69 A Capo Comes Home

Even as Tony Accardo lay on his deathbed, whatever legacy he planned to leave behind was shattered.

When it became public knowledge that Lenny Patrick would sing his song on Gus Alex, one of the credos of the Accardo regime was torn. Sharon Patrick, the lovely daughter of Lenny, was living with a friend on the far north side of Chicago. Her car was parked in the driveway. On the day just prior to the day Lenny was to testify, the car was blown up. It was a message to Lenny.

During the rule of Tony Accardo this would not have happened. The mob would come after Lenny—if they could find him, something most difficult to do these days of the federal Witness Protection Program so efficiently handled by the U.S. Marshals' Service—but they would not have come after his family, not when Joe Batters was ruling the roost. The mob was honorable then, at least to some extent. At least to *that* extent.

Now the Chicago Outfit would have to make its way, almost for the first time since it was initiated, without the guiding hand of Tony Accardo. Somewhere, in some capacity, Joe Batters had been involved since 1926. Now, almost *seventy* years later, he was no longer available. I recall that when I testified in 1983, Accardo had been a strong member, if not *the* leader, of the Chicago mob "for parts of seven decades." I was told that Joe was incredulous. "How can I have been that when I'm only eighty?" But if you think about it, it was true. By the time of his death he had added almost another decade.

And one of the ways the FBI had discovered who the new bosses of the Outfit were was by following Accardo in 1990. They had watched as he met with the new boss and his new underboss, thereby learning initially who they were. The regime of Joe Ferriola lasted only a short while. He was gone in 1989, dead of natural causes. Then a new regime took over. It would be the last one to be granted its authenticity by Joe Batters.

Later in 1992 Joe Lombardo came back to Chicago. He had served most of his sentence in the Pendorf case and was granted parole. Immediately, most mob watchers in Chicago jumped on his return. He was termed a "natural" to take over the mob.

Rosalind Rossi, the fine *Sun Times* reporter, quoted me in her piece on November 12: "If there was a written resumé, his would be great. There's a void and he's the natural to fill it."

Lombardo had been serving his time, not in Marion, the tough federal prison, but in the FCI, the Federal Correctional Institution in Bradford, Pennsylvania. He had been sentenced to sixteen years in the early Eighties, but was out early since the federal mandatory guidelines had not yet been set. These days federal sentences have no chance for parole, just time off for good behavior. And that is small time.

Bob Fuesel of the Crime Commission was quoted in Rossi's article as saying: "From all indications, Lombardo is the logical choice to be the leader of the mob in Chicago. I think he is going to be the one to lead the mob into the next century."

Rossi's piece in the *Sun Times* continued: "William F. Roemer, Jr., a retired FBI agent and mob author who spent decades chasing the Outfit in Chicago for the FBI, said Lombardo worked as a *capo* or captain of two of the mob's major areas of concern—Las Vegas and the Teamsters Union.

" 'Those are things that make a mob boss,' Roemer said. 'He'd be the best candidate they could possibly find because he's done everything—he has corrupted, he's done gambling and he's done the mob heavy work.'

"Lombardo has never been convicted of murder. But Roemer says he was a prime suspect in 'some of the biggest gangland killings in the last 20 years. They include the 1973 slaying of renegade lawman Richard Cain, the 1974 murder of mob witness Daniel Seifert, the 1977 slaying of Chicago millionaire Ray Ryan and the 1983 slaying of Allen Dorfman, charged with Lombardo in the Teamsters (Pendorf) case.'

" 'Such alleged exploits,' Roemer said, 'give him a certain respectability in his circle.'

"Roemer said the late mob titan Anthony Accardo coached his underlings to 'keep your head down,' meaning keep a low profile, don't excite the media or law enforcement. 'That's what I would expect Lombardo to do,' Roemer said."

And that is indeed what Lombardo chose to do. He was not the clown the media thought he was. He is still at home in Chicago, in the same house in the 2200 block of West Ohio where John Bassett and I arrested him a couple decades ago, waiting for his parole to expire. Then it may well be another story. Then Joe may step up and hold his head up high.

In the meantime, he allowed himself one jump into the limelight—more or less. As John O'Brien, the well-respected dean of crime reporters in Chicago today, wrote in his piece in the *Tribune* on December 11, 1992, Lombardo "advertised." John opened his article by saying, "Call it a preventive strike, self-indulgence, a waste of money or an intrusion on truth in advertising.

"One way or another, Joseph P. Lombardo is sending a message, making a statement. The reputed Chicago organized crime boss, in a series of classified ads appearing this week in three newspapers, including the *Tribune*, tells his story in 60 words.

"The convicted rackets figure, paroled last month after 10 years in prison for plotting to skim $2 million from a Las Vegas casino, has gone on record to say:

"He isn't a 'made' member of the mob. 'I never took a secret oath with guns and daggers, pricked my finger, drew blood or burned paper (in my hand) to join a criminal organization.

" 'If anyone hears my name used in connection with any criminal activity, please notify the FBI, local police and my parole officer, Ron Kumke.' "

"The Clown" had struck again. Could anybody that goofy be considered to be material for the top spot in the Outfit? In the

Chicago family of La Cosa Nostra? He even seemed to be mocking the initiation rites of the eastern families of the LCN.

Again I will say that Joe Lombardo is no clown. Tony Accardo would never have allowed him to be the capo in charge of Las Vegas and the mob's control over their "bank," the Central States Pension Fund of the Teamsters Union, if he had believed Lombardo to be mentally deficient. As I was quoted as saying in the Rossi article in the *Sun Times*, "This guy has done it all." I do believe that when his parole expires in 1999, we will see Joe Lombardo's head come out of the sand. At this point he can still be returned to prison if he is seen associating with known felons or known mobsters. Don't expect that to happen.

70 Accardo's Successors

Tony Accardo's last gasp as "The Man" with the ultimate power in the Chicago family of La Cosa Nostra, the Outfit, was to put his mantle around two guys. Two guys who he hoped, but did not expect, would lead the once-proud family back to greatness. They were Sam Carlisi and John DiFronzo.

To show you how much the attrition had set in, let me give you a very brief synopsis of their backgrounds. Sam is called "Wings" because he had been a courier for Joey Aiuppa. A message boy. A gofer. I remember well the days I'd look right past Carlisi. Joey Aiuppa used to operate out of the Towne Hotel in Cicero. The hotel had a nice parking lot. In the parking lot was a small hut which served as the cashier's location. You paid your parking fee to the guy who stood in that hut. He was there even when it was twenty below zero. You know who he was? Wings. Of course, he also doubled as the appointment secretary-driver-bodyguard for Aiuppa. When Aiuppa went to prison on the Strawman II case in Kansas City, Wings, who was left without a boss, moved up a little under Joe Ferriola. Now that Ferriola had died, Wings was left in one of the two top spots. That is the history of Sam Carlisi.

John DiFronzo had been the boss of what is called the Elmwood Park street crew, which had a proud tradition because it was the stepping-off spot for one of the great all-time bosses of the Outfit, Jackie Cerone. But before John DiFronzo took over that spot, before he was "made," he got his nickname. I hadn't been aware of this, since we weren't tracking burglars off the Organized Crime Squad at C-1, but I got the story from Sandy Smith, the veteran *Tribune*, *Sun Times*, *Time* and *Life* reporter. DiFronzo's nickname, which he seems to be proud of, is "No Nose." The story DiFronzo tells goes like this: he was in a shootout with the cops. After he got a few of them, one of them got lucky and shot his nose off. Wrong! Nice story. That's glamorous, maybe even a little sexy, at least in mob circles. According to Sandy, this is how No Nose really got his nickname: he was a burglar, a common, ordinary thief. His "expertise" was down pat. He would go up Michigan Avenue and spot a nice fur store. Then, when he had scouted it to see that there were no cops around, he would smash the plate glass window of the shop, jump in, and within seconds, grab a fur piece off the mannequin, jump back through the broken window and into his car parked at the curb. Away he would go, burglar alarm or not. It would all be accomplished in a matter of seconds, not even a minute.

Now, one day, things didn't go quite so smoothly. He smashed the plate glass, jumped onto a mannequin, freed it of a high-quality fur coat, and then jumped back to go out the window. You guessed it. He sliced his nose off on the glass window he had broken on his way in. The cops traced the trail of blood, gave DiFronzo his nose back and pinched him. A doctor pinched his nose back on so that it is hardly noticeable, but it stuck—both the nose and the nickname.

These are what was left of the mob leadership when Joe Batters, the proud old Tony Accardo, came to the end of the line.

Let me tell you something else about DiFronzo. Accardo was no sooner in his grave than another of his edicts went down the drain. No Nose put his brother into narcotics. Not just dealing it, in fact, but growing it. One of the mob's juice victims had a gigantic house in the northwestern suburbs. He couldn't pay up. The mob had a remedy. They had found that in the mansion of this guy's house he had a huge basement. So they put it to him, an offer he couldn't refuse. They cultivated a huge patch of marijuana down there and put No Nose's brother in charge. One of the mob's guys involved in the deal subsequently became a CTE, a top echelon criminal informant, and then a cooperating witness. The whole bunch was indicted and then convicted. But No Nose's brother took it on the lam. As I write this, he has been a fugitive for over a year.

Now, in one respect, I'd like to feel he's missing because he followed in the footsteps of Chris Cardi, the guy who was convicted on Joe Batters' watch, went to prison and then was trunk music when he got out. The only reason I say that is that I would hope that the ban against narcotics is still in effect even though Joe is gone. But I'm told by people like Lee Flosi, the recent supervisor of the third tier organized crime squad of the FBI in Chicago, that my hopes are in vain. The Outfit is in fact now involved in dealing dope, according to Flosi, a guy who should know.

Actually, I'm being too hard on No Nose. He was arrested in his home in Long Grove in January of 1992. The FBI agents who searched his home incidental to the arrest there found that he had one book in particular in his library—*Roemer: Man Against the Mob*. Pete Wacks, my former fellow squad partner in Chicago, was one of the agents who participated in the arrest. He chided me. "We found it on the nightstand beside his bed. It probably put him to sleep at night!" Nonetheless, the man can read.

Art Pfizenmayer, the fine Chicago FBI agent who was one of the key agents in the Pendorf case in Chicago, had now gotten an "office of preference" transfer to San Diego. When he did, due to his reputation and that of the squad he had worked on in Chicago, he soon became the supervisor of the O.C. Squad in San Diego. Art had been around the block, more than just once or twice. He had broken in on C-1 when I was still on it and soon made his mark.

Now he got a whiff of the odor in San Diego. He smelled the Chicago mob! Out on the beach in San Diego. The case had begun when Joe Batters was still in charge, in 1987. Chris Petti had been placed in San Diego by Tony Spilotro. In 1987 Petti, who was now answering to Donald Angelini after Joe Batters had, in 1986, sanctioned Spilotro's killing in the cornfield, got a call from Chicago. He was told that there were several people in the western part of the country who had been juice debtors of Spilotro. He had loaned them six for five, the usual deal. Pay $6 for every $5 borrowed—every week. Borrow $10,000 and out pay $2,000 "vig," vigorish, interest, every week until the entire principal is paid off. Nice, if you can get it. And the mob does.

The call came from a mob figure new on the Chicago scene,

Mike Caracci, a relative of Donald Angelini. Donald had taken over most of the responsibilities of Spilotro in Las Vegas and the West Coast. Caracci instructed Petti to go about collecting the Spilotro juice loans from the delinquent debtors who thought they could get away with it now that The Ant was dead.

So Petti, with the help of John Spilotro, Tony's brother, and a couple hoods on the coast named DiNuccio, two brothers, began to squeeze these guys. One was Joe "Pigs" Pignatello. (I knew Pigs in Chicago. He had been the driver for Sam Giancana when I knew him. I remember the time I went to Pig's house in Chicago and we took turns trying to find out who had the strongest handshake. I think it was a toss-up.) When Petti, John Spilotro and the DiNuccio brothers began to put muscle on Pigs and the others to cough up what they owed to Tony Spilotro, the FBI got involved. First, they put an undercover agent in the deal. Then they made use of "roving taps." They tapped public phones that the mobsters were using in the San Diego area.

They found out something else at the same time. They found that the Chicago Outfit, under the aegis of Angelini, was attempting to muscle in on the Rincon Indian Reservation in North County. It even got a little hairier than that. A guy named Silberman, who had been the financial manager for Jerry Brown, the governor of California, got involved in an attempt to launder money. Art Pfizenmayer and the case agent, Charley Walker, now had a hell of a case.

The phone taps picked up some interesting mob techniques. Nothing new though. Joe Pigs threatened to go back to Chicago for help when the boys in San Diego began to twist his arm. He was told: "If you don't go back with any money, just buy a one-way ticket!" Another debtor was told: "If you don't have that money, you're as good as dead!" That guy, however, escaped Chicago's clutches. He "belonged" to the Detroit mob. They would take care of him. Caracci called off the Chicago muscle on that guy.

Phil LeVelle, the ace reporter for the San Diego *Union Tribune*, summed it up in his piece on January 11, 1993. He wrote that "Federal prosecutors have showcased the trial as an example of the Chicago mob's ability to project power far from its Midwest base. . . . The trial threatens to disrupt the top leadership of the Chicago mob known as the 'Outfit,' a crime family whose command structure has been battered in recent years by deaths and vigorous prosecution.

" 'This trial is a watershed event in the Chicago mob, because if it's successful, you're going to be taking down at least three of the very top people in the Chicago mob today,' said retired Chicago FBI agent William F. Roemer, who now writes books on organized crime from his home in Tucson.

" 'It is historic, no question about it,' Roemer said."

The reason I said three people was because Art had instituted a surveillance after receiving information on a tap. Carlisi and DiFronzo had come into San Diego to oversee the deals their people had become involved in. These were the two top guys in the Chicago Outfit; on a couple other occasions, Donald Angelini came in to supervise the situation. These three guys were the trio I referred to. Carlisi and DiFronzo, the boss and underboss, and Donald, the capo in charge of the West Coast and Las Vegas for the Chicago mob. Whatever might be said of them—and Angelini ranks up with the best of all times in the brains department—these were the power now in what was left of Tony Accardo's family.

Although one of the jurors was pretty loud about it when he left the courtroom after the verdicts were announced, it was a mixed bag. "I hope they got a message," he said. "Tell the Chicago mob to stay out of San Diego!" The trial had lasted ten weeks. I guess the juror's message was received but, unfortunately, Wings flew. The jury had hung on him. No Nose and Donald went down, however. They would subsequently be sentenced to thirty-seven months in prison.

I was quoted once more in the San Diego *Union Tribune* by LaVelle. " 'When they got DiFronzo . . . they got a major mobster in this country. He's the guy in charge of Chicago.' "

In reviewing the trial testimony, I guess the juror was right. Caracci said at one point: "They wanna get a foothold down where you're at (San Diego), I'm tellin' ya." They didn't get it.

Obviously, the Chicago mob was now in further disarray. Carlisi hadn't been convicted but soon he would be. He and his street crew would be convicted of gambling charges in Chicago in 1994. He went away, possibly for what remains of his life.

Donald did his time, and as I write this, he is in a halfway house in Chicago, about to get out. I hope he knows enough now to stay out of the Outfit and to use his fine intellect to do something legitimate. He could.

The real kicker, however, came when DiFronzo appealed his conviction and won. He was released on "time served" in mid-1994 when the Ninth Circuit Court of Appeals in San Francisco ruled that he had been sentenced under the wrong guidelines.

No Nose returned to Chicago, unlike Donald and Joe Lombardo, free as a bird with no parole restrictions.

It is the opinion of those in the third tier of the FBI as I write this that DiFronzo is the boss once again. That would almost have to be true, if only by default. In fact, one of the only real challengers, a guy who must have felt he was going to command the Outfit until No Nose got his break—Marco D'Amico, a strong capo—is in the MCC now. He and several of his crew were indicted in the late fall of 1994 on gambling charges. It looks like he will be out of the game for many years to come.

So it is that in 1995 we have come a long way from the days when Tony Accardo, the strongest, most capable boss ever, had the Chicago family of La Cosa Nostra in its prime. A long way down.

Am I saying that we have won the fight? No. Not yet. DiFronzo, maybe Lombardo in a few years, maybe Angelini, if he doesn't wise up, maybe his buddy Dominic Cortina, and even a guy named Joe Andriacci could turn things around if left to their own devices. Andriacci is related to Lombardo. There are those who believe that Lombardo is taking a chance, very cautiously and surreptitiously meeting with Andriacci with his "suggestions" as to how the Outfit should function. In other words, Lombardo feels that if he gets caught talking to his cousin, he can plead "family business"—blood family, not mob family. That's a long shot, but maybe.

In other words, it may be Joe Lombardo—no clown—who is now the consiglieri of the Chicago LCN. Yet although Lombardo is nobody's fool, even though he'd like the public, the media and law enforcement to believe that he is, neither is he a Tony Accardo. Joe Batters would "have more brains at breakfast than Joe Lombardo had all day," to use a favorite expression.

There can be no doubt that when the Chicago family of La Cosa Nostra, The Outfit, lost The Man, it lost somebody who was irreplaceable, indispensable. No matter who might fill his slot, he would never fill his shoes. Even if Capone, Colosimo, Torrio, Nitti, Ricca, Giancana or any of the other Chicago mob bosses had been available at this time, they wouldn't be The Man Tony Accardo was.

When they made Joe Batters, they threw the mold away. All of us in law enforcement heaved a sigh when he left. Thank God! In many ways it was bittersweet. He was the last link to Capone. He was a guy who certainly wasn't all bad, keeping the mob away from families and from the drug trade. But he was the guy who brought the Chicago Outfit into so many productive enterprises and made it a model of efficiency as no one else had. Under Tony Accardo the Chicago mob became the best—read "worst"—family of La Cosa Nostra any time at any place. That is why I say "Thank God" he is no longer around. At the same time, however, "Rest in Peace, Joe Batters, God Bless You and Have Mercy on Your Soul."

Epilogue

It is difficult to overestimate the fascination the American public has with mobsters. This was most recently illustrated to me when I received a phone call at my home in Tucson from John Binder in early October 1994. John, a University of Illinois-Chicago professor, is the most able president of the Merry Gangsters Literary Society in Chicago. The Merry Gangsters are a group of mostly highly educated professionals in Chicago who have an interest in the Prohibition era, the gangster era. I am an honorary member.

John called to tell me that the Merry Gangsters were invited to a special cocktail party to be held on October 14, 1994, at 1407 Ashland Avenue in River Forest. I sure recognized that address. I had never been inside, but I had been outside many times. It was, of course, the former address of Tony Accardo when he was at the height of his power. He had purchased it in 1963 and sold it in late 1978.

It seems the public would be invited to the Accardo home on Saturday and Sunday, October 15 and 16. The invitation was to inspect and purchase many of the furnishings Joe Batters had left behind when he sold the Accardo Ashland Avenue abode and moved into a much smaller condominium.

I accepted John's invitation to come into Chicago and speak at the cocktail party the night before the two-day sale. It was my first opportunity to get inside Accardo's house, something I had hoped to do when I interviewed the ill-fated Van Corbin, the contractor. It was interesting to sit in Tony's basement at his desk (which sold ten minutes after the sale opened the next day for $10,000), to sit at his thirty-chair conference table where so many murders were sanctioned, to enter the vault where he had cavalierly left $275,000 when he left for Palm Springs, and to inspect the kitchen where he had cooked for his mob pals, like Jackie Cerone, Paul Ricca, Gus Alex, Sam Battaglia, Joe Aiuppa and Butch Blasi.

I didn't go back the next day. (I went down to South Bend that day to cringe when Brigham Young University beat Notre Dame in football.) But when I returned to Chicago that evening and turned on the TV at the home of my good pals from the FBI, Bill and Lori Dougherty, I was amazed to witness the mob scene at 1407. Almost 1,000 people had lined up before the doors were opened that morning. They bought everything in sight which at one time might have belonged to The Man. Even the teacups he drank from were sold—individually. Thousands more came during that Saturday and again on Sunday. Just to mingle, mostly, in the ambience of the boss of the Chicago mob. To get a vicarious thrill, I guess.

Even the NBC national news did a big feature on the affair, including an interview with me. The local TV stations did likewise. It was good to talk on camera once more with a favorite of mine, John "Bulldog" Drummond of the CBS affiliate in Chicago, WBBM-TV.

I was further reminded of the public's fascination with the aura of notorious gangsters when Joe Bonanno, Accardo's longtime adversary on the national Commission of La Cosa Nostra, celebrated his ninetieth birthday in mid-January 1995.

In its edition of January 16, 1995, the Arizona *Daily Star*, the only morning newspaper in Tucson, featured the story. One half of its front page, mostly above the fold, continued on one half of page two, with appropriate photos, was devoted to the big story of the day.

Three hundred people, mostly in tuxedos and formals, attended Bonanno's birthday party at one of Arizona's biggest resorts, the Westward Look. A United States senator and the governor had sent telegrams, according to the story. The party was attended by people from all over the country, including politicians, lawyers, priests, actors, businessmen, even authors. Bonanno's speech brought the crowd to its feet in a standing ovation when he shouted: "Extreme justice is extreme injustice!" Whatever that meant.

The key word uttered time and time again by the other speakers in regard to their hero was "respect." Wow!

Here is a man who, I suspect, has murdered many and who sanctioned the murder of many others, in addition to the other crimes spelled out in the files of the New York FBI office and the Tucson office. I always perceived him as a hot-winded bragger who did nothing in his life of any real value. He was a charter member of La Cosa Nostra when it was founded in 1931, was the boss of one of the five New York LCN families (which was noted for bloodshed) and was also a charter member of the Commission when it was founded in 1931.

Yet when he throws a birthday party for himself, he is honored as if it had been the second coming of Abraham Lincoln. What a world we live in!

Joe Batters must have turned over in his grave when he looked up and saw the homage being paid to his fellow-Commissioner—a man for whom he never had the slightest respect.

We discovered what Bonanno called his "buco," his safe, hidden in the cement under the floor of his bedroom closet when we raided his house in Tucson in 1979. I wonder what that will sell for if and when it is put up for sale as Accardo's possessions were. I suppose the public would go crazy bidding for it!

The Chicago *Sun Times* had previewed the auction of Accardo's Ashland Avenue abode on its front page on October 8 with a picture of "Accardo's home furnishings." Zay Smith, the fine *Sun Times* reporter, tickled my funny bone with his article:

"Mobster Tony Accardo never got the chair.

"But he had a great sofa."

Smith reported the results of the sale and the fact that the house itself was up for sale at $1.25 million. "It's not exactly a fixer-upper."

I was quoted several times in the article about the history of the house. Then the article concluded: "Roemer, who is working on a biography of Accardo entitled *Accardo: The Genuine Godfather*, will be on hand to share legends about The Man who died at age 86 in 1992. 'Me, I'd go for the conference table, except I'm not going to buy anything,' Roemer said. A lot of very important mob business happened at that table.

" 'A lot of things were said at that table that caused a lot of people to die. A house like that has a great many memories.' " I guess. Tell me about it!

Appendix A

The following history of organized crime in Chicago appeared in the November/December 1994 issue of *Real Crime Book Digest*.

I have been asked by Jim Agnew, the editor of RCBR to write the history of organized crime in Chicago since its inception. This is the fourth time I have been requested to do so. The first time was by Robert F. Kennedy when he became Attorney General in 1961. Then, as FBI agent assigned to J. Edgar Hoover's Top Hoodlum Program, I had access to the files of the FBI, to my informants inside the mob and especially on the conversations I was overhearing on the microphones I had helped place in mob headquarters in Chicago. I occasionally heard Tony Accardo talk of his formative years and regularly heard Murray "The Camel" Humphreys discuss his days with Al Capone, Nitti and Ricca. Accardo had been a bodyguard of Capone and a shooter in the St. Valentine's Day Massacre in 1929. Hump, who discussed his salad days incessantly, had been close to Capone and had been designated "Public Enemy Number One" in 1932 by the Chicago Crime Commission after Capone was sent away. So my task was easy. Bob Kennedy was most pleased with the product.

Then, after I retired from the FBI after 30 years as an agent, I was retained in 1983 to compile the history of the Chicago "Outfit" as a consultant for the Chicago Crime Commission and to use it to supplement my testimony on their behalf before the U.S. Senate Permanent Subcommittee on Investigations.

Then, in 1990, I once again prepared such a history to be included in one of my books.

I explain all of this to show the reader that I "have been there." Not really, not all the way, but at least vicariously, from the lips of mobsters who actually were and who were talking openly to colleagues, completely unaware that I was keenly attuned to their conversations. This was a vantage spot perhaps no other has been privy to.

Origins of the Mob

We can begin a discussion of the origins of what continues to be organized crime in Chicago in World War I. Then Jim Colosimo, in order to eliminate competition for his night spots and houses of prostitution in Chicago, put together a very loose, poorly disciplined group of thugs and thieves of Italian and Sicilian extraction. There was little formal organization involved until Johnny Torrio, who had joined Colosimo in Chicago in 1910 after being raised in crime in New York, put together an organization along the lines of the Sicilian group of criminals called "The Mafia." Many of the underlings in the Colosimo-Torrio band of thieves had belonged to the Mafia in Sicily. As part and parcel of this organization Torrio brought a young New Yorker who had "made his bones" there by the name of Al Capone. Capone had done some heavy work and had the reputation there of being a resourceful, aggressive young gunman with a future.

Murder of Colosimo

When it became evident that the Volstead Act would be passed in a year or so, Torrio became alarmed that Colosimo did not appear to see the potential for his gang during the upcoming Prohibition Era. Colosimo, at least in the eyes of Torrio, seemed to be about to waste the opportunity presented. He therefore commissioned Capone to kill Colosimo in 1920, a job successfully accomplished by the youngster who had acquired the nickname "Scarface" from the scars on the left side of his face.

With the demise of Colosimo, Torrio assumed the leadership of the Chicago mob. With the help of his young lieutenant who had made his leadership role possible, Torrio set out to accomplish two things. First, he enforced a tight discipline and secondly, he enlarged the membership. Although initial eligibility mandated Sicilian origin, Torrio brought in members who were not Sicilian, who were from Italy originally.

Prohibition Brings Boom

When Prohibition set in, the opportunities were almost unlimited. Now Torrio's organization became big business. As the workload increased, so did the need for new members. Some were not even Italian. These would include men such as Jake Guzik, a Jew with the nickname "Greasy Thumb," and Murray "the Camel" Humphreys. Both were to obtain power in the Twenties inside the mob. As a result of this genesis of the Chicago "Outfit" many powerful mob leaders in Chicago in coming decades would not be from either Sicily or Italy, something unique in Chicago compared to other cities.

Capone Becomes Boss

Then Capone got greedy. Mainly for the same reason Torrio had wanted Colosimo out of the way, now Capone wanted his mentor, Torrio, dispatched. He made an attempt on Torrio's life. Although wounded, Torrio did not die. He saw the handwriting on the wall, however, and turned over the leadership to Capone soon after he was able to leave the hospital.

Now, under Capone, the Chicago outfit became perhaps the most tightly disciplined and the most wealthy organized crime group in the country. This was especially true compared to New York City in the Twenties. The forces of Joe Masseria were fighting those of Salvatore Maranzano in New York and there existed turmoil in the Big Apple.

Capone had rivals in Chicago, however. Some of Italian origin, some Irish, some German. One by one, however, he came to terms with them, ordinarily by the use of violence such as the St. Valentine's Day Massacre in 1929 when his men, led by an Italian thug with the unusual nickname of "Machine Gun Jack McGurn," wiped out most of the "Bugs" Moran Gang, or when his men shot and killed another rival, Dion O'Banion, in his flower shop on State Street. Chicago was noted in the Twenties for the thousand or so gangland killings, most done by Capone's boys to forge their preeminence as the city's top gangsters.

Then in 1931 came La Cosa Nostra. Maranzano's mobsters killed Masseria and consolidated their power in New York. Then Maranzano was himself killed. But before he went, Maranzano formed La Cosa Nostra, "this thing of ours" in Italy. He formed five families in New York City and put his imprimatur on Capone in Chicago, not that Capone needed any authority from anyone in his old stomping grounds—he had taken what he wanted in the Windy City.

The Commission

Along with La Cosa Nostra came "The Commission." Maranzano set it up. That is what he called it. It was then, and is today, the ruling body of organized crime, of the LCN. The general council, so to speak. Always the five LCN families in New York (now called the Gambinos, the Colombos, the Bonannos, the Genoveses and the Lucheses) were reported on The Commission. Always Chicago, always Philadelphia, New England, Detroit, and usually Buffalo, Pittsburgh and Cleveland. The Commission has no right to interfere in the internal affairs of a family but, instead, arbitrates any disputes between families.

IRS & Capone

In the late Twenties the IRS began to focus on Capone's guys. First they got his brother and then his top gun, Frank Nitti. Then, they got Capone. For tax evasion. What is called a "net worth and expenditures" case. They were able, thanks to their case agent assigned to the job, Frank Wilson, to show that his lifestyle greatly outspent his acknowledged income on his tax returns. When Capone went away in 1932, it would be for the rest of his life, at least as far as Chicago was concerned. He would die of the ravages of syphilis. In later years Eliot Ness would be perceived by much of the public as having been responsible for "getting Capone." That is Hollywood. He and his "Untouchables" had little to do with the conviction of Capone. He did a job diminishing Capone's income from bootlegging—after all, Ness was a prohibition agent—but did almost nothing to bring Capone to justice.

Nitti Becomes Boss

Frank Nitti succeeded Capone. Nitti had been with Capone most of the way. He realized that Capone had brought much of his problems on himself by his high profile, his high style of living and his penchant for publicity. Nitti learned this. He kept his head down. He hid his light under a bushel basket. And that of his men. The mob flourished under Nitti and the Chicago Outfit quickly switched gears. With Humphreys and Guzik showing the way, they went into labor racketeering in a big way. Many of the local unions in Chicago were targeted and many came under the dominance of the Outfit in the Thirties. The mob's lifeblood, however, soon became gambling. Mostly on horse races from "offices," bookmaking joints, set up all over the territory covered by the Outfit—from the Wisconsin state line on the north to Kankakee to the south, and from Lake Michigan out past Aurora to the west. Hand in hand with gambling became "juice," the Chicago colloquialism for loan-sharking or shylocking as it is called elsewhere. Prostitution was frowned on in the Outfit but it flourished in their night clubs and strip joints.

Hollywood Extortion Case

Nitti and his men stayed *sub rosa* until 1943, when he and several of his top men, including his underboss, Paul "The Waiter" Ricca, were indicted (in New York, of all places) for extortion of every Hollywood movie studio.

Nitti and Ricca dominated the Stage Handlers Union and the Movie Projectionists Union through their fronts, George Browne and Willie Bioff. Upon his indictment in 1943, Nitti went out onto the Illinois Central Railroad track near his west suburban home and shot himself in the head with his .38.

For a short time, Ricca, true name DeLucia, took over as the Outfit boss. But soon he was convicted in the Hollywood Extortion Case. He and his fellow convicts in that case would be sentenced to ten years. But in one of the major scandals of the Truman Administration, they were released immediately as they became eligible for parole—after just three years, even though there had been a superseding indictment hanging over them which mandated they would not be paroled. I heard Humphreys discuss the situation more than once. He bragged how he had gotten to Tom Clark, then the Attorney General, who would later be rewarded by being appointed by Truman to the Supreme Court and whose son, Ramsey Clark, would be successor down the line as Attorney General—where he followed in his father's footsteps.

Accardo Becomes Boss

By the time Ricca was released, however, another had taken his place. His underboss, the guy given his nickname by Al Capone. When Tony Accardo killed two of Capone's foes with a baseball bat, Capone told his pals: "This kid is a real Joe Batters." It would stick. From then on Tony Accardo might be known as "The Big Tuna" in the media, but to all who knew him, including me, he was known as "Joe Batters." I never called him anything but Joe. Tony Accardo would become, in my estimation, the best boss the Outfit ever had, including his mentor, Al Capone. Under Joe Batters the mob flourished. The killings went on, especially to take over policy and numbers on the South Side from the blacks, but not the convictions. Accardo was the acting boss from 1943 to 1946 and then the official boss from 1946 to 1957. Those were the best days of the Chicago mob. Accardo ruled with an iron fist but more with a loud voice and the big black stick behind his back. The mob not only moved into the black neighborhoods but into Las Vegas and Reno. They made the "street tax" a big thing, taking a half interest in even the independent bookmakers and big cuts from every burglar, thief, extortionist, abortionist and many of the restauranteurs and nightclub owners in their territory. The money rolled in and there were few problems. Almost none from law enforcement. Joe Batters' regime was most rewarding.

Murder of James Ragan

Here I should tell you that when I say there were almost no problems from law enforcement, there were absolutely none from the FBI. In 1946 a race-wire operator who was being hounded by Accardo's men came to the FBI. He became a walk-in informant. He knew the mob and its players. Up until then J. Edgar Hoover had not believed that he had jurisdiction to investigate organized crime. He realized there were mobs in New York, Chicago, and the other major eastern cities, but he did not possess information indicating that they transcended state lines thereby giving FBI federal jurisdiction, the interstate character needed to enforce federal laws. But now the walk-in, a man named James Ragan, was too good to ignore. A case was opened and code-named "CAPGA." It was an acronym for "Reactivation of the Capone Gang." Reactivation? That gives us a real insight into the mind-set of law enforcement in 1946. As if the "Capone Gang" had dried up and blown away but may now be blowing back. A tribute to Tony Accardo and the way he was guiding the ship which was the Outfit. No turbulent seas for them under Joe Batters. For several months the FBI dug into their investigation of the Outfit in Chicago. They put wiretaps on the phones of some of the mobsters and on one in the barbershop at the Morrison Hotel, then the mob's message center. They seemed to be ready to accomplish something. Then the mob hit Ragan. Shotgunned him in his car on the south side. Didn't kill him. But when he was recuperating in the hospital, they did. They poisoned him. Now the FBI lost its prime witness, its reason for the investigation. They quit the investigation: Closed CAPGA. Reassigned several agents focusing on the Outfit to the cases J. Edgar Hoover considered more important at the time, such as car thefts, bank robberies and kidnappings.

Into the 1950s

Accardo kept things in high gear during the early and mid-Fifties. He put the mob in Havana in joint ventures with the New York families who had bribed Batista to allow casino gambling there, and in Nevada. In Chicago the mob never had it so good, especially in bookmaking. Horse racing and boxing, not yet baseball, football, or "buckets," were the prime focus of the gamblers but the income was great. Graft was big and Accardo was strident that Humphreys, Guzik and their "connection guys" must put politicians, cops, labor leaders and judges "on the pad" (corrupt them for favorable treatment). And they did. "The West Side Bloc" of politicians under the control and/or influence of the Outfit was instrumental in paving the way for easy going for the mob. Things were smooth, so smooth. So smooth that Accardo decided he had had enough. Enough power and enough money. He decided to step down. Voluntarily. He suggested that a young man who had made his bones and done some fine things inside the Outfit be appointed his successor. He was. The year was 1957 and the young man was Sam Giancana.

N.Y. Mob Wars

I was also a young man in 1957. Thirty-one. What a year that would be!

First, internecine warfare broke out in New York. In the spring, Frank Costello was shot. Then other top mobsters were killed. And then, in the fall, it was the turn of Albert Anastasia, "Double A" as Humphreys always referred to him. He was the boss of one of the five New York families, perhaps the most powerful after Costello stepped down when he was shot earlier in the year. Whenever I'm in New York, I stop in at the Park Central Hotel, an Omni Hotel now, awed with nostalgia to reminisce where AA was killed in the barbershop as he was getting his daily shave.

Apalachin

That was what we might call Act I in 1957. Act II came when, as a result of the warfare in New York, a meeting was called of the top leaders of La Cosa Nostra from all over the country. As many as eighty of them! It took place in a small village in western New York which was about to become famous. Heretofore unheard of, it would now go down in the history books. Its name was Apalachin. It became famous when Edgar Croswell, a New York State Trooper, became suspicious and led a raid on the home of Joe Barbara, a legitimate businessman there. Croswell rousted most of the participants. They turned out to be famous names. Not to the FBI, who had hardly heard of them, but to the media who had. It became a real media event. It stirred up so much interest that J. Edgar Hoover couldn't ignore it.

The mob didn't coexist over state lines? There was no interstate travel? No federal jurisdiction? Then how come eighty of the very top gangsters in the country had such an interest in each other that they would travel, some of them thousands of miles, to converge in a small village in the state of New York? J. Edgar Hoover couldn't fight that logic. He found a peg. A vehicle to send his troops into action—really for the first time except for a few isolated instances, like CAPGA in Chicago and the investigation of the acid attack on national columnist Victor Riesel in New York City in 1956—against organized crime. 1957's Act III opened. Hoover decided that the Hobbs Act, passed in 1940, could be the peg upon which he could latch onto jurisdiction to initiate his long delayed fight against organized crime. Now Hoover decreed that its elements gave the FBI the jurisdiction it needed to fight OC. It had been passed in 1940 but not discovered until 1957.

Hoover Starts War on the Mob

So it was that in November 1957 Hoover sent a directive to all of his field offices. He initiated what he then called "The Top Ten Hoodlum Program," the THP. Every field office was to target the "top hoods" in its territory. In New York, there would be twenty-five. In Chicago, ten. Each target would be assigned to an individual agent, hopefully an agent who might have whatever it might take to make something of this new THP. If he didn't, he would be placed on Hoover's list. Not his A list.

Roemer Assigned to Chicago

In November of 1957 I had been in the FBI seven years. I had been assigned to field offices in Baltimore, New Haven and New York City. I had had several assignments, such as investigations of communists of the faculty of Yale University, bank robberies in a black section of Baltimore, the capture of The

Nationalist Party of Puerto Rico shooters in Spanish Harlem, those who had shot up Congress and wounded several Congressmen in 1954, and surveillance of members of the Nation of Islam in the south side of Chicago. Now I was investigating members of the underground section of the Communist Party-USA, those who had assumed hidden identities and were underground waiting for the word to sabotage strategic facilities. I was not my supervisor's favorite agent. When he was called upon to give up one agent to the squad which would now have the responsibility for the Top Hoodlum Program, he gladly gave me up.

As I say, ten of us agents, some of us with a little bit of rogue, were assigned to the Chicago THP. First, I was assigned to Gus Alex, the number two man to Murray "The Camel" Humphreys on the "connection squad." Not that we knew that then. Alex also was responsible for the Loop, Chicago's downtown area. But we didn't know that either. In fact, in 1957 we didn't even know where Gussie lived. Within a matter of several months, when Mr. Hoover decided that ten agents in Chicago were too many and cut us to five, I was assigned also to be the case agent on Humphreys.

In view of the circumstances I have outlined above, I don't think a reader should find it difficult to believe we started off as novices in the fight against the mob—not only the Chicago mob but mobs everywhere. We had never heard the term La Cosa Nostra. We had no knowledge whatsoever that there was something they themselves called "The Commission."

Hidden Mikes Planted

Slowly but surely, however, we got our act together. I led what was to become the most important advance against the mobs anywhere at the time. That was the placement of a hidden mike, a bug, in the general headquarters of the Outfit. It was in a second floor custom tailor shop on the Magnificent Mile, at 620 North Michigan Avenue in Chicago. Celano's Custom Tailors. Every day the top leadership of the Chicago mob convened at Celano's. Accardo, Giancana, Humphreys, Alex, Frankie Strongy, the underboss; Alderisio, Cerone, Ricca, Pierce and Buccieri. All of them who were upper echelon leaders. They were virgins. Never before had a hidden mike been placed inside a mob meeting place. Taps on phones, yes, but not bugs. We were there when decisions were made to murder; we were there when discussions were made on which judges, cops and public officials had been corrupted; we were there every month when the tally was made of the income from the previous month; and we were there when guys like Dalitz and Roselli and Caifano came in from Las Vegas to report on their activities out there. It was my baby, I was the "case agent," the guy who had the "ticket," the assignment card for this penetration. We code-named that mike "Little Al." After all, these were the successors to Al Capone, weren't they? Some had been with him from the start, like Accardo and Ricca and Hump. It is from this mike I garnered much of what I have written in the early pages of this piece.

Giancana Now Boss

It was not our only mike, however. We put "Mo" in the special headquarters of the boss, Sam Giancana. We put "Shade" in the headquarters, across from City

Hall, at 100 North LaSalle, of the Regular Democratic Organization of the First Ward, the conduit of orders from the mob leaders and the "connection guys" to corrupt politicians and cops. We even had "Plumb," a mike in the residence of Humphreys, who hated to go out in the winter and stayed at home where he discussed his agenda each morning with his bodyguard-driver, Hy Godfrey.

LBJ Pulls Mikes

These bugs were great. We installed Little Al in 1959, and the others in the early Sixties. They stayed in and were most productive until July 11, 1965. Then LBJ ordered them pulled. They were "violating the civil rights of the mobsters." Really. I didn't make this up. That is what the President said.

Fall of Momo

Giancana stayed in power until 1966. His was a return to the high profile days of Al Capone, unlike the years of his immediate predecessors Nitti, Ricca and Accardo. His high profile included a red-hot affair with one of the McGuire Sisters, one of the top singing acts of the time. That heated up the media. Then I led what we called "lockstep" surveillance of him. I was on his rear end from morning to night, just a foot away, even on the golf course and even in the men's room. Then he took us to court for thereby violating his civil rights. And won! Then we took him to court in an unprecedented manner. We granted him immunity—giving him absolution for all his crimes. This took the Fifth Amendment away from him. He couldn't incriminate himself if he couldn't be held responsible for any of his crimes. Still he refused to testify. We put him in jail—for contempt of the federal grand jury.

When Giancana came out, a year later, the mob had had enough of his style of leadership. Accardo, who had become the consiglieri, the man with the veto power over even the boss, replaced him. Giancana went into exile in Mexico. When he came back, eight years later, the mob rubbed him out. Killed him with eight shots to the head in his basement in 1975.

Battaglia Runs the Crews

Accardo replaced Giancana with Sam "Teets" Battaglia to run the day-to-day Outfit affairs in 1966. He lasted about a year. He went to prison, only to be released to die soon thereafter.

Alderisio Takes Over

Then it was the turn of Felix "Milwaukee Phil" Alderisio. We got him in about the same time it took to get Battaglia, a year. I've seen the photo of Alderisio, who had been the mob "hit man" before his elevation to boss, being led into jail by three anonymous FBI agents in dozens of publications, including the next day on the front page of the Chicago *Sun Times*. The guy on Alderisio's left is me.

Cerone Next

Now Accardo replaced Philly with his protégé, Jackie Cerone. I knew all these guys from personal confrontations on several occasions, but especially, I guess, Cerone. A topflight guy for a mobster. Intelligent, articulate, well read, well dressed, a weight lifter with a handsome profile, he was a cut above most. Still is. But we got him in about the same time as his immediate three predecessors. Maybe I should say Lou Bombacino got him. Lou, who became a good pal of mine, testified as what we call a "cooperating witness." He sank Cerone and three of his best guys. But the mob got Lou. Blew him up in his Caddy in Arizona after they located him in hiding.

Accardo Returns

It was now 1971. The mob was desperate. But they had the best guy in the hole. Accardo himself. He didn't want to come back. But he had to. Not alone however. The mob would run now AAA. Accardo; my old target whom I never got, Alex; and Joey Aiuppa. That lasted just long enough for Accardo and Alex to train Aiuppa and saddle him with the job. It was no longer something a lot of top guys lusted after. After all, look at what we had done to each of the four guys who took the top spot after Mr. Hoover got us involved in the Top Hood Program. Bang, bang, bang, bang.

Operation Pendorf

In 1978 I had moved on, to Arizona to take on Joe Bonanno, one of the original 1931 New York mob bosses who was still running Brooklyn, now by remote control from Tucson. My successors at the Chicago FBI, mainly Pete Wacks and Art Pfizenmayer, then threw themselves into Operation Pendorf—the penetration of Allen Dorfman, the Teamster official with access to the Pension Fund. They placed mikes all over the place, especially in the International Tower near O'Hare off the Kennedy Expressway. As a result, Dorfman, Roy Williams, the president of the Teamsters, and Joe Lombardo, a big boss of the LCN in Chicago, were convicted.

Operation Strawman I & II

Then it was the turn of Bill Ouseley, one of the finest agents ever, in Kansas City. He was the case agent on Operation Strawman I and Strawman II, two cases having to do with the skimming of Las Vegas hotel-casinos by the top guys in the Chicago, Kansas City, Milwaukee and Cleveland LCN families. These included Jackie Cerone and Joe Aiuppa, the two top bosses now in Chicago. After Cerone returned from prison in the mid-Eighties, these guys all went to prison—for what should be the rest of their lives. What a blow to the Outfit.

Tony Spilotro

Soon thereafter it was Tony "The Ant" Spilotro's turn. Spilotro had been sent out to Las Vegas to oversee the interests of the Chicago Outfit as their enforcer. In fact, my biography of his life has just been published—*The Enforcer*. I write of my many conversations with this pissant—and of his attempts to ambush me. Spilotro had ruled Las Vegas for Chicago from 1971 to 1986. Then he got too big for his britches. They found his beaten body—and that of his brother—

buried alive in a cornfield in northern Indiana in 1986. That was the end of Tony the Ant. He joined his namesake.

Ferriola New Boss

Now Joe Ferriola became the Chicago mob boss. Just before I left Chicago for Arizona, I had a quiet sit-down with Joe. As I left Chicago, I warned my pals in the Bureau to watch out for him—he was the next boss-to-be. I was right. But Joe died soon after he took over, in March 1991.

Bosses Switch

Now Tony Accardo, still in charge after parts of eight decades in the mob, turned to Sam Carlisi. And to John "No Nose" DiFronzo. These guys, in my opinion, were a long drop down from their predecessors. But then the Outfit had run out of highly qualified guys—attrition had set in.

The FBI got DiFronzo and several other top guys in 1993 in a case supervised by Agent Pfizenmayer, now the OC supervisor in San Diego after working the Pendorf case in Chicago. Carlisi was indicted in that case, conspiracy to skim a casino in an Indian reservation in southern California, but was acquitted. His time would soon come, however. In late 1993 he was convicted in Chicago after an FBI investigation of his gambling empire, and is now in federal prison. DiFronzo was paroled this August.

New Mob #1???

The question in 1994 is, who has succeeded Carlisi and DiFronzo? Many believe it is Joe Lombardo, released from his sentence now in the Pendorf case. But I have some problems with that. I know Joe. I arrested him once. He's no clown, that being his media name. He's now on parole. If he is found consorting with mobsters, he goes right back into the slammer. He's not that dumb.

Lombardo, however, has a cousin who is a top guy in the Outfit today. Joe "The Builder" Andriacci. It seems to be the best information today that Andriacci is running the mob in Chicago—after taking suggestions (orders?) from his cousin, Lombardo. Could well be. After all, attrition has really arrived in 1994 and Tony Accardo, finally, is no longer able to consult. He died a peaceful death, after never serving a night in jail, in May 1992. (Editor's Note: Chicago's premier columnist, Irv Kupcinet, recently printed that DiFronzo now heads the Mob, on information provided by Bill Roemer.)

The Chicago Outfit has a glorious history—from its perspective. But let me tell you one thing. I can't imagine any qualified mobster aspiring to the top job in the Outfit today. Any halfway intelligent thug only has to look into that history to see where he is headed, should he become a top hoodlum in Chicago today. A decade or two of nice living and then the rest of his life in prison—to die there. That is the real history of the Chicago Outfit—from my perspective.

Appendix B

The following chronology of the gaming industry in Nevada was prepared by William F. Roemer, Jr., in March of 1987 after Roemer was retained by a Los Angeles law firm as an attorney on their defense team defending a libel suit.

HISTORICAL CHRONOLOGY OF THE
GAMING INDUSTRY IN NEVADA

Prepared for Gibson, Dunn & Crutcher
By William F. Roemer, Jr.
March 1987

1931
Legislation is passed by Nevada Legislature authorizing all forms of gambling in Nevada. Local control is authorized.

Late 1930s
JOHNNY ROSELLI is dispatched from Chicago by FRANK NITTI, JAKE GUZIK and MURRAY HUMPHREYS, Chicago mob bosses, to West Coast to oversee Hollywood and related interests of Chicago mob on West Coast.

Mid-1940s
BUGSY SIEGEL, New York mobster, is sent to Las Vegas by New York mob leaders MEYER LANSKY and LUCKY LUCIANO in order to build hotel-casino on Las Vegas Boulevard, subsequently to be known as "The Strip."

1943
ROSELLI, NITTI and other Chicago mob leaders indicted for involvement in "Hollywood Extortion Case," extortion of movie industry through use of labor unions controlled by Chicago mob. NITTI commits suicide.

1946

SIEGEL opens the Flamingo on the Strip, the first hotel-casino there.

ROSELLI and other Chicago mob leaders paroled by Truman Administration resulting in major scandal. Upon release, ROSELLI sent by Chicago mob to Las Vegas to oversee their potential interests there.

1947

BUGSY SIEGEL victim of gangland slaying in Beverly Hills.

SIEGEL is replaced by GUS GREENBAUM who subsequently is also a victim of gangland slaying, this time in Phoenix.

Construction begins on another Strip hotel, the Desert Inn. WILBUR CLARK is initial owner but Desert Inn is soon taken over by MOE DALITZ and his associates from Cleveland. This group previously operated illegal bookmaking in Cleveland area and in Northern Kentucky. DALITZ, former rumrunner previous to that in Detroit.

1948

MEYER and JAKE LANSKY open Thunderbird as undisclosed owners.

1949

The International Brotherhood of the Teamsters Union initiates the Central States Pension Fund, which is to become the largest source of funding for Las Vegas casinos. JAMES RIDDLE HOFFA is introduced to Chicago mob leaders by PAUL "RED" DORFMAN with result HOFFA is eventually elected international president of the Teamsters with support of Chicago mob. ALLEN DORFMAN, stepson of RED DORFMAN, becomes conduit between Chicago mob and Central States Pension Fund and prime mover in loans to Las Vegas casinos.

1950

Desert Inn opens on Strip.

The Kefauver Committee holds hearings focusing on DALITZ in Las Vegas.

1952

The Sands opens on the Strip. New York mobster DOC STRACHER is owner.

Mid-1950s

Strip expands with building of the Riviera, the Dunes, the Royal Nevada, the Stardust and other hotel-casinos. Riviera controlled by DALITZ group, while Stardust, built by Los Angeles gambler TONY CORNERO, is eventually taken over by JAKE "THE BARBER" FACTOR, a loose associate of HUMPHREYS in Chicago. FACTOR eventually leases the operation of the casino at the Stardust to DALITZ group.

1957

Tropicana opens on Southern edge of Strip. When FRANK COSTELLO, New York mobster, is shot in New York, search of his pockets found to contain financial record of Tropicana in handwriting of LOU LEDERER, Chicago hoodlum associate who is licensed owner of Tropicana. Indication is that COSTELLO has substantial undisclosed interest in Tropicana.

La Cosa Nostra leaders from all over the country meet in Apalachin, small upstate New York town. Discovery of this meeting leads to initiation by J. Edgar Hoover of Top Hoodlum Program, bringing FBI into investigation of organized crime *per se* for first time.

1958

Chicago mob sends JOHNNY DREW, Chicago gambling boss, to Las Vegas to take charge of Stardust Hotel.

1959

Nevada Legislature creates Gaming Commission with orders to keep organized crime members and leaders from casinos.

DALITZ and his associates obtain $1 million loan from Central States Pension Fund of the Teamsters Union for the Stardust.

1960

DALITZ summoned to Chicago by SAM GIANCANA, FRANK FERRARO, TONY ACCARDO and MURRAY HUMPHREYS. Meet in Chicago hotel for entire weekend with result DALITZ thereafter subservient to Chicago mob. In addition to Stardust, Teamsters Central States Pension Fund makes large loans to DALITZ for Fremont and Desert Inn.

MARSHALL CAIFANO, aka JOHNNY MARSHALL, Chicago mobster, sent to Las Vegas by GIANCANA, et al., as their representative in Las Vegas with orders to enforce Chicago edicts in Las Vegas.

Nevada Gaming Commission compiles "black book," CAIFANO included. This is device commanding casino operators to bar those listed in black book from premises.

1961

FBI initiates installation of microphone and other electronic devices in selected casinos and hotels believed to be controlled by organized crime. Installation is made only upon express authorization in each instance by J. Edgar Hoover but are basically illegal, not admissible in evidence.

1962
Advent of HOWARD HUGHES and his SUMMA CORPORATION in Las Vegas.

1963
FRANK SINATRA, owner of Cal Neva at Lake Tahoe, entertains SAM GIANCANA, top leader of organized crime in Chicago, at Cal Neva and eventually gives up ownership there after investigation initiated into his association with GIANCANA and his entertainment of GIANCANA at Cal Neva Lodge.

1964
STRACHER convicted for tax evasion and voluntarily exiles himself to Israel.

HOFFA convicted for manipulating Teamsters Pension Fund.

Mid-1960s
The FBI in Las Vegas, Chicago, Miami, New York and New Jersey conducted an investigation entitled Vegmon which stood for Vegas Money. This investigation was initiated upon the receipt from electronic surveillances in Las Vegas casinos indicating that skimmed money was being delivered by courier to mobs in the above cities. The FBI conducted extensive physical surveillances of suspected couriers and of IDA DEVINE, the wife of IRVING "NIGGY" DEVINE, the owner of the New York Meat Company in Las Vegas, who was observed by the FBI in a situation indicating that she had delivered the skim to recipients in the above cities. In Chicago, for instance, she was observed by the FBI debarking from a train in Chicago and being greeted there by GEORGE BIEBER, an attorney known to be closely associated with Chicago organized crime leaders.

1966
Teamsters Pension Fund makes $20 million loan to owners of Caesar's Palace for construction.

Nevada successful in defending use of black book against CAIFANO.

PAUL LAXALT elected Governor of Nevada. LAXALT immediately goes to Washington where he is briefed about organized crime and the members thereof in Nevada by

J. Edgar Hoover and his top associates. Hoover then sends instruction to DEAN ELSON, Special Agent in charge of the Las Vegas office of the FBI, to brief LAXALT with contents of lengthy report on skimming activities in Nevada which had just been prepared in October 1966 by FBI. ELSON does so.

RUBY KOLOD and "ICEPICK WILLIE" ALDERMAN, executives of the Desert Inn, were convicted with Chicago mob leader, "MILWAUKEE PHIL" ALDERISIO of the extortion of Denver businessman ROBERT SUNSHINE. During the course of this trial, it was developed that the FBI conducted extensive microphone installations in the Las Vegas casinos which led to confirmation of hidden interests on the part of organized crime leaders throughout the United States, but particularly in Chicago, and of the skimming which took place on behalf of these organized crime interests. One of these devices was uncovered at the Fremont and resulted in a suit brought by EDDIE LEVINSON against the FBI. However, this suit was settled out of court before coming to trial.

1967
Desert Inn, Sands, Frontier and Castaways purchased by HOWARD HUGHES.

1968
Landmark purchased by HUGHES. HUGHES attempts to purchase Stardust but is blocked by SEC and United States Justice Department due to antitrust laws.

1969
Legislation passed in Nevada allowing publicly traded corporations to own hotel-casinos.

1971
Chicago mob replaces CAIFANO, who has been convicted of extortion, with TONY SPILOTRO. SPILOTRO, as successor to ROSELLI and CAIFANO, has instructions from Chicago mob to enforce their control over those in Las Vegas who are acting in their behalf.

1972
ALLEN DORFMAN is convicted in New York for kickbacks involving Central States and is sent to prison.

ALLEN GLICK purchases the Hacienda on far Southern tip of Strip. GLICK is eventually discovered to be front for FRANK BALISTRIERI, the leader of the Milwaukee family of La Cosa Nostra, with Milwaukee being a satellite family of Chicago.

1973

SPILOTRO who has been using gift shop at Circus Circus as his base of operations is forced out of Circus Circus by Gaming Control Board.

1974

SPILOTRO, DORFMAN and JOE LOMBARDO are indicted for embezzlement of Central States funds. LOMBARDO is Chicago capo whose responsibility includes control for Chicago of their interests in Las Vegas and liaison with Central States Pension Fund and DORFMAN.

GLICK obtains $62 million loan from Central States Pension Fund for the Argent Corporation which he sets up to buy the Stardust from PARVIN-DOHRMAN, controlled by Chicago hoodlum associate DEL COLEMAN.

At this point in time, Central States Pension Fund of Teamsters holds 56% of loans for the large hotel-casinos in CLARK County, Nevada (Las Vegas).

1975

Central States Pension Fund makes loan to PERLMAN BROTHERS, owners of Caesar's Palace.

SAM GIANCANA and JIMMY HOFFA victims of gangland slayings during summer of 1975.

Gaming Control Board issues license to MORRIS SHENKER to operate Dunes. SHENKER is St. Louis attorney who had represented mob figures there.

FRANK "LEFTY" ROSENTHAL, who had been dispatched by Chicago mob to Las Vegas a couple years earlier to operate the hotels under ARGENT banner (Stardust, Hacienda and Fremont), is forced out of Stardust by Gaming Control Board.

JAY VANDERMARK is discovered to be running slot skim at Stardust by Gaming Control Board. VANDERMARK'S son murdered in Mexico, and VANDERMARK has never been heard of since.

1978

Chicago office of FBI initiates "Pendorf" investigation which eventually leads to conviction of ALLEN DORFMAN, LOMBARDO and Teamsters president, ROY WILLIAMS, for bribery of United States Senator HOWARD CANNON of Nevada. Pendorf investigation includes Court-authorized microphone surveillances in Central States headquarters in Chicago, Intelligence Division of Las Vegas Police Department, and other strategic places developing information showing close control by Chicago mob of gaming interests in Las Vegas.

Ruling "commission" of La Cosa Nostra issues edict granting Chicago mob primary rights to gaming interests in Las Vegas while "grandfathering" in previous rights held by Eastern interests. Noted that Las Vegas previously was considered open city by LCN. Commission ruling granted Atlantic City to Eastern mobs. Noted that legal gambling had just been authorized in Atlantic City.

1979

Gaming Control Board in Nevada forces GLICK to sell Stardust. Licenses AL SACHS and HERB TOBMAN at Stardust. Chicago mob continues control of Stardust.

1980

JOSEPH YABLONSKY appointed Special Agent in charge of FBI office in Las Vegas. YABLONSKY initiates intensive drive against organized crime in Las Vegas which continues throughout his tenure there through 1982.

1982

FBI in Kansas City initiates "Strawman" investigation. Part one of Strawman involves organized crime control of Tropicana Hotel and eventually leads to convictions of leading Kansas City mob chiefs and shows control by them of Tropicana and of skimming activity there. Part two of Strawman involves control by Kansas City, Milwaukee, Cleveland and Chicago mobs of ARGENT hotel-casinos, namely the Stardust, Hacienda and Fremont. Part two of Strawman resulted in convictions of JOEY AIUPPA, the top leader of organized crime in Chicago, JOHN CERONE, the underboss of organized crime in Chicago, two Chicago capos, FRANK BALISTRIERI, the Milwaukee boss, and the top leadership in Kansas City, along with a leading member of organized crime in Cleveland. All sentenced to lengthy prison terms which will probably result in their spending the rest of their lives in prison. Pendorf and Strawman convictions hailed as landmark investigations involving organized crime interests in Las Vegas.

1983

In January 1983, ALLEN DORFMAN victim of gangland slaying in Chicago suburb.

1984

Nevada Gaming Control Commission forces SACHS and TOBMAN to sell Stardust Hotel; appoints BOYD FAMILY as trustees to operate Stardust. BOYD FAMILY also owns Sam's

Town and California Club. BOYD FAMILY eventually finds Stardust Casino, now unskimmed under their trusteeship, to be most productive enterprise and purchases Stardust and its sister casino, the Fremont.

SPILOTRO involved in murder trial in Chicago and based on testimony of former associate, FRANK CULIOTTA, is acquitted. However, he is soon indicted with members of his "Hole in the Wall Gang." SPILOTRO also defendant in Strawman trials but is severed. SPILOTRO undergoes bypass heart surgery in Houston.

1986

SPILOTRO victim of gangland slaying in June. Beaten bodies of SPILOTRO and his brother MICHAEL found in shallow grave in Northern Indiana cornfield. Speculation of authorities indicates SPILOTRO murdered by Chicago mob for following reasons: SPILOTRO had lost control over GLICK, CARL THOMAS and JOE AGOSTO, who were his responsibility in Las Vegas and who all became government witnesses in the Strawman investigations and were instrumental in guilty verdicts. Also because SPILOTRO involved in narcotics activity in Las Vegas. Also because of high profile of SPILOTRO in Las Vegas which diminished his capacity to operate without detection. Also because he remained a defendant in the Strawman case after having been severed in the Hole in the Wall Gang case which had resulted in a mistrial in 1986.

WAYNE NEWTON, who was the subject of a series of four reports on NBC in 1980–1982 linking him to FRANK PICCOLO and GUIDO PENOSI, was awarded $19.3 million in damages after he won a libel action against NBC in December. NEWTON is a Las Vegas entertainer and the former owner of the Aladdin Hotel.

Appendix C

The following article, entitled "A Place in the Sun, Las Vegas . . . From Capo to Corporate," by William F. Roemer, Jr., appeared in the *Illinois Police and Sheriff's News*, the official publication of the Combined Counties Police Association, in its issue of Autumn, 1994.

A gangster made grass grow in the desert—an oasis out of sand, brush and nothingness. Dusty old Highway 91 cut right through the heart of Las Vegas, a mean, miserable town on the periphery of civilization when New York–honed Bugsy Siegel was sent west in 1943 by Meyer Lansky and Frank Costello, the Prime Minister and the Chairman of the Board of "Big Apple" organized crime, respectively.

In the hot desert sun, the mob's "advance man" drew up a bold and imaginative plan to lure the high rollers from the West Coast and great Southwest to a sin capital on the scale of Havana, Cuba, the haven of eastern gamblers, crime bosses and thrill seekers until Fidel Castro put an end to everyone's good time by winning a revolution in the winter of '59.

Lansky, the financial genius of Charlie "Lucky" Luciano's powerfully fluid New York operation, had traveled to Havana in 1938 to finalize a deal with Fulgencio Batista to assume control of gambling operations shortly after the U.S. Government-backed Cuban dictator seized the two casinos from the local military, which had no idea of how to run this kind of business. The Cuban Army ran the casinos for nearly two years, but the profits were not to Batista's liking, so he invited his American friends down to his Caribbean hacienda to help straighten things out.

Under the astute Lansky's tutelage, the Cuban gambling Mecca flourished like never before. The island nation became a most popular destination point for American café society, showbiz stars and high rollers who flocked to the majestic Hotel Nacional, overlooking the entrance of Havana Harbor. Lansky built a casino inside the walls with the help of International Hotels Inc., a Pan Am subsidiary, marking the first (but certainly not the last) time a legit corporation entered into a partnership with a fast-on-the-move mobster.

President Batista was a pompous, strutting martinet in the hip pocket of the New York City racketeers. He was a power-hungry feudal lord who kept his people in abject poverty while hoarding untold riches for his personal pleasure. And of course Batista was more than happy to oblige Lansky in his plan to lure wealthy American tourists to Cuba as long as there was something in it for him.

The experience of operating Cuban casinos greatly aided the enterprising Lansky and Siegel when they went west and established similar gaming ventures in Las Vegas. The money earned in Cuba provided them with the seed money and means to do so. The trick of the trade—the sine qua non—was the ability to skim the casino profits in the countinghouse. The technique was perfected in Havana in the 1930s and elevated to an art form by the time Siegel arrived in Vegas to sniff out new business ventures and try to capitalize on postwar land values, which were rising by the day.

Gambling was legalized in Nevada in 1931, but it remained pretty much a local amusement appealing to itinerant cowboys and ranch hands who poured into Reno, the "Biggest Little City in the World," on Friday nights for a weekend of carousing and hell-raising in the local "buckets of blood." In Vegas, the El Rancho and the Last Frontier catered to Army recruits from the nearby gunnery school. Strictly small-time stuff. It took Ben Siegel, backed by Lansky and Frank Costello's financial wherewithal, to build a casino with a touch of class—a place to gamble in a majestic setting with pretty showgirls, cocktail waitresses, plenty of gourmet food and big-name entertainment. The Flamingo was the first world-class Las Vegas resort built by the hoods of America. It was not to be the last.

The Siegel-inspired pleasure dome opened on December 26, 1946, but it was not the immediate success the impatient eastern "backers" hoped for. A torrential downpour ruined opening night, and triggered a run of bad luck for Benny "Don't Call Me Bugsy" Siegel.

His girlfriend, one Virginia Hill, had been salting away mob money earmarked for construction for some time, and her penchant for skimming ultimately cost Bugsy his life. Five bullets fired from a .30-.30 carbine ripped through Siegel as he read the paper in the living room of Virginia's Beverly Hills home the night of June 20, 1947.

Within a matter of days the New York mobs seized control of the Flamingo and sent Siegel's lonely love, Virginia Hill, on her merry way. Operating under the direction of Moe Sedway (one of the original partners listed in the "Nevada Project Corporation," which supplied Siegel with his funding), the Flamingo became an instant moneymaker and soon the high rollers across the country arrived to frolic in the dry desert air. Then a guy named Wilbur Clark, who had a piece of the action down in Havana, began work on the Desert Inn, about a half-mile north of Bugsy's place on the same side of Highway 91. Right after that the Thunderbird opened, and suddenly the mob controlled a lucrative semi-legit enterprise, at least by the standards and statutes set by the State of Nevada and the City of Las Vegas. The wolves were in the chicken coop.

In 1949 Moe Dalitz and his Mayfield Road Gang moved west to Vegas from Cleveland in order to drive out the unlucky Wilbur Clark. Clark had encountered serious financial troubles which idled construction crews laboring on his uncompleted Desert Inn.

Oddly enough, it wasn't until after the Senate Kefauver Hearings in 1950 began focusing on the national organized crime network that the Chicago guys entered the game in Las Vegas.

In the 1930s Al Capone had a passing interest in Bill Graham's Bank Club in Reno, but they failed to recognize the potential of Nevada gambling until the eyes of Tony Accardo opened to the possibilities of fast money and loose law enforcement out West.

Accardo's lucky break came when a Los Angeles gambler named Tony Cornero began building the Stardust—located on old Highway 91, which by now was called Las Vegas Boulevard South, or more commonly, the "Strip." Before the Stardust could open, Cornero died, and that event proved most fortuitous for Chicago. Murray Humphreys, who was my special responsibility during the years I worked on the F.B.I.'s Top Hoodlum Program in Chicago, hired Jake Factor, brother of cosmetics tycoon Max Factor and an underworld dabbler, to "front" the Stardust for the Chicago Outfit guys.

It soon became quite clear to agents like myself that Chicago had reached an accommodation with Moe Dalitz and the New York families in order for them to run the Stardust (for the blue-collar, "dinner pail" gambler), the Desert Inn (serving the high-roller trade), and the Riviera. These were the three major hotel-casinos in the late 1950s, and the deal that granted autonomy to the Chicago Outfit, we learned, was cut in early January 1961 when Dalitz and his partner Morris Kleinman came to Chicago to confer with Tony Accardo and Sam Giancana.

The next ten years was a period of remarkable growth and expansion for Las Vegas and its Chicago benefactors. The Outfit added the Hacienda, the Sahara, and the Fremont (the biggest downtown casino) to its already sizable holdings, and if ever there was an adult playground blending glitz, glamour and sleaze into one appealing package, it was Las Vegas in the 1960s. Frank Sinatra and his fellow "Rat Pack" showbiz pals headlined the Stardust, knowing full well whom they were working for. Complimentary rooms and free booze were liberally dispensed to vacationing Americans by the Outfit "hoteliers," deeply engrossed in the lodging and hospitality business. Not even the murderous impulses of Tony "The Ant" Spilotro, a thug of the first order who dumped five of his victims in the desert in the early 1970s, failed to scare away the tourists who came to partake in the Vegas experience—a happening, if you will.

The "change" in Las Vegas—the transfer of the hotel-casinos from mob ownership to corporate America—was slow to occur. But once it started and continued to evolve, things would never be the same again in America's gambling capital. I suppose one can trace this whole metamorphosis to the arrival of the reclusive billionaire Howard Hughes and the influence he wielded over politico Paul Laxalt, then the governor of Nevada.

Hughes' point man in those days was Bob Matheu, who convinced the governor that there might be a spot for him in the organization later on. If he could somehow convince Nevada legislators to overturn a state law barring public corporations from casino ownership.

In time, the law was changed to Howard Hughes' wants and satisfaction after a battery of lobbyists, including retired tax commissioner Robbins Cahill, whose duty was to win passage of the casino act, put the arm on the State Legislature. The strange and mysterious Hughes bought up six of the nicest hotels in Vegas from syndicate bosses. Moe Dalitz was a canny mobster who agreed with the wily Meyer Lansky that the glory days would soon be coming to an end. Change was down the road.

Dalitz sold the Desert Inn to Howard Hughes in 1967, thus paving the way for ambitious entrepreneurs cut out of the Hughes cloth to overrun the town during the junk bond, merger and acquisition frenzy that consumed Wall Street in the 1980s.

Meyer Lansky realized a profit of just over $1 million when his point man, Jack Entratter, peddled the Sands to Howard Hughes for $14.6 million in 1967. Lansky undoubtedly considered himself fortunate for cutting such a good deal, but the real money was yet to be made by pedigreed MBAs from America's prestigious schools of finance and business administration (Wall Street preparatory schools), who had a lot more on the ball when it came to structuring a corporation than the gangsters of yesteryear.

The value of prime Las Vegas real estate and the luxurious new hotels about to go up on the Strip soared in the next decade. The real suckers in this game of real-estate high finance were the old-time mob bosses whose split of the Hughes sale in the late 1960s was mere pin money to a high roller like Akio Kashiwagi, who routinely dumped hundreds of thousands of dollars in a single night of gambling at the Dunes before he was hacked to death by Japanese *yakuza* in his native land sometime later.

Steve Wynn, the son of a compulsive gambler who has a keen appreciation for the bottom line, replaced Dalitz, Benny Binion, and the muscle of a Spilotro as the Casino King of Vegas. He is the owner of Mirage Resorts, Inc., whose holdings include the Golden Nugget, the Mirage, and Treasure Island. His counterpart in Atlantic City is Donald Trump, who also subscribes to the gospel of junk bond financing. Wynn is on a mission. The mission is to "sanitize" Vegas and make money . . . lots and lots of money. Drive out the sin and sleaze in order to make the town attractive to vacationing mommies and daddies from mid-America who see nothing wrong with pushing their kids around in strollers on the Strip. Thus far he has succeeded—possibly beyond his own well-thought-out dreams. The glitter of the new Las Vegas epitomizes modern America.

Key federal prosecutions of leading mobsters from Chicago, Cleveland and Kansas City in the 1980s aided Wynn in ridding Vegas of the lingering gangster elements. Convictions stemming from the Department of Justice operations Pendorf and Strawman I and II devastated mob rule in the 1980s—especially the Chicago influence.

Meanwhile, Wynn had already established a working relationship with junk bond king Michael Milken as vast amounts of capital to finance these casino ventures flowed in before Milken became the most famous (albeit the richest) felon in American history. Together Wynn and Milken accomplished with the stroke of a Wall Street pen what the mobsters of yesteryear finalized with a bullet and a gun.

It's a booming business—a brilliant one of entrepreneurial skill—that is operated with greater savvy and sophistication than ever before. Fortunes are made and lost in less than a heartbeat, and the town the mobsters built has come a long way toward respectability. They have marketed and sold the total package of a "Ma and Pa" Disneyland as suitable entertainment for the whole family.

It would be exceedingly naive to believe that all of a sudden, a decade or so later, the town of Las Vegas is stripped clean of its criminal element. Because nowadays, it is almost impossible to tell just who the real crooks are. One thing is for sure. The appeal is to Main Street America. Think of it as "Leave It to Beaver Strolls Down the Strip."

Index

421

If you liked ACCARDO: THE GENUINE GODFATHER, you won't be able to put down

THE ENFORCER

Spilotro: The Chicago Mob's Man Over Las Vegas

by William F. Roemer, Jr.

Bugsy Siegel built Las Vegas. But it was Tony "The Ant" Spilotro who ran the show, keeping the gambling capital of America booming. William F. Roemer, Jr., veteran FBI agent and scourge of the Cosa Nostra, tells the shocking story of how a teenage wiseguy grew up to become "the man" in Vegas.

THE ENFORCER
by William F. Roemer, Jr.

Published by Ivy Books.
Available in bookstores everywhere.